P9-DVV-628

The
HEART *of a*
SOLDIER

The
HEART *of a*
SOLDIER

A True Story of
Love, War,
and Sacrifice

CAPT. KATE BLAISE
WITH DANA WHITE

GOTHAM BOOKS

GOTHAM BOOKS
Published by Penguin Group (USA) Inc.
375 Hudson Street, New York, New York 10014, U.S.A.
Penguin Group (Canada), 90 Eglinton Avenue East, Suite 700, Toronto, Ontario
M4P 2Y3, Canada (a division of Pearson Penguin Canada Inc.); Penguin Books Ltd,
80 Strand, London WC2R 0RL, England; Penguin Ireland, 25 St Stephen's Green,
Dublin 2, Ireland (a division of Penguin Books Ltd); Penguin Group (Australia), 250
Camberwell Road, Camberwell, Victoria 3124, Australia (a division of Pearson Aus-
tralia Group Pty Ltd); Penguin Books India Pvt Ltd, 11 Community Centre,
Panchsheel Park, New Delhi - 110 017, India; Penguin Group (NZ), cnr Airborne
and Rosedale Roads, Albany, Auckland 1310, New Zealand (a division of Pearson
New Zealand Ltd); Penguin Books (South Africa) (Pty) Ltd, 24 Sturdee Avenue,
Rosebank, Johannesburg 2196, South Africa

Penguin Books Ltd, Registered Offices: 80 Strand, London WC2R 0RL, England

Published by Gotham Books, a division of Penguin Group (USA) Inc.

First printing, January 2006
10 9 8 7 6 5 4 3 2 1

Copyright © 2005 by Kate Blaise
All rights reserved

Gotham Books and the skyscraper logo are trademarks of Penguin Group (USA) Inc.

LIBRARY OF CONGRESS CATALOGING-IN-PUBLICATION DATA
Blaise, Kate, 1976–
    The heart of a soldier : a true love story of war, love, and sacrifice / Kate Blaise
with Dana Whiter.
        p.   cm.
    Includes bibliographical references and index.
    ISBN 1-59240-177-5 (hardcover : alk. paper)
    1. Blaise, Kate, 1976– 2. Iraq War, 2003—Personal narratives, American.
I. White, Dana. II. Title.
    DS79.76.B58 2006
    956.7044'3'092—dc22   2005021107

ISBN 1-592-40177-5

Printed in the United States of America
Set in Sabon with Avenir
Designed by Sabrina Bowers

Without limiting the rights under copyright reserved above, no part of this publica-
tion may be reproduced, stored in or introduced into a retrieval system, or transmit-
ted, in any form, or by any means (electronic, mechanical, photocopying, recording,
or otherwise), without the prior written permission of both the copyright owner and
the above publisher of this book.

The scanning, uploading, and distribution of this book via the Internet or via any
other means without the permission of the publisher is illegal and punishable by law.
Please purchase only authorized electronic editions, and do not participate in or encourage electronic piracy of copyrighted materials. Your support of the author's
rights is appreciated.

*To Chief Warrant Officer 2 Mike Blaise and all the
soldiers like him who, on any given day, get up in the
rain, dark, and danger to go to work. Not for some
high ideal but for their brothers and sisters in arms.
You are not forgotten.*

ACKNOWLEDGMENTS

I could not have written this book without the assistance of numerous people to whom I am very thankful. First and foremost, thanks to God, who guides me daily and gives me the strength to find my new path in life.

This book would not have been possible without Susan Reed and Sarah Turcotte of *Golf for Women* magazine, who offered me the opportunity that led to this project. My agent, Mark Reiter, took a chance with a novice author. Lauren Marino at Gotham Books believed this story should be heard and has worked hard to bring it to the world, along with Hilary Terrell. I appreciate all of their efforts and professionalism.

A special thanks to my father for the numerous files he kept of my military career, particularly his detailed research of the war in Iraq, which he kept in binders for the day that I might "decide to write a book about my experiences."

Thanks to my family and friends, who have assisted with memories, good humor, and patience over the past few months. The town of Macon welcomed me back home with open arms when I needed a quiet place to write and heal. Many thanks to Terry and Cheryl Blaise for their patient reading and rereading of the manuscript. Their love and support kept me smiling.

Friends with whom I served in the 101st Airborne Division provided invaluable encouragement and support, particularly Chip O'Neal for his humor, ideas, and fact-checking; and Jesse White, who inadvertently started me down this road by bringing some golf balls and a sand wedge to Iraq.

A special thanks to my sister, hero, and friend, Lindsey, who dug through her often painful memories and answered my questions without hesitation. She was always there with positive words of encouragement, and her confidence in me energized me daily.

Thanks also to Tim Merrill and Scott White for their detailed accounts of a combat pilot's life in Iraq. I was riveted by their stories and grateful for their willingness to open up about their missions and accomplishments.

Three talented civilians, Barbara Gogan, Ursula Liang, and Priscilla Eakeley, helped to ensure that the manuscript was as accurate as possible.

Finally, a heartfelt thank-you and applause to my collaborator and—after months of digging through memories with me—my friend, Dana White. She pushed and prodded me to tell this story, and I am grateful for the opportunity to work with her. I'm proud to have found a friend in her and her family: David, Eli, and Jesse Tuttman.

If, in the end, there is any merit to this book, it is due in large part to the people listed above.

CONTENTS

The
HEART *of a*
SOLDIER

PROLOGUE

TODAY I AM TWENTY-SEVEN, and I'll celebrate by washing my hair and getting some sleep.

It's been another long night at the Tactical Operations Center (TOC). With four other soldiers, I monitor the fighting in the volatile city of An Najaf, tracking missions and dispatching medevac choppers as needed. I've gotten about ten hours of sleep since the war started, and I ache for a deep night's rest, the kind you see in mattress commercials back home, from which the person wakes up stretching and smiling, refreshed and ready for anything.

Our convoy had crossed the border into Iraq on March 27, an ant trail of three hundred Humvees, supply trucks, and fuel tankers following on the heels of the infantry. We inched north toward Baghdad—a slow, hot, often harrowing odyssey through the land that time and democracy forgot. We passed mud huts, bombed villages, and burnt-out tanks from Desert Storm. And always the people, trying to sell to us, steal from us, or just stare at us—especially the men, and especially at me, a woman in authority, a female beamed down from Planet America.

After crossing from Kuwait, we found ourselves in a forlorn border village, scarred from decades of poverty and war. Scores of people, mostly young and mostly male, pressed close to our vehicles, eyeing our bottled water and food, looking for a chance to rush us. At one point three young men threw huge chunks of scrap metal into our path in an attempt to slow us down. My NCO, Sgt. First Class David McDaris, a Desert Storm veteran, yelled, "Hold on!" and barreled right through it. We kept our weapons locked and loaded and pointed out our windows, but the people seemed unimpressed, and I wondered what had happened to them that a loaded gun in their faces didn't faze them.

Under no circumstances were we to stop. The fedayeen had ambushed other U.S. convoys, and we had been briefed on their techniques, some of them particularly effective. For example, they would kidnap a child and hold a gun to his or her head, threatening to shoot unless the child's mother stood in the road to stop the trucks. We were under orders to run over everything in our path, including human beings, and I prayed that neither my soldiers nor I would be put in such a position.

We stopped only once before An Najaf for a little sleep and a bathroom break. The sight was almost comical: hundreds of soldiers running into the desert, trailing long tails of toilet paper behind them.

Outside An Najaf we learned that the infantry was engaged in heavy combat in the city, so we set up camp for a couple of weeks. In a matter of hours a vast tent city sprang up in the desert, occupied by six different units.

Surrounded by a barbed-wire perimeter and a six-foot earthen berm, the Brigade Support Area (BSA) is a safe zone where soldiers can rest between battles. It is secure but by no means impenetrable. The BSA is set up in a rough circle, like a pie, with each unit occupying a slice. My office, the Tactical Operations Center (TOC), is a large tent in the middle of the circle, and all the units come to us for up-to-the-minute information. My desk is a long folding table stacked with Army manuals, a phone roster with all the unit numbers in our Brigade Combat Team, and a military telephone.

I share the night shift with Sgt. First Class McDaris, whom I call Sgt. Mac, and we share a tent as well. It's close enough to the TOC that we can get there quickly if need be, yet isolated enough that we can rest undisturbed during the day. Sgt. Mac built it, teaching me the basics of field craft along the way. He took two Army-issue camouflage blankets and tied them to tent poles to create a small V-shaped tent, anchoring it to the ground with stakes. It's big enough for two cots placed two feet apart, under which we store our gear. The sides of the tent stop just shy of the tops of the cots, so there is always a small breeze or a gust of sand blowing over us. The tent's back wall is an Army poncho, but the front is open. The upside of this configuration is that it lets air circulate. The downside is that anyone who passes by can watch me sleep. But by this point I don't care, privacy being one of the many luxuries I have learned to live without.

April in Iraq runs hot and cold. The desert nights are chilly, but the days are a furnace. At 10:00 A.M., when my shift ends, it's already eighty—not the heat of summer yet, but the start of a ceaseless, burning sun that will drive us close to crazy in the coming months. That and the sand, as far as the eye can see, the coarse, brown, gritty kind better suited for construction than beach towels. A fine film of dust coats everything; you could live in an airtight canister and still look like an extra in *Lawrence of Arabia*. Our tents are Army green, but only a few hours later the sand has camouflaged our equipment and ourselves, as if claiming us as its own.

After briefing the day shift, Sgt. Mac and I slog back to our tent. It has been weeks since I've washed my hair, and I'm determined that this will be the day, my one indulgence on my birthday. While Sgt. Mac hits the rack I dig some Pantene shampoo out of one of my bags, grab a bottle of water I've saved up, and go to work. I take off my helmet and my bulletproof vest. I unsling my M-4 and take off my bayonet, my two canteens, two hundred rounds of ammo, and a gas mask. I take off the small backpack containing my chemical suit and boots, gloves, a test kit, and syringes full of vaccines for various gases and biological agents. I set the shampoo and water bottle on the tailgate of my Humvee, unbutton and remove my desert camouflage top, and in a brown T-shirt quickly scrub my arms and neck with baby wipes. Then I bend over and pour some water on my hair, just enough to get it good and damp. I quickly work the shampoo through my hair and rinse it out with the last of the water.

Afterward I feel reborn. By the time I hit the cot, my hair is almost dry.

It's too hot for real sleep, too hot for dreams. After a few minutes I fall into a fitful doze, but then a voice tugs me back to consciousness. "Kate! Kate!"

I realize it's my friend, Capt. Tony Boniface, who works the day shift at the TOC. Now he's here, shaking my shoulder and yelling my name. What's he doing in my tent? He should be at his desk.

"Kate, throw your boots on and get to the helipad! Mike just radioed that he's on his way!"

This message takes a few seconds to sink in. I have seen my husband three times since being sent to Kuwait in February. We're both in the 101st Airborne, but Mike is a combat pilot, a tip-of-the-spear warrior, and I'm a transportation logistics officer who helps to oversee medical support, maintenance, and supplies. After we entered Iraq, we were prepared to not see each other for a year. But now he's coming here? I can't believe it. I pull urine-stained boots onto bare feet, exit the tent, and start shuffling toward the airfield, remembering that not only is it my birthday, it's the day after April Fools' Day.

The swath of sand where the birds land is 150 yards from my tent. I haven't taken the time to tie my laces, so between my loose boots, the deep sand, and my stupor, I slog like a sleepwalker toward the helipad. As I get closer, two OH-58D Kiowa Warriors fly into view and gently land. Their rotors whip up the sand and send the tents around us flapping madly. Each Kiowa holds two pilots, though in their helmets and brown flight suits they all look alike. But the pilot who climbs out of the cockpit and removes his helmet wears a familiar grin. He runs toward me across the sand. His face has a two-day growth of stubble, and he looks tired from long hours of flying in heavy combat, but I can tell it's Mike, my Mike, and so I try to run.

Mike reaches me, throws his arms around me, and lifts me off my feet in a bear hug. I feel simultaneously self-conscious and blessed. I'm hugging my husband while most other soldiers won't see their spouses for months. Yet at the same time, I am, for one small moment, nothing more than a wife celebrating a birthday, even if it is in the middle of a war.

"Happy birthday!" Mike yells over the helicopter engines. "The colonel gave me permission to stop by and say hello! I can't stay long!"

I wish we had a few hours to sit and discuss our experiences over beef jerky and warm water. But I've been given a gift of two minutes. For now, that will have to be enough.

"I love you," he tells me. "Be safe." He gives me a quick kiss, another hug, and turns to go. I feel him leave my arms. I say the same words back. He waves from the cockpit as the bird takes off, taking him, my birthday gift, away. I stand there in the sand and watch the sky until his helicopter is out of sight.

CHAPTER 1

WHERE WE WERE

AUGUST 2004, MACON, MISSOURI

I WAS A SOLDIER. My husband was a soldier. Our last name, Blaise, is pronounced "blaze," as in fire.

As I write this it's late summer, and another birthday, my twenty-eighth, has gone by. I'm sitting in the living room of my father's farm-house, gazing out at two hundred acres of soybeans, corn, and wheat ripening toward harvest. My father, Steve Decker, and I are a lot alike, and I love the farm as much as he does. Before he moved out here full-time, he used to work the farm on weekends, and sometimes, though not often enough, he'd bring me with him. Heaven was sitting on a tractor in a freshly plowed field, smelling the tilled earth, pretending to drive. Dad likes to say he wants to die sitting on a tractor with a beer in his hand. He knows that this is where he'll spend the rest of his life.

But my future is less certain. Where am I going? What is home? How will I recognize it? You sacrifice a lot of personal liberties when you put on an Army uniform; you go where you are told, do what you're ordered to do, fight an enemy you're ordered to fight. But that lack of freedom also makes things easier in a way. Many of your big, life-altering decisions are made for you. Now I have to make them myself. The future is an open book, but I'm still learning the language it's written in.

I don't watch the war on the news. I'd rather hear about it from friends who are still in the service. Politicians deal in hypothetical scenarios and political positions; soldiers deal with the grim realities the politicians can't, or don't care to, see. And the media—they see what they're allowed to see. I know what I saw, but it's still developing in my mind, like a photo taken with a Polaroid instant camera, blurry and gray. I can't make sense of it all yet. It's too soon. I'd prefer to let my mind drift back to the year I spent there, the hardships I endured, the men I helped to save, the people whose lives I helped to make better, at least for a while. The times I spent with Mike.

If I apply myself, I can think back even farther, to the day that brought us to Iraq.

———

Three years ago, Mike and I were stationed fifty miles apart in South Korea.

I was a new officer based at Yongsan Garrison in Seoul, the U.S. military's headquarters in Korea. This was my first posting since going on active duty after three years in the ROTC. Mike, a Kiowa pilot, was stationed at Camp Stanton, one of twenty-two Army posts clustered along the DMZ; the post is so primitive that he received an extra $150 a month in hardship pay for living there. It was his first posting as a pilot, though he'd been on active duty for six years, having enlisted at the age of nineteen. Mike was a member of the 4th Squadron, 7th Cavalry, an air division that flew security for the 2nd Infantry's tanks and infantrymen as they patrolled the border with North Korea. That made them the first line of defense should the North Korean military get any big ideas. If any part of the world was poised to go up in flames, conventional wisdom held that it would ignite here.

I was twenty-four and a second lieutenant; Mike was twenty-six and a chief warrant officer. Because I was a commissioned officer, Army regulations dictated that Mike had to salute me and call me ma'am. I never felt this was important, but in public Mike insisted on doing both, despite the ribbing he got from his fellow soldiers. "Do you salute your wife when you get up in the morning?" they'd ask. Mike said no, but when asked why he saluted me when he didn't have to, my husband replied, "My wife has worked hard to become an officer. I salute her out of respect for the effort she's put in."

After getting married in 1997, we had signed up for the Married Army Couples Program. The program makes an effort to keep military couples together; it worked well for some, but we weren't one of them.

In late 2000 I was finishing up my college degree at Austin Peay State University in Clarksville, Tennessee, near Fort Campbell, while Mike attended flight school in Alabama. We had been apart for two years, seeing each other only on weekends and holidays. An ROTC graduate, I had requested and received Fort Campbell as my first post.

Since the senior officer in a marriage dictates where the spouse is stationed, Mike was supposed to come to Fort Campbell as well. We thought that we would finally be together, just like a normal couple. We had even started house hunting.

Six weeks before he graduated from flight school, Mike was informed that he was being sent to Korea instead. There were no explanations—the Army tells you what to do, and you do it.

"I've been separated from my wife for two years," he told his superiors. "There has to be a way to keep me stateside."

But it wasn't as if he had a choice. "What about Kate?" he'd asked.

"We'll send her to Korea, too."

"Forget it, you're on your own," I told Mike when he called to give me the news. But, of course, I didn't mean it.

"We can't put you in the same place as Mike," my branch manager told me.

"As long as we're in the same country," I replied. "That's better than clear across the world."

I arrived in Korea in January 2001; Mike arrived in April. He was getting to do what he loved: fly a helicopter on the front lines. I, on the other hand, was a military intelligence officer, a job for which I was ultimately ill suited, having been trained in transportation logistics. I could have fought to get a better job as a truck platoon leader, but it would have meant living farther away.

As a logistics unit, the 498th Corps Support Battalion spent a lot of time playing war. I would evaluate concocted threats, report to my battalion commander on the enemy's potential capabilities, and decode the "intelligence" to fathom their goals. We did these drills with other units and conducted actual missions, setting up camp in the woods, decked out in our nuclear/biological/chemical gear, poring over maps and acting on invented intelligence reports. Back at the garrison, I conducted one inspection after another, making sure the companies in the battalion were safeguarding sensitive information according to military regulations.

Housing at Yongsan Garrison was limited, so home in Seoul was a rented apartment in a relatively new three-story concrete building. The landlords, an elderly Korean couple who spoke no English, enjoyed making me native delicacies and keeping an eye on my apartment. When I first moved in, the wife was curious about Western ways and never missed a chance to enter the apartment and linger over my government-issue furniture. That stopped after I adopted a stray dog, Scout, who wouldn't allow people in when I was gone. By most standards, I was living the good life. Korea was a party assignment for a lot of soldiers, many just turned eighteen and away from their parents for the first time. Seoul was full of drinking districts that catered to the U.S. military, though aside from sightseeing and going out for a beer now and then with friends, I kept my own head down and did my job, living for Friday nights, when I'd head north to see Mike. Because he was usually locked down on post, I would go to see him.

The trip took two hours. I'd drive there in a used Hyundai I'd bought from another soldier, or I'd take mass transportation, riding the subway to its last stop on the outskirts of Seoul, followed by a thirty-minute taxi ride to Camp Stanton. There, Mike and I would spend two days trying to remember what it was like to be man and wife—some aspects came back to us more quickly than others—even if our short time together did take place in a room with all the charm of a prison cell. Mike's room had a bathroom with a shower and tub that doubled as a kitchen sink, a small TV with three English channels, a hot plate, a mini-fridge, and a twin bed that barely contained us. Mike was a big guy, a former high school football star with thighs so thick he had to squeeze into his chopper, and I invariably spent my nights up close and personal with the wall.

Tucked between rocky, heavily treed hills, Camp Stanton was like any number of small towns back home in Missouri: Blink and you'd miss it. In the winter, it froze; in the summer, it baked. Three hundred soldiers were posted there, the same population as Atlanta, Missouri, the flyspeck of a town where Mike grew up. The camp consisted of an airfield, a barracks, a tiny library, a barbershop, a gym, and a small grocery store that sold canned goods, chips, and DVDs. A catwalk over a road connected the barracks and the airfield, where the helicopters were parked within full view of a Korean cemetery carved into a hillside, its headstones visible for miles.

Needless to say, there was nothing to do; an American '80s big-hair band would come through for a few nights, but the primary form of entertainment was drinking. The chief warrant officers lived in the three-story Bachelor Officers Quarters. The Army had given them money to fix up one room on each floor. On the top floor, they built an old-fashioned diner complete with an old stove, a toaster oven, and well-worn vinyl booths. On Sundays they'd gather there to cook a big breakfast and shoot the shit. No one got around to doing much on the middle floor. The ground floor featured the soul of the post: a bar called the Babushka. The bar itself was built out of old bunk beds and scrap lumber. Camouflage nets and Christmas lights hung from the ceiling; a pool table occupied one corner, a jukebox another. A Korean artist painted murals depicting the history of the Air Cavalry, which went all the way back to the horse cavalry units of the Civil War. The Babushka was an oasis. With the jukebox blasting out George Strait or Twisted Sister, and if you could forget for a moment that you were within gunshot distance of ten thousand North Korean soldiers and within missile distance of a million more, you could swear you were in a bar in your hometown back in the States, wherever that happened to be.

————

The second week of September, I was sent north to Camp Casey for the week to take a class on antiterrorism measures. Since the post wasn't far from Camp Stanton, my boss let me stay with Mike during the course. A whole week: It was like Christmas in September. We looked forward to sharing meals, small talk, and beers at the Babushka.

The course was a sort of Terrorism 101. Along with twenty other officers from various posts in Korea, I would learn how to recognize a terrorist threat and to differentiate the profiles and goals of the various terrorist organizations.

The first day of class was Monday, September 10. I traveled by bus to Camp Casey, where I spent the day discussing homegrown militant groups in the United States.

After class I took a bus back to Camp Stanton. Mike was out flying, so I settled into domestic mode. I prepared his favorite meal of boiled potatoes, green beans, and porterhouse steak, bought at the large Army grocery store in Seoul. I boiled the potatoes and beans on the hot plate and marinated the steaks for Mike to cook on a communal grill outside. The tub was piled high with dirty dishes, so I ran hot water and washed them.

It was late by the time Mike got back. He was the type of husband who enjoyed skating the fine line between being in trouble with his wife and making her laugh. As usual, he greeted me with a grin and a smart-ass comment designed to elicit from me either a chuckle or the look of exasperation I reserved just for him. "I knew if I left those dishes there long enough you'd get around to washing them," he said, tossing his helmet on the bed. This time I laughed.

Over dinner we discussed our upcoming vacation. We'd opted against returning home to Missouri for our midtour leave in November and had chosen instead to take a dream vacation in Australia and New Zealand. It would be the honeymoon we never had. We both loved the outdoors, and we looked forward to hiking, snorkeling on the Great Barrier Reef, and visiting the local pubs. After dinner, Mike took a shower and I turned on the TV.

Searching for one of the few English-speaking channels, I flipped past a Korean soap opera, a popular Korean dance show, and the Camp Stanton movie channel. I got to CNN and saw the image of a massive skyscraper, consumed by smoke and flames. Figuring it was a commercial for a new movie, I paused to watch. The special effects seemed amazingly real, and I thought it might be a movie that would interest Mike and me, since we both enjoyed action films.

I turned the volume up. A newsreader came on the screen, and as his words sunk in, so did the realization that this wasn't a movie. It was real, it was America, and it was live. I recognized the New York City skyline and the World Trade Center, one of its towers ablaze.

Just as all that was registering, a commercial jetliner entered the screen, banked hard, and plowed into the second tower, setting off a massive explosion and fireball. My first thoughts were for the passengers on the plane, and my heart sank as if attached to a lead sinker.

"Mike, come here, you've got to see this!" I yelled.

"I'm showering!" He sounded aggravated.

"No, Mike, you've got to come here and see this!"

"I got soap in my hair!"

I saw people jump from the burning towers. I saw the Pentagon smoldering. I couldn't articulate what was happening; all I could do was yell for him to come. Finally he recognized the urgency in my voice. I'll never forget him standing in the bathroom doorway, dripping onto the carpet, a towel around his waist, saying, "What?" and my answering, "Look at that!" and then the look in his eyes as he saw what I was seeing, a scene too incomprehensible to process.

"Where is that?" he asked.

"That's New York! That's real, that's happening, that's going on right now!"

Everyone has their "where were you?" moment. My paternal grandmother, Helen Decker, can tell me where she was when she learned that Japan had attacked Pearl Harbor: at home in Galesburg, Illinois, reading a book and listening to the radio. The first thing she thought was that it meant her new husband would be drafted, and she was right. Her son, my father, remembers where he was when news broke of JFK's assassination: in an industrial economics class at the University of Missouri-Columbia. And I can remember where I was when the United States kicked off Desert Storm: at a high school basketball game in Centralia, Missouri. As a freshman, I kept the stats for the boys' basketball team. I was sitting in the bleachers with my pencil and notepad, scribbling numbers, when the announcer came over the loudspeaker and said U.S. forces had reentered Kuwait. Then he stopped the game and asked for a moment of silence for our soldiers. A hush fell over the crowd, and I closed my eyes and said a brief prayer. I remember wishing I were older so I could join the fighting, so I could be one of the people putting their lives on the line to help others. That was the moment I knew for sure that I wanted to be a soldier.

Yet now the country I had pledged to defend was under attack, and there was nothing I could do. Mike and I sat dumbstruck on a bed in a room on the other side of the world, helplessly watching, able only to ask each other over and over, "What would we do if we were there?"

Suddenly someone was banging on our door, then on every door on the floor. I opened it to see ashen-faced soldiers stalking the hallway, alerting everyone to wake up and turn on their TVs. Soon the hallway was crowded with soldiers trying to get in touch with their families on cell phones or sitting at laptops in their rooms, trolling for an Internet connection. Communications in Korea were dicey on a good day; tonight, they were impossible. The frustration was palpable—as was the fear. If New York and the Pentagon were in flames, what was going on in Korea? What were we not seeing?

Then the siren began to wail.

A military alert siren sounds like nothing else. Take every emergency sound you can think of—ambulance, fire truck, tornado warning—and stir them together. Then add the sick feeling you get when you know there's bad trouble afoot, and that's what it sounds like. This was a drill every soldier in Korea practiced for: the day when hostilities with North Korea boiled over. This was the first time I'd heard the siren when it actually meant something, making it more ominous still. That I was away from my unit and my combat gear only compounded my sense of helplessness and concern.

For pilots the siren means, *Grab your gear and get ready to fly.* For Mike, it meant the moment he went from husband to warrior, the way Clark Kent enters a phone booth a mere mortal and emerges a superhero. Mike jumped into action. He pulled on a flight suit and black leather boots, jammed a bulletproof Kevlar helmet onto his head, and strapped a 9 mm to his side. He grabbed his flight helmet and flight vest with the bulletproof lining, as well as pouches packed with survival gear in case he got shot down.

Each company had a designated meeting place in the building adjacent to its hangar. Mike ran into the hallway, joining his fellow pilots, who sprinted across the post to the catwalk, taking the stairs two at a time. I ran as fast as I could, trying to keep up. Once at the meeting place, I stood next to Mike, one of three women in the unit and the only wife there. I felt out of place in my plain basic duty uniform while everyone else wore flight gear; I didn't even have a weapon or Kevlar to make me feel soldierly—not that anyone noticed. Our eyes were fixed on the television in the office, which was replaying the collapse of the towers over and over.

The first thing the Army does in a time of crisis is count heads. The company first sergeant called out names in alphabetical order, and each soldier called out "Here!" in return. Then the company commander, a soldier about Mike's age and with about as much life experience, walked to the front of the room. He told us not to try to use the phones because the lines were clogged, and that they would let us know what we needed to know when we needed to know it.

"The post is shut down," he said. "You can't leave. We don't know what's going to happen, so go back to your rooms and keep your gear close."

Mike and I waited for him to tell us something CNN hadn't, to give us some glimpse into what was in store for us, but he knew no more than we did. We didn't yet know who had attacked us and why, but this much was clear and no one had to say it aloud: Our lives as soldiers—and as a couple—were about to change forever.

I have a series of photographs from Iraq on my laptop, which I carry with me everywhere. There I am after a rocket attack on our last base near Mosul, surveying the damage with other officers. That's me getting promoted to captain; there's Mike and my sister, Lindsey, an MP in the National Guard, who had come up from Baghdad for the occasion. That's me at my "home," a bombed-out building we called The Heap, and that's a tubful of "clean" laundry water so dirty it begged to be photographed.

My favorite photo is of Mike and me. It was taken in June 2003, nearly two years after 9/11. In the photo, Mike and I are standing in a field outside Mosul, rifles slung over our shoulders, smiling into the camera. Behind us is an outdoor shower, just like in *M*A*S*H*, right down to the bag of water warming in the sun. Mike's cousin nicknamed the photo *Iraqi Gothic*, because we resemble that old couple in the 1930 painting by Grant Wood, only we are soldiers and young.

The photo offers clues to Mike's personality. My husband loved to flaunt authority, within limits. In this picture, his uniform is hardly regulation. He's wearing a tan flight suit not quite to Army standards; his sleeves are rolled up, and he has removed his name and rank. His hat isn't authorized, either—in the desert you're supposed to wear a desert-colored one. Before becoming a helicopter pilot, he'd been in a Scout unit in the infantry, and that's the hat he used to wear. Scouts are a tight-knit group, and that floppy green hat had sentimental value, especially now that he was scouting from the air for soldiers on the ground. Ask him about the hat and he'd tell you a story.

Mike liked to buck convention when it came to uniforms. In the winter of 1998, right before his first overseas posting as an infantryman, he moved out of his barracks at Fort Campbell, Kentucky, and packed all his belongings in his red pickup. He stopped in Columbia, Missouri, to pick me up from college on the way to Macon. His dress uniform (called Class As) was lying in the passenger seat, so I relocated it to the bed of the pickup for the trip, thinking it would be secure. We got to Macon to find his uniform had blown out of the truck. The next day he and his mom, Peg, went looking for it. They found the uniform at a Department of Transportation work shed, where someone had turned it in. It had been run over a few times, and one of the jacket's shoulder seams was ripped. Mike got the uniform cleaned but not repaired. At inspections his platoon sergeant always ordered him to get the rip sewn up. "Roger that!" Mike would say, but he wouldn't do it. Explaining the rip was too good a story.

That photo tells you a few more things about Mike. If you look closely, you'll see a scar above his left eye. Mike loved to hunt, and he got that scar shooting targets with his grandfather's old .270 Winchester: The rifle kicked back with such force that the scope branded him for life. You'll notice that he has his arm around me, as always—Mike was the affectionate type. As for the big smile—well, Mike always had one of those. He loved to make people laugh and possessed a truly original sense of humor. In fact, he was the morale officer for his squadron, the guy you could always count on for a laugh when the chips were down.

To be honest, I'm describing this photo from memory. I have lots of photos of Mike on my laptop, but I can't look at them yet. I mean, I look at them, but I don't really see them. I keep telling myself that the day will come when I can, but right now I'm afraid of what will happen if I look into his eyes and allow myself to drink him in. Still, I like that one photo so much that a tiny copy of it hangs from the rearview mirror of my Chevy Tahoe. It's in an oval frame, with my wedding picture on the other side—a memento made for me by a kind woman at Fort Campbell who makes them for all the widows. Right now, it's enough to drive Mike around with me, knowing he's there, knowing I'll catch a glimpse of us when I glance in the rearview mirror.

When I was deployed overseas, I always wrote home about my experiences. E-mails, letters, you name it—my laptop got a workout. In Iraq I e-mailed my family and friends several times a week or whenever I could get an Internet connection. It's in my nature to share how I feel and what I'm going through, so it makes sense that I would share the story of Mike and our life together, in wartime and in peace.

But this book is about more than Mike and me. I also want to set a few things straight about today's military. Despite what you see on TV, the U.S. Army is made up of two types of soldiers: those whose job is to fight and those who provide support. Mike was on the front lines, fighting; I was backing him up, along with hundreds of capable, well-meaning, idealistic soldiers. Our combat experience is rarely shown on the evening news, but it's essential.

Second, the military isn't what it used to be, thanks partly to the large number of women who are choosing it as a career. Being a woman in the U.S. Army is far more nuanced than being a man—and in some cases, not necessarily less dangerous.

When you're married and in the military, as Mike and I were, the whole idea of a two-career household takes on new meaning. Of the almost seven years Mike and I were married, we spent about two actually living under the same roof. But we made our long-distance marriage work in the only way we knew how: through sheer Missouri tenacity and faith in each other and God. When Mike and I fell in love in high school, we couldn't have predicted that we'd end up married to the military as well as to each other, or that world events would send our fates marching in new and dangerous directions. But we were soldiers, true to our country and true to each other.

More than anything, I want you to know Mike. To risk your life for your country is an extraordinary thing, and when a world leader sends soldiers to war, Mike is the kind of person he gambles with: a good man, a patriotic man, a country boy with nice manners who says please and thank you and loves to work on his old Chevy. The kind of man America is made of.

CHAPTER 2

MIKE

I KNEW I WANTED to date Mike Blaise the first time I saw him cry. It was late November 1992, and I was sitting in the bleachers at Sainte Genevieve High School, huddled against an icy rain with my friends Natalie Thompson, Nancy Ellis, and Mollie Meisner, watching the Macon Tigers play the Sainte Genevieve Dragons. It was the sectional championship, the biggest game in our school's history. We had a lot riding on the outcome personally—Natalie's dad, Walt Thompson, was the team's coach, and Nancy was dating its star cornerback, Robert Henry—but so did the entire town of Macon, most of which, it seemed, had driven the three hours to cheer on the Tigers.

High school football runs a close third behind God and family in Macon, and that season the Tigers had given God and family a run for their money. The team had won its first game in September, and it had kept on winning. Every week, whether the team was playing at home or away, the bleachers would be packed with Maconites clutching hot dogs and cups of cocoa from concession stands that had never seen such business. Even standing room was scarce. The town didn't miss a game—it was an unspoken pledge between the team and the fans. Whatever the weather, we traveled wherever we had to as long they kept giving us a show on Friday nights. The team pressed on into the fall, each successive victory a gust of wind behind their backs, blowing them ever closer toward the state finals.

A lot was on the line. The Tigers had already made school history by advancing further than any other team. But they wanted it all. If the Tigers won here in the semifinals, they would go to state for the first time. If they lost, they would go home.

Mike was a part of the reason the Tigers had gotten this far. At six feet and 220 pounds, he was one of the best defensive linemen in our conference—pretty good for a farm boy who hadn't touched a football until he was fourteen years old.

Mike grew up in the rolling farmland outside Macon with his parents, Terry and Peg, and two younger siblings, Josh and Kristina. When Mike was eight, they moved into a double-wide across the road from the Blaise family farm. It was owned by Terry's dad, Virgil, whom everyone called Grampy. Mike grew up feeding the horses, cleaning the dog pens, calling in the hogs. He drove a tractor long before he drove a car. He went to school in Atlanta, Missouri, population 400. Mike's class could fit in a thimble: fifteen kids, all of whom had risen through the academic ranks together since kindergarten. Ten miles from Macon, Atlanta is one of those tiny towns in northern Missouri that are hanging on for dear life. Their downtowns are boarded up and the residential streets are dotted with abandoned houses; here and there you'll spot a roof sitting flat on the ground, as if the house beneath it just got tired of standing and, with a sigh, collapsed.

When Mike was in eighth grade, his parents divorced after sixteen years of marriage. Peg moved to town to start over. Terry, who drove a feed truck at the time, moved to Macon as well, figuring that living in the same town would make it easier to share custody of their three kids. That meant that Mike and his siblings would have to move as well, and Mike wasn't happy about it. Relocating to Macon meant leaving behind everyone and everything he'd known. Later he'd say it was for the best—he got to play football, and he got to meet me.

With a population of five thousand, Macon is a thriving metropolis compared with Atlanta. It is the county seat, a tight-knit rural community with an ethanol plant, a Toastmaster factory, a ConAgra Foods processing facility, a few fast-food joints, and a small Amish community. The big events in town are the annual tractor pull at the fairgrounds and the exotic animal auction at the Lolli Brothers Livestock Market. There used to be a drive-in movie theater until the spring of 2004, when a tornado blew down the screen. Seeing this as a sign, the owners made good on their long-standing plans to retire.

Macon is the kind of place where the scent of fertilizer drifts on the evening air, where all the pickups are American-made, and where everyone waves when they drive by, whether they know you or not. If you don't like waving back, don't come to Macon.

Every kid in town goes to one school: Macon County R-1 (that stands for Reorganized District 1). Our school had one thing Atlanta doesn't: a football team. As boys tend to at that age, Mike sprouted into a man overnight. He grew from a short, soft kid into a human oak tree solid and strong, with broad shoulders and thick, muscular legs. Mike made the junior varsity squad as a starting lineman, moving up to varsity as a junior, and it was no coincidence that in his senior year the Tigers had their best season ever.

Having attended Macon R-1 my entire life, I had a close circle of acquaintances, but it did not include Mike. I'd see him in the hallways now and again, but he was a year ahead of me, so our social circles rarely intersected. Still, I knew everyone by name, so I knew who Mike Blaise was and that he was on the football team. I also knew that he belonged to a group of pranksters that included Robert Henry and Brian Walters. There wasn't a lot to do in Macon on weekends or any other day of the week, so Mike and his buddies spent Friday and Saturday nights "cruising the block." On Saturday nights, the old downtown, which occupies about three square blocks, would be bumper to bumper with kids in cars. The parking lot behind Sherry's Flowers was a favorite meeting spot. If you saw someone you knew, you'd say, "Meet me in the back parking lot," and you'd go back there to talk, to flirt, maybe to pass a bottle. My parents, Steve and Marie Decker, considered cruising the block a big waste of time and gas. "Why put miles on the car for no good reason?" they'd ask rhetorically. But I'd manage to make it down there anyway, and if they disapproved, they never let on. At least they knew where I was, and besides, I never caused trouble.

So I knew Mike by name and reputation. I knew him, above all, because my friend Natalie had a crush on him. Natalie was girly, big-hearted, and liked by everyone—except, of course, the one boy who wouldn't look at her twice. Mike knew of Natalie's feelings, but there was one big problem: She was the coach's daughter and thus off-limits as far as he was concerned. We didn't know this at the time; he simply seemed shy when it came to girls. Natalie eventually got tired of trying and moved on, and as her friend, I moved on with her.

I was a stick-skinny straight-A student with glasses who played softball and ran track. A tomboy, I usually had a black eye or a scabby knee. When it came to unrequited love, I was a grazer. The object of my infatuation changed daily, which I figured improved my chances of actually finding a boy who would like me back. Natalie and I would sit at school dances in the cafeteria, working up the courage to ask our respective crushes to dance. We'd dance with a guy friend or play it cool at the refreshment table, casually sipping 7-Up and Coke from red plastic cups, waiting for the slow songs to end while our eyes scanned the room for the boys in question.

Mike came back into my life two years later. It was the summer of 1992, and my other good friend Nancy dragged me to dinner at Pizza Hut with her boyfriend, Robert, the Macon Tigers' star cornerback. Robert dragged along his best friend, Mike. I remembered him as Natalie's long-ago crush, the quiet, unassuming football player.

I saw a different side of Mike that night: sly, sarcastic, and hysterically funny. I can't recall one joke he told, but he had us in stitches throughout the meal. He never made eye contact with Nancy or me, and his combination of shyness and humor intrigued me. I was hooked and curious.

A few days later, I was working my regular job at the C & R Market on East Briggs Drive. It was my second summer there; I'd started at age fifteen, to earn some extra spending money, and was quickly promoted from checkout girl to the customer service desk, also known as "the booth." I'd spend hours a day standing behind a long wooden counter, cashing paychecks and tallying up the store profits. As a high school student, I got paid far too little for such an important job, but I had a reputation for being a girl responsible beyond her years, and the store's owners knew a good deal when they saw one. It was my first job and I took it very seriously, as I did everything.

That afternoon, I was counting out money and chatting to a coworker when a shadow crossed the counter. I looked up and there was Mike, check in hand. He didn't seem to recognize me. He simply slid the check across the counter without a word. I counted out his cash—about one hundred dollars. He said thank-you and left.

Every Friday for the next few weeks Mike came in to cash a check for his weekend spending money. He never seemed interested in talking; if anything, he seemed oblivious to my presence. I, on the other hand, always enjoyed seeing him. I liked his look. His hair was dark brown and so were his eyes. Everything about him seemed larger than life: his shoulders, his hands, his well-muscled arms deeply tanned from a summer spent working as a farmhand. When football season got under way, my friends and I attended every game as always. But this season I found myself scanning the field for number 66. Game after game I watched him, as the Tigers rolled toward the sectional final.

Unfortunately, the game against the Sainte Genevieve Dragons did not end happily for the Tigers. The Dragons were known as football giants, and we were simply outmatched. The game and a light rain had turned the field swampy, and while the Dragons celebrated, the Tigers sat in the quagmire, heads in their hands, or simply stood like muddy statues, heads bowed, mirroring the dismay of the Macon fans. At seventeen, these young men had personally brought Macon together, and by losing, they felt as if they'd let down the entire town.

Finally, the Tigers pulled themselves together and headed for the locker room, but not before making one final gesture. As the players walked off, they raised their helmets to the stands in a salute to their fans. When the stadium lights hit the boys' faces, I could see that they were visibly upset yet trying valiantly not to show it. And then I saw Mike walk past, head erect, rubbing his eyes. I had seen him before, but at that moment, I *really* saw him: a big defensive lineman crying over a bitter disappointment, unembarrassed by the fact that everyone could see him.

After the game, Nancy's mom drove us back to Macon. About halfway home, I turned to my friends and announced, "You know who I'd like to go out with? I'd like to go out with Mike Blaise."

———

Nancy and Robert happily set the wheels of romance in motion. When Robert asked Mike if he'd be interested in dating Kate Decker, Mike responded, "I don't know who she is. Is she fat?" (Mike was not a shallow person, but he was in high school and, well, I have no further excuses to make for him.) Later, when Nancy told me that Mike had had no idea who I was, I was shocked. He didn't remember eating pizza with me or cashing checks at the C & R. I had failed to make any impression whatsoever, and had I known this at the time, I might have called the whole thing off.

Mike would have to see me for himself. To get to my locker, I had to walk past the lockers where the senior boys loitered between classes. As I passed by, I spotted Robert whispering to Mike and slyly pointing me out. I felt a little like a prize steer being inspected before auction, but a happy one when I heard that Mike had immediately said to Robert, "Yeah, I'd like to go out with her."

The following evening, the school was hosting a basketball game followed by a dance. Robert assured Mike he would set the whole thing up; all Mike had to do was show up. Instead, Mike did one of the classiest things you could expect from a high school kid: He told Robert that the only way he'd go out with me was if he asked me himself.

After a flurry of notes, it was decided that Mike would meet me at my locker after school. I lingered there, nervous and excited, until the school was empty of kids. Finally, as I was loading my book bag, I heard someone clear his throat. There stood the most nervous person I had ever laid eyes on.

"Um, I was wondering, would you, um . . . ?" Mike's voice trailed off and his eyes found the floor. "How would you . . . um . . ."

Clearly I would have to take matters into my own hands. "Yes, I'd really like to," I said. He smiled, and the tension evaporated.

In small-town America, there is no such thing as a secret. Pretty soon the entire school knew of our date. My younger brother, Joe, who was thirteen at the time, got wind of it and decided to intervene.

"You shouldn't let Kate date Mike," he told my father. "He drinks too much, and he'll be a bad influence on her."

On the first count Joe was correct—Mike's capacity for alcohol made him a local legend. The most infamous story involved him naked except for cowboy boots, belting out Garth Brooks into a fan as if it were a microphone. You couldn't do something that noteworthy in Macon without the entire town knowing about it in five minutes flat.

My father replied that he knew Mike's parents to be good people and that my seeing Mike was all right with him.

The next evening, Nancy came over after school to help me get ready. The prettiest girl in school, she was well versed in the feminine art of primping. We spent hours in front of the bathroom mirror, giggling, while Nancy worked her magic. She applied more makeup than I'd ever worn and teased my long hair to within an inch of its life, spraying it into place and enveloping the bathroom in a cloud of Aqua Net. I put on a good sweater and jeans with black flats. The result, when I looked in the mirror, was a person I had never seen before and would never see again.

Nancy oohed and aahed over my new look. Needing an impartial opinion, I walked downstairs to show my mother.

It was only December 4, but already the house was ready for Christmas. This was my family's favorite time of year. The Thanksgiving leftovers were barely cold before Mom would haul out the boxes of ornaments and decorations, and with everyone pitching in, the house soon looked as if Santa himself had consulted on the interior design. A Christmas tree blinked in a corner. On top of the TV was Mom's artfully arranged collection of small silver-plated figurines. There were about two dozen in all, each engaged in some wintry activity: building a snowman, pulling a load of wood on a sled, or just skating along in twos and threes atop a mirror that doubled as a frozen pond. Each was brightly painted and thin as a dime, finely detailed down to the flowing scarves and tiny skates. My great-great-grandmother had sent the figures from Germany many years ago as a gift to her granddaughter, my mother's mother. Mom treasured them. Each year one of us kids would take turns placing them just so, lingering over the position of each figurine, as if we were placing ourselves in the scene as well.

Mom was nestled in her usual spot on the sofa, reading a mystery novel, looking as if she, too, had been set in place with great care. Now that two of my three older sisters were married and out of the house, she had more time to herself.

She looked up from her book and smiled. "You look beautiful, honey," she said, because she knew that that was what I needed to hear.

With four daughters, my parents were experienced at meeting first dates. I'd seen the drill with my older sisters: Using interrogation techniques worthy of FBI agents, our parents prodded and pried the young man to see if he was worthy of dating a Decker girl. Since my father was out of town on business this time, the task fell to my mother. So I wasn't surprised when she said, "You have to leave Mike alone with me for ten minutes so I can see what kind of young man he is."

I cringed inside. I worried he'd get so tongue-tied that Mom would think him incapable of carrying on an adult conversation. But once again, Mike surprised me.

Mike arrived for our date at the appointed hour, one of only two times he would ever be on time in the history of our relationship. (The other was our wedding.) I answered the door that evening with equal parts eagerness and dread. Mike looked great—he was dressed simply, in blue jeans and a button-down shirt over a T-shirt. It was twenty degrees outside, but he wasn't wearing a coat. Mike generated so much body heat he glowed like a coal-burning stove, a fact that would continually astonish my mother in future years. His eyes took me in with a gulp, though he seemed as nervous as I was.

I invited Mike in, pointed him toward the living room, and left him to his doom. I hid out in the bathroom, counting the clock ticks until I felt enough time had passed that I could go in to rescue him.

When I entered the living room, I found Mike and Mom sitting on the couch, laughing and talking like old friends. Mom told me later that Mike had broken the ice by commenting on her skating figurines. His first words to her when he sat down were "Those are really neat." From that moment on, Mike could do no wrong in my mother's eyes. Their relationship skated along, always in sync.

First dates can be unbearably awkward, but ours may have set some sort of record. The basketball game was slow paced, and we found little to say about it; I don't even remember who won. Afterward the crowd moved to the cafeteria for the dance. The party committee had cut out paper snowflakes and taped them to the cinder block walls, along with festive plastic greenery. A DJ spun records in one corner, and folding chairs lined the room's perimeter. I hoped the dance would be more fun than the game, though I didn't like dancing much. As it turned out, Mike didn't either. We sat against the wall and tried to talk over the music while my friends flitted by and giggled, "Why aren't you dancing?" The floor was packed with small circles of girls laughing and dancing, one brave guy in the group.

Mike and I stayed put, struggling to make small talk. Finally, he said, "Do you want to get out of here?" He didn't have to ask twice.

We hopped into his blue Oldsmobile Cutlass Calais, bought with all those paychecks he cashed at the C & R. "Where should we go?" I asked as he started the car.

"The Christmas lights are nice," he said. "Let's go check them out."

With that comment, Mike stole my heart—I had loved to drive around town and look at the lights since I was a kid. Mike usually drove fast, but that night the roads were icy, so he took it slow. We toured the residential streets, admiring the elaborate twinkling displays and listening to country-western on the radio. Afterward we rented Nintendo football and went to my house to play. Mom stayed upstairs reading, taking herself away from her book long enough to bring us brownies and refills of iced tea. Mike and I agreed to go to a movie the following night, and he left without trying to kiss me good night.

Things between us got serious rather quickly. We soon became known around school as a couple, and we were inseparable. Having my first serious high school boyfriend earned me entrée into an elite sorority. I was now one of the girls wearing her boyfriend's letter jacket in the hallways and trying to make his class ring fit my skinny finger by wrapping it with string. I felt very grown-up.

We entered into the traditional high school dating rituals: study sessions, weekend dates, late-night phone calls. We double-dated a lot with Nancy and Robert, going to movies at the drive-in or eating at the Country Inn Cafe, the local greasy spoon. I made it quite clear to Mike that I was saving myself for marriage, and while that didn't always make him happy, especially as time wore on, he respected my feelings.

At sixteen, I hadn't dated a lot, but I knew this much: I could only be with someone who understood the importance of family. Mike was close to his and willing to become a part of mine, even from the very beginning. He already knew my sister Lindsey—both seniors, they shared an algebra class, where he'd always ask to copy her homework. But it was some time before he met Anna and Wendy, since they lived out of town. After failing to head off that first date, Joe again became uninterested in my life and got on fine with Mike. He and Mom clicked immediately, of course, but my father can take a while to warm up to people. The two found common ground in their mutual love of farming, and Dad liked Mike's country-boy manners— he'd take time to inquire after an elderly person and carry a stranger's groceries if she needed help—and over the years they grew close.

Our families were very different. Both were close, but in their own way. The Deckers, all seven of us, were fiercely protective yet not physically demonstrative. We loved one another's company, but we didn't spend a lot of time handing out hugs or saying "I love you." The Blaises, on the other hand, were the most touchy-feely people I'd ever met.

If your boyfriend's family doesn't like you, your chances of sticking around for any period of time are slight. Fortunately, I got along well with Mike's parents. Peg was a pretty woman with a blond ponytail down her back. When she and Terry met, her father was an executive at the Toastmaster factory, which made them one of the better-off families in town. A talented equestrian, she gave up a scholarship to a prestigious college near St. Louis to marry Terry. He was twenty-one; she was eighteen. They lived in a couple of different houses outside town while Terry worked as a farmhand; Mike, their oldest, came along in 1974. He had his dad's sturdy build and his mom's brown eyes and fine features—in fact, their profiles were almost identical.

I found Terry to be a warm, emotional man, with blue eyes that didn't hide much. He met his second wife about a year after moving to Macon. Cheryl Adair's husband had left out of the blue, leaving her with two kids. She and Terry met at RadioShack, where he had taken a part-time job and Cheryl was working the Christmas rush. They have been happily married for almost two decades.

Terry loves to tell stories, and Mike's childhood was a favorite subject. They had a little routine: While Terry spun his yarn, Mike would roll his eyes and shake his head in mock dismay. Many of Terry's tales involved church. Mike's irreverence was legendary, even in places where reverence was a prerequisite. He had grown up going to Mount Zion Methodist, a tiny country church surrounded by fields in the middle of nowhere. His father and his father's parents had grown up attending Mount Zion. The church must have felt like a second home, because Mike was known to drop his overalls and relieve himself off the front steps. (Fortunately, he was just a little boy at the time.)

As places of worship go, Mount Zion is a casual place—you can wear whatever you like, and the Sunday service is short on ceremony and long on community fellowship. During every service, the preacher asks if anyone in the congregation would like to come up to the front of the church and sing a hymn. Mike has an uncle named Dale Wilson, who is married to Terry's sister, Linda. Dale, a professional singer of some local repute, sang regularly. One Sunday morning when Mike was about five, Dale requested that his little nephew be allowed to sing. He took Mike to the front, sat him on his knee, and asked Mike what song he'd like to perform. Instead of "Jesus Loves Me" or "Go Tell It on the Mountain," Mike chirped, " 'War Is Hell (On the Homefront, Too).' " It was an old T. G. Sheppard country-western tune about a military wife who finds comfort in the arms of another man while her husband is off at war. To a chorus of chuckles, Dale told Mike they'd work on something more appropriate to sing the following Sunday.

For me, Terry's stories opened a window into their past, shedding light on the family influences that had shaped Mike's interests and character. According to Terry, Mike had an uncle who sparked his interest in flying: Peg's brother, Bob Rasmussen. During the Vietnam War, Uncle Bob was one of the fabled Wild Weasel pilots whose job was to root out North Vietnamese surface-to-air missile sites by flying low overhead, inviting missile fire; a strike force behind them would then take out the missile sites. To a kid hearing his uncle describe these life-and-death adventures, flying sounded about as exciting a profession as there was in the world.

———

Before Mike was a soldier and a helicopter pilot, he was a teenager whose primary interests were farming, football, drinking, and driving at an excessive rate of speed. He'd scream down the roller-coaster back roads, pushing his Cutlass so hard that the car actually caught air off the hillcrests until I laughed out of both anxiety and glee.

Mike liked engines and other loud things, but he didn't like school. He never skipped class, but he didn't exactly apply himself, either. He'd failed English in his junior year, and that seemed to scar him. He didn't think of himself as smart, and somewhere along the line he convinced himself he was of average intelligence. He was wrong, of course. For one thing, Mike was like a human telephone book. I never bothered keeping an address book or pen handy because if I wanted someone's phone number, all I had to do was ask Mike for it. He could recall the makes and models of hundreds of muscle cars and knew everything there was to know about country-western music.

He wasn't too shabby at singing it, either. One day, a few weeks after we'd begun dating, I arrived at school to find the place buzzing about something that had happened the previous afternoon. Mike belonged to the school safety club, though I suspect this had less to do with his concern for his fellow students and more to do with the fact that you got to miss class to attend meetings. They took place in the auditorium, which had a stage. Mike's friends were goofing around with the microphone and convinced him to start the proceedings off by singing. I don't know which song Mike performed, but it was no doubt by Garth Brooks, his current favorite. Afterward, everybody in the room turned to one another and said, "Was that Mike Blaise? He seemed like such a quiet boy."

Mike came across as shy until you got to know him. In fact, he was a social animal. He made friends with ease, something I couldn't do. It was Mike who'd strike up conversations with strangers, Mike who'd see an interesting face and want to learn more about the person behind it, Mike who'd stand and talk with a group of old men outside a grocery store while the milk he'd just bought grew warm.

But Mike became my favorite person, not for his virtues but for his flaws. He wasn't perfect, and I didn't want him to be. I was perfect enough for both of us. I excelled in school and sports, obeyed my parents, was elected student body president at the end of my junior year. I had my father's stoic personality, and I needed someone who could tap into my fun-loving side: a good bad boy, if there can be such a thing. Mike fit the bill. No one has ever made me laugh so hard. We had a good time, no matter what we were doing. He always seemed to enjoy being around me, and that made me feel special. He loved to tease me, to see how far he could push me before I got mad. A few months after our first date, he started calling me Chubby, and the nickname stuck. Oftentimes he'd put on one of his funny voices and say, "Kate is Chubby," over and over while trying to tickle me. He was always touching me, holding me, pulling me close. Mike coaxed out my affectionate side, but he could also pick on me to the point that I got impatient. When I lost my temper and told him to leave me alone, he'd laugh and say, "You know, there are women out there who'd kill to have someone touching them all the time."

"I'm sure there are," I'd say dryly, though I never worried about Mike's attentions straying elsewhere. He never dated anyone but me.

And he was always a gentleman. He soon learned that I hated to get into a cold car in the wintertime, and so a few minutes before we left anywhere, he made sure to go out and start the engine and turn on the heat.

A few days after our first date, a friend from school died in a car accident. Mike picked me up and took me to the visitation at the funeral home, along with Robert and Nancy. He helped me into my coat when I was ready to go and bought us ice cream at Hardees on the way home. Afterward, we sat in the car for an hour and talked about life and death. That Christmas, though we'd been dating only three weeks, he gave me a gold locket in the shape of a heart. He didn't know me well enough to know I didn't care for hearts; nevertheless, for months I never took it off.

My seventeenth birthday rolled around in April. Mike had overheard me telling my mother how much I needed a new dress for some upcoming school events. On my birthday, he appeared with a dress box wrapped with a big red bow. Inside was a navy blue dress with white polka dots and buttons up the front. When I held it up to my body, I could see it would fit perfectly. It surprised and pleased me that Mike had not only driven all the way to the mall in Columbia to shop for me, but had picked out something I actually liked. When I asked him how he knew what size to get, he sheepishly replied that he'd shown the salesgirl my dimensions with his hands.

Like a lot of young couples, Mike and I had a special place. His mom owned a nice piece of land on the outskirts of town, where she stabled horses and lived with her second husband, Gary "Rat" Bloomberg. (It was Rat who gave Mike the hat that would become his trademark: a red baseball cap that bore the logo from J&B Scotch whiskey. Mike always wore it backward and was rarely without it.) Peg lived on a gravel road, and at the end of that road someone had laid a few boards across a narrow stream. We called the boards "the bridge," and we called the stream the Chattahoochee, after the Alan Jackson song, "Way Down Yonder on the Chattahoochee," which was popular at the time. There was a tree and a grassy spot, and when we wanted to be alone or say good-bye, we'd come down here and sit in the shade and talk. It wasn't much but it was ours, a place to go before we had to go home. Every meaningful conversation we ever had before our marriage we had at the bridge.

Mike was easy to talk to, and he wasn't afraid to express his emotions. At the bridge he talked about how painful his parents' divorce had been and how he'd taken it personally, as if he himself were responsible for not holding the family together. Months after we got together, we were sitting at the bridge, and I told him about seeing him cry after losing the game to Sainte Genevieve, and what a strong impression that had made on me.

"I wasn't crying because I was sad," he said. "I was crying because I was pissed off. It seemed like we gave up before we should have, and that's what bothered me the most."

Mike never gave up. When he made up his mind, he was as inflexible as an oak in a windstorm, more apt to break than bend. He generally could see only one solution to a problem and wasn't willing to listen to other options. I first saw the full extent of his stubbornness the night of his senior prom.

Prom night in Macon is quite a shindig. The dance is held in the school gym, but first there's the Grand March. Everyone in town stands along the sidewalk that connects the middle school to the high school. An announcer says the couple's names into a microphone beauty-pageant style, and the kids walk down the sidewalk into the gym while the proud parents and friends applaud and snap photos. As Mike and I walked into the gym we saw Mike's dad, Terry, and his stepmom, Cheryl. Terry took some picture of us, and then he pulled Mike aside for some last-minute instructions. "Be careful," he said. "Kate's dad has entrusted you with his daughter, so take care of her." These words infuriated Mike to no end. He became convinced his father didn't trust him, and no amount of arguing the contrary could change his mind. He spent the rest of the night fuming over the conversation.

Mike was also a creature of habit. Every Christmas, including our first together, he'd watch his favorite movie, *National Lampoon's Christmas Vacation*, reciting all the punch lines by heart. He spent New Year's Eve doing the same thing—playing cards and drinking at his best friend Mark's house—and getting him to break that routine was like trying to turn an ocean liner. He and Mark had met their freshman year. They had a lot in common: Mark was also the new guy in school, and his parents were divorced as well. Of all Mike's friends, Mark was the one Mike always stayed in touch with, always made a point of seeing when he came home to Macon.

But Mike's tenacity was one of his greatest strengths, the glue that held him to his principles, even if it did almost torpedo his football career. The summer before his junior year, the football coach had decreed that whoever didn't come to the July camp and lift weights the rest of the summer wouldn't play that season. Mike was torn. He had his summer job at a huge farm owned by the Kemp family; he loved making a good wage just as much as he loved football. After a lot of soul-searching, he decided he couldn't let the Kemps down, so he told the coach he couldn't come. Later, when Mike walked into the football office after a summer of hard labor, the coach took one look at him and considered adding bale slinging to his football program. Mike played that year and went on to earn All-Conference honors.

Six months after our first date, in June 1993, Mike graduated from high school. He'd been offered a football scholarship at a small four-year college in Quincy, Illinois. I urged him to accept it, but Mike didn't think he was up to the challenge academically. "What would I study?" he asked. "Besides, I wouldn't know a single person there." But no number of pep talks from me could convince him of his true intelligence; he had to discover it for himself, though it would take years.

Instead, he enrolled at Linn State Technical College, two hours away, to study auto mechanics. He had always enjoyed tinkering with cars, but beyond that, he'd never seriously considered what he wanted to do with the rest of his life. He planned to live near school during the week, sharing an apartment with Mark and Brian, and come home on weekends. We had one summer to be together before he left.

I'd grown up in Macon, and I was a city slicker compared to Mike. I taught him townie skills like cooking and playing tennis, and on a fine Saturday in July, he taught me to ride.

Mike's mom had two horses, a gentle mare named Shotsy and a fiery stud named Cracker. Peg had owned Cracker since before Mike was born, and he was like a very large family pet. Cracker was a beautiful horse—tall and white, with light gray dapples and intelligent brown eyes. He had a regal way of standing and looking at you, as if sizing up whether you were worthy enough to ride him.

Cracker and Shotsy were stabled outside town. That day they were grazing in the paddock together, but when Cracker spotted Mike, apples bulging in his pockets, he began to prance around excitedly. "Cracker can be pretty spirited when you first saddle him," Mike told me. "I have to ride him a little bit to calm him down."

Mike offered an apple to each horse. They ate them immediately and nuzzled his hands for more. Mike lifted the saddle and placed it gently on Cracker's back, murmuring softly all the while. At first Cracker's nervousness had intimidated me, but now he seemed calmer, and I felt my confidence rise. Mike cinched the saddle and put on the bridle and swung up onto the horse. As if he'd flipped a switch, Cracker took off bucking all over the field with Mike on his back, riding him like a rodeo star. After a minute or so, Mike brought the horse to a trot and then a standstill. I eyed Cracker warily and wondered what I'd gotten myself into.

Mike turned out to be a great teacher. He was calm, patient, willing to explain every detail. He started with the basics—positioning of the feet and hands, how firmly to hold the reins. He told me what to do if Cracker ran or galloped: "Lock your legs tight around his stomach and hold on. Don't let the horse know you're nervous." He also told me the best way to fall off if that was my only option: "Roll into a tight ball, protect your head, and get out of the way as fast as you can."

I hooked my boot in the stirrup; Mike lifted me onto the horse and then hoisted himself up behind me. I felt safe knowing Mike was there in case Cracker decided to pull something funny. Mike clicked his tongue and touched his heels to Cracker's flanks and we took off at a gentle trot. This was the pattern our lessons would take: We'd ride together for an hour, walking or trotting, until finally I began to ride solo. Then we'd spend afternoons riding Cracker and Shotsy. We stayed in the pasture or galloped along the dusty dirt roads, drinking in the fresh air. It always surprised me how willing these powerful animals were to let us throw a piece of leather onto their backs, climb on, and be carried around a field when they could have flung us off so easily.

CHAPTER 3

THE CENTER OF THE UNIVERSE

WHEN IMPORTANT PEOPLE enter your life, they bring with them, if you're lucky, others who can affect you just as profoundly, who broaden and enrich your experiences and actions. So it was with Virgil Blaise, Terry's father and Mike's grandfather. Mike and I had been dating only about a month when he said, "I want you to meet Grampy." I could tell it was important. In fact, to understand Mike, you needed to meet his granddad.

The Blaises had lived and farmed in northern Missouri as long as anyone could remember. They grew up here, got married here, settled here, and died here. Mike's ancestors emigrated to the United States from Germany in the nineteenth century, settling in Iowa for years. Then the Great Depression hit. Hoping to improve their prospects, the family moved to northeast Missouri and took up farming when Grampy was a few years old. He had to drop out of school at sixteen to help feed himself and his family, and he hired himself out as a farmhand before moving to Macon as a young adult.

Grampy was a fixture on Macon's agricultural scene. He owned five hundred acres, where he raised livestock and farmed oats, sunflowers, and milo. His small white house, impeccably maintained, stood near a gravel road; it had a garage off to the side and a barn and a chicken coop out back. Behind them, pastures rolled to the horizon. Grampy had a long, healthy relationship with the local Amish community; a young Amish girl looked after his house, and every summer Grampy hired some women to harvest his grapes, paying them partly in jam. One of his favorite events was the annual Old Time Flywheel Reunion at the fairgrounds, a sort of beauty pageant for vintage tractors and farm machines that have been lovingly restored by their owners.

When his family moved across the street, Mike would spend every spare moment at Grampy's house, following him around the farm, a stocky shadow in beat-up overalls. Grampy taught Mike to drive one of his three tractors, a red Farmall from the 1950s, and promised Mike that someday it would be his.

After Mike's parents split up and move to Macon, Grampy provided some much-needed stability. Terry and Peg worked out a compromise where Mike could spend the summers at Grampy's place; as soon as school was out, he'd pack up in his belongings and move in with him. When Mike turned fifteen, he started working summers at the Kemp farm. It was a man's day of work, feeding the cattle, sorting and giving shots to the hogs, helping to bring in the harvest. Mike excelled at physical labor, and though the days were long and the work hard, he loved it. He'd spend the evenings playing cards or sitting on the porch with Grampy, who would lend him a pipe so they could talk and smoke together.

Over the years, Grampy's became the place where Mike went when life wasn't going well, when he wasn't getting along with one of his parents, or when he just needed a break. It became my refuge as well, and even when Mike and I could agree on nothing else, we could both agree that Grampy ruled.

If Grampy's house was the center of Mike's universe, then the kitchen was the center of Grampy's. His house had a living room and three bedrooms, though you'd never know it, they got so little use. The kitchen was the focal point of family dinners, holiday gatherings, and that all-important autumn ritual, the opening day of hunting season. After a morning of shooting deer or at least thinking about shooting deer, every hunter in three counties would show up at Grampy's kitchen for breakfast. One by one they'd stomp the snow off their heavy boots and enter through the side door, faces red from the cold. As the door opened and closed, the smell of clean, fresh air battled with the thicker aroma of cooking bacon. Terry would fry the bacon and make the gravy while his brother-in-law Dale whipped up the pancakes and Dale's son Larry toasted the bread. I would set the table and make biscuits while Mike got started on frying the eggs. As the hunters trickled in, they took seats around the kitchen table and began to tell tall tales and compare the morning's kills. I can picture Grampy now, sitting in the midst of it all, smoking his pipe and smiling—the godfather of the hunt. After a hunter was done bragging about the deer he'd bagged, Grampy would grab his Polaroid camera and traipse outside, where the prize was tied to the roof or thrown in the truck bed. No matter if it was a monster buck or a little doe, Grampy would snap the hunter's picture with his trophy and hand the picture over as a souvenir. Then he'd reassume his position at the kitchen table, which is exactly where I found him that winter day Mike took me to meet him for the first time.

———

Right after Christmas, we drove out to Grampy's house for a family dinner. The first snow of the winter covered the rolling hills and the thick stands of woods. In the fields, corn stubble poked up through the whiteness like whiskers. Horses and sheep stood quietly in the snow or nibbled on hay bales. Smoke curled from the chimney into the late afternoon sky.

Mike parked in the short driveway, and we entered through the side door. Everyone else was already there, hovering around the stove or setting the two tables that had been placed together to accommodate the crowd. Terry and Cheryl were there. So were Josh and Kris; his aunt Linda and uncle Dale, and their three kids, Larry, Lisa, and Stephanie. (Mike was especially close to Stephanie; she was only two weeks younger than him, and they'd grown up together. At five, they were devastated to learn that they were related and thus could never get married.)

Grampy sat at the head of a long table, talking and smoking a pipe. When he saw us he rose with an ease that defied his seventy-seven years, and it was as if a farmer in a Norman Rockwell painting had stepped out of the canvas to greet us. He wore a faded flannel shirt with rolled-up sleeves, brown slippers, and light blue Key overalls. A red tin of pipe tobacco was stuffed into the top pocket. He smelled of the outdoors, of wood smoke, of tobacco and coffee, and I'd come to think that if I could bottle that scent, I could put Ralph Lauren out of business. His white hair was cut into a spiky, military-style crew cut. His skin was tanned a dark brown from working outside, and his fingertips were worn smooth from years of hard labor. But the features that captivated me were his eyes. They were the lightest shade of blue and were filled with humor and intelligence. I had never seen eyes that literally twinkled. Above them perched black, wing-shaped brows that looked ready to fly off his face.

Mike introduced me to his grandfather. He shook my hand and said, "Hello, I'm Grampy."

I'd brought him a Christmas gift, a jar of honey wrapped with a ribbon, to which I'd tied a plastic reindeer ornament. Grampy graciously accepted it and later put the reindeer in his china cabinet, where it stayed as long as I knew him.

The family was a well-oiled domestic machine and set about finishing dinner. Within minutes we were seated and eating pork tenderloin, homemade egg noodles, biscuits, and green and brown beans from the garden. Dinners at my house tended to be a relatively restrained affair, but this meal was a festival of teasing voices, laughter, and clinking utensils. The hubbub kept up throughout dinner, and I listened as the talk swirled around me.

After dinner, Mike assumed dishwashing duty while everyone systematically began clearing the dishes and putting things away. The leftovers were stored in the fridge for Grampy's meals the next day, and the tables were wiped down and dried so we could play cards. I sat there waiting for the decks to come out. Instead, everyone drifted into the living room and draped themselves on the furniture and the floor. What in the world were these people doing? As I would discover, the siesta gene ran strong in the Blaise family.

Grampy must have seen the look on my face, because he opted to stay in the kitchen and visit. He lit his pipe, shuffled the deck of cards and dealt out two hands of four-point pitch, a card game that involves teams, betting and bidding. I grew up playing pitch with my family, so he was thrilled that I already knew the rules.

"My house is your house," he told me. "I'll show you where everything is in the kitchen once, but after that, you should feel enough like family here to help yourself to whatever you want." Since this house was the single most comforting place I had ever been in my life, those words warmed my heart.

"This has been a good old house," Grampy went on. "I always say to Terry, when I die, make sure someone's always living in it. Don't leave it empty. I hate the sight of an old house falling down. If nobody wants to live in it, push it down. Better that than let it fall over."

The spirit of Grampy's late wife, Fern, was very much in evidence, from the sewing rack on the wall to the stories everyone told about her.

"I met Fern at a church social," Grampy told me. "The single women would fix a supper basket, and the single men would bid on the baskets and the company of whoever fixed that particular one. I saw Fern and asked, 'Which basket is yours?' I bid five dollars, a whole week's wages, and won the basket."

After a bit, I asked, "Virgil, would you like anything to drink?"

He chuckled. "Call me Grampy, everyone does," he said. In my own family you don't call people by names that aren't theirs, so I was a little surprised. But "Grampy" was so surely his name that anything else felt wrong. He asked for what I would come to know as his signature beverage: a cup of black coffee with one ice cube to cool it off.

After about an hour, the family began to rouse itself and gather in the kitchen. Grampy got up and put a pan on the stove. He dropped in butter, milk, sugar, and cocoa powder and a few secret ingredients, let it heat to a boil, then drizzled it over bowls of vanilla ice cream, which everyone consumed along with vast quantities of Mountain Dew and coffee (I passed on the coffee, which I never acquired a taste for). Grampy's "fudge," as they called it, was the most delicious dessert I'd ever eaten. Afterward, fueled by sugar and caffeine, we sat at the tables for pitch. It was a boisterous game, full of trash-talking and bragging. I can be reserved, but I got into the spirit of it. They teased me, too, and by the afternoon I felt like one of the family.

In the coming years, Mike and I would spend as much time at Grampy's house as we could. There was something about the place that drew us to it—a certain timelessness, a sense that no matter how much we changed or the world changed around us, Grampy's would be the same. There were always Snickers bars in the candy jar and smoke curling from his pipe and hot coffee brewing on the stove. He even talked about the same topics all the time: the people he grew up with, the lessons he'd learned over the course of his life. Grampy's aphorisms rang with an eternal truthfulness:

"The good old days weren't all that good; people need to be happier with what they have now."

"Be respectful to everyone, even if you don't like them."

"Before you can appreciate the good things, you have to know what they are."

One of my favorite sayings of his was "You've got to bid to win." This was Grampy's motto: to truly live, you have to keep moving forward. He was a firm believer in not looking back and second-guessing your actions. He once told me that his big regret in life was quitting school to help the family during the Depression—especially since it meant giving up basketball. But that was the most you would ever hear him say on the subject of regret.

That first day, Mike and I crunched through the snow to the Cutlass in the sharp light of a late winter afternoon. Grampy followed us out. Right before I got in the car, he gathered me into a big bear hug and said, "Come back soon." The hug took me off guard. But I hugged him right back and got into the car, where Mike was already sitting, coatless as usual despite the cold. He shook his head and looked at me, completely incredulous.

"Why'd you call him Virgil?"

CHAPTER 4

SOLDIER DREAMS

WANTING TO BE A SOLDIER isn't a particularly ladylike fantasy, but then I've never been a conventional girl. No matter how often I wear a dress, at my core I'll always be a tomboy, crazy for sports and crazy about my dad. As a kid I lived for the evenings when he'd trade his briefcase for the old four-fingered glove from his high school days and join my sister Lindsey and me in the yard. I became a serious softball player in junior high, famous for my speed around the bases. I ran track in middle school, specializing in the sprints. In eighth grade I won the hundred-meter dash at the Conference track meet, surprising no one more than myself. With my short hair and scabbed knees, I was often mistaken for a boy, though I didn't mind. I never considered being female a barrier to getting ahead in a man's world. I was certain I could play major league baseball someday, and that I would work around the locker room issue if I became a good enough player.

Even then, I had the personality for the military. I stayed cool under pressure. I wasn't squeamish or giggly or helpless, and I felt comfortable around boys. Guys were people you hung around with, not people you dated. That attitude toward men changed, of course, but I never lost the ability to be "one of the guys," a skill that proved invaluable in the U.S. Army, where men outnumber women forty to one.

I can lay my interest in the military square at my father's feet. I loved my mother with everything I had, but he and I forged a special bond. Like him, I tend to be serious and comfortable with silence. My looks, too, favor Dad's side of the family: tall and skinny, with gray eyes, dark hair, and a long face. Of his five children, I was Dad's favorite—"the perfect child," as he calls me to this day.

As a civil engineer for the state of Missouri, Dad traveled a lot.

His job encompassed everything from troubleshooting oil spills to overseeing the installation of sewage systems in tiny communities. It was an important job, one that allowed him to make a positive difference in people's lives. When he was home I did everything I could to monopolize his time. I'd follow him around the house, grabbing any chance to spend time with him. He loved to watch old war movies on TV; on weekend nights I'd find him in the living room, glued to some World War II classic like *To Hell and Back* with Audie Murphy, *The Bridge on the River Kwai, Sands of Iwo Jima*—anything with John Wayne. Dad liked films about the Vietnam War like *Platoon*, but felt they were too intense for me. The old movies made war look far more glamorous, and those I was allowed to watch. I'd sit quietly on the sofa or behind his easy chair, hoping he wouldn't notice me and decide the movie was too adult. We would silently watch actors re-enact the great conflicts of Europe and the South Pacific, and over time I came to know the difference between a Gatling gun and a Sherman tank.

I knew Dad had been in the Army, and I knew where the evidence was hidden. With Mom's permission, I'd go into the finished basement where their hope chest served as a coffee table. I would open the lid, releasing the spicy scent of cedar into the room, and dig through the lace doilies, old letters, and the topper off their wedding cake until I found what I wanted: Dad's dress uniform, neatly folded, and a small tin that contained his ribbons and medals. I'd take each medal out of the box and ponder its significance, wondering what feat of valor my dad had performed to earn it. I did not know until many years earlier that my father had done the same thing with his father's uniforms, or that he would badger his father for stories about his military service, just as I did.

Like his own father, Dad was stingy with details, but over time I've pieced his story together. It unfurls, as with so many American families, as a story of service to God and country, and that story begins with the Civil War.

My great-great-great-grandfather, James Randall, was a soldier in the Union army. Born in New York State, he moved to Wisconsin with his family as a boy and spent his teenage years hired out as a farm and factory laborer. On October 5, 1861, he enlisted in Company B of the 14th Wisconsin Volunteer Infantry for the duration of the Civil War, and after a six-month training period traveled from

St. Louis, Missouri, by boat down the Mississippi River with his regiment. Their destination was Tennessee. They encamped at Pittsburg Landing, near the town of Shiloh, and on April 6, 1862, Randall found himself in the middle of what he later called "one of the most desperate battles of the war." Confederate forces surprised the Army of the North, and after a bloody battle that cost twenty thousand lives on both sides, the South withdrew, thus prolonging what many had assumed would be a short war in which the Union would triumph. It ultimately did, of course, but not before a million men had died over the next four years.

Aside from the occasional bad back and bout of ague (cured routinely with quinine), Randall suffered no injuries in battle. Though he had only about twenty months total of formal education, he chronicled the last year of his Civil War service in his diary and in his letters to his wife, Martha, back home in Oshkosh. Randall distinguished himself in battle time and again, yet described his adventures with a matter-of-fact understatement, punctuated by mundane remarks on his health and the weather that belied the horrors he had surely seen. He participated in the burning of Atlanta and was part of General Sherman's march to the sea. He and a thousand other troops followed Sherman five hundred miles to Savannah and from there to the coast of South Carolina. Along the way the Union army destroyed almost every Southern asset they came across, from railroad tracks to plantation houses, driving one more stake into the heart of the dying Confederate rebellion.

"I would not boast of what I have done," he wrote in his last letter to Martha upon leaving the army, "but I believe I have performed my part in this war, at least in length of service, and I am glad I had the inclination and courage to do this."

After the war, Randall returned to Wisconsin and his patient wife, who gave birth to their first child, Lena, a year later. Randall had lung problems, and thinking a warmer climate would help, he, Martha, and their daughter moved to Missouri in the spring of 1868. After searching for a suitable farm, they ended up in Macon County and bought 185 acres of land outside Callao for thirty-five dollars—"a high price for unimproved land," he later wrote. Over the years he and Martha had three more children and moved to a larger farm.

In 1888, Lena married a young, well-respected farmer named Peter

Decker. They settled on the 250-acre Decker family farm near Callao, which Peter's parents had started when they arrived from Michigan ten years earlier. Peter Decker built a second farmhouse for his bride up the road from the original dwelling where his parents lived.

Eventually, James and Martha Randall retired to Chicago. In 1901, at the age of sixty, he wrote down his life story, drawing on memory and his Civil War diary and letters. In the years before he died, he made four handwritten copies of the book, which were passed down through the generations, father to son. My father counts his copy as his prize possession.

Like the journal, the farm stayed in the family as well. My father's father, Charles Decker, was born and raised there, along with his brother Billy. Grandpa Decker joined the Marines at twenty-nine when his draft number came up. It was after the attack on Pearl Harbor, and he ended up driving a truck on Saipan and Okinawa in support of the South Pacific operations. Dad's mother, Helen, was pregnant with him at the time, and Dad was walking and talking by the time his father came home from the war in 1945. Dad has an old photo of Grandpa Decker holding him when he first got home, wearing his old fatigues because those were the only clothes he had. "Grandpa Decker never talked much about his war service," Dad says. "He didn't think it was that interesting."

After the war, Grandpa Decker took a job driving a bus in the Quad Cities area of Iowa. He wasn't that interested in farming, but Billy was, and everyone figured he would take over the farm someday. But when Billy, who stayed in the Army, died in a trucking accident in 1949, Grandpa Decker moved back to run the farm, though not very enthusiastically. "Mother wasn't thrilled about it," Dad recalls. "The house was so old you could throw a cat through it."

Along with his sister Teresa, Dad grew up on the farm and attended school in Callao, the valedictorian in a class of twelve. But he didn't see much future in farming and wanted to be off on his own. He attended the University of Missouri-Columbia (nicknamed "Mizzou"), where he made it to ROTC brigade commander, the highest rank a cadet officer could attain at the time. In 1967, he graduated with an engineering degree, got his commission, and was assigned to Frankfurt, West Germany. He took a six-month deferment before going overseas and worked on a dam project near Rathbun, Iowa. There he met Marie Schupmann, a beautiful high school student with a quick mind and lustrous blond hair that fell to her shoulders. A year later they were engaged.

My father left for West Germany, returning to marry my mother nearly a year later. She went back with him. He was twenty-three; she was nineteen and had never left the Midwest before going to Frankfurt. Dad spent an uneventful tour in an intelligence slot: "As long as the East Germans and Russians stayed where they were, it was calm."

Dad's second tour of duty could have been in Southeast Asia. He would have had to leave his young bride behind, and while he liked the idea of a military career, he loved his wife more. So when his two-year commitment was up, he left the Army and returned to the University of Missouri for a master's degree in engineering. He and Mom moved to the family farm, which Grandpa Decker had taken over running in the 1960s, and proceeded to have their series of kids. "We planned to have a baseball team," Dad likes to joke, "but we decided a basketball team would have to do."

Mom and Dad had six children in eight years. First came Anna in 1970. She was followed by Peter in 1971, Wendy in 1973, Lindsey in 1975, me in 1976, and Joe in 1978. Peter did not survive. Sickly since birth, he was about a year old when he stopped breathing while Mom was changing his diaper. My parents did everything they could, but Peter died before they could make it to the hospital. He is buried in Callao, in a tiny graveyard alongside my father's ancestors. Peter will always be a member of our family; visit Dad's house and you'll see him in the family photo collage on the wall, along with the rest of us.

My family lived on the Decker farm. We lived in one house, Dad's parents in the other. Our old home was charming but a bit too rustic and small for modern family living. It lacked both air conditioning and a furnace—an oil stove provided heat—so we froze in the winter and sweltered in the summer. Dad didn't want to dump a ton of money into improvements, and after I came along they decided it was time for a bigger place, in Macon. When I was a few months old, we moved to a new subdivision a few blocks from the school, where my parents had built a house on Crestview Street. Only a few other houses were finished, and over the next few years more families built homes and moved in. The neighborhood was a regular kids' paradise: There was a park three blocks away, big hills for sledding, a creek for hunting frogs. Being so young, I had no opinion about the move whatsoever, though my sisters were excited to be in a house where they could sleep two to a room instead of three.

People called us the Decker Girls, and each of us had a unique personality. Anna was the musical one with a remarkable singing voice. Wendy was studious and artistic, with strong convictions and beliefs; when she made up her mind, she stuck to her guns, and I always admired her for that. Lindsey was the middle child and wild as a hare. I came along eleven months later. Joe was born after the move to town, and Dad was thrilled to have another son. I was less than thrilled to have competition for Dad's affections, and I resented Joe for being a boy. When we were young, Joe and I rarely got along. When I was six and he was four, we were playing a game where we took turns dressing up as ghosts and trying to scare the snot out of each other. At one point Joe got angry and shoved me hard; I fell and hit the corner of a dresser. Joe got a spanking, but I got a black eye and a tiny scar that still graces my left cheekbone.

————

Along with war movies and baseball, the farm was another thing Dad and I had in common. It was our favorite place in the world. Dad had worked there most of his life—planting, harvesting, keeping the place up and running against great odds. Small farms die at a frightening rate, and in our area many survive by partnering up. Grandpa Decker's neighbor, Charles Hall, had a much larger farm where he raised livestock as well as crops, and the two men shared equipment, advice, and labor. Today Dad and Charles's youngest son, Chuckie, do the same. As close as blood brothers, they share the pure joy of tending and coaxing plants to flourish and grow.

Growing up, we kids would help out in any way were allowed, whether it was operating the wood splitter, tossing hay bales off wagons to fill in erosion ditches, or just sitting in the tractor, pretending to drive. (Dad never let me drive one for real, something I was desperate to do.) I loved the sounds and smells of the farm, and the way you could stand at the highest point and see for miles.

This was my idea of the perfect Saturday. Lindsey and I would pile into Dad's truck for the ten-minute drive to the farm. Once there, we girls would head straight for the old hay barn. Built in 1910, it was huge to us then and is still huge to us now. The lower level has stalls for horses and dairy cows, and above, at the top of a steep, narrow ladder, sits a hayloft the size of a basketball court. Lindsey and I weren't often allowed up there because there was a big hole in the loft floor, which allowed you to bring the hay down into the livestock stalls. Dad was afraid we'd get to running around, forget about the hole, and fall through. He didn't realize that the hayloft was like a church to us. Up there, we didn't feel the desire to run and jump. Instead, its deep, brooding silence instilled in us a sort of reverence. We'd lie on our backs, breathing in the fresh, clean smell of hay, gazing up at the high-beamed ceiling and saying nothing. Swallows nested in the eaves, and it was so quiet we could hear their wings move the air and sometimes the soft mews of newborn kittens nestled in the hay. Though the barn was used only for hay storage and the stalls stood empty, the mechanism for delivering the hay from stall to stall—a series of bins that run on a track system connected to the ceiling—was still intact on the lower level. I marveled at the ingenuity of my ancestors who dreamed up the system. Sometimes a driver would pull the big red grain truck into the barn and we could climb down inside the back of the truck and forage in its corners for soybean kernels to chew on. Then we'd take a few rides on the tire swing out back and maybe head to the livestock sheds across the road to see if any new piglets or calves had entered the world.

If it was summer, Grandpa Decker would take us to the Callao Harvest Fiesta and then take us out to the farm to spend the day with him. It was even better if we got to spend the night. I loved the noisy red-winged blackbirds that woke me up in the morning and the smells of Grandma Decker's kitchen. Lindsey and I would gorge ourselves on her molasses cookies, help her pick cherries or sort through a big pan of gooseberries, picking out the best ones for pies. Grandpa always wore overalls, and we loved to sit on his lap while he watched his favorite soaps, and root through his pockets for something of interest, especially his big silver pocket watch that loudly ticked off the seconds.

In 1984, Grandpa got cancer. He and Grandma retired from farming and moved to town to make medical care easier. Dad took over the farm full-time. He did his engineering job during the week and spent weekends working the farm. When Joe was old enough, at about age eight, he was the one who got to go with Dad to the farm a lot, much to my dismay. I would be stuck at home cleaning the house, imagining Joe doing all the chores I should be doing, and fuming with envy. I'd get even madder when Dad would talk about passing the farm on to his son someday, just as his ancestors had done, and how proud it would make him to have another Decker farming the land. What really burned me up was that Joe seemed less than enthused about the idea. Why should he get the farm when I loved it so much more? I was Dad's favorite, after all. But there was one thing I could never be, as much as I tried: his son.

Missouri summers play out to the piercing wail of the tornado siren. Like sentries watching for an enemy attack, Dad and I would stand on the front porch of our house, scanning the sky. If it was dark and menacing, he'd say, "When it turns that color, it means hail." If the sky was the greenish-yellow of an old bruise, he'd say, "When it turns that color, it means go in the basement." If the sky was that color and the siren started to scream, it meant get in the basement *immediately*. Mom and Dad would round up us kids and hustle us downstairs. We'd sit down there playing checkers and cards while the rain thrashed and the wind roared with the sound of a freight train passing by. I was never afraid; for me, it was an adventure. I'd imagine myself a soldier in a foxhole with bombs exploding around me, just like in the war movies Dad and I watched. When the siren stopped screaming, we'd emerge into the freshly scrubbed air. I loved sitting on the porch after a terrible storm: Everything smelled so fresh and clean afterward, as if God had just done his laundry.

We had some close calls. Lindsey was born in April 1975, when my parents were still living on the farm. When the baby was ten days old, Mom drove her to the doctor in Macon for a checkup, leaving her mother, who was visiting from Illinois, at home to watch Anna and Wendy. Dad was at work in town when the tornado sirens went off. The radio said the twister was on the ground about twenty miles west and heading due east, toward Macon. Dad drove home as quickly as he could get there. "I'd never seen a sky like that in my life," Dad recalls. "It was black and boiling—just awful." He got everyone down in the basement. Hail the size of softballs began to fall, and Dad thought about his wife and Lindsey, out there in the weather. "There were no cell phones back then," he says. "You just had to hope." Mom kept her wits about her. She took cover from the hailstorm under an underpass, cowering in the car with Lindsey in her arms, until the hail let up.

Some of that wild weather must have gotten under Lindsey's skin, because she grew into a sort of wild human tornado. She was only eleven months older than me, and we looked enough alike to be twins. As kids we were about the same height, brown-haired, skinny-legged, and athletic. But in middle school, Lindsey began to change. She started wearing makeup (even though she wasn't supposed to) and using a curling iron. And she, well, *blossomed*. Her interests shifted from sports to boys, and she began to skip school and sneak out of the house. Our house had only three bedrooms: Our parents had one, Anna and Wendy shared another, and Lindsey and I shared the third. Joe bunked down in the finished basement behind a screen that Mom put up to give him some privacy from the television and constant foot traffic. Eventually, Dad finished off part of the garage to give Lindsey and me our own space so Joe could take our bedroom. The fact that the garage had its own door only made it easier for Lindsey to sneak out at night. She'd push her car out of the driveway and start it up once she hit the street. There was always a party going on somewhere, and even if there wasn't, she'd drive around town, reveling in her freedom. I can't count the nights she'd creep unsteadily back into our room, exhausted and smelling of beer. She never had to ask me not to tell Mom because she knew I never would.

I didn't have to—our parents were perceptive people. After Anna and Wendy left home, they moved Lindsey back upstairs, next to their bedroom, so they could keep an eye on her. Nevertheless, she always seemed to be grounded, confined to her room, or deprived of some vital pleasure, such as the telephone. When she was seventeen, she was driving with a boyfriend. They got pulled over, and the cop spotted one can of beer rolling around under her seat. She was arrested for underage drinking, and Dad hired a lawyer who got her off.

"I had no hope for her," he says today. "She was wild. But once she got out of high school and realized that life wasn't going to be all that easy, she settled down and became a good kid." Indeed, most people in town were shocked when Lindsey, instead of meeting the bitter end so many had predicted, actually made something of her life.

When it came to partying, I took a characteristically rational approach. I liked to drink with my friends as much as the next girl, but I saw the wisdom of having fun without inviting trouble. This won me my parents' trust and ultimately a good dose of freedom.

So when I told my parents that the boys' varsity basketball team

needed someone to travel with them to away games and keep the sta-
tistics, they agreed, though I was only fifteen. The boys' and girls'
teams always played the same school on the same nights, so we'd all
pile into the bus for the long trip to Hannibal, Shelbina, or Mon-
roe City.

And so it was that I found myself in Centralia on January 16,
1991, jotting down fouls and missed free throws while in the Middle
East, American forces moved to recapture Kuwait from Saddam Hussein. When the announcer stopped the game and said our forces had
gone in, he asked for a moment of silence. I said a prayer for them. I
remember thinking how amazing it was that our soldiers were helping to free the Kuwaitis from Saddam Hussein's occupation. They
were Americans who wanted to improve the lives of others, people on
the other side of the world. These soldiers were willing to die so that
strangers could live in a free society.

I wanted to be one of those soldiers. I wanted to help people, to
give something back. I didn't care how much I got paid as long as I
felt good about what I was doing. Maybe I'd seen too many antiseptic
war films, but I didn't think about the dangerous parts of military life.
All I knew was that it was a noble career, and that as with most noble
pursuits, a certain amount of sacrifice would be involved. I was more
than prepared to make it. At the same time, I was beginning to feel
the pull of life beyond Macon. I loved my family and my hometown,
yet I wanted to get out and see the world, experience everything it had
to offer.

Within days, all the trees in town sprouted yellow ribbons. Dad
and I sat and watched news coverage of the war on CNN for hours. It
didn't consist of much except briefings by generals Norman Schwarz-
kopf and Colin Powell—both of whom I admired tremendously—and
reporters cringing as Scud missiles struck cities behind them. The Gulf
War was over practically before it had begun, but it left an impression. The next time America went to war, I wanted to be in the middle
of it.

Ironically, Lindsey had her own ideas about joining up. At the time,
the Missouri National Guard had a program that allowed seventeen-
year-olds to sign up with the Guard with their parents' permission. They
were required to complete the first half of basic training during the
summer between their junior and senior years and the second half the
following summer. One Friday a month during the school year, they

attended a drill just like a regular soldier. On those days, they were required to come to school in uniform. Those teenagers were always an
impressive sight; the uniforms made them look much older and more
experienced than they were. This appealed to Lindsey. She couldn't
imagine giving over her entire life to the Army, but she'd give them a
piece of it. Maybe, she told me, joining the Guard might help give her
some direction.

But when she shared her notion with Dad, he squashed it immediately. Being in the military is no party, and he felt she lacked the disci-
pline to take it seriously and understand the commitment she would
be making. "She can't stay out of trouble," he'd grumble. "How
could she stay in the Guard?" He had a point, though she would ultimately prove to him she could do it.

Personally, I kept my soldier dreams to myself. I wanted to follow
my father's footsteps into the Army, but wasn't sure how. How would
I get to where I wanted to go? I was too young to devise a plan of action, too young to do more than think about it. Dad had always said
we were lucky to enjoy so many freedoms, and he thought his kids
should understand how blessed we were. "When you grow up," he'd
tell us, "you should give something back to your country." And so we
have, but I don't think he ever dreamed that he'd one day have two
daughters leading soldiers in a war zone in the Middle East.

CHAPTER 5

MEMORIES OF MARIE

MY MOTHER DID AN ADMIRABLE JOB of raising her children long before Dr. Phil came along. Organized, industrious, and more patient than five restless kids deserved, Marie Decker didn't need a made-for-TV guru to tell her that the best life is lived according to three guiding principles: faith, family, and good grooming. Church was mandatory, and so were chores. Every Saturday she would assign each of us a room to dust and vacuum from top to bottom. If the room wasn't clean by the end of the day, our social plans for the evening were scrubbed. Because my father traveled so much for work, Mom was the main caregiver, and Dad freely admits that she is the reason we turned out as well as we did. She signed us up for piano lessons, gave us books for Christmas, and sang with us in community theater productions of *Show Boat* and *Annie*. She was the keeper of the holiday rituals, the tuning fork that kept our family in key.

Mom was pretty, and she smelled nice. Her skin was pale as ice milk and soft as corn silk, thanks to the Oil of Olay she applied religiously twice a day. Her favorite perfume was Emeraude. She kept her dark blond hair combed and glossy and wore it in a bob for much of my childhood. She also wore glasses, as did we all. She was small— about five feet three—and well muscled from carrying all of us kids around. She stood erect, with great posture, and had a natural sense of leadership. Dad says her nickname in high school was Captain. As a girl, she'd taken a lot of ballet lessons, performing in local productions in Junction City, Kansas. She retained her elasticity into adulthood, and would amaze us with stories of how she could once put both feet behind her head.

Oh, but she could get riled. Mom was very strict, but we knew it was out of love, not meanness, and that her rules existed to protect us. The highest compliment I can pay her is that she was always there. If you came home with a great report card, she was there to congratulate you. If you staggered home after midnight with beer on your breath, she was there to give you hell.

And she was there when you were under the weather; in fact, that's when she was at her best. She'd stay home from school and devote herself to our care, and we in turn relished our time alone with her, even if we did feel lousy. I had mono as a kid, and for three weeks she tucked me into the orange recliner in the living room and brought me a TV tray with my favorite ramen soup and Chicken-in-a-Biscuit crackers. Then she'd sit and watch *Perry Mason* with me until I fell asleep.

Only after the children were pretty well raised did Mom permit herself to work outside the home, as a teacher's aide at Macon R-1. "She had a knack for working with disabled children," recalls Dad. "She had the patience of Job and a practical, commonsense approach to relationships with these kids. And she really loved doing it."

Mom also liked working at the school because she had the same hours we did. In the mornings she'd stand in the kitchen in her fuzzy blue bathrobe systematically packing our lunches for the day. She'd set out twenty slices of bread on the counter and, with the efficiency of an assembly-line worker, slap on toppings according to each kid's particular likes and dislikes. We always had a well-balanced meal: sandwich, fruit, chips, cookies, and money for milk only, no soda. In the afternoon she was always the first home from school, ready for a "how was your day?" and a fresh batch of her famous magic cookie bars.

Mom had the biggest heart imaginable. She tried to help those who didn't have the advantages in life that she felt every kid deserved. One of those kids was Tiffani Shelton. I'd known Tiffani since kindergarten; we had grown up together, giggled over young romances, and competed on the softball field. Only two months older than me, Tiffani was a talented pitcher. Her parents pushed her hard to excel at the sport, and when Tiffani rebelled against the pressure, her parents kicked her out when she was only a sophomore in high school. Tiffani needed a place to live. "She can stay with us," Mom said. For two years, Tiffani split her time between our house and a small apartment downtown, joining the Army after high school. A medic for four years, she stayed in touch with us and visited during holidays. Now my family says we have five girls instead of four. Six years ago Tiffani had a daughter, Athena, to whom she gave the middle name Marie, after my mother.

————

Mom came by her maternal skills naturally. She was born in Detroit Lakes, Minnesota, where her father, Frank Schupmann, was a Lutheran minister. Tragically, he drowned during a church picnic, leaving his wife, Mary, with five children under the age of four, including a set of twins. As the oldest, Mom helped to raise them while her mother, a devout Lutheran, struggled to cope with the hand God had dealt her. Mary moved the family to her hometown of Junction City, Kansas, where her parents ran a drugstore, Sargant's, which had been in the family for three generations. (Family lore has it that Wild Bill Hickok used to hang out there.) When my mother was in her teens, her mother married William Koslowske, who worked for the Corps of Engineers, and they landed in Rathbun, Iowa. That's where she was living when, in the summer of 1967, a young civil engineer named Steve Decker pulled into town to work on the dam project.

Mom had a story she liked to tell us about how she and Dad met. He was washing his new Chevrolet Chevelle SS 396 when one of the secretaries who worked on the dam project for the corps saw the car and stopped by to talk. He was vacuuming the interior at the time. When the secretary called his name, he looked up, but his eyes slid right past the girl who was speaking to her passenger, the prettiest girl he had ever set eyes on. "I really turned his head," Mom would say, laughing. "He did a double take." She was only seventeen and he was twenty-two; thus her parents were not thrilled at the idea of their dating.

Marie's brother, Philip, was fifteen at the time and loved baseball. When Dad spent an afternoon teaching him to throw a curveball, Mom's parents decided that if Marie's young man didn't mind playing catch with their son he must be okay.

Dad asked her to marry him before he left for West Germany. The wedding took place a year later, while he was home on leave. When Mom returned with him to Frankfurt, it was her first airplane ride.

"Marie was very studious and smart," Dad recalls. "She appreciated fine literature and good books, thanks to the influence of her mother."

Mom's life mirrored her own mother's in certain ways. Both had four daughters and one son to look after. And for both, Lutheranism was a driving force in family life. Dad took Mom's faith when they married, and they gave it to us.

When I sift back through my memories of Mom, I tend to settle on Saturday nights. Getting five kids ready for church was a big job, one she didn't like to leave for Sunday morning. I can see her standing at the ironing board, pressing our frilly dresses and laying out our outfits on the beds, from dresses to socks, just as she did with the slices of bread. Our patent leather shoes sat in a row by the fireplace, freshly shined and ready. One by one she'd plunk us in the bath, wash our hair and clip our nails, and put us to bed. The next morning, at 6:00 A.M., she got us dressed, gave us breakfast, and hustled us into our Pinto wagon. We'd call dibs on the best seats, but Lindsey and I always got stuck in the back. At least we could lie down, so it wasn't all bad.

Dad always drove to church, and because we were Wisconsin Evangelical Lutheran Synod, the drive was long. The closest church was Grace Evangelical Lutheran, an hour away in Columbia. It was a tiny church, and for a while the pastor held services on folding chairs in his basement while a bigger church was being built. After Sunday school, we'd take our places for the sermon. We had to sit quietly and listen, curled on Dad's lap if we were small enough. Mom said she taught us to behave in church by sitting us on her lap and helping us through the rituals of singing and liturgy.

After church, as a special treat, Dad sometimes took us to Pizza Hut or Dairy Queen. We'd sit chattering away, chewing with our mouths closed, keeping our elbows off the Formica tables, saying please and thank-you and wiping our lips daintily with our napkins— supernatural behavior for four girls and a boy, all under the age of ten. Several times, when Dad went to pay for our meal, he found that a stranger had already done so because he was so impressed with our manners.

Mom loved her life, but there was a part of her that would have liked to have seen more of the world. She didn't see as much of Europe as she'd hoped when Dad was posted in Germany, and after the kids came there wasn't the time or the money for extended vacations. Our idea of a big family vacation was a baseball game in St. Louis and a night in a motel with a swimming pool. She found her escape through books, especially Agatha Christie mysteries, and in a spare moment, of which there weren't enough, she could be found curled up with a book and indulging her sweet tooth with caramels from her private stash.

Maybe that's why she placed so few limitations on her kids. As far as she was concerned, nothing was impossible and being a girl was no barrier to advancement. "You can be anything you want to be," she'd say, "as long as you set your mind to it."

And trust me, her daughters took those words to heart.

––––––

Anna, the oldest, was the first out of the house. Like Mom, she is petite, but her voice is huge. It was always a shock to hear so much voice coming from one so small. She went to college on a scholarship in piano and voice, and later toured Europe with her college choir. While attending a school music conference, she met a student from Wentworth Military Academy named Mike, and in April 1991 they got married.

The marriage bug must have been contagious, because two months later Wendy followed suit. She had just finished high school and was planning to attend college. Her boyfriend, Chris Roberts, nineteen, had joined the Air Force out of high school. They'd dated for a couple of years, and Chris, while on leave, asked for permission to marry her. My parents said yes on one condition: that they wait until Wendy was out of college. Not long after, Wendy went with Chris's mother to visit him in Oklahoma, where he was stationed. After she came home she was sitting in the living room, discussing the trip with Mom. I sat on the floor, listening.

Something must have triggered Mom's maternal radar, because she suddenly looked hard at Wendy and said, "You got married, didn't you?"

My parents were furious. I remember tears, slammed doors, threats of an annulment. Chris rushed home from Oklahoma to explain that he and Wendy wanted to get a posting overseas, but they needed to be married to put in for one. Besides, Anna had just gotten married and they figured Dad would have balked at having to shell out so soon for another wedding. My parents contacted a lawyer about an annulment, but finally they calmed down. We had a small reception for the newlyweds at the house, and then Wendy moved to Oklahoma with

Chris. Thirteen years later they are still going strong. They live in Florida, where Wendy is a high school history teacher, and have two beautiful children, Isabel and Henry, whom Dad adores.

Despite Anna's and Wendy's adventures in matrimony, I was not particularly precocious when it came to boys. I was sixteen before I had a real romance. In May 1992, I went on a two-week school trip to Panama City, Florida. I learned to scuba dive, sunned by the pool, and stayed up late gabbing with the other girls in my hotel room. I came home both exhilarated and exhausted. I also came home with my first boyfriend, Joey, who lived forty-five miles away. He was a football player: big, strong, and handsome. He was also the boy who gave me my first real kiss—a stolen moment in Florida between rounds of Ms. Pac-Man in the hotel arcade. After I got home, we continued our romance by telephone and on weekend dates.

That summer was to be the Decker family's first big vacation together, ten days visiting relatives in Colorado. Mom had really been pushing for it. It was the first real vacation she'd ever planned, and Wendy and Chris had come home from Oklahoma to go with us.

But the day before we were supposed to leave, I woke up with a sore throat and a spleen enlarged to the point where you could see its outline through my skin. The doctor diagnosed me with mono and wanted me admitted to the hospital immediately. He was also stumped. I'd had mono years earlier, and it's unusual to get it twice. Maybe, he said, the trip to Florida had worn me down.

My parents debated what to do. Finally Mom said she'd stay home and nurse me while the rest of the family was away, and the doctor agreed. She cheerfully sent them on their way and proceeded to care for me in the quiet, empty house. I will never forget how willing she was to sacrifice her cherished escape to stay with me. On the other hand, I think she loved the vacation of having the house to herself. I slept most of the time while she devoured one mystery novel after another. Joey, my boyfriend, stopped by occasionally with ice cream and flowers; he spent hours by my sickbed, keeping me from expiring from boredom. I repaid him by breaking his heart.

By August I was feeling myself again, if a more fragile version. Eager to put my invalid days behind me, I went back to my job at the C & R. That was the summer Mike would walk through the door with his paychecks and into my life. By December 1992, we were a couple.

From the night Mike first admired her skaters, Mom cared for him as one of her own. She always had a batch of his favorite iced tea—brewed in the microwave with lots of sugar—in the fridge, and his favorite foods seemed to find their way to the table whenever he visited. I could always find the two of them sitting in the kitchen, heads together in conversation. She'd be leaning on her elbows, hanging on his every word.

In August 1993, when Mike went off to Linn Tech, she cooked him a big farewell dinner and hugged him good-bye, as if she was sending her own son off into the world, even though she was going to see him every weekend. He planned to work for the Kemps on the weekends through the winter, so he'd drive home on Friday nights and return to Linn on Sunday evenings.

On those weekends that Mike couldn't make it home, I'd go see him. I had my driver's license and the hand-me-down Volkswagen Rabbit that at one time or another had belonged to every girl in the family. By this time, my friend Natalie was dating Mike's roommate Brian, so we both had good reason to get in the Rabbit and drive to Linn.

Soon after Mike left, I missed a menstrual period. Then I missed my September period, too. I wasn't worried. I had stuck to my vow of abstinence, so I knew I wasn't pregnant. I chalked it up to being extremely active and busy. I was student body president, and so the first few weeks of my senior year were filled with meetings, assemblies, and party committees. I was playing softball and organizing a student blood drive. For the drive, I decided it would have a theme from my favorite show: *M*A*S*H* (I'd seen every episode at least twice in reruns). All the student volunteers dressed like military surgeons, and I wore one of Dad's old Army shirts and his dog tags. I loved signing people up to give blood, knowing it could help keep someone alive.

I missed my October period.

That same month, I began to have what I thought of as "temperature problems." At night, I'd wake up twisted in sweaty sheets. I'd get so overheated it was all I could do to keep from stripping down to my Skivvies. An hour later I'd be in a deep freeze. This started happening several times a week. While the episodes didn't interfere with my daily activities, they did make it difficult to concentrate in class.

Mike didn't know what I was going through. I tried to pretend everything was normal. I was young, or maybe I was in denial, or both. I'm the kind of person who has trouble asking for help. If there's a problem, I feel I can solve it myself, through sheer force of will if nothing else.

That Christmas, Mike wanted to give my parents something nice. He couldn't afford much, but he could afford a day of hard labor. Knowing we had a woodstove in our basement, he went out to the country, chopped a load of wood, threw it into the back of a truck, and unloaded it behind my house. Mom already thought he was God's gift, but that gesture sealed the deal, and his act of generosity was rekindled with every log Mom threw on the fire.

The holidays came and went. In January 1994, my temperature problems got worse; the episodes became more frequent and intense. It was time to go to Mom for some answers.

"How long has this been happening?" she asked me with deep concern.

"Six months."

"I can't believe you haven't told me about this sooner," she said, her voice suddenly turning angry.

Now, Marie Decker was a great mother, but she'd had three daughters go through puberty by the time I got there, so she must have assumed I would have come to understand my changing body through osmosis or something. "It's not stuff you and I talk about," I replied meekly.

She scheduled an appointment with our family doctor in Macon, who referred us to a specialist in Columbia. Six trips and dozens of tests later, he gave me the diagnosis: premature ovarian failure (POF). My ovaries had shut down, sending me into menopause. My temperature problems were in fact hot flashes. At the age of seventeen, I had the hormonal status of a fifty-year-old woman. To keep my body in a premenopausal state, I'd have to take estrogen for the rest of my life.

POF is almost unheard of in someone my age. The doctor theorized that it had been triggered by the mono I'd had in the summer of 1992. He has kept my records in case he wants to write a paper on me someday, and every doctor I've seen since uses the word *fascinating* to describe my case.

After we got the bad news, Mom drove back to Macon. We said little in the car. When we got home, she sat me down and asked, "Do you understand what this means?"

"I think so," I answered.

"It means you can't ever have children."

Her words didn't really sink in. Having kids wasn't something I'd thought much about. But she uttered those words with the deep sadness of a woman who understood that I would never know the joy and pain of bearing children, as she had. She said them, also, with a touch of guilt: Maybe they should have admitted me to the hospital when I had mono for the second time. I believe she always felt bad about my diagnosis, as if there was something she could have done to change the outcome.

"We could have taken the illness more seriously," Dad would say later, but I don't blame anyone. My condition is simply part of the story that was written for my life.

When Mike called to ask after me, I told him what the doctor had said. "In other words, I'm not going to be able to have kids." I said it without emotion.

"Are you okay?"

"I'm fine."

"Don't let this discourage you," he said kindly. "You'll be a great mom someday. There are plenty of kids out there for you to adopt."

It was the best thing Mike could have said, and he never wavered from that attitude. Mom worried that I was too young to grasp the ramifications of my condition, and she was right. The full repercussions wouldn't hit me until years later, after Mike and I were married and I seriously began to consider motherhood. Not until after I realized what a great dad he would have been.

Looking back, I was too young then to realize that every life has defining moments, and that this was one of them. There would be more defining moments, just as surely as tornado season arrived in May. You just had to hang on tight to something or someone, cover your head, and hope for the best.

I went on estrogen, and by the end of February 1994, my hot flashes were gone. I started feeling like my old self again. When I looked in the mirror, I saw not a tomboy or a sick person, but a woman. I had long since replaced the eyeglasses with contact lenses, and the style-challenged girl Mike had first gone out with no longer looked like she needed a magazine makeover. I'd grown my hair out, and it was quite long, a wavy brown curtain reaching to the middle of my back. I never thought of myself as pretty, though Mike and Mom told me I was.

As my senior prom approached, I had a very definite idea of how I wanted to look. I wanted to wear a simple black dress, to wear my hair in long loose curls, and to carry a single rose, not a fancy corsage that would break Mike's budget. On those occasions Mom and I clashed it was usually over clothes, but this time she deferred to me. She picked me up early from school one afternoon, and we drove to Columbia to shop for the dress and to have lunch. I'd never had her undivided attention like this, and I think she realized that time was running out for us, that soon I'd be gone to college, too. We found the perfect dress in a small boutique, a black halter style with two vintage rhinestone clasps at the bodice. It was a little too short to reach the floor, but Mom had the answer. She knelt down and took the hem in her fingers, then turned her head and looked up at me. "I'll sew a piece of satin ribbon on the bottom," she said. "No one will ever know."

CHAPTER 6

HUNTING

GROWING UP, I have to say my favorite game was guns. I'm not sure where the game came from or who thought up the rules; maybe it was just one of those things that kids inherently know, like certain off-color jokes and the "Old MacDonald" song. What kid doesn't grow up pretending to assassinate her best friends? When playing guns, I never thought of myself as a cowboy or an Indian or a soldier. I just liked the idea of shooting, even if the weapon in question was my index finger.

My compatriots in guns were Lindsey and our next-door neighbors, two brothers named Rodney and Jeremy, who were the same age as us. I always partnered up with Jeremy, and Lindsey paired up with Rodney. Jeremy and I were the bad guys, Lindsey and Rodney the good guys. In other words, we played against type. We usually played in the boys' yard, but all of Crestview Street was fair game. The object was simply to avoid being seen, shot, or captured.

A giant evergreen provided ample cover. Jeremy would lurk behind a nearby bush, ready to back me up. I'd give him a nod and then peer around the trunk, on the alert for a movement or noise of any kind, the sound of a breaking branch, a whisper. I'd scan the yards, the street, the bushes covered with tiny red berries that, when squished, left juice on your hair and clothes that looked like blood and was murder to wash out.

Lindsey would usually make a break for it. She'd dart across the yard, running for the cover of the bushes. I'd point my finger, take aim, and shoot. One word, yelled loudly, stood in for the actual gunshot: "Bang!"

Lindsey would keep running, ignoring the fact that she'd been hit. Instead of falling down dead, she'd drop to the ground, roll onto her side, and return fire. Our game would inevitably devolve into a shouting match over who was deader. But we'd also be careful to keep our voices low enough so that they wouldn't carry through the open windows of our house. If Mom heard us yelling she'd bring us inside and punish us for fighting, and then we'd *really* be dead.

Rodney and Jeremy would holster their fingers and stand off to the side, knowing better than to intervene. When Kate and Lindsey Decker went at it, it was best to let the argument burn itself out. We were extremely competitive with each other, yet we didn't stay mad for long. We'd get our differences out in the open and then put them behind us just as quickly, friends again. Before long we'd be back at it, taking aim and taking prisoners. Each team had its own hangout where we could hold a captive, but you had to leave him or her there to go looking for the captive's teammate, who would sneak back to free his or her partner. This cycle of catch and release could go on forever, which it did. On warm days, we played guns incessantly after school, stopping only when Mom called us in for dinner.

I wanted to learn to shoot a real gun. For this I blame my childhood crush, the Lone Ranger. Lindsey and I loved to watch the old black-and-white TV show, and I soon became infatuated with the masked stranger who helped strangers anonymously, leaving only a silver bullet behind to show he'd been there. When we role-played the TV show, Lindsey was always Tonto, even on Halloween. Mom reconfigured a paper bag into an Indian vest, snipping the bottom to look like fringe. I wore a black mask and a blue shirt and strapped on my plastic six-shooters. I even had a Lone Ranger sleeping bag, which I'd proudly roll out at slumber parties, next to the other girls' Rainbow Brite and Care Bears bags. And even though we didn't need his help, I was convinced the Lone Ranger would show up at our house. I waited for him to appear the way other kids waited for Santa Claus. One day, I found a silver plastic bullet out in the yard. How it got there I'll never know, but I was convinced it was a sign. Wendy and Anna, who were too old for such delusions, laughed at me, and Joe was too young to care. Only Lindsey believed me.

In middle school, an officer from the Department of Conservation came to class to teach us the basics of hunter safety. Shortly after that, all the farm boys in my class started talking about "goin' huntin' " on the weekends. I envied the boys and their stories. I wanted, more than anything, to go hunting, too. But Dad didn't hunt anymore, and shooting at deer wasn't high on my girlfriends' social agenda. For years hunting sat on my list of things to do someday, should I ever get a chance. Mike gave me that chance.

One day in November 1993, when Mike was home from Linn Tech for Thanksgiving break, he happened to mention that he and his dad went hunting every year. In fact, they were going in a couple of weeks. This was before my diagnosis, before I'd told anyone that my body was going haywire. But I wasn't going to let a few hot flashes stand in the way.

"Take me with you," I said.

"First you'd better learn to shoot," he replied.

We used his .270 Winchester, handed down from his mother's father, Grandpa Rasmussen. It was long and heavy and it packed quite a punch. We drove out to a local conservation area and set up some targets, which were actually paper plates on which Mike had drawn circles with a Magic Marker.

Just as he had done when teaching me to ride, Mike took a patient, methodical approach. He ran me through the rifle's components and showed me how to load and unload and how to fix a jam. Then he showed me the basics of shooting: how to control my breathing and pull the trigger between breaths. "Don't jerk the trigger," he instructed. "Squeeze it slowly."

I shouldered the rifle and peered down the sight with one eye, bringing the bull's-eye into the crosshairs. Mike stood behind me, holding the rifle still, so close I could feel his breath on the back of my neck.

"Steady," he said.

I squeezed the trigger. The shot echoed over the field and the rifle bucked backward with such force I would have fallen over had Mike not been there to catch me. I nicked the paper plate, which indicated to me that I was a terrible shot. But Mike was excited that I'd even hit it my first time out. He had me hoist the rifle and go through the drill all over again. This time he stood off to the side. I was on my own.

I counted my breaths and squeezed the trigger slowly. The bullet leaped from the barrel, and the butt of the rifle recoiled into my shoulder with such force I yelped. Then I did it again and again until my shoulder was raw and we were out of plates.

Mike collected the targets, some of which you could see daylight through. He proceeded to drag them out to anybody who'd show the slightest interest: my parents, his parents, Grampy. "She's a natural!" he said proudly.

Two weeks later, when Mike was home for the weekend, he and his dad picked me up at 0400 and we headed out to Grampy's farm. The late fall weather had been unseasonably cold and snowy, but the sky was clear, the stars sharp as knives. I wore a new pair of hunting boots and brown coveralls borrowed from Dad. Mike lent me the required orange vest and hat, and my outfit, burdensome yet warm, was complete. I couldn't yet hunt with a gun because I didn't have a permit, though I've had one every year since.

Between our friends and families who lived out in the country, we had plenty of land to hunt on. Each family had its assigned area. We joined up with Mike's uncle Dale and his cousins Larry and Stephanie, setting up in small groups along a hillside overlooking some timber. Mike and I were paired together, and every now and then he would quietly explain some finer point of the hunt.

"If you see a deer headed in our direction," he whispered, "let me know as quietly as you can, and move out of the way."

I nodded my head in the affirmative.

"Keep quiet and listen. You can tell one's coming because you'll hear it panting from a long way off as it runs in our direction."

"Okay," I whispered. I believed just about anything Mike told me if he said it with enough conviction.

I put my senses on high alert and tried with all my might to hear the sound of a deer panting. I listened so hard I thought my eardrums would pop with the effort.

A few minutes later, Mike took a plastic bag of saltines out of his pocket and began to eat them, crunching loudly as he chewed.

"Be quiet! I won't be able to hear the deer panting," I whispered urgently.

Mike erupted into a stifled guffaw, and I feared bits of cracker would shoot out of his nose. "I can't believe you believed me," he said, almost crying. I punched Mike in the arm and made him promise not to relay the story to a single soul. He only laughed some more, and I knew Grampy was going to hear about this when we got back to the house.

In the afternoon, after breakfast and a short nap, we headed back out into the cold. We took turns walking through the woods to push the deer toward waiting hunters; after the big breakfast, we needed the exercise to stay awake. As evening fell we climbed into the deer stands that each family had built in the trees. There we sat and quietly waited for a monster buck to slip out of the shadows and into our gun sights, though that day none did, as if the deer could sense us quietly waiting.

———

My last semester of high school flew by. I was accepted to the University of Missouri, where I planned to follow Dad's footsteps into the ROTC. At eighteen, I wasn't thinking about marriage. I was going be a soldier and Mike was planning to fix cars for a living, and I never saw those paths intersecting. From what I could tell, he didn't either. I saw my future laid out like a field prepared for planting; all I had to do was put the seeds in the ground and pray for rain.

Mike wasn't so sure of his path in life. As his freshman year in college came to an end, he told me he didn't want to go back to technical school. He'd gotten out of his hometown only to discover that he wanted more out of life than fixing cars. Something was driving him to see what else he could do. I had been sensing that Mike's heart was not really into being a mechanic, and I was glad he'd found the confidence to begin searching out what would truly make him happy.

It was a time of change for both of us. Two days after I graduated, my parents moved from the house in Macon to the farm, taking Joe and me with them. Since Grandpa Decker had died of cancer in 1984, Grandma had stayed in Macon. My parents moved into my grandparents' old house, which had been empty all those years. It was my last summer at home, my last summer at the C & R. Mike went back to the Kemps, but we were living on opposite sides of town.

That summer I finalized my plans for my freshman year at Mizzou. I was assigned a dorm room and scheduled my classes, including an ROTC class my second semester. Meanwhile, Mike was off hunting for his calling in life, but his calling came to him.

The recruiter was driving around the country lanes outside Macon in June, lost. He saw a young man by the side of the road fixing a tractor and stopped to ask for directions. He got out of his car and walked up to the farmhand, whose hands were covered in oil and grease. The recruiter, a staff sergeant, told him that he was on his way to pick up another kid up who was joining the Army, and did he know where the address was?

The farmhand pointed the guy in the right direction. By now the sergeant had noticed that he was a strapping kid, big and strong, about nineteen or twenty years old. And since he was good at his job, the recruiter asked, "Have you ever considered joining the Army?"

Mike shrugged. "Not really."

I can see Mike squinting up at the man in uniform. He takes in the brass buttons and the ribbons and the hand extended to him to shake. Mike wipes his palms on his overalls so he won't get the officer's clean hands dirty. The recruiter tells Mike his name and asks Mike for his. The sergeant sees an opening, and before long Mike is leaning against the fence, listening intently and nodding.

I often think what a strange coincidence it was, this Army recruiter showing up out of nowhere. It was as though Mike's uncertainty about his future had sent out some sort of homing signal that led the man straight to him, a desperate, high-pitched sound only he could hear.

The sergeant worked out of a recruiting office in Moberly, about thirty miles away. Mike asked me if I'd go there with him, and I agreed. I was getting a bad case of Army fever, and I was eager to meet and talk with some of these men in green.

The sergeant wore a casual-dress Army uniform with shiny boots and ribbons on his chest. He was in his late twenties and had the confidence of a used car salesman. He welcomed us courteously, asked us to take a seat in his office, and offered us water or coffee. Then he sat down behind his desk and asked Mike what direction he wanted to take in the military.

"I was thinking I want to try the military police. I think police work is something I might be interested in after the Army," Mike said.

"Aw, you don't want to do that," replied the sergeant, and he began to list the reasons: "Most police academies don't take men who have come from the military police. The rules and laws are so different it's harder to teach them. They'd rather recruit infantry soldiers." The recruiter leaned in a little closer. "Why don't you consider the infantry? You're a big, strong guy."

"I don't know that much about it," Mike said, shrugging.

The sergeant led us to a small room to watch a short film about the Green Berets, also known as the Special Forces. It was a typical recruitment video. There were flags flying, patriotic songs, and fresh-faced boys talking about the exciting and rewarding life that was the Green Berets. The part that really captured Mike's imagination was when they described how only the best were chosen to be Green Berets. They were a brotherhood of the Army's elite, directed to do good in the world.

From the moment Mike saw that film, I knew that he was going to join, if the Army would take him.

Mike's decision shocked his family. Not only had he never discussed joining the Army, it meant he would be leaving Missouri. No Blaise had ever left Missouri. Only my dad was openly enthusiastic. Mike's decision to serve his country earned Dad's respect. However, knowing a bit about the infantry, he did try to explain to Mike what he was getting into by going that route—the hardship outside the glory. Being a ground soldier is one of the most demanding and dangerous professions that a man can choose.

We drove out to Grampy's place so Mike could break the news to him.

Grampy looked a little like he'd been punched. He ran his fingers through his cropped hair and tamped his pipe on the fence. "You're going to leave us," he said, more of a statement than a question. "Are you ready for that? To be gone for months or years?"

"I know what it means," Mike said. "I think I'm up for it."

"It's not an easy life," Grampy told him.

"I know," Mike said. "But it feels the right thing to do."

Grampy paused. "I'll miss you every day," he said with a sigh and gave Mike a hug.

By the end of the summer, my relationship with Mike started to deteriorate. It was my fault, mostly. I saw four years of college stretching ahead of me, with my boyfriend living in another state or even another country. I was curious about dating other people and wanted to see what it felt like to be single for a while. We were both going through some big life changes, and instead of leaning on each other we began to pick fights. We were both stubborn and strong-willed, but my hostility just seemed to confuse and dismay him. My behavior wasn't fair—he was leaving for basic training, the most intimidating, challenging, and stressful event of his life, unsure of where we stood. Meanwhile, I would be living it up away from home for the first time, with access to parties, booze, and boys.

On August 28, 1994, Mike took the oath and joined the United States Army. The recruiter picked him up at his mother's house and drove him to Kansas City, where he was shipped off to Georgia for basic training. I wasn't there to say good-bye.

CHAPTER 7

THE ACCIDENT

WHERE WERE WE the day that everything changed?

It was September 30, 1994. Dad had taken the day off work to haul soybeans for Chuckie Hall. He was down in the river bottom, helping to load the crop into a truck, which he would then drive to town and deposit in the grain elevators at Quincy Soy. Anna was living in Louisiana, Missouri, with her husband, Mike. They had been married for two years, and he had a job as a state highway patrolman.

Wendy was in England. Chris had gotten a four-year posting at RAF Croughton, a British air force base outside London, but that day they were vacationing in Greece. We had to call the American Red Cross to track them down.

Lindsey had been living on her own for three months in Columbia, working at a bank and taking night classes at the community college. That evening, however, she was at the farm. Mom had called Lindsey and asked if she could take her shopping for stuff for her new apartment, so they had made plans. The two had had their differences, and Lindsey was excited that Mom had reached out, had seemed determined to understand her.

Joe was with Mom in the minivan. She had picked him up from Grandma's house, and they were on their way home after stopping in town for takeout Chinese.

I was at my new job at a computer store on the Mizzou campus. We had just closed up shop to do inventory.

Mike was in his first month of basic training and thus about as accessible as Wendy and Chris were in Greece. It would be weeks before I knew that he was aware of what had happened.

The two of us were still in touch. I was writing to him once a week about what was happening in Macon, how his friends were doing, the latest football scores, what my classes were like—busy talk designed to take his mind off all he was going through. I signed my letters to him simply "Kate." As far as I was concerned, we had broken up before he left yet remained on "good terms." I saved the letters we wrote to each other in the early days of my freshman year, and when I read them now it's quite clear that the connection between us, while tenuous, was still there. It was also there in the photographs that I tacked to my dorm room walls: Mike riding horses, at the prom, at my graduation party. He had been the biggest part of my life for two years, and it didn't seem possible to simply erase him.

Mike called when he got phone privileges—once, maybe twice— but the conversations were awkward and short. The way I saw it, his lack of communication underscored my decision to break up with him. I didn't understand until much later that the military leaves little time for romance. I couldn't fathom the challenges and hardships he was facing—I imagined basic training to be a thrill ride, like Outward Bound, when in reality it is a twelve-week stint in hell that stretches would-be soldiers to their physical and emotional limits.

While Mike was being screamed at, deprived of basic needs, and learning the art of killing people, I was settling into college life. I lived in the girls' dorm with a roommate who spent most of her time at her boyfriend's apartment. (The campus had coed dorms, but my parents were having none of that.) I knew which showerhead worked the best in the communal bathroom and the best time of the day to score some hot water. Nancy moved into the dorm next door, and we were ecstatic to be so close—if nothing else, we could share the cost of our pizza obsession. My classes—freshman basics like math, science, and history—were fun and challenging, and I was meeting a lot of new people. In other words, our new worlds could not have been more different.

My dad had struck a deal with all five of his kids: He would pay all our college tuition and room and board for two years, but we had to pay for books, clothes, and spending money. After two years we were on our own. I had gotten the job at Computer Spectrum to supplement my income and to begin saving for the lean years.

My coworkers were a fun bunch, and on the day that everything changed, we were cutting up and not in a big rush to do inventory. The phone rang, but I didn't think much of it—our phones rang constantly. We had several lines for technical support, and they were always lighting up with calls from students desperate to retrieve their term papers from ruined hard drives. I was standing on a ladder counting computer cables when someone hollered at me to take line one.

I picked up and said hello. Then I heard Lindsey say my name and start to cry—a scared, shaken-to-the-core sobbing that set my teeth to chattering and my hands to shaking. A lightning bolt of adrenaline shot up my spine. I was afraid to ask what happened because I knew it wasn't good.

"What's wrong?"

She began to babble in the run-on sentences of panic and fear. "Mom and Joe have been in an accident. Kate, Kate, it's terrible. Kate, I was right there. I didn't know what to do. There was so much blood. They're air-lifting Mom to Columbia. Dad and I are leaving to drive up to the hospital. Someone has to be there when she gets there."

All I could say was "Okay. I"ll get my stuff and leave right now."

Time suddenly slowed to a crawl. I could sense my coworkers, one by one, stopping what they were doing to stare at me. My mind struggled to process what Lindsey had said. An accident? What did she mean? What had happened to Mom?

I told Lindsey I'd leave for the hospital immediately. She said she'd call Anna, Grandma Decker, and Aunt Teresa, Dad's only sibling. Her boyfriend would drive her and Dad to Columbia. "I'll be there as soon as I can," she said, trying valiantly not to crumble. "But it'll take an hour." I hung up the phone with a racing pulse and a heart that had turned to ice.

It took days, weeks, and years for Lindsey to tell me everything she had seen that day. Even now there are things that are easier not to remember.

Mom and Joe were coming from town after picking up dinner at the Chinese restaurant. From what I pieced together later, they had been arguing. Joe was a high school junior at the time, and like a lot of teenage boys, he didn't get along with his dad. Joe had evolved into someone Dad couldn't understand: a laid-back kid with long hair and a love of rock music, not farming. Mom was the one who kept Joe in line, always riding him about his grades and urging him to take responsibility for his actions.

Our farm sits off a country highway. A small gravel lane leads to the house; to get to it, you have to make a left-hand turn. After moving back to the farm, Dad had put in a new mailbox, but the postal service mandated that it be on the right side of the highway so the postman could shove in the mail as he drove past. This meant we had to park in the lane, get out of the car, and walk across the road to get the mail. It would have been easier to pull over onto the shoulder, roll down the car window, and get the mail before turning into the lane, but Dad sternly warned us against doing so. The mailbox sat on a curve, making it difficult for an oncoming vehicle to see you until it was right on top of you.

And Mom always did as Dad said, until that day. Maybe she was distracted. Maybe she was tired and just wanted to get the mail—a grocery store circular, some bills, maybe a postcard from Wendy—and get home. Whatever the case, she pulled up alongside the mailbox, close enough for Joe to reach in.

As she pulled back onto the road, she didn't see the grain truck rounding the curve. The truck driver saw her minivan and switched lanes to go around it. At that moment, Mom turned left into the lane.

Lindsey was on the phone when she heard a knock on the door. She opened it to find a young man in a highly agitated state. "I need to use your phone," he said urgently. "There's been a really bad accident at the end of your lane." Lindsey ended her call and handed the phone to the young man, whose name was Chris. He dialed 911 and gave the details to the dispatcher. After he hung up the phone, she asked him what had happened. "One of the vehicles is a blue minivan," he said. "Do you know anyone who drives one?"

But Lindsey was already running.

She got there before the paramedics, before the highway patrol, before anyone. The impact had crushed the driver's door and pushed it into the interior. Mom sagged badly behind the console, unconscious and bleeding from the head. Joe was conscious yet incoherent. Lindsey yelled at him to get his attention and to see if he was okay, willing them both to be okay. "Run to the house!" she yelled. Joe took a few steps and fell. Chris, who was back at the scene, came to his aid. Lindsey crawled into the passenger seat and tried to hold Mom up. Passersby who had stopped to help suggested they pull Mom from the vehicle.

"Don't move her until the paramedics get here!" Lindsey yelled, worried Mom might be paralyzed. Lindsey knew she was alive: She could hear her breathing, a liquid sound.

It took fifteen minutes for the ambulance crew to get from Macon to the accident. While paramedics extracted Mom from the car, Lindsey, forgetting it was harvest season, asked a passerby to call Dad at the office. When he wasn't there, a neighbor tore off to look for Dad and eventually found him at the river bottom loading a truck full of grain. By the time a neighbor screeched to a halt at the farm and told Dad what had happened, Mom was already at Macon's Samaritan Hospital, the same hospital where she had given birth to me. There, the doctors quickly realized that her injuries required a level of care they couldn't offer. As Mom was loaded into the helicopter, Dad and Lindsey began the hour's drive to the University of Missouri hospital in Columbia. Joe was transported there in an ambulance.

The Mizzou campus was only three blocks from the hospital. One of my coworkers at Computer Spectrum named Eric drove me there. On the way my mind raced with questions and scenarios, none of which I cared to consider for more than a split second.

The front desk would tell me nothing, not even whether or not my mother was there. It seemed like hours before anyone else showed up, and then they came all at once: Dad and Lindsey and Lindsey's then-boyfriend. Now that Dad was here, the admitting nurse told us Mom had been rushed into surgery. We decided to concentrate on Joe since we could get to see him right away. Joe was lying down in an exam room, cut up, disoriented, and shaken to the core. We tried not to ask a lot of questions, and he didn't feel like talking. He received a CAT scan and some stitches. Diagnosed with a concussion and bruises, he was held overnight for observation. He would fully recover, physically at least.

By the time Anna and her husband arrived two hours later, we didn't have much to report. Everyone was in shock, but no one was crying—we didn't yet know if there was anything to cry about.

Throughout the whole ordeal, I never shed a tear. When I was little, my sisters would always say they knew that something was really wrong if I was crying. I unconsciously adopted that philosophy for life. I figured if I didn't cry, then things couldn't really be that bad. My refusal to cry was my way of willing Mom to live.

We paced the waiting room, paced the halls. Every time a door swung open, we looked up, hoping it was someone who could tell us something, anything. In an effort to locate Wendy and Chris, Dad dialed the first of his many calls to the Red Cross. Finding his daughter and her husband gave him a mission, and he threw all his nervous energy into the task.

Family and friends occupied the ICU waiting room as the minutes and hours ticked by. We sat without speaking. Once in a while someone would attempt a little small talk that would quickly sputter.

During one of those silent stretches, an incident that had occurred a few months earlier entered my mind. Our farm had been sitting empty for so long that the local creatures—coyotes, raccoons, skunks, deer—had become accustomed to coming and going as they pleased. My parents' room had a door that opened onto the front porch, and their bed was positioned so that, from the bed, they could see directly out the door. One night Mom woke up, glanced at the porch, and saw two yellow eyes peering in at her. She sat straight up and made out the shadowy shape of a coyote. "Steve!" she cried out, frantically clutching at my dad. He ran for his shotgun, but by the time he got back the coyote had loped off. They slept with the gun in a corner of the room for the next few weeks just to be on the safe side.

Sitting in the waiting room while Mom fought for her life, I found it hard not to think of that coyote as some sort of omen, a shadowy figure stalking her. A day after we came to live in the hospital, Dad was allowed to see Mom.

Anna went with him because she was the oldest. I knew from the way they looked when they came out that our lives as we had known them were over. We had crossed the threshold into a new reality, and the door had closed behind us.

My father's expression was stunned. He looked at Anna and said, "She just looks so bad," and then he began to sob. The only other time I had ever seen him cry was at his father's funeral.

Eventually the surgeon came out to brief us. When Mom hit her head on a support post inside the van, her brain had crashed against the other side of her skull, causing a blood clot and swelling. The surgeon had removed part of her skull in an effort to reduce the pressure on her brain. "Even if she wakes up," he told us, "we have no idea how much damage has been done."

Another day went by, and Mom remained unconscious. We prayed, the town prayed. Occasionally, a doctor would join us in the waiting room but could tell us very little. Finally, a few days into our vigil, Lindsey and I were allowed to see her. "Talk to her," the doctor told us, "as if everything is normal."

The ICU was a crisp, white world filled with beeping machines. My eyes traveled over the room, looking for Mom. I had a hard time finding her; it was if someone had thrown a sheet over the room's contents, concealing them. Then I saw her eyes, which were closed. Her head was wrapped in bandages and she was on a respirator. Tubes snaked from her stomach, throat, nose, head, and arms. The atmosphere was so hushed that I hardly dared to speak.

I approached the bed. I wanted to take her hand, but I didn't want to disturb the IV. "Mom?" I said, and even though I whispered, my voice seemed to boom, as if amplified. Lindsey, still traumatized by the accident, began to shake and tear up. Seeing Mom like this was a shock to our sensibilities. Numb, we linked arms and prayed as hard as we could. When I opened my eyes and looked toward the bed, Mom seemed to have disappeared again into the tubes and the bandages and the sheets. I stood in silence, trying to find her.

Mom was in a coma for two weeks. With every grain of good news came an avalanche of bad. Such as:

"She's waking up, but it looks like the damage is more severe than we thought."

"She moved her finger, but don't get excited—it probably means nothing."

Dad remained hopeful and optimistic. He slept at Lindsey's apartment or in the waiting room on a bench and took showers in the hospital basement. When Joe was released, he moved in with Grandma Decker in Macon so that Dad could spend his time at the hospital. I stayed in my dorm, which was the building next to the hospital. Dad insisted that we try to keep our normal routines, so I went to as many classes as I could and worked some. Natalie, Nancy, and Mollie came from their various colleges to sit at the hospital with me. We all became more familiar with the hospital and its rules than we ever wanted to be. Before long, we could find the elevators, soda machines, cafeteria, and waiting rooms with our eyes shut. We knew the names of the nurses and the shifts they worked. We knew the names of other patients and their life stories, told to us by other anguished families. We learned what all the beeping machines did. Most of all, we began to understand how delicate the brain is, how easily harmed.

Two weeks after the accident, Wendy and Chris finally arrived. They had traveled thousands of miles from Europe to get here, worried that they'd arrive too late. Mom was still alive, but any hope that my sister and her husband had brought with them quickly faded when they saw her. She was living on the margin between life and death; if she didn't make it, at least we would all be together now that Wendy and Chris were back. A cold comfort, but we grabbed on to whatever solace we could to keep us afloat.

On October 14 or thereabouts, I arrived at the hospital from class to some big news. "Mom opened her eyes," Dad told me, yet he looked so grim that we knew better than to rejoice.

"We're not out of the woods yet," said the doctors, who tended to say things like that. We thanked God for small miracles and continued to hope.

After Mom woke up, my visits to her bedside were more upsetting than when she'd been in a coma. When I looked in her eyes, something was missing: that spark, that essence of the woman I had known. When I knelt to smile at her, she didn't seem to recognize me. Everything that should have been familiar to her wasn't. Only two of us were allowed in at a time, for five minutes every hour; with such a big family, each of us had to wait our turn, and each time I went in I hoped I would be the one to say or do something to lift the fog from her memory. Dad spent every waking hour by Mom's bedside. He talked to her, touched her, comforted her—did everything he could to pull her back to him.

———

Meanwhile, I hadn't heard a word from Mike. This shocked me, given how close he and Mom had been. I began to wonder if he knew what had happened. A few weeks after the accident, while I was in Macon visiting Grandma Decker, I ran into Mike's dad, Terry. He told me that Mike had called and that he'd told him the whole story. I waited and waited for some word from him, but it didn't come, and finally I got tired of waiting.

My friend Eric from the computer store had a roommate, an ROTC student named Gregg. I'd go to Eric's apartment to watch movies, and soon Gregg had me in his sights. He began to come to the hospital and sit with me while I waited my turn in the ICU. Sometimes he took me to dinner or out for ice cream. He tried to get me to open up about what I was going through. I enjoyed his company, and I was vulnerable. When he made it clear he wanted to be more than a friend, I said no. I told him that I still cared about Mike and that I wouldn't feel right about dating him until Mike came home and we were able to talk things through. But time passed, and I didn't hear from Mike. Gregg was there; he liked my company and everything else about me. To be wanted was an intoxicating feeling. I also needed some stability, some sense of normalcy in my world, and Gregg seemed to offer that.

I wrote a letter to Mike expressing my anger over his lack of communication. A few days later, Gregg dropped me off at my dorm. He walked me to the door, and as I turned to go inside, he grabbed me and kissed me. I figured there was no turning back.

A month after the accident, Mom was moved from the ICU into a private room. She was out of danger but still unresponsive. Dad had almost a year of sick leave saved up, and he began to cash it in. One weekend he decided he needed to make sure things were still standing in Macon. I invited Gregg to come with us and have dinner. After we visited Mom, they dropped me off at the dorm and waited in the car while I ran upstairs to pack a bag. As I was walking out the door the phone in my room rang. It was Mike.

"I got your letter," he said in a voice that was both hurt and angry.

"It's really good to hear from you," I said. "But some people are waiting for me." If I had taken the time to speak with him then, our wounded relationship might have been mended much sooner. But the Army allotted him only enough time for us to get angry and to say things to each other that we didn't mean. I hung up the phone feeling that that conversation had severed whatever connection we had left.

Gregg and I dated for only two weeks. He liked the thrill of the hunt, but after he bagged me the thrill was gone. I was also a good girl, and he quickly discovered that he wasn't going to change my mind. One day he simply stopped calling. The next thing I heard, he was dating other girls. I had never been dumped before; I couldn't believe someone could do this to me. I felt like the stereotypical good girl who had been given some rope and used it to hang herself.

The protocol with brain injuries is to begin rehab as quickly as possible in order to slow or reverse the damage. In early December, after weeks in intensive care, Mom was moved to a rehabilitation center in the hospital for six weeks. She couldn't speak and responded to stimuli by blinking or moving her body a little. Dad and Joe were the only ones who could get any reaction from her. She knew enough to know that Joe could have been injured, and seeing him seemed to reassure her that he was all right. Sometimes she recognized me, sometimes she didn't.

The rehab unit was next door to my dorm. I'd spend every evening there, usually accompanied by Nancy. I wanted to make sure that I was the last one to see Mom before visiting hours were over. Yet I hated the visits. I hated what had happened to her, hated the growing certainty that the mother I'd known and loved wasn't coming back. But I also knew that had it been me lying in that bed, she would never have missed a night. So at eight o'clock I would head over and sit and ramble on to her about my day and my classes. Finally, I had to drop math and French because I fell so far behind.

Mike's dad called often to check on Mom's progress and on me, and in November Terry called to see if I wanted to go hunting with him again. I was excited and a little surprised that he asked, given the situation with his son and me. But a break from the hospital routine sounded great.

I went home to Macon for the weekend. On opening morning of hunting season, Terry picked me up at 0400, just as before. We stationed ourselves in the Blaise family deer stand. Terry called it "Old Faithful" because it had been there forever, and everyone who had ever hunted from it had always seen a deer. To this day I have yet to see one while sitting up there.

We sat in Old Faithful all morning and saw nothing but squirrels. We laughed and talked, our closeness still intact. Terry asked me if I heard from Mike regularly and did I want a ride to his basic training graduation? After a while it became obvious that he had no idea that Mike and I were no longer a couple.

Grampy was his usual self that year. His reassuring presence and good humor reminded me of happier times. We talked about Mike and basic training and how we hoped he was holding up. "Mike's a strong kid," Grampy said. "He'll be fine." Like Terry, Grampy had no idea that I wasn't seeing Mike.

After the traditional breakfast, I dragged Mike's sister, Kris, outside. "Does your family know that Mike and I have broken up?" I asked her.

"I had no idea!" she said. "Nobody does."

"I guess Mike decided not to tell you," I said. "Please keep it to yourself." And she did. But the revelation got me to wondering if Mike still held out hope that we would work out.

Mike graduated from basic training in mid-December. His parents drove down to Fort Benning for the ceremony. I badly wanted to go along but felt there was no place for me there. I'll always regret missing that event.

Nancy and Robert, the friends who got Mike and me together, were still dating, and in early December Mike called to let them know that he'd be home for Christmas leave in a week. The two of them invited Lindsey and me to go to dinner with them at the Olive Garden. The thought of seeing Mike after all that had passed between us made me anxious to the point of nausea. How would we react to each other?

In a way, getting dumped by Gregg was the best thing that could have happened to me. With Mike, I'd always felt as if I had the upper hand in our relationship, that he loved me more than I loved him. But rejection is the great equalizer. I realized what an exceptional man Mike was and how lucky I'd been to have him. Mom's accident taught me several things, too. One, that life can take a 180-degree turn with such speed it leaves you reeling and questioning your own goals. Two, that one change of routine, no matter how small, can have tragic, far-reaching consequences. Three, that I wasn't as self-sufficient as I thought I was. I'd always hated to admit that I needed anything. But I needed Mike in my life. I needed to laugh again.

Before we went to dinner, Nancy came to my dorm room and asked me if I knew what I wanted. I told her I wanted Mike. She simply said, "Okay, then let's go."

I saw him for the first time outside Nancy's room. We said an awkward hello and Mike asked after my family. Though he was dressed the same as always—jeans, T-shirt, a baseball cap, no coat—he looked different. He was leaner and his hair had been shorn close to his head in a military haircut nicknamed a "high and tight." He walked with more confidence and had an air of worldly wisdom about him, like a boy who'd survived his ritual rite of passage and returned home a man. Although he wasn't twenty-one yet, Mike ordered a bottle of wine at the restaurant and wasn't carded. But behind that mystique, he was the same old Mike. He kept us in stitches all during dinner, entertaining us with impressions of his drill sergeants and of Army life. It felt incredible to laugh again, to forget for a few hours about the previous weeks. Mike sat across from me, yet he rarely glanced in my direction. It was like that night at Pizza Hut three years before: I might as well have been invisible.

When we got back to the dorms, he said a quick "See ya," and I headed to my room. Mike went to hang out with Nancy and Robert in her room; I could hear them laughing through the walls. A few hours later, there was a knock on my door. It was Mike; he wanted to see my mother. "Could you take me over there tomorrow night?" he said, all business.

"Call me when you get into town," I said as nonchalantly as I could.

The next night he and Terry showed up in a new red Toyota pickup Mike was test-driving. The three of us went to dinner at some generic chain restaurant and sat and talked long after our plates were empty, a breezy conversation that felt like old times. They had a lot of questions about Mom, and I tried to prepare Mike as best as I could for meeting her. I knew it wouldn't be easy for him, and I was right.

Dad was there as usual. Thrilled to see Mike, he gave him a quick hug and shook his hand and congratulated him on getting through basic. He pumped Mike full of questions about the Army for a few minutes, then stood off to the side and caught up with Terry. Mike got his first good look at Mom, and it was disconcerting. Her head had been shaved for surgery, and the left side was caved in where her skull should have been. He took two steps toward Mom's bedside and crouched so he was at eye level with her.

"Hi, Marie, it's me," he said. "It's Mike."

Mom's eyes swung toward Mike's face. She tried to speak, but the words were merely sounds, garbled and incoherent. It was hard to tell if she recognized him or not. Shaken, Mike glanced up at me, then tried again.

"I'm sorry I couldn't get here sooner, but I've thought a lot about you," he went on. "I've been in infantry basic training. When I heard what happened, my whole platoon said a prayer for you." He paused, waiting for a reaction, which did not come. "I sure did miss your iced tea while I was there."

He spoke to her for another minute or so about Army life. He smiled and laughed, but it was an act. When he rose to stand, I could see his hands were trembling. "I didn't expect anything like this," he murmured to me. He was beginning to understand that my family had endured its own sort of boot camp.

We left the hospital in the red truck and dropped Terry off at his vehicle. Mike was quiet. I knew he wanted to talk, but he wasn't sure where to begin, which questions to ask first.

"I'll take you home," he said, and by the time we got to the dorm it seemed the natural thing for him to come up for a while. We talked for hours leaning against opposite walls, sharing our stories of the last few months and trying to fathom how life could have changed so much in such a short time.

"Kate," he finally said. "I want to forget the past few months and start over." Then he walked over to my side of the room and gave me one of those famous hugs and kissed me. At that moment I knew there would be times he would make me angry, times he would drive me up the wall, and times he would make me laugh. But there would never be a time when I didn't love him.

Christmas rolled inevitably toward us, but without Mom, we had little enthusiasm for the holiday. She was the one who spent countless hours ensuring the house was decorated, the skaters were put up, and all the Decker traditions were faithfully carried out. This year, Christmas would be spent at the rehab center.

It was also my first Christmas Day away from home. An older friend of Lindsey's from her job invited us to dinner at her house. Lindsey, Joe, and I went. They were kind people, but eating without Dad and trying to be cheerful made the situation feel even more alien. We spent the evening at the hospital with our parents. Wendy, who had stayed with us for two months, had returned to England with Chris, but Anna and her husband came up. We had hung Christmas decorations and lights in Mom's room, which was filled with flowers and gifts. Dad had set up a small wooden nativity scene on her nightstand, and we exchanged gifts. We sat and unwrapped them quietly. At one point a nurse came in wearing a Santa hat.

After six weeks in rehab, Mom showed little improvement. She had no short-term memory, and her long-term memory went on and off like a faulty light switch. Her left side was slightly paralyzed, and she was confined to a wheelchair. The doctors took Dad aside and told him they'd done everything they could, but her brain damage was too severe. They suggested that he try a more specialized rehabilitation hospital where she could get one-on-one care. They recommended one in Carbondale, Illinois, six hours away.

"What could I say?" Dad told me later. "No, I don't want to try that? Or, yeah, we'll try that. We'll try everything."

In January 1995, Dad had Mom admitted to the rehab hospital in Carbondale. He stayed with her for a few days and turned around and drove home. For the first time in thirty years, they were living apart, though only Dad knew it. He hated being away from her, hated living alone out at the farm, which held so many memories. In a way, it was the worst fate that could have befallen him: His wife was alive, but she wasn't his anymore.

By the end of January 1995, we'd all begun to settle into our new reality.

Anna and her husband went back to their lives in Louisiana, Missouri. Anna called a few weeks later to give us some good news: They were expecting their first child. But she would have to navigate those scary and exciting waters without a mother of her own.

Wendy was back in England. She got a job as a teacher's aide at a school on the Air Force base and started working toward a teaching degree. She kept in constant contact via telephone, and not a conversation went by where she didn't fret over how far away she was.

Dad bought a single-story house in town with the hope that Mom would eventually get to come home. He spent weekdays at work and weekends in Carbondale. He lost a lot of weight and began to look haggard and worn. If he talked to anyone it was usually me, but he never complained or discussed what it was like to lose his wife.

After a few months at Grandma Decker's, Joe moved back in with Dad. With everyone's energy directed toward Mom, Joe felt alone and neglected. He had no one to talk with or release his anger and sorrow to. He carried it with him, and the burden got heavier and heavier.

I'm not sure Lindsey ever recovered from the accident. If anything, it sobered her up. She went back to work at the bank, but I sensed in her a new seriousness, an acknowledgment that life isn't something to be treated carelessly.

Mike was now stationed at Fort Campbell, Kentucky. An infantry private first class, he became his platoon's M60 gunner. At twenty-three pounds, the M60 machine gun is the largest, heaviest handheld weapon in the Army's arsenal.

I took a closer look at myself. I wasn't pleased with many of my decisions over the past six months. I had used my mother's accident as an excuse to be angry, self-absorbed, and irresponsible. Now that Mike and I were back together, I vowed to get the rest of my life on track. I made an appointment to talk to the ROTC recruiter on campus to find out what I had to do to become a full-fledged cadet, what I'd wanted to do all along. I was ready to sign my life over to the Army after college.

Mom was permanently disabled. While she regained her speech and some body movement, her left side remained paralyzed and she began to have terrible seizures. For the last ten years her condition has been the same. Blessedly unaware that anything has happened to her, she has the sweet, slightly confused nature of a lost child in the company of friendly, concerned adults. There are days when she knows I'm Kate, and days when she doesn't recognize me at all. Her long-term memory stops at about 1986. In her mind, we still live in the house on Crestview Street, and I am permanently ten years old, playing guns and limping home with scraped knees that need Bactine and a Band-Aid. But sometimes, in the muddy waters of Mom's memory, the distant past rises to the surface and she is a little girl again. She is a ballerina on a stage, dazzling in tulle and a tiara, and she is dancing.

CHAPTER 8

CAMOUFLAGE

NO GIRL FORGETS her first uniform. In January 1995 of my freshman year, I stood in my dorm room and ironed my green camouflage basic duty uniform (BDU) until it creaked and spit-polished my black boots until they gleamed. I pulled on the pants, buttoned the stiff shirt, tugged on the boots and laced them tightly, a task that took almost ten minutes. My cadet rank identified me as a freshman and my insignia said simply ROTC, but when I pinned them on, my hands shook. My brain whirred with fears and concerns. What if I put them on wrong? Would I remember when, who, and how to salute? If an upperclassman told me to do push-ups, would I drop and do them or simply vomit on his boots? Yet despite my nerves, I knew from the moment I put on that uniform that a business suit would never work for me. I walked into the dorm bathroom and gazed at myself in the mirror. The young woman who smiled back at me in her spanking-new BDUs wasn't a soldier yet, but she was finally on her way.

My first ROTC class, military science and leadership, was a two-part course. In the classroom we learned such infantry skills as basic land navigation, military courtesy, rank structures, and what to do in case of ambush. Every Thursday afternoon we put our book learning to practical use in labs. The new cadets were issued BDUs for lab days, and we had to wear them all day to class. Wearing that uniform for the first time around campus made me feel almost bionic. I felt a lot of eyes on me. I could tell what other students were thinking: "What in the heck is she doing wearing this getup to class?" If they didn't get it, that was their problem.

You'll scarcely find an eighteen-year-old girl who has a true sense of herself, let alone in one who is coping with the aftermath of a family tragedy. Mom's new identity as an invalid recast the family roles—Dad became the caretaker, Anna and Wendy and Lindsey the helpless bystanders, Joe the guilt-ridden survivor. I thought I knew who I was—an officer in training. Little did I know that the accident and the Army would intersect down the road and cause me to put my soldier dreams on hold.

For freshmen, Army ROTC was an elective, like creative writing or cooking. Nancy and I had become better friends than ever, so I talked her into taking the class with me. "It's something we can do to-gether," I told her, "and we'll get to do fun stuff like rappelling. Plus it'll count as your P.E. credit."

Of the thirty people in our ROTC class, there was only one other woman, though I can't remember her at all. Nancy, on the other hand, was a girl you didn't soon forget. She didn't exactly fit the tom-boy, soldier-girl stereotype. A former homecoming queen at Macon R-1, Nancy had dark brown hair, brown eyes with long dark lashes, and a voluptuous figure that made men's heads swivel when she walked by. But Nancy was up for anything, so she agreed.

In one of our first labs, we learned to "camo up." Because a bare face stands out like a full moon in the dark, the purpose of camou-flage is to make oneself invisible, to hide our human identities and be-come one with the woods.

Each camo stick was the size of a tube of lipstick, but the colors were strictly Army issue: brown in light and dark, green in light and dark, and black. Unlike lipstick, the camo sticks were not the least bit soft—it is like trying to color your face with a frozen crayon. We were taught to warm them up with a lighter for five seconds and rub the melted tip on our cheeks. When the heated camo touched our skin, it singed our faces. First we put the black camo around our eyes and the features that stood out, like the forehead and nose. Then we painted the greens and browns on our cheeks, chins, the backs of our hands, our necks and ears, and any skin that showed. Done incorrectly, it looks like you have a black cross on your face; it must be shaded and blended, as if you're painting a canvas.

If putting the face paint on was a pain, taking it off was a chore. After the lab, Nancy and I stood in the dorm bathroom and ran through a week's supply of clean washcloths, rubbing our faces raw. We emerged from the ordeal red-faced but also wiser: Later we found out that the older cadets bought civilian camo, used by hunters, from Wal-Mart and washed it off with women's face soap. Learning to use the Army-issue sticks was a rite of passage, though it seemed more like a hazing.

A few weeks into the class, our NCO told us to show up for a lab in our BDUs and with our faces camo'd up. We were going to learn land navigation. Nancy and I were determined to camo up correctly on our own. My dorm room had a mirrored vanity cabinet on each opposing wall, one for each roommate. Nancy and I each took a mirror, our tubes of camo at the ready. We had to move fast—it dried quickly—and we spent an hour alternating between warming up the sticks and cursing that there had to be an easier way. At one point I flashed back to Nancy helping me get ready for my first date with Mike, and I laughed out loud.

"What's so funny?" Nancy said, wincing in pain.

"Oh, nothing," I answered, and refocused on the masochistic exercise. Eye shadow, mascara, and lipstick were one thing, but this was something else completely. When we were done our faces looked like a bundle of brown sticks lying on a bed of green leaves. Our hard work paid off: Our instructors singled us out for our fine work.

In the classroom we'd learned to use a compass, to count out steps to track our distance, and to read a map. I was ready for the real thing. The cadets were given the grid coordinates to ten points, or locations. Each point was marked with a small sign bearing a letter of the alphabet. We had to plan our route and record the letter on the sign to prove we'd found the spot. Then we had to find our way back, all within a certain amount of time.

The second I set off I felt I'd found my calling. I loved being in the woods and relying on myself to find my own way. I loved the absolute silence, the feeling of walking straight to a certain point and finding exactly what I was looking for. It resembled a treasure hunt, only the reward was tired legs, blisters, and a sense of a mission well done.

During other labs we performed squad maneuvers, where groups of five or six would move quietly through the woods as a fluid team, each of us wearing a heavy rucksack and toting a plastic M16, nicknamed a "rubber ducky." It seemed like a natural extension of guns, my childhood game, taken to a new, more serious level.

Rappelling, on the other hand, was a leap of faith. We'd learned some basic knots and how to tie and check a Swiss seat—a rope tied around your legs, butt, and waist that was then hooked into the rappel ropes. The first time, we headed to some cliffs outside town. It was a balmy spring day, and the rocks were warm from the sun. I hooked in just below the ledge and assumed the L position, with my legs straight out in front of me pressed against the cliff face. I dangled there with nothing beneath me but air, gathering my courage. I was nervous and excited but focused on my instructor, who awaited my signal. Once settled, I waved at him and pushed off, becoming briefly airborne. Down I went, pushing off and falling, pushing off and falling, trusting the knots and my nerve would hold. I hit the bottom exhilarated and eager to do it again. I hiked up that cliff at least three more times before it got dark.

Nancy had fun, too, but not as much as I did. She enjoyed the people and the rappelling, but she didn't much like walking through the woods with forty pounds on her back. We'd always known that she wouldn't sign up for the long haul, and at the end of the semester she took her A and moved on.

———

There was another aspect to my military education, one that was taking place in the real world of working soldiers. While I studied how to be a soldier in college, Mike was the real deal. While I was learning to rappel down some puny cliffs, Mike was learning to rappel out of helicopters. While I was studying officer etiquette and protocol, he was saluting officers and following their orders, no matter how absurd or unreasonable. While I was going on my glorified treasure hunts with my rubber ducky in the woods of Missouri, he was practicing squad movements with live ammo in the woods of Tennessee. While I was studying the military tactics I'd need to get my ROTC credits, he was perfecting the lethal skills young soldiers need to know to win battles and stay alive.

Fort Campbell—all 105,000 acres of it—straddles the Kentucky-Tennessee border about sixty miles from Nashville. Most of the post lies in Tennessee except for the post office, thus its Kentucky address. The post is next to the town of Clarksville, but it is a small city unto itself. Between the soldiers and their families and civilian employees, more than 100,000 people live and work there, making it the Army's third-largest military population. The post has the infrastructure to support itself, including seven schools, several stores, a gas station, 4,100 family housing units, a hospital, an airstrip long enough to accommodate a space shuttle landing, and a railroad line for transporting trucks, helicopters, and other armaments and supplies.

Fort Campbell is home to the 101st Airborne Division (Air Assault). The 101st Screaming Eagles are the only air assault division in the world; soldiers learn to fight after being inserted into the combat zone by helicopter. Like all infantrymen, Mike was required to attend Air Assault School, and he went immediately after arriving at Fort Campbell. It's a ten-day course and it's tough. There are tests to take, information to memorize, and daily physical fitness challenges, such as marching ten miles with thirty pounds on your back in less than three hours.

Mike was a private first class in the 1st Battalion, 187th Infantry Regiment, also known as the Rakkasans. The 187th is an infantry airborne division that was created at the start of World War II; its paratroopers became the most successful airborne fighters of the war. The 187th got its nickname while serving as part of the American Occupation Force in Japan. During maneuvers, when the soldiers jumped out of airplanes, the Japanese would point to the sky and shout "Rakkassan! Rakkasan!" their word for parachute. It translates roughly to "falling umbrella"—a lyrical name for a brigade whose current mission is "to deploy thirty-six hours worldwide as part of a joint multinational or unilateral task force to destroy enemy forces or seize and retain terrain, to control land, people and resources."

Even in peacetime, being an infantryman is a dangerous job. Soldiers get injured or killed in training accidents or, more often, while driving too fast or drunk off post. A big sign by Fort Campbell's front gate tracks the number of fatalities in a year, along with the number of days the post has gone without an accident. The soldiers are rewarded with extra days off when they go a certain number of days without a fatal accident. Since they go to the field for weeks and months at a time, they also get days off for working more hours than the average civilian wage slave. About once a month Mike's platoon had Friday and Monday off, and Lindsey and I tried to pick those long weekends to drive down to Clarksville.

Lindsey and I had a routine. On Thursday afternoons we'd meet at her apartment, throw our overnight bags into her blue Pontiac Sunbird, and head out by four to miss the St. Louis traffic. At St. Louis we'd catch the interstate down through Illinois and Kentucky to Fort

Campbell. For 423 miles we had nothing to do but drive and talk. With 50 miles to go, we'd pull off the interstate at the Kentucky Lake exit, where there was a huge truck stop. We'd freshen up in the ladies' room, checking our faces in the mirror, fixing our makeup, and brushing our hair. We wanted to look presentable for the boys who were waiting for us.

Across the street from Fort Campbell's front gate sits a strip mall with businesses that cater to a soldier's every need, from uniform alterations to life insurance. Mike and his buddies always met us by the big white sign for U.S. Cavalry surplus. As soon as Lindsey and I saw the red letters reading U.S. CAV, we could practically taste those first cold beers.

No matter what you may have heard or read about young G.I.s, I can tell you that Mike's buddies were good guys, fun-loving and respectful. They were all about the same age, though at twenty, Mike was the youngest of the group. They treated Lindsey and me like celebrities—I think we reminded them of their sisters and girlfriends back home.

They went by last names only. Flint was short and stocky, with light brown hair and a perennial tan. A sergeant, he cared about his guys, though he didn't hesitate to dole out helpings of tough love if necessary, and he'd do anything for you if asked. He had a thing for Lindsey, and she liked him, too. Byrd was tall, hilarious, and miserable in the Army. He wore expensive clothes and knew how to turn on that Georgia charm. He couldn't wait to get back there, but like a lot of the guys, he didn't seem to have any idea of what he'd do once he got there. Bower was a sweet, fair-haired guy, quiet and grounded and determined to make a success of the Army. He had a serious girlfriend whom he later married. Mike's roommate, Gomez, would clear out when I visited. He was a broad-shouldered, dark-eyed Nebraskan who was waiting for his wife to arrive from back home so he could move out of the barracks. He never did figure out how to put away his laundry; it lay in heaps on his bed, and I always had to resist the urge the fold it.

They'd be standing by that U.S. Cav sign like a receiving party, waiting for Lindsey and me to pull up so we could hit the town. We'd pile into Mike's truck, his buddies piled into theirs, and we'd head out for the night. There was always a party or a barbecue in town, and sometimes we'd drive the sixty miles to Nashville to hook up with a group of G.I.s partying in a rented hotel room. Mike and his buddies really cut loose on weekends. The hours were long and the work could be tedious, so they played as hard as they soldiered. There was more than one night where I can't remember how we made it back to post.

Mike's platoon lived in a barracks near the intersection of Air Assault Street and Desert Storm Avenue. It was a long, homely cinder block building, four stories high and painted a sickly brown inside and out. The floors were covered with old linoleum tile, the kind you find in many schools and mental hospitals, but those tiles gleamed thanks to the soldiers' constant waxing and mopping. The barracks themselves smelled of old, musty Army equipment, twenty types of male soap, and hundreds of pairs of male feet. His platoon occupied an entire floor, and each floor had several dozen small rooms that held two bunks apiece. The place was old enough that each room had its own myths and lore. Jimi Hendrix had been stationed at Fort Campbell when he was a paratrooper in the early 1960s. Rumor had it his ghost still walked one of the floors, and the guys would debate which room might have been his. The bathroom was large, decrepit, and exceedingly ugly, though its floors gleamed from the frequent moppings. Mike would stand guard at the door while Lindsey and I took our morning showers, letting the hot water wash away our hangovers.

I got to know soldiers who weren't in Mike's immediate circle. Across the hall from Mike lived a guy named Majarado, who was fresh from a Los Angeles gang. He'd been given the option of going to jail or joining the Army. Sometimes Majarado joined us, but mostly he hung out with other Latino soldiers. For some reason, Majarado liked to talk with me. If I caught him in the right mood he'd tell me harrowing stories about growing up in L.A. Sometimes he'd pull out his photo album to show me, but instead of pictures of friends and families, it contained images of funerals held for friends and rival gang members. I couldn't even imagine the world he'd come from.

Mike was having a blast in the Army. He bitched about it like every other soldier, but he loved it. When Mike and his buddies talked shop I would eagerly listen in. Lindsey herself was seriously considering joining the National Guard, and she was as curious as I was. The soldiers seemed to speak a different language, full of acronyms and mysterious phrases: "The time space and heading was off on the M60"; "we got a FRAGO to the OP-ORD, but the LT says we'll still

SP around 0400." I wanted to understand what they were talking about, to soak it all in: the culture, the lingo, the equipment.

One weekend, we were sitting on Mike's bunk, hanging out. The platoon had just come back from the field, and all of Mike's gear was piled in the middle of the room. "What's that for?" I asked him, pointing to something that resembled a vest.

"Well, I'll just have to show you," he said. He bent over and picked up a Kevlar. "This is a flak vest," he said, and he put it on me. "And this is a web belt." He put that on me, too. And so it went, from ammunition belts to helmet. By the time he was done, about thirty pounds of gear hung on my body. He laughed and grabbed a camera to snap a picture.

I have a lot of photos from those visits. In one, the guys are standing in the barracks, drinking beer. They've all got their arms around each other, and they're laughing. That's the way I like to remember them.

Every one of them is out of the Army now, either by choice or chance. Flint became an Air Assault School instructor and eventually got out and went back to New York. Byrd got married and stayed in for another tour; last I heard, he'd gotten out and had moved back to Georgia. Gomez got out and is selling cars. Bower was killed in a training accident when a live grenade went off. Majarado did his time, served honorably, made rank, and got out. He wanted to go back to L.A.; he had plans to become a firefighter and was motivated to make a difference, he said. A few months later, Mike and I heard from him, and he had fallen back in with his old crowd.

Over the course of that year, Lindsey and I visited Mike about a dozen times. Those weekends were some of the best times I've ever had. We all hated Mondays, when we had to go back to our other lives. At dawn, Mike and the rest of his platoon would head out for their dawn P.T. run. If Lindsey and I were lucky, we'd stay long enough to hear the morning cadence being called as we headed dead-tired back to Columbia.

————

It so happened that the route to and from Fort Campbell passed through Carbondale, so Lindsey and I would stop in and see Mom both coming and going. Even weekends when I didn't see Mike, one of us would tag along with Dad and Joe on the five hours to Carbondale.

Mom was living in a large house with a kitchen, a living room, and three bedrooms, two people per room. There was round-the-clock nursing care and a steady stream of therapists. With their help, Mom had recovered her speech and some motor skills, but her memory was deeply flawed. She could recall some people and incidents quite clearly, but then suddenly her memory would hit a glitch and skip over months and years at a time, like the needle on a scratched vinyl record. Sometimes she remembered all five of her children in great detail, only as much younger versions of ourselves—I was Kate, but it was hard for her to fathom me being nineteen, not nine. Mom has one brother and four sisters, just as she herself has one son and four daughters, so she would often confuse us with her siblings. When I'd correct her and say, "Mom, I'm not Jane, I'm Kate," she would laugh at me. "You're trying to trick me," she'd say, refusing to believe that I was her daughter.

She was no longer the mother I had known. She didn't laugh the same, didn't look the same. The liquid IV diet, combined with her sedentary life, was turning her once-muscular body soft. Her silky skin was now rough and dry, and her hair, always neatly combed in the past, had grown in darker and coarser. Worse, she cried all the time. For no apparent reason the tears would start to fall, a soft, quiet sobbing that went on for several minutes. We were told it wasn't unusual for brain-damaged patients to cry, that it was part of the healing process. Still, it was disconcerting to sit there and listen to her, obviously in distress, unable to comfort or help her in any way. We couldn't take her for a drive because the car ride exacerbated her disequilibrium. Any sudden motion or movement startled her, and she'd cry out, feeling as if she were being pushed off a cliff.

Wendy, who lived with her husband on a tiny RAF base an hour from London, felt cut off from everyone. But she and I had always been close, and I kept her up-to-date via phone and e-mail, which was just becoming popular.

At one point, she floated the notion of my visiting her and Chris in England. At first the idea seemed out of the question—I would have to leave ROTC, for one thing, and I was hoping to get a full-ride scholarship at Mizzou, just as Dad had done. I'd already completed a set of interviews, a thorough physical, and a long application. Yet I couldn't help fantasizing about how fun it would be to see Europe.

In June 1995, two things happened almost simultaneously to force my hand. First, Mike got orders for a one-year tour at Fort Kobbe in Panama, commencing in January 1996. A week later, I learned that

I'd been awarded a three-year, full-ride ROTC scholarship at Mizzou. When I called Dad to give him the news, he was excited and incredulous at the same time. "I guess you're serious about this," he said.

He was right, and yet he wasn't. I had always wanted to be in the Army, and I had always wanted to see the world. I saw myself as a traveler sitting at a crossroads, puzzling over which road to take.

Ultimately, it was a choice between Mom and Dad. By getting that scholarship, I was living my father's life. My mother, on the other hand, had always dreamed of traveling; when she didn't get to see as much of the world as she hoped to, she passed her dream to us. Her accident had changed me, changed all of us. I had a clearer sense of the fragility of life, of how quickly everything can change, even for the best of people, like my mother. I would live the life she would have wanted. The Army would be there when I got back.

I called Dad not a week later to tell him I'd changed my mind. He seemed to understand. "Be sure this is what you want," he said. Yet I could hear a certain lack of surprise in his voice, as if he wanted to say, "You never were serious about this, were you?"

My ROTC recruiter was more direct. "If you turn this scholarship down," he said, "you'll never be eligible again." His implication was clear: Leave now and I was out for good. It was a chance I'd have to take.

In June, I packed up my belongings and left Mizzou, never to return. I moved home for the summer with Dad and Joe at the farm and got a job as a park ranger with the U.S. Army Corps of Engineers at Long Branch Lake. It's a popular recreation area outside town, with a nice swimming beach, fishing, hiking trails, and boating. It was a federal job, so the pay was pretty good—nine dollars an hour—and I got to be outside all day. In the fall, I would get an apartment in Columbia with Lindsey and Nancy, go back to my old job at Computer Spectrum, and take a few night classes at Columbia College, where Lindsey was a junior.

That summer, Mike and I had our first talk about marriage. We had an unspoken understanding that we'd get married eventually; the question was when. I was interested in his thoughts on the subject before he was sent to Panama and I left for England.

One evening, when he was home from Fort Campbell for a week, we sat at the bridge and discussed our future.

"We've been doing this long-distance thing for a while," I said. "Are we going to keep doing this? What do we want here?"

Mike was completely taken off guard. "Kate, I don't think I'm ready to get married."

"Well, what are you ready for? You're going to leave for a year, and what are you going to do when you get back? Are we going to pick up right back where we left off? I need a plan here."

"I think we can keep things going like they are. I don't want to get married."

"Neither do I—not right now. But we need to talk more about this."

Later, Mike told me that that conversation got him to thinking. He hadn't considered asking me to marry him because he didn't think I would say yes. But since I'd brought it up, he'd begun to think that maybe I would. That maybe getting married when he got home from Panama wasn't such a bad idea after all. Heck, it sounded like a plan.

———

In September 1995, a year after her accident, Dad brought Mom back to Macon. She had made great strides the first three months in Carbondale. But after eight months, the staff told Dad that they had done all they could for her.

Dad moved Mom into a nursing home in Macon, but we wanted her at home. We hoped that her belongings—her wedding dishes, the yellow couch from the seventies—would trigger something. Dad had bought a single-story house in town to accommodate Mom's wheelchair. Her sister Zoe, who was living in Chicago at the time, offered to move to Macon with her three school-age girls to care for Mom full-time. Dad instantly agreed to the plan.

Aunt Zoe and the girls went to live out at the farm. She sent her oldest daughter to Macon R-1 and home-schooled the two younger girls at our house in town so she could be with Mom during the day. At night, Dad took over as caretaker. This was his new identity, and he performed his duties heroically. Aunt Zoe would cook dinner, and they'd all sit together and eat. Dad would try and coax some food into Mom, and then he'd give her a bath and get her to bed. Several times during the night, he'd help her to the bathroom. In the morning, Aunt Zoe and the girls would arrive and Dad would go to work. That was the rhythm of their days.

Unfortunately, Mom's return didn't go as planned. This wasn't the house she'd lived in for eighteen years, so she felt completely lost.

"Where's my stuff?" she'd demand of Dad.

"This is our home. This is our stuff," he'd reply patiently.

"Quit teasing me. Where's our stuff?"

And she began to suffer seizures. The doctors couldn't find a medication to relieve them. I never saw one, but they were terrifying episodes that required medical care. Dad lost a lot of weight during this time, but he never complained.

On a blustery, snowy day in early December of that year, Mike moved out of Fort Campbell and I moved out of the apartment in Columbia. He picked me up there, and we drove the last hour home to Macon together. Mike had thirty days of leave before being shipped out, and we planned to spend as much of it together as we could. He would leave for Panama shortly after New Year's; I'd leave for London a week later.

Mom wasn't at the new house when I got there. She had had surgery to replace the piece of skull that had been removed after the accident, and was recuperating at the nursing home for a few weeks. It was the second Christmas since the accident. Dad had put up a tree and hung about ten ornaments on it. But he had also set the skaters out, and it was nice to see them gliding along once again.

On December 23, Mike arrived to take me to a party at his mom and stepfather's house. We visited with Dad for a while, but when it came time to leave, Mike asked me, "Will you run outside and start the truck and turn the heat on?"

"Why?" I said. "Don't you always do that?"

"I think it'd be really nice if you'd do it this time."

"That doesn't make sense. Why do you really want me to do it?"

"Kate, please. Just trust me."

"Oh, all right." I picked up the keys and headed outside toward the truck. When I passed the living room window and saw Mike and Dad shaking hands and grinning broadly, everything suddenly became clear, especially since he didn't mention the conversation when he got to the truck.

Christmas Eve dawned warm and sunny. I'd planned to go to

Mount Zion with Mike for Christmas Eve services, but I felt like death warmed over. In fact, I hadn't felt this poorly since I had had mono. I was burning with fever, my body ached, and my throat hurt so badly I could hardly swallow aspirin. Dad was torn between staying with me and being with Mom at the nursing home. Mike said he'd stay with me in the afternoon. "If she gets worse," Dad told him, "take her to the emergency room." I knew what he was thinking: Look what happened last time she was this sick. Dad had become more cautious since the accident, and this time he wasn't going to take any chances.

Mike brought some movies over, and then Natalie came over to visit. I lay on the couch, miserable, trying to watch *Star Wars*. When it came time for Natalie to leave, Mike walked her to the car. He came back looking as if he was about to face a firing squad.

Mike had a plan, but it wasn't panning out. Outside, he'd told Natalie that he'd planned on asking me to marry him that evening at the bridge at his mom's house. Then he'd take me to church for Christmas Eve services and tell everyone the good news, but I was clearly too sick to go. "What should I do?" he'd asked her. "The ring is the only present I got her, and I don't want her to get suspicious."

"Ask her anyway," Natalie said.

Back in the living room, Mike walked toward me, took a ring box out of his pocket, and got down on one knee. He opened the box, revealing a marquise-cut diamond set among many smaller ones. (He had bought it with his mom a few days earlier at Sim's Jewelry in town.) Then he simply said, "Kate, will you marry me?"

My response was immediate. "Yes," I said, adding a Mike-style punch line: "You must really love me because I look awful right now."

Right after Mike slipped the ring on my finger, my fever soared and nausea tumbled over me. "You're going to the ER," he said. He bundled me up into a coat, a stocking hat, and gloves. I vomited out the side of the truck all the way there. At the hospital, I lay on an examining table with what turned out to be a nasty case of strep throat. I held up my hand, admiring the way the ring sparkled in the harsh fluorescent light.

"What a pretty ring!" a nurse said admiringly.

"Thanks, I just got it ten minutes ago!" I said weakly. I was engaged.

———

When Mike and I said good-bye after Christmas, we knew it would be a long stretch until we saw each other again. He was heading to Panama for a year, and I to England, where immigration let me in on a four-month tourist visa.

Wendy and Chris lived in a modest house on post. I slept in their spare room on a foldout couch. Wendy was working with disabled kids at the American School and was active with the base theater group. When I wasn't sightseeing in the area or going to London to ogle the crown jewels and the stoic Beefeaters, I volunteered at the school library and played a dead body in an Air Force production of *Arsenic and Old Lace.*

Through the theater group I met a married couple named Mary and Lloyd, American civilians who worked on post. Lloyd was about forty with long brown hair, a nutty sense of humor, and a passion for rock climbing. Once in a while he'd call me up to go climbing with him and his friends in the Lake District. This was serious technical climbing, with pitons and ropes. Lloyd would set the route up the cliff, and I'd follow, picking my path carefully. I learned how to find the right hand-hold, where to put my feet, how to push with my legs to conserve my strength. Afterward we'd head to a pub and drink a pint or five.

Chris, Wendy, and I took several extended trips together. We traveled to Scotland for a long weekend, where the wild, rugged countryside impressed me far more than man-made wonders like Buckingham Palace and even Big Ben. In late March, Chris got two weeks leave, and the three of us spent it on the Continent. We took the ferry across the Channel to Belgium and stayed in Bruges for a few days. I had been indifferent to going there, but I ended up loving this small, elegant city threaded with canals. The weather during our stay was crisp and cold, the food in the restaurants simple yet delicious. At one memorable meal, we enjoyed mussels plucked that morning from the North Sea. They were brought to a table in a huge, steaming pot along with an immense plate of French fries. We ate both with liberal doses of vinegar. April 2, 1996, was my twentieth birthday, and for breakfast Chris bought me a Belgian waffle from a street cart, freshly made and steaming in the crisp morning air.

From Bruges we drove across Europe. We visited castles in Austria, Anne Frank's house in Amsterdam, and got lost in Germany on the way to Italy. I never did make it to Paris or Venice or other wonderful European cities. This, I discovered, is the trouble with traveling: No matter how much I saw, it only awoke in me a thirst to see more. I wrote letters to Mike, detailing all my adventures. Sometimes I sent him cassette tapes onto which I narrated my experiences. Mike was never a big letter writer, so we talked as often as we could on the phone. As a communications specialist, Chris had access to all sorts of special codes, and gave one to Mike so that he could call me at the house for free by accessing a military operator.

We often got cut off in mid-conversation, but I heard enough to know that Mike wasn't too happy about his first adventure abroad. While I had the benefit of staying with family in a wealthy country where English was spoken, Mike was in a place where he had no grasp of the native tongue and where there were no family members to lean on when the harsh realities of life outside Macon hit home. "Kate, you can't believe how poor the people are here," he said. "Today, while we were on maneuvers in the jungle, we stumbled upon a family living in cardboard boxes." I urged him to explore his new home, to go places. But Mike was stubborn in that regard. He would land in a rut and stay there, and nothing could get him to do something new. Like so many soldiers who get homesick and bored, he looked for diversion at the bottom of a beer bottle.

Mike did make a couple of friends. One was James Brady, his assistant gunner. Young and smart, Brady was tall and weighed next to nothing. Another new friend was a G.I. from Nashville named Doug Johnson, though everyone called him Johnny. He'd been in Panama for six months, so he took Mike under his wing and showed him the ropes. Johnny loved God, his family, and football, so he and Mike hit it off right away. Johnny played the guitar and loved to sing country music. He heard Mike singing one day and convinced him to sing where people could actually hear him. And so Mike's love of karaoke was born. Johnny taught him a few songs on the guitar, and they spent hours drinking beer and singing.

I liked Johnny right away, too. He'd often slip a letter in with Mike's, or he'd grab the phone from Mike and chat me up. I was grateful Mike had found such a good friend so far from home. Johnny told me they'd made a videotape of the two of them performing together, and to be sure to look at it when Mike got home. As I recall, we never did watch it. I threw it in a cabinet with our wedding video and forgot about it, only to have it resurface years later, when it could hurt me the most.

————

I returned from England in the late spring. I wasn't especially eager to move back to Macon, though I was anxious to see Dad, Grampy, and Lindsey. I went back to my job at the lake. The Corps of Engineers had offered me my park ranger position back and promised to extend it through the winter months as well. Add in planning the wedding and helping to care for Mom, and I had plenty to fill the eight months until Mike got home. Aunt Zoe was still there caring for Mom during the day, which left the nights to Dad and me. Lindsey came home on weekends to help out, but Joe had a harder time dealing with it. Now in his senior year, he had fallen in with a rough crowd, and he spent most of his time with them. He'd grown his hair, gotten a couple of tattoos, and taken up smoking. Left to his own devices, he did what many teenage boys would do: He ran wild.

After Joe graduated from high school, Dad figured the only way to set him on the straight and narrow was to get him out of town, away from all the bad influences. He marched Joe down to the recruiting office in Macon and signed him up. My brother was shipped off to basic training at Fort Leonard Wood in southern Missouri.

Joe made it through basic and in fact did quite well. In October, we drove down to his graduation. The tall kid with the high and tight didn't look like Joe. He had more confidence and self-respect, which was good to see. He was assigned to Advanced Individual Training in military intelligence at Fort Huachuca in Arizona. A couple of months into it, he came home for Christmas leave and fell in with his old friends, and he went back with a bad attitude. The Army has a low tolerance for such behavior as not showing up for guard duty, and so Joe was discharged. He came back to Macon, moved back in with Dad, and got a job working the night shift at the Toastmaster factory.

Grampy's was my home away from home. He'd stuck the letters I'd written him from England on his refrigerator with magnets, where they stayed for years. I cooked him dinner on Wednesday nights, just like always, and on the weekends I went over there to bake cookies and play cards. Those afternoons together, sitting and talking, helped to sustain me. Grampy was thrilled that I'd officially be part of the family soon; when Mike had told him he'd asked me to marry him,

Grampy had hugged him and said, "Congratulations. You did the right thing."

In late November, when I told Dad I was participating in the usual hunting ritual at Grampy's, he replied, "Please come out and shoot some of my deer—they're eating up all the crops."

I wanted to use the old .270 that I'd learned to shoot with, so I called Peg and asked if she'd mind my using Mike's gun that year. She readily agreed, and I picked it up later that day. Terry and I headed to a great hunting spot on a farm that neighbored Grampy's. We took our positions in one deer stand; Dale was in another, and Dale's son Larry was in a third. The season had been slow, with little to shoot at; now it was the last day, and the sun was fading fast.

A good hunter's intention is to drop the animal where it stands, with as little suffering as possible. No one wants a prolonged hunt for a wounded deer, least of all the deer. There are different camouflage scents and deer calls a hunter can use to lure a deer in, but they're generally reserved for bow hunting. To kill a deer with a rifle, you don't have to bring it in close as long as you are a decent shot. It's a waiting game, pure and simple. And so we waited until, when the light was almost gone, a doe trotted out of the woods about 175 yards away and began nosing the corn stubble. It was far away and a bit small, but it was a deer all the same.

"Terry," I whispered, "I want to take a shot."

"It's a long shot, but go ahead," he whispered back.

I raised the rifle sight to my eye, brought the doe into the crosshairs, and squeezed the trigger. The shot echoed over the snowy fields. When I saw the doe sink to her knees and topple over, I couldn't help but give a triumphant yell.

The four of us clambered down from our stands and traipsed across the field to my prize. Upon closer inspection it was the smallest deer I had ever seen, but it was mine; a spot of blood on its chest proved I'd killed it instantly.

If I was going to hunt, then I was going to go the whole way. I borrowed Terry's knife and, following his instructions, worked through gutting the deer. Starting at its rear end, I made a long cut from butt cheek to neck, steering the knife gently around the stomach and other vital organs. "Nick that stomach," Terry warned, "and it'll send a lot of unpleasantness all over you and your kill." As I cut, I made sure to keep the white fur off the meat because it makes it harder to clean later. To remove the organs, I put down my knife, stuck both hands into the deer's steaming abdominal cavity, and dragged the entrails out on the snowy, blood-spattered ground for the coyotes to snack on later. Lastly, I made a small slit through the back leg near the hoof and tagged my prize for transport. We loaded the animal into Terry's pickup and drove back to Grampy's.

There, the other hunters greeted me like a conquering hero. Dale and Larry burned up the phone lines, calling family members to "come see Kate's deer." My deer wasn't much to look at, but everyone understood the excitement that comes with your first kill. Grampy was as proud of me as if I'd bagged the Loch Ness monster itself. He ambled out with his Polaroid and snapped several pictures of me posing with my catch. Then we sat down for hot coffee and candy bars, the adrenaline still pumping through me as I told and retold the story. I felt like I was standing on top of a mountain, on top of the world.

Later, Terry and I skinned the deer, cut it up, packaged it, and put in a big freezer in his garage. I stuck one of Grampy's Polaroids in an envelope with a note and sent it to Panama. After Mike saw it, he called to tease me. "You sure it's a deer, not a dog?" he said wryly.

But I knew he was proud. When he got home two months later and even for years after, he loved to tell his buddies about his girl-friend the sharpshooter who, at the tender age of twenty, had taken down a deer with a single bullet through its heart.

CHAPTER 9

THE END OF WAITING

MIKE AND I WERE MARRIED on May 31, 1997, at the Crossroads Christian Church, next door to the John Deere dealership in Macon. I had planned a simple wedding, from the flowers to the dress: a beaded sleeveless bodice and a tulle skirt that puffed slightly from the waist, scattered here and there with sequins. Lindsey picked it out for me when we went to a bridal store in Columbia. The dress was too froufrou for my taste, but I tried it on to humor her. When I came out of the dressing room, she said, "You're going home with that one." It cost six hundred dollars, the most expensive single item at the wedding. I could have worn my mother's dress, but it was ivory. I felt I'd earned the right to wear white.

I asked Lindsey to be my maid of honor, and Natalie, Nancy, Mollie, and Wendy to be my bridesmaids. On the day of the wedding, we set up shop in the basement, spreading our cosmetics across several folding tables. Anna played makeup artist as the others giddily zipped themselves into their sleeveless green dresses. It was hot for May, and our cheeks were so flushed with excitement and heat that blush seemed like gilding the lily. My long brown hair was pulled back into a sleek, tight bun. Lindsey helped me into my dress, put a penny in my shoe, adjusted my veil, and did the checks for something old and something blue.

For the most part, Mike had helped me plan the wedding by telephone. In Panama, he had decided he wanted to be in a Scout platoon, and he wanted to be a Ranger. Now he was back at Fort Campbell, making good on his new career goals.

The Scouts are a step up from the regular line infantry. Their job is to move forward of the line units to perform reconnaissance on terrain and enemy positions. There was one Scout platoon in the entire battalion; it got better equipment, better missions, and more respect. A Ranger is an infantry soldier who, simply put, has better training and more specialized skills. Rangers are given priority on high-profile missions, which are often more specialized and more dangerous. Most Scouts wore Ranger tabs or were preparing to attend Ranger School to get one.

Mike approached his goals with the single-mindedness of a football player training for the big game. In Panama he had run a lot for lack of anything else to do, whittling off what was left of his baby fat. He was in the best shape of his life and had no trouble meeting the fitness demands of the Scouts. By the end of March, after a month-long hazing and evaluation process, Mike had found a home with a Scout unit, which short-listed him to attend U.S. Army Ranger School in Fort Benning, Georgia.

I had wanted a military wedding, but since the groomsmen were mostly his high school friends, we settled on rented tuxes. His best man was his friend Brian, Natalie's ex. His groomsmen were his brother, Josh, his buddies Mark and Robert (Nancy's ex), and Brady, his assistant gunner from Panama. Mike and I didn't have the time or money for a nice honeymoon, so we opted to spend a couple of days in a bed-and-breakfast in Ethel, a tiny town twenty miles from Macon. It was called the Recess Inn because it was in a renovated nineteenth-century schoolhouse. Afterward we'd return to Macon, pack up our few household belongings, and move down to Clarksville, where we'd found a two-bedroom apartment near Fort Campbell for six hundred dollars a month. Mike would go back to work in his new Scout platoon, and after the summer I'd start at Austin Peay State University and return to my ROTC training there.

On the eve of our wedding, given Mike's history of tardiness, we put several plans in place to ensure he made it on time. We went so far as to tell him the wedding was an hour earlier than it really was and to assign various family members as escorts. To my surprise, Mike arrived at the church before I did, dressed and ready. I could hear him talking and pacing upstairs, prattling nervously. He greeted family members as they arrived, and everyone who walked in asked him if he was nervous, which I'm sure didn't help. It was the kind of gathering you get only at weddings and funerals: about three hundred people ranging from friends and loved ones to aunts and uncles we hadn't seen since we were in diapers. Tiffani Shelton, our surrogate sister, couldn't make it; she was a specialist in the Army stationed in South Korea.

Another notable absence was my mother.

Six months earlier, in December 1996, Dad had finally acknowledged that he couldn't keep Mom with him any longer. The demands of her care were too great, her seizures too frightening. He found a Lutheran nursing home in Hannibal, and Aunt Zoe returned to Chicago, saddened that in the end she hadn't been able to make a difference.

Dad and I had driven Mom to the home. Her bare-bones room had a bed, a nightstand, and a bureau. We immediately set out family pictures to make it homier and spent the day getting her settled. We had dreaded this for weeks, but Mom seemed interested in what was going on, and Dad and I were more concerned and upset than she was. We left her with the promise that we'd visit her in a few days. We drove home in silence, speaking only to reassure ourselves that we had done the right thing and glossing over the merits of this particular institution.

As for the wedding, Dad had left it up to me whether to bring her. After a lot of internal debate, I decided it was best if she stayed in Hannibal. I had several reasons. Her vertigo made car travel frightening. People who hadn't seen her in a while would have wanted to say hello, but they would only have bewildered her. And her new appearance would be hard on those who hadn't seen her since the accident. But mostly, I wanted Dad to enjoy the day without spending the whole time worrying about Mom, who wouldn't have understood the significance of the event anyway. When Dad walked me down the aisle and lifted my veil, we both knew, without speaking, that someone very important was missing.

Given what my family had gone through the past two years, it felt good to be gathered in happiness for a change. We had pulled through some hard times, and now we had good times to look forward to.

Mike and I stood at the front of the church holding hands while his uncle Dale and cousin Larry sang an old country song. The congregation wore a skim-coat of perspiration in the warm church. During the song I looked up at Mike. He gave me his infamous sly grin and began to slowly rub his sweaty hands up one of my bare arms. It was all I could do not to burst out laughing in front of God and everyone.

The Lutheran ceremony lasted for about thirty-five minutes. At one point Anna sang "The Lord's Prayer," her beautiful high soprano filling the church. I recalled being an eighth-grader and attending a winter concert at a lovely old church in the middle of nowhere. It was so cold I could see my breath, but when Anna started singing I felt nothing but immense pride at her talent, just as I was feeling now.

Mike and I recited the vows just as we'd rehearsed them the night before, knowing we were making those promises not only to each other but to God as well. We said the words "till death us do part," believing that moment to be too far in the future to even contemplate. Mike slipped the ring on my finger, and I slipped on his simple gold band. Soldiers tend to leave their wedding rings in a drawer when they're at work because they can snag on heavy equipment. So when I'd asked Mike what kind of ring he wanted, he'd replied, "The cheapest and plainest you can find, because I won't wear it very often." We bought him a ninety-nine-dollar gold band at Wal-Mart, special-ordered to fit his size 13 finger.

When time came for the kiss, Mike really laid one on me. "That was a bit much," his cousin Lisa told him later, laughing.

I fell into being Kate Blaise with great ease, as if she had been sitting inside of me, waiting to be called outside. It didn't seem strange to write *Blaise* instead of *Decker*. Instead, it seemed like the most natural thing in the world.

Our reception was held at an old military academy in town that had been converted into apartments and banquet rooms. We had catered finger foods and beer, and there was a DJ for dancing. We followed the traditions to the letter. When it came time to cut the cake, it took every ounce of self-control Mike possessed not to smear it all over my face. At her toast, Lindsey told stories about our childhood misadventures and how Mike used to cheat off her math homework.

A few weeks before the wedding, Mike, Lindsey, and I had been discussing the DJ when Lindsey asked us, "What's your song?" Mike, without skipping a beat, said the first song that popped into his head: " 'The Gambler' by Kenny Rogers." Lindsey laughed and I rolled my eyes and promptly forgot about it. Lo and behold, when it came time for our dance, the DJ said, "This song is dedicated to the newly-weds," and the first notes of "The Gambler" filled the room. I knew life was always going to be fun with Mike around.

Our wedding then became like any other, full of dancing and drinking and high spirits. If I had my wedding pictures, I'd describe how nice everyone looked in their tuxes and wedding finery. But the photographer we hired went bankrupt before we could order prints and left town with the negatives. So I'll close my eyes and describe the partygoers from memory.

There are Anna and Mike dancing with Brett, my flower girl and the first of their three daughters. And Wendy and Chris, living in Texas now that Chris was out of the Air Force, taking a spin on the dance floor. And Joe, handsome in his tux with his short trimmed hair, wandering the edges of the gathering. He would leave Macon within the year and wander from one job to the next, hoping to make it as a musician. There is Lindsey, about to graduate from college and join the National Guard, the only daughter left unmarried. Out of frame somewhere is Curt, her future fiancé, whom she didn't even know at the time—he'd crashed the wedding with friends and a twelve-pack of Bud Light. There's Dad, smiling and shaking hands and kissing babies, and Grandma Decker, who'd brought food even though I'd told her repeatedly that the reception was being catered. There are Nancy and Natalie and Mollie dissolving into giggles whenever the topic of my honeymoon night came up. They were all dating the men who would become their husbands, and we'd always remain friends, no matter how far from Missouri I traveled. Mike's parents, Terry and Cheryl, were there, as was Peg, now divorced from Rat, though Mike insisted his former stepfather come anyway. There's his brother, Josh, chatting up some girls as usual. And finally, Grampy in a coat and tie, tapping his foot to the music and no doubt wishing that overalls were acceptable wedding attire.

Around 11:30 P.M. we made ready to leave the reception. Throwing rice is taboo in Missouri because birds can choke on it, so everyone pelted us with birdseed as we left the church. We hopped into Terry's Ford Thunderbird, borrowed for the occasion, and drove to Ethel. As Mike drove we chattered about a million trivial things to fill the tension. We'd waited a long time for this night.

It was past midnight when we arrived. The innkeepers had left us a note of welcome and lit oil lamps in our room. After eight hours my dress was heavy, itchy, and somewhat bedraggled, and my heavily lacquered hair was stiff as a bird's nest. "I've got to take a bath, I'm filthy," I said. Mike went into the bathroom and turned on the water in the claw-foot tub and poured in some fancy bubble bath.

"Go look in my suitcase," I said.

He left the room. When I shimmied out of my dress and let my hair down, birdseed spattered over the wood floor with a sound like rain. I got in the tub and Mike returned with a present, which he unwrapped before me. It was a Bible with his name engraved on the cover. "I've never had my own Bible before," he said.

He leaned against a wall, and we talked softly about the day. But I was so overwhelmed by excitement and nerves that the conversation didn't stick. Finally Mike went into the bedroom and I got myself ready for the big moment. I dried my hair and combed it out, leaving it long and damp down my back, and put on an ivory slip bought from Victoria's Secret for the occasion.

Most women, if they're being honest, will admit that their first time isn't exactly transcendent. After, I lay in bed staring at the ceiling, saying nothing, wondering why in the world I'd saved myself for *that*. Finally I glanced over at Mike. He looked at me with a big grin and said, "Well, was it as good for you as it was for me?"

Then he started laughing, and I joined in. We both knew it could only get better, and it did.

CHAPTER 10

MARRIED TO IT

IT DIDN'T TAKE LONG for me to learn that marriage and the military have a lot in common. You have to make compromises in both, and the result is often far from ideal. You are answerable to another person in everything you do; not only does that person play a role in every decision, he sometimes makes the decisions for you. You must learn to accept sacrifice and compromise, to prioritize what comes first, what second, what you have to let go of altogether. Both marriage and the military challenge you, push you, force you to adjust to unforeseen hardships. You can decide whether to push back, when and how hard, and if doing so will jeopardize everything you've worked for.

Ask a new bride for a word that, in her opinion, sums up what marriage is about, and she might say togetherness. In our case, it was separation. For the first three years of our marriage, Mike and I lived together for only about a year total. The longest stretch was six months in 1998, when he left the Army for six months and enrolled in college. Those three years opened my eyes to the fact that assumptions I'd made going into both marriage and the military didn't necessarily hold up. I had to face the fact that as an Army officer, I'd be a woman in a man's world. Worse, I had to learn to be alone.

That summer, at the age of twenty-one, I found myself in a new town, with a new apartment, a new set of friends, and of course a new husband. Our furniture, on the other hand, was old, a motley collection of castoffs and hand-me-downs. We had a tiny TV from my college dorm, a bed and two dressers from my dad, a lopsided recliner from Peg, and two stained sofas we got for free from a fellow soldier in Mike's platoon. Our only new item was an entertainment center from Wal-Mart, which Mike assembled, cussing all the while. His contribution to our home decor was a John Deere banner that his Rakkasan buddies had "liberated" from a dealership in Clarksville as a going-away present when he'd left the unit. Ever the farm boy, Mike took it everywhere—even to Panama—and he draped it on a quilt rack in our bedroom.

Married life brought its inevitable adjustments. For our first nice meal in our new apartment, I made, as all new brides do, a fancy dish: honey chicken. After eating it politely, Mike informed me that he hated meat with sweet stuff on it. I told him he didn't fold towels correctly; he told me I didn't store leftovers the way his mom did. He loved to watch vintage car shows on the Discovery Channel; I liked comedies. I was compulsively organized and prone to making to-do lists; Mike liked to stack things anywhere and everywhere. I jumped out of bed ready to go; he was cranky as a bear for the first half-hour after waking up. He had a penchant for napping I didn't share. He would rope me into taking a thirty-minute snooze with him, but I'd toss and turn, trying to fall asleep until he finally kicked me out of bed. As a big man with a volcanic body temperature, Mike could sleep only with a fan blowing on him full force. I weighed considerably less and was relatively cold-blooded, so I'd burrow deep beneath the covers to escape the breeze. Yet we always went to bed at the same time and fell asleep in mirror positions of each other: on our stomachs, our right legs drawn up. I'd tuck my hand under his stomach just to remind me that he was there.

Mike spent much of that summer in the field, and in July he attended a two-week course required for soldiers hoping to attend Ranger School. I spent that summer turning our apartment into a home and getting to know the guys in Mike's platoon and their wives, who were invariably young mothers new to the military. I got a job at a Zales Jewelers in the local mall, where I worked nights and weekends during school to supplement our income. As an average specialist, Mike earned no more than $1,200 a month. Grampy had instilled in Mike the dangers of debt, so we wanted to make it through college without taking out a lot of loans. If we couldn't pay cash for something, we went without. We didn't have a credit card.

In September 1997, I started my sophomore year at Austin Peay State University, majoring in political science. Established in 1927 and named for the governor of Tennessee of the time, Austin Peay is in the heart of Clarksville, a stone's throw from the historic downtown. The

200-acre campus has stately brick buildings and a small football stadium where the Austin Peay Governors lost one game after another.
Peay is pronounced like the legume, and the school cheer of "Let's go,
Peay!" didn't help to inspire a winning performance. A bad football
team is a sin in the South, but the school had other things to recommend
it. I liked the small classes, where every professor knew my name; and it
was at Austin Peay that I found a new passion. One of my ROTC re-
quirements was to take a military history course, so that fall I signed
up for a class on World War II with Dr. Malcolm Muir, one of the country's foremost military historians. White-haired and distinguished, he
brought the military to life in a way those old movies I watched with
Dad never had. I'd always enjoyed history, but Dr. Muir made me
love it, and over the next three years I took every class he offered.

Austin Peay's ROTC program was first-rate. It was headquartered
in a vintage armory that had been an auditorium at one time. The
wooden basketball court and balcony bleachers were still there, but
the cadets had built a small rappel tower in one corner and converted
what had been the stage to a lounge and study room. That's where
everyone hung out. I could always find a parking space outside the
armory—maybe non-ROTC students wouldn't park there out of fear
of being recruited. Most of my fellow cadets were former enlisted soldiers who wanted to become officers. There were only five other women
in my class, four of whom planned to be Army nurses.

As I was beginning my first semester at Austin Peay, Mike learned
he'd gotten a slot in Ranger School for that October. It was a great career opportunity—a Ranger tab opened doors. He'd need to be one if
he wanted to apply to an elite force like the Green Berets, a goal of his
since he'd seen that recruitment video years earlier.

In a way, the U.S. Army is the Boy Scouts on steroids: It's about
acquiring new skills and collecting badges. Soldiers attend one school
after another to earn new qualifications, and when you graduate, you
get a patch to sew on your uniform on the left breast. Some posts, like
Fort Campbell and Fort Bragg, place a lot of importance on the number of school patches you have. First impressions are important, and a
patch-heavy soldier is often immediately assumed to be "high-speed"—
a top-notch soldier with ambition and drive. Being a Ranger carries a
very high cool factor, and I was justifiably proud of Mike—he really
wanted this, so of course I wanted it for him. I didn't understand what
he was getting himself—or me—into.

U.S. Army Ranger School is the ultimate survival test: a three-month, three-phase exercise in controlled sadism that tests every muscle and mental fiber a soldier possesses. Phase One is three weeks of mud, sweat, and tears. It's one grueling test after another, such as a combat water survival test, a sixteen-mile foot march, and night and day land navigation tests. The school then moves to the mountains of northern Georgia, where the soldiers suffer through three weeks of mountaineering and survival training, and then put their new skills to use during field-training exercises. Ranger School ends up in the swamps of western Florida for eighteen days. At each phase, soldiers learn how to survive and conduct missions in that particular terrain. They sleep, live, and train outside, no matter the weather, their only supplies those they can fit in their rucksacks and carry on their backs. They get little food and even less sleep. At the end of each phase a soldier is required to lead his squad and to complete a mission.

After the excitement of Mike's acceptance passed, we had to figure out how we were going to pay for all the extra equipment the school required. We tightened our belts even more and haunted the local military surplus stores. He'd need several sets of basic duty uniforms, so we bought ripped, ragged ones, which I spent hours patching.

Two nights before Mike left for Fort Benning, we laid all his gear out on the living room floor. He had to fit four pages' worth of stuff into a rucksack and two duffel bags, so he'd roll and reroll each item of clothing into as tiny a ball as possible and stow it away, while I marked off each item with a fat orange highlighter. As he did so, I was taking mental notes of his technique so I could apply it to my ROTC field exercises. I didn't want to be one of those cadets who threw her stuff on the gym floor and asked for help packing. The next morning, Mike packed up his truck and drove the eight hours to Benning.

After the first week of Ranger School, the soldiers are released for the weekend to spend time with their spouses. I got a ride with a college friend who was going down that way; I would drive our truck back. Mike and I spent two days relaxing in a Super 8 Motel near post and repacking every piece of equipment. He wasn't looking forward to eating one Army Meal Ready to Eat (MRE) a day, so his primary task was to consume as much steak, potatoes, and salad as he possibly could.

In those rare moments outside the room when he didn't have his mouth full of food, Mike brought me up-to-date on the week. During the opening-day brief, his class had received a piece of unnerving news. In the past, if a soldier failed any one of the three phases, he had to repeat it with the next class, a contingency known as "recycling." There is no shame in recycling; it's quite common, and if anything, you seem tougher because you have to stay out in the wilderness and starve for another three weeks. But the two hundred or so men in Mike's class had arrived to find that the school's new commandant, a real hard-ass, had created a new standard. "There'll be no more repeating a single phase," he told them. "If you don't pass a phase, you have to repeat the entire course from the very beginning."

"Does this make you even more nervous?" I asked Mike.

"Nah," he said between chews. "I'll be fine."

After each phase, the students are released for a few hours to wash their clothes, eat some real food, and see their families. Between my classes and the simple fact that we couldn't afford the gas, we knew we wouldn't see each other until December. Mike and I went for our usual quick good-bye: a hug and a kiss followed by a promise to call and write when we could. Then he waved and smiled in that impish way that assured me all was well in Mike's world.

Right after Mike left, Lindsey, who had just graduated from Columbia College with a degree in criminal justice, moved down to Clarksville to live with me for two months while he was gone. In January, she planned to make good on her long-standing desire to enlist in the National Guard and attend basic training. Lindsey and I are very competitive, and a part of her wanted to prove to Dad that she wasn't just a party girl, that she could hack it in the Army, too. She never considered active duty because she didn't want to surrender complete control of her life. She wanted to serve her country, but in typical Lindsey fashion, she wanted to do it her way.

We figured that living together would be just like old times, but we'd both grown up too much to recapture our past harmony. Lindsey found a telemarketing job, and when she wasn't cold-calling people to convince them to buy something they didn't need or want, she was obsessed with basic training. I was married, in college, and working in retail, which I didn't particularly like. Zales attracts a big military clientele in the market for engagement rings. We worked on commission, and I hated watching other salespeople pressure the soldiers into buying more ring than they could afford "on the payment plan."

In my free time, I wondered about Mike and wrote him letters in which I'd update him on what the family and I were up to. "Don't ask me how I'm doing because I won't be able to answer," he'd told me, so I made a point not to.

The letters he did write to me were filled not with accounts of how he was doing or feeling, but with thoughts on food. He'd describe his favorite dishes and all the elaborate meals he'd prepare when he got home. Mike, who had up till now never had much of a sweet tooth, revealed a new obsession for Reese's Peanut Butter Cups. I talked to him twice on the telephone, in the hour between Phases One and Two. Once, he called me from a pay phone at Shoney's, where he was about to give them a run for their money on the all-you-can-eat buffet. He called me thirty minutes later while doing his laundry to tell me he'd thrown up his dinner in the Shoney's parking lot. He wasn't the first: The Shoney's binge-and-purge turned out to be a Ranger School rite of passage as well.

Lindsey left Clarksville a couple of weeks early, at the beginning of November. We'd spent most of the time at each other's throats and were both relieved when she moved on. Suddenly I was living completely alone for the first time in my life. Though I had made a lot of friends in ROTC, most of them were married with children. I'd been married less than a year, but my relationship with Mike had come to resemble our pre-matrimonial days, full of absence and longing.

Mike was scheduled to graduate from Ranger School in early December. Terry, Cheryl, and my dad planned to pick me up on the way to Fort Benning for the graduation ceremony. I was packed and ready to go days early. I was bringing along an extra pair of Mike's BDUs, onto which I'd sewn the Ranger tab, bought in a store on post.

Three days before we were to leave for Benning, I was sitting in the kitchen when the phone rang. It was evening.

All he said was "Hey."

"You're not supposed to be calling me," I replied, surprised. But something in his voice was off. Mike sounded like a different person: hollow, flat, and angry. "What's wrong?" In a few quick sentences, he explained.

"They gave us two patrols at the end of the Florida phase," he said. "I didn't do too well on the first one, but the second went smoothly and I ran out the woods yelling *Ranger* with all the other guys. Then, when I went to my instructor for his out-brief and evaluation, he failed me on the second patrol. Kate, they're sending me and about twenty-five other guys home."

"I don't understand," I said, but he was silent. "Let me come get you."

"No, I have to take the bus."

After we hung up I snipped the Ranger tab off his BDUs. I felt as if I had jinxed him by sewing it on prematurely.

I have never seen anyone so dispirited as the bedraggled man who stepped off the Greyhound bus in Clarksville two days later. He'd lost more than thirty pounds, and his cheeks were hollow. I couldn't believe the Army would do this: ship one of its soldiers home along with a bunch of life's losers, including two drunks who'd been throwing up the whole trip.

All I could do was hug him and take him home.

When we got back to the apartment, Mike threw his bags of gear, which smelled of three months' worth of sweat and sacrifice, onto the deck and didn't look at them for weeks. His first thoughts were of a hot shower, a cold beer, a thick steak, and a soft bed. When he got undressed I saw his ribs for the first time in my life, and his feet looked like raw hamburger. Mike stood in the shower for about an hour, and when he got out I suggested we go to the grocery store. That was a mistake. As we walked the aisles, Mike filled it with mounds of perishables—meat, milk, fruit, vegetables—that would surely expire before we could eat them all. When the cashier told me the total— more than a hundred dollars—I cringed but paid it.

Mike set about preparing the meal with the focus of a brain surgeon. He spent an hour seasoning the steaks and slicing the potatoes just as he liked them, then cooking them just so. Then he sat down in the easy chair with his plate on a television tray to devour his feast, but a few bites into it, his chin hit his chest and he was out. This was the pattern for the next two weeks. He would doze off in the middle of conversations and at all times of the day. He'd fix large, elaborate meals only to fall asleep or feel full after a few bites.

Mike was a different man from the one I'd said good-bye to at Benning. Instead of talking and telling jokes, he was now more inclined to sit quietly watching TV. Sometimes I'd suggest we go out to a movie or dinner at our favorite restaurant, the Black Horse Pub downtown. "I just want to stay here," he'd say grimly before shutting down completely.

A few nights after he got home, I woke up to find Mike's side of the bed empty. I found him asleep outside in the winter chill, curled up in his Army sleeping bag on our little deck. The next morning he told me that after two months of sleeping outside, the apartment was just too warm. He slept on the deck, on and off, for a week. "Come out here with me," he begged me one night. "The bag will keep us warm." But I could feel the wind infiltrating the cracks in the boards between us, and after shivering for an hour I went inside.

Little by little, stories of Mike's ordeal leaked out. He talked about falling twenty feet to the ground flat on his back when his climbing ropes slipped; nodding off over his rifle until his forehead hit the rifle sight and jarred him awake; slogging through sand three feet deep in Florida. But mostly he talked about his fellow soldiers and food. He described how he and his buddies would concoct recipes pieced together from random MREs. If they got cocoa powder, they'd hold on to it for weeks, hoping to eventually get peanut butter so they could make a delicacy called Ranger pudding. Sometimes I'd find him mixing these concoctions at home, as if his taste buds, having been acclimated to such makeshift fare, now longed for it.

Meanwhile, I was knee-deep in military history at school, and those lessons put Mike's condition into a larger context. If three months in simulated combat situations could do this to a man, what must soldiers endure over years of real fighting?

By Christmas, Mike was laughing and talking again, but he'd never really be his old self again. Ranger School had drop-kicked any last vestige of boyhood out of him. From that point on, Mike was a man, and like many men, he was disillusioned that life hadn't met his expectations. It didn't help that the new no-recycling rule had been bent for a couple of officers in Mike's class. "I was only a specialist," he said. "They figured I had time to come back."

Having been in the Army for five years, Mike's reenlistment period was approaching. In order to return to Ranger School, he would have to reenlist in the infantry. "I'll support you if you want to start all over again," I said.

At the same time, it was dawning on me what a dual-career military marriage was going to mean. Our house would be not a home but a way station between schools and training stints. It wasn't the life I'd imagined as an idealistic kid in that gym in Centralia, when patriotism overcame pragmatism.

"Maybe I should go into the Guard or the Reserves," I suggested to Mike once. "Or maybe I should reconsider the whole Army thing."

But Mike would have none of it. "Your goals are as important as mine," he said. "The Army is what you've always wanted. It's going to be tough, but I won't let you give up on it." Over the years he stuck to that philosophy, the quiet presence at my back, pushing me to succeed, reassuring me that we could weather any storm.

Instead, it was Mike who left the Army. He decided to complete his term of duty through 1998 and then enroll at Austin Peay with me. He wasn't sure he'd return to the Army, but if he did, he'd need more schooling to advance. "Sometimes," he told me, "God has a way of showing you the right and wrong paths in life. Maybe I should be doing something else."

That something turned out to be helicopters. Mike had entertained the idea of flying since he was a kid, but he'd gotten the fever bad in Panama, training in jungle warfare. He loved the feeling of flying low with the doors open, and he admired the skill and courage of the pilots. Sometimes, while we were driving on post, he'd tilt his head skyward as helicopters passed overhead. "That could be you up there," I'd tell him. He'd just grin and keep looking up.

———

In July 1998, it was my turn to leave home. I headed for a five-week ROTC Basic Course at Fort Knox, Kentucky. The course was designed to give freshmen and sophomores from around the United States a taste of Army life, and even though I was going to be a junior, I had to attend to make up for the year of ROTC classes I'd missed. That way, I would be eligible for the two-year full-ride scholarship I was hoping to get.

Fort Knox is home to the Army's armored division and of course the famous gold depository, but I didn't see much of the place. The van deposited me at an older section of post, where I was in-processed. I was then marched to our quarters at the basic training barracks and introduced to the rest of my platoon. Like me, most of the other cadets were young, wide-eyed college students determined to join the Army or at least find out what it was all about. Unlike me, most were male and single. In my platoon of about sixty people there were only eight women. We were all handed over to four drill sergeants, who would lead us over the next five weeks. They yelled some and smoked us some, ordering us to do jumping jacks and push-ups and sit-ups. While they didn't tolerate screwups, they also weren't allowed to abuse us too much.

This was my first full-time foray into Army life, and I reveled in it. I loved the dawn wake-ups, the bad mess hall food, even the marching. The camp curriculum covered some of the same skills I'd learned at Mizzou, such as rappelling and land navigation, but I also got to fire a variety of weapons, including Mike's specialty, the M-60. Lying on the ground, firing that monster with another cadet feeding the chain link ammunition, made me feel like I could mow down anything. Mike's old Winchester suddenly seemed utterly inadequate.

Both Mike and Dad came to my graduation. I won a couple of cadet awards at the camp, and when Dad saw that Army general pinning them on my chest, he thought, *She's really serious about this.*

I returned home full of patriotic zeal and ambition. I wanted to be high-speed. I was offered another full-ride ROTC scholarship, but to get it I had to commit to four years of active duty and another four to the inactive ready reserve. Certain I'd spend at least twenty years in the Army, I signed on the dotted line without a moment's pause.

I began to think about what branch of the service I'd apply for. My ultimate goal was to be a platoon leader, preferably in a combat arm. The infantry was closed to women, so what was next? Air defense, perhaps. Women can do that. But women are very limited in terms of which posts they can get assigned to, and Mike and I knew that we had to make it easy for the Army to put us in the same place. I could be an engineer, but I couldn't be a combat engineer, so I couldn't be on the front lines. I wanted to be in a combat unit that wouldn't hold me back. Aviation, a relatively new branch for women, seemed the way to go, and it offered the option of becoming a helicopter pilot. I submitted the required forms. I was confident I'd get to be whatever I wanted, just like Mom had always said.

But there are no sure things in the Army. I was about to learn the hard way that I could control my destiny only to a point.

In November 1998, I showed up for my flight physical at the Fort Campbell Aviation Clinic. Since pilots must have perfect vision, the doctors pay special attention to eyesight and hearing. After the exam, the doctor called me into his office and delivered some bad news. He explained that when I looked through binoculars, my eyes took a split second too long to focus on objects at a distance. It wasn't correctable, even with my contacts in. I was automatically disqualified from aviation.

This news blew a hole in my self-assurance. I floundered. Mike commiserated, but when it came to coming up with an alternative branch, the decision was mine. I talked it over with some of my friends who were prior service infantry. They advised me to consider logistics, specifically transportation. Getting supplies to the front lines had been crucial in Vietnam, and I figured leading convoys to bring desperately needed supplies was a mission I could do well that would still have some flair.

It was a time of transition for both of us. In the same month as I got my bad vision news, Mike got his exit papers from the Army. He signed up for ROTC and basic freshman classes at Austin Peay for the upcoming semester.

Without Mike's Army salary, we were transformed into starving students overnight. My ROTC scholarship included a housing stipend, so Mike and I packed up our borrowed bed, our stained sofas, and the rest of our meager belongings and moved to the campus married couples housing. It was a first-floor cinder block apartment with a tiny wall heater that was always on the blink. But the place was rent-free, so we couldn't complain.

We were students together for only one semester, and it was almost like being a normal married couple. We were poor, but we were happy. We saw each other regularly, studied together, and ate meals together, even if they did consist mostly of ramen and toast. I left town only to travel to shooting competitions for the college rifle team, which had recruited me during the fall semester. I'd never heard of precision air rifle in Missouri, but it's a popular college sport in the South. Ours was a new program, and we were competing against established teams, some with former Olympians. At home, I studied hard and graded papers for a history professor to help pay the bills, while Mike got a job at JCPenney assembling bicycles at night.

In early 1999, an unlikely source of income came along, courtesy of Mother Nature.

January 22 was supposed to be just another busy day. We had gone to bed early the night before because I had a P.T. test in the morning: sit-ups, push-ups, and a two-mile run. In the middle of the night, a howling wind woke me up, but I quickly fell back to sleep. The next thing I knew, the sun was hitting my face. I grabbed the alarm clock—it hadn't gone off and I'd missed my test. "Shit!" I yelled and threw my clothes on. "Mike, wake up, you're going to be late to class. I'll drive you." As I rushed around the apartment, I noticed that we had no power whatsoever. This struck me as strange, and I made a mental note to call the campus housing office. As I pulled into our street, I spotted a steel girder beam wrapped around a telephone pole like a giant bow. This didn't seem right, either.

I turned onto the main street of campus and found myself facing a gauntlet of tree branches and debris. Swerving madly, I saw that the wall of the football stadium had collapsed in the street. Oblivious, Mike had his head down, gathering books and papers for class. I braked to a stop and said, "I don't think you're going to class today." The building that housed his classroom was missing its roof.

We had slept through the most powerful tornado ever to hit the region. Miraculously, no one had been killed or injured, but the twister had left the campus and the downtown in ruins. Nothing was left of a century-old church except the front wall. The historic courthouse, Clarksville's pride and joy, was a pile of rubble. The building on the other side of the Black Horse Pub was gone completely. Bricks littered the street like confetti. The scene resembled the photos of ruined French villages I'd seen in Dr. Muir's classes. "This looks like a war zone," I said, astonished at the devastation.

Clearly this was going to be big news. We drove to a friend's house to call our families and assure them we were okay. But when we tried to return to our apartment, the police told us the area was blocked off. We couldn't afford a hotel room, so we went to stay with friends in Nashville for two days, watching the coverage on CNN until we were allowed to return home.

For weeks Clarksville was a massive cleanup and construction site. My ROTC battalion pitched in to help with the cleanup, sorting through rubble, separating bricks from tree branches and trash. A local construction company was paying a hundred dollars for a pallet of usable bricks, so in our spare time Mike and I sorted through a mountain of bricks near our apartment, salvaging the intact ones. We'd come home covered in red dust, looking as if we'd been attending a Halloween party dressed as the planet Mars. We used a few of the bricks to prop up the hand-me-down recliner, which had lost a leg. "Our chair is up on blocks!" Mike said, laughing.

Between our various jobs we made enough to pay the bills and buy groceries. We also kept a jar into which we tossed our spare change, and when it was full Mike would cash it in for a can of Foster's Lager the size of an oil drum. Then he'd sit back in our propped-up recliner, take a deep breath, and pop the can open, relishing the soft hiss of releasing air before taking his first long drink.

Besides me, the woman who had the biggest influence on Mike's evolution from soldier to officer was our ROTC battalion commander, Lt. Col. Robin Mealer. She was in her forties, short, with cropped brown hair and a powerful presence; when Lt. Col. Mealer was in the room, there was never any mistaking who was in charge. She was fair, honest, and no-nonsense, always willing to tell you how it was. Not everyone liked her, but everyone respected her. She was also an aviator (as was her husband, a retired Special Operations warrant officer); she flew Chinooks, the Army's largest helicopter. Lt. Col. Mealer became my role model because she didn't think of herself as a "woman in the military," and neither did I. We considered ourselves soldiers in the Army.

She took Mike under her wing and offered to help with his application paperwork, or "packet," should he decide to apply to flight school.

When it came to becoming an officer, Mike had two options: commissioned or noncommissioned. The latter, also known as warrant officers, float between the enlisted ranks and commissioned officers. Like Mike, many warrant officers are former enlisted soldiers. Highly respected, they perform all kinds of jobs in the Army, from maintenance to aviation to supply, and are generally considered experts in their chosen field. Enlisted soldiers affectionately refer to them as Chief.

The freshman ROTC course quickly convinced Mike that being a commissioned officer wasn't for him: too much paperwork, too many meetings, too little contact with soldiers. With Lt. Col. Mealer's help, Mike completed his packet for the two-month Warrant Officer School at the U.S. Army Aviation Center in Fort Rucker, Alabama. If Mike got accepted, he'd have to move to Alabama for at least a year. I was contractually obligated to the ROTC department at Austin Peay, so I'd stay in Clarksville, six hours away.

"If I get accepted, I'm not sure how I'll do with my study habits," he told me, laughing. But he was being modest. The high school kid who'd been too insecure to attend a four-year college got As and Bs in all of his classes and finished the school year with a GPA of 3.8.

In the summer of 1999, I had to attend a five-week Advanced Camp in Fort Lewis, Washington. Since I would be gone so long, Mike moved back to Macon to live with Grampy and await word on his application to Warrant Officer School.

Advanced Camp is a crucial milestone in a cadet's quest to become a commissioned officer. Those who do well are recommended for active duty officer status after college; those who don't are taken aside and urged to reconsider their career paths, though this doesn't happen as often as it should. I felt confident I'd make the grade, but what was supposed to be simply a tough five weeks became my first encounter with the fact that not everyone took kindly to being ordered around by a woman.

When I arrived in Seattle, I boarded a bus with two dozen other ROTC cadets who'd flown in from all around the continental United States, Hawaii, and Guam. Thousands of cadets cycled through the Advanced Camp each summer; there were about two hundred people in my group. We were broken down into eight platoons of fifty people each, and then broken down again into squads of ten. Over the next five weeks I did everything with my platoon: eat, sleep, learn, and test. There were about eight women, including me, but that number was soon reduced when, at the requisite physical, one of the female cadets turned up pregnant and was quickly sent home.

For my part, having to take estrogen every day to stave off premature menopause threw me into a medical no-man's-land. "There was a time when we wouldn't have let you stay in the Army," the doctor told me. As it was, he had to vouch for me before a board of officers so I could remain at the camp and remain in the Army.

Fort Lewis dates back to World War I, and our antique two-story barracks looked like a set from the film *From Here to Eternity*. The boys bunked on the top floor, the girls on the bottom. The variety of women the Army attracts has never ceased to amaze me, and our little group was a microcosm of female types: There were girly-girls, a tough girl, a nerdy girl—and me, who embodied characteristics of all three types. Yet I quickly realized I had little in common with them. At twenty-three I was older and married to boot, a fact the other girls found endlessly astonishing. "But you're so young!" they exclaimed (though by Macon standards, getting married at twenty-one was average, if not a tad old). The girly-girls bonded immediately; averse to cliques, I wasn't interested in becoming "best friends" overnight. I was focused on becoming an officer and didn't need or have time for anyone or anything else. I probably came across as standoffish, but a few years of being married to the Army had taught me how quickly people come and go in the military.

Every day a different cadet would be selected to run the platoon for twenty-four hours. Each squad had a leader for twenty-four hours as well, and a panel of experienced officers scored us on various leadership criteria. Everyone knew they would get their chance to shine or fail. I was a platoon leader twice, at the beginning and the end of camp. As such, I was in charge of my fellow cadets' every waking moment, from morning formations to maneuvers to cleaning the barracks. I'd led platoons at Austin Peay, so I knew I was up to it. This time, however, I was leading fifty peers whom I barely knew. We were forced to rely on one another quickly, to pull mutual trust out of thin air even as our egos clashed.

I was determined to prove that I could pull my weight. Every cadet got to take a turn carrying a twenty-three-pound M-60 on a mission, but the instructors offered to cut the girls some slack. "It's pretty heavy," they said. "It's okay if just the guys do it."

Of course, I was adamant about carrying it. The instructor slung it around my neck and I set off on a march. I carried it for the required one mission, and they were right: It was frickin' *heavy*. I'm so stupid, I thought. No one would have thought less of me if I hadn't carried it, but I was always doing things like that.

"Hanging in there, soldier?" one of the instructors remarked as he trotted past. I threw him a look and kept on trudging.

We spent the last ten days of camp in the field, sleeping outside without tents, wearing full camouflage the entire time. I'd never seen anything like the woods of Fort Lewis. We were at camp almost ten days before the fog lifted its skirts to reveal Mount Rainier. When it wasn't raining, the steamy air was thick with mosquitoes, and the woods were riddled with anthills so high they came to my waist. Trillions of ants had forged a vast trail network through the pine needles; when I looked down, the forest floor resembled a big-city freeway at rush hour. The rain was relentless to the point where my boots and BDUs seemed about to sprout moss. Our only creature comforts were the Porta-Johns parked around the forest. After a few days of this, all I craved was dry clothes and a warm bed. I had to force myself to stay motivated with every squishy step.

My strongest leadership trait was my ability to get along with people so that they would want to do what I said. But in the case of one male cadet, my personality wasn't the issue, my gender was. I don't remember his name, what he looked like, or where he was from. But I'll never forget what he said.

I was the platoon leader that day, and he was a squad leader. I had called a quick meeting to map out our day. The guy didn't agree with one of my decisions—I can't recall what it was—but it was my call to make, and after a few minutes of heated debate I went with my gut.

He started to walk away, then turned and spoke to me with fury in his voice. "We don't need your kind around here," he practically spat. "I don't know why you think you need to be in the Army."

I was pretty sure he wasn't referring to the fact that I was from Missouri.

My face burning, I threw his buddy a look that said, "What's he doing?" The friend took him aside to talk him down while I grappled with my response. This was a direct challenge to my command and my gender. I had to get this guy to realize that I didn't give a rat's ass whether he liked me, women, rainbows, or baseball; he was going to do what I told him to do. "That was incredibly immature," I finally said in measured tones. "And frankly, I don't care what you think. I'm in charge, so just do it."

That cadet and I never did get along. I'm not sure his ideas about women were ever going to change, but at the end of the day he was standing in formation and following my orders just like everyone else.

After Advanced Camp, I headed home to Macon to join Mike, who was working for a local electrician. I visited Mom, something I didn't get to do often enough—though she couldn't recall one visit to the next—and spent quality time catching up with Dad, who was planning to move back to the farm. Mike and I bunked down in the second-floor bedroom at Grampy's; and when Mike wasn't working, we fished, drank beer, and did a whole lot of nothing. Our big project was painting Terry's barn across the street. Grampy would amble out and smoke his pipe and hold forth on his favorite topics. Meanwhile, Mike would be thinking up ways to accidentally dump paint on me.

In late July, after much nail biting, Mike got his letter of acceptance to both Warrant Officer School and flight school. He had to report at the end of August, almost exactly six years to the day after he had joined up the first time. That summer was the longest stretch Mike would ever spend in Macon again.

Sometimes you can stand in a field and watch the past recede behind you, like the view out of a car's rear window. That's the way that summer felt. While Macon's familiarity was comforting, we were getting older and getting on with our lives, moving ahead to the point where the touchstones of our youth were irretrievable. Right before we left town, Cracker developed a twisted bowel and Peg had him put down. Working for the Kemps, Mike had seen his share of life and death in the animal world, but that horse was a friend, and Mike cried for him unashamedly, the same way he'd cried after losing that football game years earlier. By the time we got to Peg's, it was too late: A guy with a backhoe had already dug a hole and lowered Cracker into the ground.

—————

That fall, I began my last year of college and Mike went off to Warrant Officer School. It was like basic training times twenty. The candidates were given four minutes to get up, get dressed, brush their teeth, and get downstairs into formation. They had to roll their socks on a special board and scrub the drains in the barracks showers until they gleamed like mirrors. If a superior passed them in the hallway, they had to glue their heels and elbows against the wall and stand at attention. There were endless papers to write on military protocol, history, and weapons. Mike was allowed limited contact with the outside, so I spoke with him three times on the phone. He was able to sneak out an e-mail from an instructor's office computer. It was three sentences: what he was up to, a joke, and "I love you!" I can see him now, hunting for the keys while keeping an eye on the door.

Between classes and the rifle team—I'd been named captain and had received a small scholarship—I stayed busy enough to hurry time along. Just as I knew he would, Mike made the cut and graduated on November 16, 1999. He would start flight school a few weeks later, so he needed to be settled in by the time classes started. I drove down to Fort Rucker, Alabama, to help find him an apartment.

Mike's only criterion was that he live close to the gates so he could sleep as long as possible in the mornings and still arrive at work on time. We drove to the nearby town of Daleville, which calls itself the Gateway to Fort Rucker, and stopped at the first apartment complex we came to. The buildings were an ugly dull brown with cracked, flaking paint and an abandoned feel that made a morgue seem lively. The manager showed us a modest one-bedroom with shabby carpet and a dingy kitchen. The rent was a mere few hundred dollars a month, and Mike, not one to waste time, declared he would take it. But when we went to fill out the paperwork, we discovered why the apartment was so cheap: They were state-subsidized apartments for lower-income families. As we walked away, the manager called us back and offered Mike the place. "I can't turn away a good renter when most of these places stay empty year-round," she said.

We had barely enough furniture for one apartment, let alone two. Mike took our only nice chair, a La-Z-Boy that Dad bought us after he'd almost broken his neck in the recliner on blocks. We bought an air mattress, a used washer and dryer from a military couple heading to Germany, and a desk from Wal-Mart. We had one car at the time, a used Saturn coupe, and Mike needed a vehicle to drive back and forth to the post. After balking at dropping thirty grand on a new truck, he bought a red 1970 Chevy long-bed, step-side pickup truck for four thousand dollars. It was in excellent condition but a gas-guzzler, and Mike would dream of fixing it up someday. He was generally allowed to leave Fort Rucker only on holidays, so I was the one who spent weekends driving back and forth.

Mike's apartment complex was home to an odd, threadbare assortment of people. Across the hall lived a nice young man whose hobby was flying radio-controlled helicopters and airplanes. Next door lived a retired Army veteran named Floyd. He liked to sit in the yard—and I use that term loosely—and talk Mike's ear off while Mike barbecued his dinner. Across the parking lot lived Keith, a tall, slender guy in his thirties who was deaf. He was very friendly and eager to make Mike's acquaintance, as if he could sense my husband's soft spot for children and the disadvantaged. "I'm going to be his friend and help him however I can," Mike told me on the phone. They'd go to dinner once in a while, and sometimes during my visits we'd take Keith to the movies with us.

Keith's reliance on Mike soon became a problem. Keith's window faced Mike's, and he'd sit and wait for Mike to get home from class at night. Mike wouldn't have hurt Keith's feelings for the world, and he'd draw the blinds and throw a blanket over the windows so Keith would think he had gone to bed, when in fact he was reading by the light of a small desk lamp.

Mike's best friend in flight school was a fellow student named C. D. Foster. C.D. had served in the Army's elite Ranger Battalion before coming to Fort Rucker. He hailed from California and had the blond hair and laid-back attitude of a surfer. He was also a master storyteller. He kept his audience in stitches, and like Mike loved to tease those he loved best. C.D.'s wife, Stacie, had moved to Alabama with their two young sons while he attended flight school, and they decided that Mike was worth adopting. Mike spent a lot of time at the Fosters' house; he became their friend, confidant, baby-sitter, entertainer, and oftentimes cook. Mike and C.D. liked to drive to the Harley-Davidson showroom in Dothan and drool over the rows of shiny motorcycles, then stop at Hooters on the way home. One time, when they were visiting some of C.D.'s Army buddies at Fort Benning, they went to a bar with live music. C.D. asked the band's lead singer if they knew Travis Tritt's "Here's a Quarter (Call Someone Who Cares)," and if so, would they let his buddy sing it with them. They said sure. It was the first time Mike performed with a live band.

C.D. went on to fly medevac Black Hawks in Iraq, and while he and Mike never served together, they always stayed in touch. Their friendship lasted a lifetime.

Mike studied hard, but he had no aspirations to finish first in his class. Doing so would have meant giving up his evenings at his favorite local bar, The Landing Zone Lounge, where he liked to drink a few beers and sing a little karaoke. He made the grade in the classroom, but he excelled in the air. I'd talk to him on the phone and he'd still be riding high on adrenaline, chattering away about what a rush it was to fly.

During one of my weekend visits, I spotted a large Gatorade bottle on top of his refrigerator that was filled with pine needles. I took it down and asked him, "What's this?"

"I was out flying the other night," Mike answered. "My instructor had me hover among some trees. He told me to put my hand out the window, and I felt the branches of a fir tree. I grabbed a bunch of pine needles, and he said, 'That's a trophy.' " As Mike talked, his eyes lit up as if he were reliving that moment all over again. Mike was in love with flying, and there was no turning back.

———

In January 2000, Lt. Col. Mealer selected me to be battalion commander at Austin Peay, the highest rank an ROTC cadet could attain. Dad was the first person I called with the news. "Well, I'll be," he replied.

The title came with its own office and a lot of responsibilities. Under her supervision, I ran the ROTC battalion; there were decisions to be made, events to organize, and projects to delegate. The armory became a second home. I wanted to learn everything I could before being thrown to the wolves in active duty.

On May 12, 2000, I graduated from Austin Peay. I wore my uniform under my robes, and immediately after commencement I was sworn into the U.S. Army as a second lieutenant. Mike got special permission to miss a day of training and come up for the weekend. Almost everyone in our families was there except for my mother and Grampy, who had taken sick the day before, though it wasn't serious. Two members of our family were now in the Missouri National Guard: Anna's husband, Mike, was a captain, and Lindsey was, like me, a second lieutenant. Both were there in their uniforms. Mike's uniform bore his new warrant officer rank that I'd pinned on him six months before. This time it was his turn to pin rank on me; he and Dad did it together.

A few days later, I was on post running an errand when an enlisted officer walked by. He raised his arm in a salute and kept going, but I almost stopped in my tracks. It was the first unsolicited salute I'd ever received. Finally I felt like a real soldier, not a pretend one.

––––––

When I went on active duty, one of the first things Mike and I did was sign up for the Married Army Couples Program. By doing so, we knew the Army would make an effort to give us a "joint assignment" where we would be posted together or at least near each other, which in Army language means no more than fifty miles apart. Because I was the senior officer in the marriage, Mike was supposed to follow me wherever I went. That was the idea, anyway. I requested to be assigned to a forward unit in the 101st Airborne Division at Fort Campbell and got it.

My first assignment was as an ROTC instructor at Fort Knox, working at the same camp that I'd attended there a few years earlier. It was a short assignment and none too hard. But Mike and I saw little of each other that summer and even less of each other that fall, when I headed to a four-month Officer Basic Course (OBC) in Fort Eustis, Virginia, the U.S. Army Transportation Center. There I learned the fundamentals of my job as a transportation officer, from the types of trucks and boats the Army had in its inventory to how to plan and conduct missions for a platoon of soldiers. I was scheduled to graduate from OBC in December 2000, the same month Mike would graduate from flight school. He'd then head immediately to a four-month advanced training in his helicopter of choice, the OH-58D Kiowa Warrior. The smallest, most maneuverable bird in the regular Army's helicopter fleet, the two-seater Kiowa is equipped for aerial reconnaissance. Its pilots scout out enemy movements and communicate them to ground forces as well as fire on enemy positions.

After finishing advanced flight school, Mike would then join me at Fort Campbell. As far as I was concerned, that day couldn't come soon enough. For the last six months of 2000, Mike and I saw each other about once a month. We were living such separate lives that we scarcely felt married. We had separate bank accounts and separate bills. I loved that we shared our faith, and I missed having someone to sit with in church. I'm a fairly outgoing person, but Mike was the one who'd start up the conversations or linger to talk after services. Without him, I'd chat a few minutes and leave. In the evenings, I socialized with other cadets once in a while, but mostly I stayed home and studied, watched TV, read, or talked to my family on the phone, especially Lindsey. She was dating Curt, the crop insurance salesman who crashed my wedding, and it was looking pretty serious. He was a good guy, and I was happy for her.

When Mike and I did manage to squeeze in a weekend together, we fought over even the smallest things: where to eat, what movie to see. We had fallen out of the habit of being together. Our visits, though short, were extremely stressful. There was the pressure to get along because we didn't know when we'd see each other again; the pressure of squeezing a month's worth of good times into a weekend when what we needed to do was resolve countless problems and issues. There was simply too much catching up to do and too little time to do it. We were fighting and clawing to feel needed in each other's lives.

Neither of us could just walk away; I took my marriage vows far too seriously for that, and so did Mike. Divorce was not an option and never would be, but I came to understand how two people could get to that point of no return. Like a neglected house, our marriage was falling into disrepair. I counted the days until we could live under the same roof and sort through the debris of our relationship, salvaging what we could.

A couple of months into OBC I e-mailed the assignments section at Fort Campbell. Within weeks I had my dream job: leading a truck platoon and wearing the Screaming Eagle patch of the 101st Airborne, one of the most storied divisions in military history. I was thrilled, and so was Mike. He knew that this was all I had ever wanted out of the Army.

We weren't happy for long. A few days later, Mike called to tell me he'd received his first duty assignment as a combat helicopter pilot, and it was nothing to celebrate: "Kate, my branch manager told me I'm going to Korea."

I couldn't believe my ears. "You're supposed to come to Fort Campbell with me."

"There's been some kind of screwup," he said. "You'd better call your branch manager and find out what's going on."

When I called to plead my case, the manager offered me a simple solution: I could go to Korea as well. I'd have to get there four months before Mike did, and we wouldn't be stationed together. Not only would it mean another year of separate houses and weekend visits, there was no telling what kind of job I'd end up with.

Mike and I spent hours on the phone trying to come up with alternative scenarios. My first reaction was purely selfish. "I'll set up house in Clarksville and be waiting for you when you get back."

"I don't consider that an option," Mike replied coldly.

I knew he was right, but I had worked so hard for this job. Looking back, two and a half years of separation had skewed my priorities a bit. Being told to choose between my ambitions and my marriage was a test I didn't want to take. I was enraged. We had done everything asked of us: filled out the paperwork in triplicate, followed the regulations to the letter. How could this happen?

I begged. I screamed. I pleaded. But my branch manager remained adamant: my dream job at Fort Campbell by myself, or the unknown in Korea. Take it or leave it.

I took Mike.

CHAPTER 11

MOVIE GOOD-BYES

THE DRAGON HILL LODGE on Yongsan Army Garrison is a way station for American soldiers in the limbo between arriving in Seoul and receiving their first duty orders. Built with U.S. military money, it's a large Western-style hotel with a bar called Whispers Lounge ("for relaxation or romance"), a shopping mall, and five restaurants, including a Mexican place called the Oasis. I stayed at the Dragon Hill for several nights while awaiting my orders and found it, like many soldiers before me, a welcome buffer between home and the assault to my senses that was Seoul. I'd stepped off the plane in January 2001 not knowing what to expect from the country or the Army. What kind of job would I get? Where would I live? Who would my first boss be? I felt as if I was navigating new waters with no compass, no point of reference by which to orient myself, no idea of where I would ultimately land. At the Dragon Hill Lodge, it was comforting to find that I could order something as familiar as nachos, even if they did come with a side order of kimchi.

I spent my first night in a garish pink motel near the airport along with fifty other soldiers who'd been on my flight. The sink and toilet in my room sat low to the ground, the tub was bucket-sized, and the beds were so short my feet hung over the end. It was like bunking down in a dollhouse. The next morning a bus took us to Yongsan Garrison, an hour away in Seoul. Occupying more than six hundred acres of prime real estate in the heart of the city, Yongsan was a base for the occupying Japanese forces for four decades until they surrendered in World War II and the United States moved in. Apart from the high brick wall that surrounds it, Yongsan is a typical military base, with a commissary and an exchange (PX), dry cleaners, and barracks for the lower-ranking soldiers. This being Korea, however, it had some unique characteristics, as I would discover over the coming year. Throngs of protesters, sometimes five thousand at once, would gather every Friday outside the main gate, joined by specially trained policemen who kept the peace by force if necessary. Usually the protesters were college students who wanted the U.S. Army to pack up and go home. The following Friday the older generation—the citizens who remembered America's role in the Korean War—would show up to chant their appreciation for us.

The bus dropped us off at Yongsan's in-processing center, where I lined up to fill out my first round of paperwork. Afterward we were driven to the Dragon Hill Lodge. The place was distinctly lacking in bellboys, so I lugged my own bags down a long hallway to my room, along with my roommate, Jess Umentum, a friend with whom I'd attended Officer Basic and who'd also drawn Korea as her first posting. While Jess dug up some DVDs for us to watch on the hotel TV, I plopped down on the double bed and stared at the ceiling and thought about Mike, replaying the previous weeks and months in my head, though some of the memories were not exactly pleasant.

The weeks before I left for Korea had been our worst patch yet. We'd rarely seen each other, and when we did, we were often at odds. Our lack of a relationship frustrated both of us. While Mike was finishing up flight school, I had to move three times in six months. He graduated on December 6, 2000. A few days prior to the graduation ceremony at Fort Rucker, each flight class hosts a fancy ball in part to thank the spouses for all their hard work and sacrifices. Mike's entire family—Terry, Cheryl, Peg, Kris, Josh, and Grampy—finally got to meet C.D. after hearing about him for a year. Unfortunately, I was a no-show—I was in the field at the Officer Basic Course and could wrangle only one day's leave. The ball was just one more in a long string of missed occasions. But at least I made it to the graduation, where I pinned on Mike's wings. I told him how proud I was of him, and I could see in his face and the way he carried himself that he was proud of himself as well.

We had two weeks of Christmas break in Macon. Afterward, Mike would head back to Fort Rucker for a three-month course for the Kiowa and I'd head to Korea. We stayed one week with Terry and Cheryl and one with Dad at the farm. Now that he was living alone, Dad had torn down both of the old farmhouses and built a new home for himself. Mike and I also spent as much time with

Grampy as we could. But those two weeks didn't go smoothly. To go from spending one weekend a month to every waking minute together was like taking two spirited horses used to roaming freely and penning them up in the same corral. We did our best to reconnect in the short time we had, but every conversation seemed to degenerate into an argument. Another year of separation was looming, and we just wanted to get on with it, to put it behind us and finally be truly married again.

A few days before I left town, I went to visit Mom at the nursing home in Hannibal. Mike came with me as usual. We arrived around dinnertime because that's when Mom is the most alert.

When she saw me she said, "Hi, Kate." While she never could come up with Mike's name, she always seemed to recognize him on some level—a brief flicker of awareness in her eyes, a fleeting smile. We sat in the dining area while she ate, then moved into the sitting room, which had a small chapel off to one side. Some people find talking to Mom uncomfortable, but Mike always settled in for a long visit just as he would with anyone. He'd gently tease her about my sweet tea not being as good as hers or the card game he had just lost to me, and she'd giggle girlishly. Finally, I told her I was going to Korea and that I wouldn't see her for a long time. "I'll miss you," I said, giving her a hug. "I'll write you as often as I can." Mike hugged her, too, and she just nodded and smiled.

On January 5, 2001, Mike and Dad drove me to the airport in St. Louis. When I was waiting to board my flight for Seattle, with connecting service to Seoul, Mike bought me one of those soft, horseshoe-shaped neck cushions and a handheld solitaire game to while away the long hours on the airplane. Solitaire seemed like an all-too-appropriate going-away present. Nightly good-byes over the phone, emotional good-byes in airports, bus stations, and parking lots: Good-bye was beginning to seem like a permanent condition.

Hollywood has an irritating habit of elevating every emotion to a grand passion. Take the homecomings, for instance: The reunited couple fall into each other's arms, kiss passionately, and then continue on with their lives as if no time or distance had passed between them, as if they hadn't changed at all. And movie good-byes, full of tears and heartfelt promises as the orchestra builds to a crescendo—well, they bear little resemblance to the real-world farewells Mike and I had enacted time and again. We'd memorized the scene through sheer repetition: a short kiss, a long hug, a murmured "I love you," and a promise to call and write as soon as we could.

"I'll see you in March," he said, punctuating his farewell with a big bear hug. Until then, I'd be on my own again.

————

On my second morning in Korea I reported to the in-processing center to get my orders. I knew that Mike would be sent to Camp Stanton up near the DMZ, fifty miles north of Seoul, because it was the only post in the country with Kiowas. Since the Army had promised to station me no farther than that from Mike, Seoul was as far south as I could live and still be near him.

A soldier's destination and future are decided in an impersonal military office. You are handed a piece of paper with a lot of verbiage and symbols whose meaning you'll never decipher, nor are you expected to. And spelled out below all that, in big, bold letters, is the post where the soldier will spend the next year, if not more, of his or her life.

When I saw the name of the post, I was stunned. "Camp Walker in Taegu." The Army was sending me four hours south of Seoul.

As this was sinking in—or failing to—a senior NCO told me to get my belongings together. "The southbound bus is leaving in twenty minutes," he said. "If you hurry, you can still catch it and be there by nightfall."

"Look," I said. "My husband will be arriving in March, and he is going to Camp Stanton up north. I was guaranteed that I would only be placed fifty miles away from him. This assignment is going to put me a lot farther away than that."

The NCO pointed to an officer, a captain whom I did not outrank. "You'll have to take it up with him."

When I tried to explain the situation to the captain, he simply said, "Get your stuff and get on the bus."

I stood my ground and, as politely and respectfully as possible, replied that I would not be getting on that bus.

For some reason this captain decided to give a new and obviously desperate second lieutenant a chance to speak her mind. "There has to be another assignment somewhere up north," I said. "Send me somewhere that no one else wants to go. If I get on that bus and go south while we try and work something out, I'll never get back up north."

Not only did he give me a chance to speak, he actually listened: Within minutes I had stamped orders in my hand to stay in Yongsan. I was hugely relieved and incredibly lucky, though I didn't realize how lucky at the time. Yongsan was the primo spot, where everyone wanted to be stationed. It had a more Western, more relaxed environment compared with almost every other post in Korea, and a great launching pad from which to see the countryside.

I was assigned to the 498th Corps Support Battalion and given the position of S-2, or intelligence officer, a job I was not trained to do and, frankly, one of the last jobs in the Army I would have wanted. Intelligence officers often work alone and are rarely assigned jobs as platoon leaders. I would have preferred being outdoors, not stuck on a computer researching the biological threats of the North Korean Army or inspecting weapons storage rooms. But I had asked to stay north, so I had only myself to blame.

Once of the first things I did when I got my new office was to make a calendar for the duration of my stay, one sheet of paper for each month. I wrote the general date Mike would arrive (some time in March) as well as my last day in country (sometime in the spring of 2002). My calendar became a local landmark of sorts. People would stop by and count down the days until their "go home" date. Every day crossed off the calendar was one step closer to home.

A Korean Realtor found me an apartment in a high-rise building next door to an elementary school. I had a roommate, also a soldier in my unit, who was rarely home. I got around by taxi at first, but a few months into my stay I grew tired of shelling out for cab fare and was eager for more freedom. A soldier about to leave the country offered me a beat-up blue Hyundai Presto for $250. The lock on the driver's-side door tended to stick, forcing me to climb in through the passenger door, but for all that the Presto looked like a heap, it ran like an Indy car. It never broke down, never even needed a drop of oil.

I was determined to make the best of my time here. Some South Korean soldiers I worked with asked me to tutor them in English— already fluent, they were eager to learn the latest slang—and in exchange they gave me tours of Seoul, offering insights only natives can give. I got used to the vast subway system and the endless traffic and developed a taste for certain Korean foods, especially *kimbop*: cold rice, vegetables, and ham rolled in seaweed. (I never did take to kimchi, the spicy pickled cabbage.) I explored the streets near my apartment and got to know the local stores and people, though the owners would laugh at my big feet and forbid me from trying on clothes for fear I'd stretch them out.

I recounted our adventures in mass e-mails to friends and family and in letters to my parents. Mom loves to get mail, and Dad would read them to her on his weekly visits.

Eager for company, I adopted a puppy from a unit whose canine mascot had had a litter. I expected it to be a typical Korean mutt: runty, ugly and hairless—nothing to get too attached to, maybe just a companion for my year's stay. But when an adorable black-and-white puffball appeared instead, I knew I was in trouble. I named him Fozzie.

"Don't get too attached to him," Mike had warned me during one of our rare conversations. "We won't be able to take him home with us."

Those first four months in Seoul were rough. I had never lived in such a big city, let alone one with eleven million people. It was noisy, crowded, and so polluted it made me wheeze. The air was thick with coal dust and had a pungent, spicy odor from kimchi pots buried in the earth and left to ferment over the winter. The streets felt exotic yet familiar; McDonald's butted up against ancient temples and gates, and shopping malls had clothing stores that sold hip-hop fashions. Korean girls would tail me around the American Eagle Outfitters look-alike store; if I lingered over a particular blouse or pair of jeans, they would snatch it and buy it as soon as I moved on, as if I had some secret American fashion sense they coveted.

The hardest part about being in Korea was the distance between Mike and me. He was flying odd hours several time zones away, which made coordinating our phone calls difficult, so we rarely spoke. I was alone and lonely in a foreign country I didn't want to be in. To top it off, he forgot my twenty-fifth birthday.

In every marriage there is an outsider who enters your life, who makes you pause and reconsider your commitment. In Korea I met the first person who made me pause. A soldier as well, he was fun, good-looking, and, well, there. My marriage vows won out before I crossed any lines, but this near-miss taught me that even I, who thought myself immune to temptation, could easily find myself standing on the precipice of infidelity, my feet slipping.

Mike arrived in Korea early May, 2001, a month later than expected. My unit gave me the day off so I could pick him up at the reception center on Yongsan. He was sitting in a chair dressed in civilian clothes, and when he saw me, he scooped me up in his arms and squeezed me tight. It felt great to be crushed by him, to see his goofy grin and breathe in his familiar scent of Lever 2000 soap. I had my best friend back and the one person I knew who was truly *mine*. Once back at my apartment, we sent an e-mail to the family letting them know he'd arrived safely, and we signed it "Mike and Kate (together at last)."

The Army let Mike stay the night in my apartment before moving him on to his post up north. We spent the night catching up and slipped easily back into our old comfortable ways with each other. Above all, we felt a great sense of relief that we were going to be so close. That single night reinforced in my mind that I had made the right decision: Coming to Korea was no sacrifice. The sacrifice would have been not seeing Mike.

I introduced him to Fozzie, my new dog, and despite Mike's initial misgivings, they took to each other immediately. "This dog needs a manlier name," he said.

I had an idea. Not only had Mike been a Scout and was now scouting from the sky, but it was the name of the heroine from *To Kill a Mockingbird*, one of my favorite novels. "Scout it is," said Mike. "Now that's a name I can tell the guys."

———

The following weekend I took the bus to Camp Stanton, the first of many trips north. Camp Stanton was a cluster of brown Army buildings and Quonset huts scattered across the hillside, hemmed in by lush green mountains. As a new guy and junior warrant officer ("woj"), Mike was required to spend his first few months in-country flying with the more experienced instructor pilots, who would help him progress to being pilot-in-command, meaning he would be in charge of the aircraft.

Like any fraternity, the Air Cavalry has more than its fair share of rituals. For starters, Air Cav soldiers get to wear Stetson hats and spurs on their combat boots, a throwback to the days when the Cavalry rode horses, not helicopters. They usually wear the Stetsons and spurs for unit functions such as formal balls or hail-and-farewells, though on some posts soldiers can wear them to work on Fridays.

First, a soldier must endure a ceremonial hazing before he's allowed to wear either. There is the time-honored tradition of "breaking in" the Stetson: Everything from food to whiskey is poured into the hat, and the owner must then drink out of it. As soon as he pauses, his buddies pour the entire contents over his head and then place the Stetson on top.

The spurs are much harder to earn. Twice a year the Cav holds a Spur Ride, where newcomers to the unit must pass various tests. Imagine crossing a frat hazing with Ranger School and throwing in some *Animal House* antics for fun, and you'll get a good picture of a Spur Ride. Inductees face an oral exam about the history of their unit and then endure a long night of mock land navigation and combat maneuvers, such as sprinting one hundred yards uphill in their heavy nuclear/biological/chemical suits while being bombarded with smoke and fired upon with blank ammunition.

Mike's head was so big that a regular Stetson sat on his head like a cup and saucer, so he got a big Garth Brooks–style model instead. He broke in his Stetson during his first weekend in Korea at the local post bar, the Babushka.

His new troop, about thirty strong, including a few guys Mike knew from flight school, crowded into the bar. The jukebox was blasting out hard rock and the beer was flowing freely. Everyone toasted the warrant officer whom Mike was replacing, and then the time began to give Mike a big Air Cav welcome. With much fanfare and raucous commentary, they poured fifteen types of beer and alcohol into his Stetson, followed by chewing tobacco, raw eggs, and a slice or two of pepperoni pizza. Mike took a few big gulps of the stuff before being doused in the hat's goopy contents. The guys determined that I, too, needed to break in the Stetson, though they kindly left the food out. Determined to swallow the nasty brew without pausing for breath, I opened my mouth, tilted the hat toward it, and gulped. When it came time to toss the hat on my head, all that was left was a small trickle, and the entire room sent up a cheer. Afterward, one of the guys handed us each a raw egg, which we were required to swallow, shell and all, in one bite—fairly disgusting, but easily done. By the end of the night I was one of the boys.

Mike made friends easily, and with him paving the way, I soon knew everyone on post. Not long after Mike arrived, another Mike showed up, fresh from flight school. His name was Mike Young, but he soon earned the nickname Big Country. He was tall and broad—at least six feet five and as country as you could get. He opened the door for you and called everyone "sir" and "ma'am." Big Country was a Georgia native and proud of it. He had spent the last few years as a Green Beret stomping through the jungles of South America. When he and his wife decided to start a family, Mike couldn't conceive of spending all that time away from a new baby. So he switched to flying in an effort to spend more time at home, only to find himself posted to Korea.

Big Country moved next door to Mike, and it soon became apparent that the two men were born to be friends. Both had old-fashioned values: They loved to drink beer and listen to old-school country stars like Merle Haggard. Big Country was probably the only other guy on post who appreciated Conway Twitty at five hundred decibels.

In early May, a couple of weeks after Mike arrived in country, I moved into a much nicer apartment in a building owned by an elderly couple. They were sweet and kind, and brought me watermelon and traditional delicacies on all the Korean holidays.

For our fourth anniversary, Mike and I hopped a short flight to Chejudo Island, a popular spot for honeymooners off Korea's southern coast. The trip was my idea. We were both wondering how we'd get along after not being alone together for so long. But we had a blast. We stayed in a traditional bed-and-breakfast with a host who spoke three words of English. An inactive volcano rises into the clouds from the center of the island, and bright hydrangeas grow wild against the black volcanic rock. We visited waterfalls, rode in a small submarine, and lay on the beach. Those few days weren't going to make up for all our time apart, but they were a start.

––––––

Every soldier looks forward to R and R. It's a chance to shed your military identity for a while, to reconnect with family or cut loose on a dream vacation. In June, I went home for a much anticipated ten-day leave. Lindsey and Curt had gotten engaged, and I scheduled my leave so I could attend their wedding. But right before I left, Lindsey learned that her National Guard unit was being sent to Kosovo for eight months as part of the peacekeeping force. She and Curt thought it best if they postponed the wedding until after she got back. I flew home anyway. I played cards with Grampy, visited Mom and Dad, pulled the loamy air of the farm into my lungs. But home was no longer the same without Mike, and when it was time to return to Korea, I didn't mind.

In August, Lindsey's unit left for Kosovo. A second lieutenant like me, she was a platoon leader in a military police company charged with rounding up criminals and conducting raids for weapons and illegal goods. "We have run across quite a few mines lately," she wrote Dad. "When we find them, we have to call a team in, and they take them over this hill and blow them up. It's pretty cool. . . . The earth shakes and the windows rattle and you can see the fire and smoke. Hopefully that is as close as we get to anything exploding. Actually, when we were in Macedonia we saw a lot of mortars and heard automatic gun bursts all night long. It was a scary welcome."

It seemed cosmically unfair. While I was nodding off over my keyboard, my big sister, the one-time rebel and party girl, was hunting down bad guys and dodging mortar fire. I couldn't help but be jealous of her platoon time, but I kept telling myself that if I remained patient, I'd eventually get to be part of the action as well.

————

Sometimes, when Mike and I couldn't agree on something, we'd make a deal. For example, Mike had always wanted a Harley-Davidson, but at sixteen thousand dollars, it was way outside our budget. Soldiers who are deployed overseas can buy a Harley at a 15 percent discount, so before leaving for Korea, we made a pact: Mike could get himself a hog if I could travel as much I wanted while we were in Asia. He ordered a Springer Softail in a burnt orange color with lots of chrome, and in early September 2001, I went to Thailand with my boss, Capt. Steve Lewis, and some other friends of mine who wanted to get out of Seoul for a while.

We flew to Bangkok, which I found so exotic as to make Korea seem mundane. I rode an elephant, ate my weight in Thai noodles, and wandered the city tallying up Buddha statues. Like me, Capt. Lewis was a military history buff, so one day we hired a private tour guide to take us to the famous bridge over the Kwae Noi River, immortalized in the film *The Bridge on the River Kwai*. I knew the plotline from watching the movie with Dad: During World War II, occupying Japanese forces used thousands of Allied POWs as well as countless local laborers to build a rail line linking Bangkok with Rangoon. The plot had its basis in reality: The real bridge was in Thailand near the border with Burma, now Myanmar. Thousands of POWs died from disease, malnourishment, and mistreatment during the construction of the bridge, which was bombed during and after the war but eventually rebuilt. Capt. Lewis and I took a train across it and visited the cemetery where the POWs were buried, an oasis of lush green grass lovingly cared for by the locals.

Afterward, our guide drove us to a restaurant for lunch. As we were leaving, I spotted a small, toothless woman sitting by the side of the road. Something about her intrigued me, so I went to see what she had for sale on her small table. What I found took me aback: There were perhaps fifteen cracked, faded pictures of POWs working on the bridge. I could plainly see their faces, eroded by hunger, hard labor, cruelty, and endless hours in the equatorial sun. The photographs disturbed me. It seemed irreverent to sell a photo to a stranger of someone's long-lost loved one, for the equivalent of fifty cents. I wanted to ask the old woman so many questions: Where did these photographs come from? Who might have taken them? Were these men buried here? But she spoke no English and simply pointed to a sign that spelled out the price for the photographs. I bought several photos of the bridge during various phases of construction to send to Dr. Muir, my military history professor at Austin Peay, and went on my way, taking the look in those men's eyes with me. I have never forgotten them.

I returned to Korea with a Harley-Davidson T-shirt for Mike and a fierce sunburn from two days on the beach in Phuket. Mike's Spur Ride was that weekend and I'd been asked to help, so I headed up north the next day by subway, my skin so fried it hurt to sit down or wear clothes. I spent most of that night huddled by a bonfire in a blanket, cursing the sun and my stupidity. The next morning Mike got back to his room, muddy and exhausted but smiling. He had passed. He received his spurs at a secret ceremony that evening while I slept.

When I got back to Seoul, I was informed I'd have to travel up to Camp Casey, near Camp Stanton, for a one-week terrorism seminar. This came as good news because it meant I could stay with Mike while attending the class. On September 11, 2001, I arrived at Mike's room with an armload of groceries and little on my mind except our trip to Australia in November, which we needed to iron out. Then I turned on the television and saw the World Trade Center under attack. I saw it explode and collapse. What I thought at first was an action movie turned out to be too real, too horrifying for words.

Every individual and collective life contains an event that separates time into before and after. In my life, it was Mom's accident. In the life of America, it was 9/11. It was as if the grief and heartache my family felt on a small scale was amplified a billion times to encompass the entire nation. The alarm that sounded through Camp Stanton that evening was a wake-up call to a new, more dangerous and uncertain century. Mike and I knew it, every soldier standing in that hangar that night knew it. That day reminded us that we were soldiers and that soldiers are trained to fight. What we didn't know then was where and how that war would be fought, and what role we would play in it.

After 9/11, Yongsan Garrison went on a heightened alert, and security became tight at all the posts. I wasn't allowed to ride public transportation in my BDUs, so I started to drive up north to see Mike. We spent the nights in his room glued to CNN. We watched his old unit, the Rakkasans, head to Afghanistan to root out the Taliban and Al Qaeda, and we were impatient to be in the mix. Had we been at Fort Campbell, I might have deployed to Afghanistan, too, instead of sitting on the sidelines. Suddenly, our Cold War mission seemed almost obsolete. In Korea, the enemy wasn't hard to find: He was sitting a few miles over the border knowing full well we were sitting on the other side. We didn't feel trained to hunt down and kill an enemy that excelled at staying out of sight.

American soldiers were prohibited from traveling for two months. But by the beginning of November the restrictions were lifted, and Mike and I headed to Australia. Those ten days brought us closer. We hiked in the Blue Mountains, rode horses, and became all too familiar with Australia's indigenous fly population. The best times were holing up in a pub in Sydney to watch the World Series on television. That year baseball seemed more purely American than ever: the New York Yankees playing the Arizona Diamondbacks in the long shadow of 9/11. In a burst of self-sacrifice, Mike insisted that we see a show at the Sydney Opera House, and I chose a light opera called *Best of British*. At the end of the show the cast asked the Americans in the audience to stand up. About ten of us rose to our feet, and as soon as we stood, the band struck up "The Star-Spangled Banner" and the audience gave us a standing ovation. That's when we saw firsthand that the world was behind us.

That trip also proved that Mike and I were behind each other. We would always have disagreements—we were both too independent and stubborn not to—but we felt confident in our ability to work through our issues.

For the first time, we began to seriously discuss parenthood. The military encourages its forces posted overseas to perform charitable work, and Mike's unit sponsored a local orphanage. The soldiers took the children to local theme parks and hosted them for holiday meals on post. Each soldier was assigned an orphan to ensure the child got plenty of one-on-one time, and since I was there so much, I had an orphan, too, an adorable little girl. Mike loved doing things with the kids, and they awoke his paternal instincts. We began to discuss our options, including artificial insemination and surrogacy, but finally we settled on adoption.

We agreed that after becoming parents, one of us would leave the Army. Many dual military couples raise children successfully, but we didn't want to find both of us deployed and forced to send our child to live with his or her grandparents in our absence. Mike loved the Kiowa, loved playing hide-and-seek in the trees. As much as I loved the Army, I hadn't found my niche. Ironically, my long-held soldier's dreams hadn't panned out as I had planned, while Mike, who was recruited off the side of a country road purely by chance, found his job the most rewarding. When the time came, I would become a civilian as well as a mother, God willing.

CHAPTER 12

COUNTDOWN

THERE WAS A LOT to fear after 9/11, and one of my concerns was that our tours in Korea would be extended. Fortunately, the Army actually came through and ordered both of us to Fort Campbell, thanks to a sympathetic civilian in the branch manager's office. In March 2002, I left Korea for home, taking Scout with me in a dog carrier. Mike would follow three weeks later, where he'd settle in with his new unit, the B (Banshee) Troop, 2nd Squadron, 17th Cavalry Regiment, 101st Airborne Division. I found a house to rent in the country outside Clarksville. We'd saved some money—one of the upsides of being stationed abroad—so I bought a new couch and chair for our living room and threw in a thirty-two-inch television and surround sound as a surprise for Mike.

Coming home after an extended tour overseas is an adjustment on several levels. There is family to catch up with, a new home to establish, new jobs to get used to, and in my case, a husband to learn to live with again.

On the home front, some significant changes had taken place. Mike's father, Terry, had had a heart attack while we were gone; he survived thanks to emergency surgery and two well-placed stents. By the time the Red Cross notified us in Korea, he was out of the woods. Mike didn't rush home, though he spoke to him enough to know he was going to be fine. Terry was instructed to quit smoking, which he did, and he dropped some weight, too. Anna, who had three daughters by now, was struggling to keep her marriage together. Wendy and Chris now had two children, and Mike and I were their godparents. Joe had left Missouri and fallen out of touch; we thought he might be in Chicago, but he wasn't good at writing or calling, and his absence worried Dad. After Lindsey came back from Kosovo, she and Curt broke off their engagement. Lindsey said they'd both changed too much to get married.

Mike and I had a lot of reacquainting to do. While we'd both matured a lot, we'd also grown accustomed to the total freedom that comes with living alone, and that selfishness was a hard habit to break. True, our shared values and all the reasons we had fallen for each other in the first place remained intact. We slipped easily back into the familiar routine of going to bed at the same time, and my hand still fit just right under his stomach. He could still make me laugh like nobody else. But there'd been changes since we'd last lived together, three years earlier. I was working full-time now, which meant we had to divide household chores. Both Mike and I could be stubborn and inflexible, too apt to pick a path and stick with it. If something had to be done, I'd grow impatient and say, "Oh, I'll do it myself." These weren't necessarily bad qualities, but when you're working as a team you have to learn to bend. But I had grown used to being a team of one.

One night, after a long day spent butting heads over trivial matters, Mike and sat down for a heart-to-heart. He glanced at me and took a deep breath as if he were Daniel about to enter the lion's den.

"Kate, I love your independence," he said. "I love that I don't have to worry about you or the bills getting paid or anything if I go to the field. You take care of everything and I wouldn't change that about you. But sometimes that independence makes me feel like you don't need me around. And although I know that you don't feel that way, you make me feel like you do. You need to think about the fact that I need to be needed a little bit."

That statement was a defining moment. He was right. I thought hard about myself for the next few weeks and tried to change my ways. I took off my Superwoman cape and stopped trying to do everything all the time. I found myself being more patient, more cognizant of the fact that I was part of a couple. At the end of the day, it was a huge relief to accept that Mike was willing and able to share the load.

In Korea, I had asked to be assigned to the 101st's 426th Forward Support Battalion (FSB), and I got my wish. The 426th is part of the Division Support Command, the 101st's logistical arm. Logistics covers everything it takes to keep the Army's soldiers and machines running, particularly "beans and bullets"—food and ammunition. In a war, the 426th would provide medical, maintenance, and supply support to a Brigade Combat Team (BCT). We would follow the combat troops, staying far forward of the 101st's other support assets.

A lot of officers don't want to go to a forward unit because you go out to the field a lot, backing up the infantry. But I begged and pleaded to be forward. I wanted to get as close as I could to the action. I wasn't thinking about a war at that point, I just wanted to work directly with the infantry. I got my wish: I became the support operations transportation officer (SPOTO), managing the transportation for the entire brigade. Whenever we made a big move, I assisted with planning and advice. I was the go-to person for answers on everything from how to store hazmat to chaining a Humvee down on a rail car.

My boss was Maj. Kirk Whitson, the support operations officer. A fellow Missourian, he was in his late thirties, with a wife and three children whom he doted on. He loved taking care of soldiers, but he had created a good balance between love of his job and love of his family. His wife, Trina, was dedicated to helping him succeed, and in a military marriage, that spousal support makes all the difference. Knowledgeable and intelligent, Maj. Whitson was also very easygoing and affable, and we became good friends.

Mike and I kept busy. It's standard procedure for all newly assigned pilots to fly with an instructor pilot (IP) to see what additional training they need in order to become a mission-ready pilot. Mike's IP was a grade-3 chief warrant officer named Tim Merrell. Mike, a grade-2 warrant officer, had about four hundred hours of flight time, about standard for a peacetime aviator of his grade, but he needed to learn a lot of new protocols for flying in the United States, especially airspace procedures and mission orientations. That's where Tim came in. At first, Mike would come home cursing Tim because he was so hard on him. Eventually, Mike figured out that Tim was pushing him to be better, and soon he came home praising him to the heavens.

Mike spent a lot of time hitting the books, memorizing rules and procedures. "He hated getting something wrong," Tim recalls. "Mike would get real mad at himself if he did. He'd study again and know exactly what he had to do the next day."

When Mike talked about work, I noticed he was telling more and more "Scott" stories. We both knew Scott White from Korea but hadn't gotten to know him really well. One day, Mike came home from work and said, "We're going to dinner with Scott and his wife, Sonja." I hoped that we'd all get along, since it would be nice to have a couple to double-date with.

Our friendship with the Whites began over casual dinners at a Mexican restaurant in Clarksville, getting to know one another over chips, salsa, and cervezas. Over the next few months we spent more and more time together. Scott could be the poster child for Army helicopter pilots: tall, movie-star handsome, masculine without being overly macho. His nickname is Scotty Too Hottie, though the nice thing is, he doesn't really know how good-looking he is. But for those who know him, his best characteristic is his big heart—he'd do anything for you without being asked. Sonja is a petite powerhouse blond whose passion is physical fitness—you could bounce a quarter off her abs. She and Scott met in college back in Michigan, though Scott left school to join the Army. Sonja, who came from a more privileged background, has worked hard at being a military wife. When Scott was attending flight school at Fort Rucker, Sonja kept herself occupied by learning to build furniture at the post woodworking shop. They left Alabama with a new bed, a TV unit, and two benches for their dining room table. Sonja can be choosy about whom she opens up to, but once she lets you in, she shows herself to be funny and warm.

While the boys went off riding their Harleys, Sonja and I went shopping and took our dogs, Spencer and Scout, for long walks. We both had a hard time fitting into the military wife clique. As an officer, I had more in common with their husbands; at troop functions I could be found talking policy with the men, not 3:00 A.M. feedings with the women. Sonja's independence was such that she shied away from the support-group mind-set. In addition, she doesn't have children, another way she stood apart from the other wives. Sonja just isn't the play-date type. But as the only civilian among us, Sonja sometimes felt left out, especially after Mike, Scott, and I were in Iraq, leaving her behind at home to worry.

That summer, with Afghanistan seemingly under control, everyone kept close tabs on the diplomatic gamesmanship over Iraq. No one was talking war explicitly, but things began to happen on post that weren't coincidental. In August, the division conducted a massive exercise called a sea deployment redeployment exercise (SEDRE). It's a dress rehearsal for getting heavy equipment from Fort Campbell to Florida for shipment overseas. The division hadn't done one in years, so this got our attention. My NCO, Sgt. First Class Kenneth Carroll, and I went along as transportation officers to track equipment and study the operation. We loaded tons of heavy equipment—artillery pieces, field ambulances, trucks, Humvees—onto train cars at Fort Campbell bound for the port in Jacksonville. Along with a small group of soldiers, I traveled by van to Jacksonville to supervise and track the unloading of the rail cars. We shrink-wrapped the helicopters for transport, just like valuable pieces of furniture, and craned them, along with tons of other equipment, onto huge cargo ships. We met the ships in Beaumont, Texas. There, everything was off-loaded onto large trucks, which were then driven to the Joint Readiness Training Center in Fort Polk, Louisiana.

By September, Mike was mission ready, and his training became more combat-oriented: how to communicate with infantry, target practice using the Kiowa's machine guns and rocket launchers. He and Tim were paired in the cockpit permanently. Ten years older and a senior officer, Tim was a good balance to Mike's relative inexperience. Tim is quiet and extremely intelligent; he knows exactly how to push someone to find the best within himself. He exudes a sense of effortless leadership, and Mike trusted him completely.

That fall, when and where the 101st would deploy became the sole topic of discussion and speculation on post. We heard it could come before the end of the year, and the news teams from the local TV stations set up camp around Fort Campbell in hopes of discerning some scoop from our comings and goings.

On October 10, Congress passed its resolution approving the use of military force against Iraq. As the momentum toward war accelerated, so did the ramping-up process on post. The division threw all its time and manpower into training for combat operations. Mike and I went from busy to swamped. We practiced packing up and sending out our equipment time and again; we'd no sooner get our trucks and bags back to our unit when we'd start all over again. Sometimes I worked so late I slept on the floor of my office. There were anthrax and malaria shots to get, next-of-kin paperwork to check and double-check, wills to be signed.

After working on all the buildup to deployment, I was transferred to a new job. Capt. Ed Sleeper, a new arrival to Fort Campbell, had been brought into the transportation office. While we got along, we didn't need two people to do that job, so I was moved to the personnel office for the 426th. As an S-1 (the S stands for "staff," the 1 designates a personnel officer), my new job was basically administrative; every piece of paper involving our soldiers' lives went through my office. My civilian equivalent would be the personnel director for a three-hundred-person company. I was also the personal assistant to the battalion commander, Lt. Col. Duane Gamble. All this meant I was behind a desk more, which I didn't enjoy as much, but getting on staff as a lieutenant was something of a coup, since captains tended to get staff jobs. My new boss was Maj. Zeyad Suqi, a Kuwaiti native who'd been raised in the United States. Everyone his rank or higher called him Z; I called him Major.

In a wartime environment, my duties would expand to include night battle captain, monitoring the infantry's combat situation from the Tactical Operations Center. The day battle captain would be Capt. Tony Boniface. He was the S-4, which meant he dealt with all the supplies our battalion needed. We became friends during the long hours in meetings and planning to deploy. Like all the captains, Tony told me I could call him by his first name, though I never did until I became a captain myself.

By December it was purely a waiting game. I figured that not having to worry about contact lenses or glasses would come in handy when I was in the desert and throwing my gas mask on and off, so I scheduled an appointment to have LASIK eye surgery at the post hospital after our Christmas leave.

———

Mike and I spent Christmas leave in Macon, where we followed our usual yuletide routine. On Christmas Eve day, we'd drive with Dad to the nursing home in Hannibal to give Mom her presents, which she always unwrapped with the glee of a small child. We'd go to Christmas Eve service at Mount Zion with Terry and Cheryl, spend Christmas morning unwrapping presents at Dad's and dinner at his sister Teresa's house. We always spent our last night of Christmas leave at Grampy's. Everywhere, Iraq was the topic on everyone's mind and the last thing we wanted to talk about. Mike and I were sick and tired of the conjecture and rumors surrounding our deployment, so we discussed the possibility only with Dad and Terry. When friends asked if we were going, we'd just shrug and say, "It's up the air."

Mike and I had always had trouble keeping surprises from each other at Christmastime. The excitement of seeing the other's face when he or she opened the gift was too much to bear, so we often caved early. So I wasn't surprised when, a few days before Christmas, Mike cornered me in Terry and Cheryl's living room and said, "It's time to exchange gifts."

Then he handed me a mailing envelope. "Nice wrapping," I quipped, but inside was a blue box that could mean only one thing: Tiffany & Co. Inside I found a silver ring shaped like a circular piece of bamboo. I slipped it on my right ring finger and wrapped him in a big hug. "I love it," I said. It seemed like one more sign that we were finally in sync again.

A couple of days later, Natalie, Nancy, Mollie, and I gathered at a local bed-and-breakfast for a slumber party. All of us were married now; Mollie had just had a baby, and the other two were working on it. This was our chance to catch up and be girls again before world events took over.

While Mike took the husbands to a local bar and snow fell outside, the four of us stayed up all night laughing, talking, and draining one bottle of wine after another. Mollie talked about the new world motherhood had opened up for her, and how rewarding it was to watch her husband, Ryan, become such a good father. Natalie brought photos of the house she and her husband, Bradley, were interested in buying. Nancy and her husband, Brian, had recently moved to Iowa and were planning to start a family soon. When they admired my ring, I shared the story of getting the Tiffany box. "It sure beat the Han Solo Christmas ornament he gave me two years ago," I said, and the girls threw back their heads and laughed. They knew Mike's quirks almost as well as I myself did.

The next morning, I drove on snowy roads to Grampy's to meet Mike. We knew this could be our last chance to see his place with snow on the ground for quite some time. Mike's cousins Larry, Glen, and Lisa were there with their kids, hooking sleds on the back of a four-wheeler and driving through the snow-covered fields. Their gales of laughter drifted over the fields. Grampy stood outside in his heavy coat, smoking his pipe and watching the grandkids. I must have looked rough, because he chuckled and asked, "How late were you girls up last night?"

While Mike and Larry went to split and stack wood, I helped Grampy clean out his china cabinet. I liked doing things like this for him—I mucked out his smokehouse one year—because I knew I'd get to hear great stories in the process. I filled the kitchen sink with soapy water and emptied out the cabinet while Grampy gave a running commentary on each item: "That's the jelly spoon my grandma used to use; that's the soup tureen from Germany." Soon the contents were washed and drying on the counters and table. Just when I thought I was done, I spied one last dusty item hiding in a corner. I reached in and took out a plastic reindeer. It was the ornament I'd given Grampy that first Christmas I met him.

"It was tied to a jar of honey with a ribbon," he said. "Do you remember?"

I nodded my head. "You kept it all these years."

"It just has to mean something to somebody to be important," he said, and I dunked it in the water and set it on a towel to dry.

A few days later, Mike and I returned to Grampy's to spend our last night in town with him. That year, as in the past, I cooked him all his favorites: breaded pork tenderloins, green and brown beans, boiled potatoes, biscuits with homemade jam, tapioca pudding for dessert. When we left I hugged Grampy extra hard and promised him I'd come back soon. Mike and I crunched out to our new Chevy Tahoe, bought used the previous fall; he'd already warmed it up, just like old times. As we drove away I turned around and committed my last look at Grampy to memory: a freeze-frame of his overalled figure in the doorway silhouetted against the light, waving us off into the night.

We walked in the door in Clarksville to a ringing phone. It was my boss, Maj. Suqi.

"Kate," he said, "we just got word that without a doubt the division will be deploying. Stay close to your phone for the next few weeks." My stomach belly-flopped. I relayed the conversation to Mike, and we exchanged a look that said, "Here we go." The office the next day was spinning like a carnival ride. Everyone was stressed, nervous, and excited. We were going to war and there was a lot to do: endless supplies to be ordered, trucks to inspect, orders to hand out, soldiers' rooms to pack up, and on and on.

On February 6, 2003, Mike and I had our orders in our hands. We were officially going to Kuwait, where we'd sit and wait for the war to begin or not begin. He would leave on February 28, and I'd follow on March 3.

Each unit left behind a rear detachment commander, usually a junior captain or senior lieutenant who functioned as the stateside liaison with the battalion commander. He or she would also keep the soldiers' families informed and calm. It's an important job and a lot of people want it, but I wasn't one of them—why would I have joined the Army if I didn't want to deploy? In addition, I wanted to be where Mike was, even if we didn't get to see each other. So when I heard that my name was being floated for the job, I went straight to Maj. Suqi.

"I heard I'm on the list to stay behind," I said. "I'll transfer to another unit if I have to, but, sir, do not leave me sitting here."

"Don't worry," he said, laughing. "The battalion commander has already made his decision and your name's not on the list."

He must have seen the relief on my face because he added, "I didn't figure you'd want to stay here, especially with Mike going."

"You're right, but I also just wouldn't feel right about being here with you guys all in the desert. I'd hate that."

"I know exactly what you mean," Maj. Suqi replied, and we both went back to work.

On a Thursday evening three days before Mike left, he showed up at my office. He had two hours to kill before he had to be back at work. I was ready for a break myself. It was five o'clock and we were both starving. "Let's go get something to eat," Mike said.

On our way to the Subway across from one of the gates on post, we passed Charlie's Steakhouse. We'd never eaten there; it was pricey and there was usually a line out the door to get seated. We'd long promised ourselves we'd eat there when we had more money, but we'd never made it.

"Hey, we've got the time," Mike said. "We've always wanted to go there, and there's no line." There must have been a Thursday special, because the restaurant was crowded with senior citizens. With our khaki uniforms and young faces, Mike and I stuck out like Sunday schoolers at a papal coronation. We took a corner booth and each ordered a beer and the biggest steak we could afford.

What began as an impromptu dinner together became a heart-to-heart talk about life. We looked back on the twists and turns that had brought us here to this point and discussed our thoughts on this war. We both had a strong desire to use our military service to help others, and we saw Iraq as an opportunity to do that. We'd read and heard a lot about how Saddam Hussein and his sons had gassed and imprisoned their own people. No one deserved to live in that much fear. We also felt that going to war with Iraq was an extension of the war against terror, that Saddam was eyeball-deep in helping terrorists obtain weapons and plan attacks.

But we mainly discussed not politics but personal matters, particularly what we would do when we got home. Start a family. Finally spend more time with our own family. Maybe buy a house. Start saving for a boat. Basic things that many young Americans would want, whether a war stood in the way or not.

That two-hour dinner was an oasis in the craziness. When Mike asked for the bill, the waitress told us that not only had it been paid but that several other diners had fought for the privilege of doing so. We stood up and smiled at that entire restaurant, knowing we had the best job in the world.

Soon thereafter, Terry, Cheryl, and Dale arrived for one last get-together before we deployed. Grampy didn't want to come because he knew how much saying good-bye would upset him. Terry would take both the Harley and the 1970 pickup back to Macon, where he'd oversee the pickup's restoration. The three of them spent the night. Dale and Mike sat in our office, singing, while Dale played Mike's guitar. Our deployment loomed, the elephant in the room. After dinner, Mike brought up the topic his family had been avoiding. "You're gonna hear and see a lot of things on the news," he said. "But every time you hear anything about a helicopter getting shot down or crashing, I don't want you to get all worried, thinking it's me. You've seen the airfield, you've seen how many helicopters the 101st has. Think of all the other units that are going to be there. The chances of it being me are very slim. And if it is me, the chances of it being on TV before you hear about it are even slimmer."

————

The day before Mike left, I sat on his green duffel bag trying to flatten its contents so we could cram in some extra T-shirts. We were trying to act as if this was just another good-bye, but of course it wasn't. Of all our good-byes, this one was our most uncertain ever. We were heading into dangerous territory, and we didn't know when we'd see or even speak to each other next. We hoped we'd see each other in Kuwait, but there were no guarantees—it could be a year before we set eyes on each other again.

Mike took off his wedding band and set it on the dresser, next to my dog tags. "I'll give that to Dad for safekeeping along with mine," I said. I planned on wearing the silver ring he had given me for Christmas. Wearing diamonds into a country where I would be working hard and sweating would be courting trouble, and I didn't want to risk losing the ring or one of its stones.

Mike picked up my dog tags off the dresser, unhooked the chain, and slid his wedding band onto it. The ring clinked against the dog chains, a tiny musical note.

"I thought maybe you could keep it for me and give it back when we get home," he said.

I smiled, swung the chain around my neck, and said, "I won't take it off."

CHAPTER 13

INCIDENT AT CAMP PENNSYLVANIA

ON MARCH 5, 2003, I stepped off a Continental Airlines plane into a cool Kuwaiti spring. The chilly wind that hit my face was not the hot sticky air I expected, and the drab brown landscape that stretched beyond the tarmac was an ocean of rolling dust with not an oasis in sight, not one picturesque sand dune, not a speck of green. Welcome to the Middle East, land of mirages, where nothing is as it seems or as expected, not even the enemy.

My flight was one of seventy or so chartered commercial jets that ferried the 16,000 troops of the 101st Airborne from Fort Campbell to Kuwait International Airport over a period of thirty days. A fleet of small buses idled on the tarmac, waiting to take me and 230 other soldiers to Camp Wolf, the military reception camp, a sea of brown tents in a sea of brown sand. Once there, we moved our soldiers into their assigned tents—really nothing more than shade from the sun—and stacked their bags at the rear of the camp. We would be moved on to Camp Pennsylvania, our home in Kuwait, but we didn't know when. The diplomats were still working to forestall a war, but that didn't seem likely, and I knew it was a matter of when, not if, we would cross the border into Iraq.

As a personnel officer, my main job at this point was keeping track of the number and location of all our battalion's soldiers. I tracked the manifests, which stated who was going on which bus, and so on. It was like being an elementary school teacher overseeing a field trip, except my charges wore full combat gear and carried M-4 automatic rifles.

Once settled at Camp Wolf, we had little to do but wait. A few days before our deployment, Mike had left a surprise on my pillow: a portable DVD player for the trip. (I had given him a minidisc recorder so he could listen to his beloved country-western music.) I had brought a few of my favorite movies and shows—*Tombstone, Gladiator,* the first four seasons of *M*A*S*H*—but I lent the DVDs to a group of bored soldiers. Camp Wolf was a stepping-off point into the unknown, and we appreciated the downtime, even hoarded it. We didn't know when we would have it again.

The morning after we arrived, a herd of small, ratty buses pulled up, Kuwaiti drivers at the wheels. All 230 of us scurried to find our bags and load them on the buses. Each soldier was allowed to bring only three bags to the Middle East. One, an Army issue duffel bag, was en route on the ocean along with the rest of the division's equipment. That left us to carry a large rucksack on our shoulders and another duffel bag crammed with everything we'd need until our other bag arrived. Among my belongings were a few books, including *Ben-Hur* and *Band of Brothers*; six months' worth of my medication; and several photos from home: Grampy, Dad, our farm, my siblings with their kids, one of Mike and Scout. I wore Mike's ring on my neck, along with my dog tags. As the soldiers slung their rucksacks onto their backs, they looked like wounded turtles, stumbling and weaving under the weight of their barest essentials.

I flashed back to the last days with Dad. He'd helped me pack up the house and put our stuff in storage, and he'd taken Scout home with him. He watched me pack my bags, and when I hoisted my rucksack on my shoulders, I'd staggered under its weight. "That thing's bigger than you are," he'd said with a laugh. "How are you going to carry it?" Dad was proud, but I could tell he was worried, too, though he pretended he wasn't. He spoke a lot about Grandpa Randall's journal and the legacy he had left behind.

"Keep a journal," he said before I left. "You may not think it's important now, but it will mean a lot later, just like Grandpa Randall's does now."

I grabbed my bags as the soldiers were herded toward the buses, counting as they climbed aboard.

Each bus held twenty people, and none had luggage racks. We filled two rows with our green duffel bags and then filled every seat with a person and every person's lap with a rucksack. We were packed in circus-clown style. The windows were down, the air still and warm, and I hoped the buses would take off soon and coax some air into circulating. We sat silently sweating in our Kevlar helmets, flak vests, desert camouflage uniforms and weapons, sixty-pound rucksacks on our laps, for nearly an hour, and we still had a two-hour trip ahead of us.

Just as we'd reached our breaking point, the buses lurched to life and we were off.

Camp Wolf fell behind us and soon we were surrounded by desert. The passing landscape was a tabletop of dust and dirty sand that varied in color from dusty brown to chalky white. And that concludes the description of the country we found ourselves in. There was no vegetation, no water, and as far as I could see, no houses, animals, or paved roads. We were just barreling off into an endless flatness with no choice but to trust the drivers and their sense of direction.

We'd gone only a short distance when, to no one's surprise, one of the buses broke down. We were prepared for this possibility, so all 230 soldiers piled out of the buses and surrounded each bus in a defensive perimeter. While the drivers pondered the bus's mechanical problem, we sent people into a large drainage pipe for a bathroom break. The women went separately, and I squatted in the pipe with three other female soldiers. I'd never liked Porta-Johns, but I'd soon miss them deeply.

The bus problem, whatever it was, was quickly fixed and we were back on the road, which was nothing more than a wide trail of packed sand. Then, as if sensing they'd never again have 230 warriors from the world's last superpower at their mercy, the bus drivers decided to liven up the trip. Channeling Jeff Gordon, they put the pedal to the metal and began weaving in and out; veering off the trail to pass one another and then careening back to cut one another off, laughing and grinning the whole time. We came so close to the other buses that I could have touched them if I hadn't been pinned to my seat by a sixty-pound bag. I admit I was grinning under my Kevlar, enjoying the adrenaline rush and the speed (I had driven those back roads in Macon with Mike, after all), but the majority of the soldiers weren't happy. Add motion sickness to hours on a stifling bus and a growing case of nerves, and they were looking greener by the minute. Just as the bus ride was about to take a serious turn for the worse, we zipped through a large slot in a sand berm and found ourselves staring at our new home.

Camp Pennsylvania was one of several Army encampments built in northern Kuwait, within striking distance of the Iraqi border. About two square miles, it was a tent city surrounded by barbed wire and an earthen berm bulldozed ten feet high. Each corner of the camp had a concrete barrier and a bomb bunker, a crude structure made of concrete blocks that was reinforced with tall stacks of sandbags. Soldiers stood guard on concrete towers that looked like they came straight out of Sing Sing. Passing through the gates felt like entering a federal penitentiary, and we were the inmates.

The 426th Forward Support Battalion included three companies: Alpha (supplies and water), Bravo (maintenance), and Charlie (medical). We were attached to the 1st Brigade's 327th "Bastogne" Infantry brigade, consisting of three battalions with around six hundred soldiers each. Altogether we made up a Brigade Combat Team—in essence, a mini Army. In a war situation, the Brigade Combat Team takes everything it needs be self-sufficient: a Forward Support Battalion, artillery, helicoptors, engineers, and military police. Later we would bulk up even more with National Guard soldiers who helped us produce clean water, set up showers, and did our laundry and mending. The number of troops in our Brigade Combat Team totaled around four thousand, 10 percent of them women.

The battalion had sent an advance party, including most of our staff, ahead to prepare our sector. A reception committee was waiting for us, and our tents were already set up. Our new home was a prefab affair; the tents had rubber floors, and rubber mats connected all the tents outside, like sidewalks in a suburban housing tract. Leaving the mats turned walking into a slog, the deep sand clutching at your feet with every step. Every footfall churned up a little dust storm, so that we resembled camo-clad Pig Pens from the Peanuts cartoons. Each tent accommodated about thirty soldiers, and we entered them to find our cots hadn't arrived yet. We'd be sleeping on the floor, which seemed like an inconvenience until we discovered that the rubber mats helped keep the rats out.

My tent was divided in half; the females slept in the back. The other staff officers were staying in a tent next door, but since I was the only woman, they put me with the enlisted women on staff. This made me the only officer in the entire tent. Soldiers need time and space away from their bosses, so the enlisted folk were less than thrilled to see me walking through every day. And I missed being able to kick back with my peers and discuss work issues in a casual, relaxed setting. I didn't appreciate being segregated, especially since, in all my past experience in the field, I'd never seen such a thing as "girls in one tent and boys in another." Plus, I would never willingly live with ten females—that would be one hell of a reality show.

Our advance party had set up the battalion's Tactical Operations Center (TOC), a large tent outfitted with computers, radios, map tables, and a beat-up military field phone. This is where we held our daily battle update briefing on the division mission, war-gamed our route north, and discussed the role we would play should the war kick off. We assumed it would—we knew enough about the Army to figure it wouldn't send us to stand ankle-deep in sand for nothing. I was so sure I'd be in the Middle East for a long time that I made a 2003 calendar using an Excel spreadsheet, one month per sheet, stapled together in the upper left-hand corner. I kept the calendar on my desk, and as I had done in Korea, I marked off the days until I'd go home, even though I wasn't sure when that would be. That calendar would follow me for the rest of the year.

Across a small sandy field from our battalion TOC, the brigade command set up its own headquarters, which was much bigger and more sophisticated than ours. The brigade would track our movements as well as the entire division's on a much larger scale. I was always happy to run to the brigade TOC to conduct business because they always seemed to have the latest information on the world and on us.

In a war zone, your relationship with your superior officers can make or break the battle. Fortunately, I was on excellent terms with my higher-ups. At the battalion level, I worked closely with the commander, Lt. Col. Gamble; our executive officer and second in command, Maj. Suqi; and Battalion Command Sgt. Maj. Flynn Stokes, a thirty-year veteran whom I outranked on paper but not in experience. The 1st Brigade's commander, Col. Ben Hodges, was a great leader. He spoke with a drawl and raised his voice usually only to get your attention. He had to meet you just once to remember your name. He understood how important his soldiers were; we were his top priority, and we in turn wanted to make him proud. His next in command was the brigade executive officer, Maj. Kenneth Romaine. He was an extremely hard worker, the last one there at night and the first one there in the morning. These would be the men leading us into battle, and I felt I could follow them anywhere.

I had two senior NCOs who worked directly with me. Sgt. First

Class Alan Wilson, a twenty-year veteran from Alabama, kept the personnel shop running day and night. In his early forties, he had a high-pitched voice that was the source of constant amusement among his peers, especially if he got riled up about something. The company commanders sometimes found him argumentative, but Sgt. First Class Wilson was squarely in the soldiers' corner. They knew he would take care of their pay problems or help push through their leave paperwork. He knew his job and wasn't afraid to voice his opinion, so of course Mike had taken an instant liking to him, and vice versa, when they met at Fort Campbell.

I first met my other NCO, Sgt. First Class David McDaris, at Camp Pennsylvania. He would be my night battle NCO in the TOC. In his forties and close to retirement, Sgt. First Class McDaris had spent most of his career in the Army's medical field and had served in the Gulf War as part of a medevac team. He reminded me of my dad in his younger days: tall and skinny, with glasses and a vast inventory of military knowledge. You get to know people fast in a war environment, and we quickly knew we'd get along. We had the same laid-back personalities yet at the same time weren't afraid to take charge. I called him Sgt. Mac; he called me L.T.

Pennsylvania had the requisite quality-of-life services: PX, barbershop, chow hall, and a laundry dropoff that sent the socks back gray. There was a row of trailers with eight showers each for several hundred soldiers, which meant we got to shower about every three days. (We would later look back fondly on that luxury.) Rows of Porta-Johns were set up everywhere; like the toilet paper and everything else, they were brown. If you were a male and didn't feel like battling the lines, the stench, and the flies at the latrines, you could use a "piss tube," a sort of desert urinal found all over camp. Long plastic pipes were stuck in the ground, positioned at just the right height so that male soldiers could walk up, unbutton their pants, and relieve themselves quickly and easily. Men loved the piss tubes. Women stood in line.

No matter where you went, you encountered endless lines. I quickly realized it was a good idea to bring a book to read or to find a friend to talk to while I stood around. The PX line was especially long, with soldiers stocking up on cigarettes and chewing tobacco. One day I waited for six hours to buy a phone card.

The camps shared one large chow hall that served typical cafeteria-style fare: The staples were salads, "beef surprise" (it was best not to ask), and boiled vegetables. Sometimes we had ice cream, which made the entire meal worth eating. Our cooks, all men, were hired from countries such as India and Saudi Arabia. It seemed as if many of them had never seen Americans up close before, especially women with weapons who were treated as equals. When I passed through the chow line with my tray, they'd sneak a peek at me but quickly look away when I smiled or thanked them. Sometimes one of them would offer me extra food, and if I tried to say, "No thanks, it's too much," they would laugh and plop it on my plate anyway.

––––––––

This was the basic forecast for northern Kuwait: days and days of dust and dirt, followed by a bit of blue sky, followed by sandstorms for several more days and a few clear nights if you're lucky. More dust and more dirt.

The country's infamous sandstorms became a fact of life. They'd blow in without warning, powerful winds that churned up the desert until I couldn't see three feet in front of me. The wind ripped at the tent flaps, and dirt, fine as talcum powder, infiltrated the tiniest cracks in the tents, coating everything inside, including our teeth. Reading *Ben-Hur*, I would have to blow dust off the pages to make out the words. Walking through a storm after a shower, I'd arrive at my tent with a dust-caked rat's nest for hair. We wore gas masks in cases strapped to our legs—we believed the enemy had chemical or biological weapons and would not hesitate to use them—but the masks came in handy during sandstorms to help us breathe. They filtered out the dirt, camel dung, and whatever else was floating around the atmosphere.

Even inside the tents, the dust would lie thick in the air. At the TOC we'd hurriedly throw plastic over our radios, computer, and weapons in a futile attempt to keep the sand out. I wore my goggles all the time and, like a lot of soldiers, wrapped a head scarf called a kaffiyeh around my head.

Our equipment had been shipped to Kuwait, and on March 9, it began to arrive at Camp Pennsylvania by truck. We spent our days repairing and packing the trucks in preparation to enter Iraq. The weather was beautiful—blue skies and cool temperatures that held the promise of great heat. The desert had its dangers, but it possessed great beauty as well. For example, there was no transition from night to dawn; the bright light of morning simply appeared as if God had flipped a light switch. The sunrise arrived as streaks of pink across a cerulean sky, awesome above the rows of Porta-Johns. When the sun went down, the sky and sand turned orange, and the color lingered so long I'd wonder if the sun would ever disappear. Then suddenly, the sky was completely, utterly black. The moon, when it appeared, was so bright you cast a shadow. I loved to look at the desert sky at night, the inky blackness of it all. I had thought Dad's farm provided the best stargazing, but the Kuwaiti desert revealed how many stars the sky could hold, smeared across the heavens like frosting on a cake.

Always, the dust storms would return and blot out the landscape. On March 13, I was hunched over a computer in the TOC in my goggles and kaffiyeh, trying not to breathe in a gallon of dust, when I got my first inkling that Lindsey would be joining Mike and me in the Middle East. Dad usually began his e-mails with the weather and how Scout was doing, followed by the latest war news. On March 13, he wrote that Lindsey's National Guard unit was preparing to head out to parts unknown. "The trucks are getting brown camouflage," Dad wrote. "Probably not Kosovo."

———

I assumed Mike was nearby, because the entire 101st was camped in the vicinity, but I hadn't had time to track him down. Then on March 14, a week after we arrived, Maj. Whitson delivered a message.

"I saw Mike at another camp," he said. "He gave me his phone number and location in case you ever get over there." When he handed me a slip of paper, it felt like a Christmas gift, even though this was March in a predominantly Muslim country.

I got on the field phone and placed the call into Mike's troop headquarters. I reached his commander, who sent someone to find him. A few minutes later, I heard my husband's familiar voice. Over the crackling connection, I said, "I'm coming to your camp tomorrow for work. I'll try and find you."

Mike was based out of Camp Udairi, site of our higher headquarters. Soldiers were always coming in there for processing, and one of my jobs was to pick them up. The next day, Sgt. First Class Wilson and I headed there in a Humvee to turn in some paperwork and pick up some new arrivals. As soon as our small convoy passed through the gates of our camp, we found ourselves in the middle of nowhere. After the hustle and bustle of Camp Pennsylvania, the silence was surreal and the road, little more than hard-packed earth, was nearly indistinguishable from the surrounding desert. "I sure hope we know where we're going," I said to Sgt. First Class Wilson.

Udairi was only about fifteen minutes away. Like Pennsylvania, it was a tent city, only much larger and with more traffic. Nearly all the division's helicopter assets were stationed at its airfield—Chinooks, Apaches, Black Hawks, and Kiowas. They sat on a ready-made tarmac made from large rubber mats fitted together and staked to the ground, and inside huge clamshell hangars made from vinyl-coated canvas stretched over an arching metal framework. It was easy to spot the Air Cavalry's area: red-and-white Cav flags flew from their tents.

Sgt. First Class Wilson and I conducted our business and then cut our new soldiers loose to visit the PX, which had far shorter lines than the one at Pennsylvania. We then headed toward the red-and-white section of camp and quickly spotted Banshee Troop by their guidon stuck in the sand outside their tent.

I climbed out of the Humvee, anxious to see Mike, and Sgt. First Class Wilson settled into his seat for a catnap. I walked around a corner on my way to the tent and almost ran smack into my husband, who was rounding the corner at the same time, heading back from washing up and shaving.

We hadn't seen each other in two weeks, though it felt like months. We stood there just staring at each other and grinning, holding ourselves back from a hug. We were both in uniform and on post, so any public display of affection was against protocol. We just stood there and grinned some more like the newly smitten high school kids we once were. His face was sunburned, but he looked great.

"How are you?" we asked almost simultaneously.

We went inside out of the sun to sit and talk. Scott White and Mike "Big Country" Young were both there, and they seemed as excited to see me as Mike was. To them I represented a little piece of home, a reminder of their wives. Mike and I compared notes about our current levels of comfort. As per normal, the rumors had circulated to Udairi that we at Pennsylvania were living high on the hog and vice versa. They had heard we had a gym, air-conditioned tents, and a Subway (not true); we had heard they had cots and a Pizza Hut (all true). Udairi did not have any chow tents, as an electrical fire had reduced them to ashes. We compared notes on how we had traveled to Kuwait. I had Mike beat there: While he'd flown in a cramped military air transport plane, I'd scored a business-class seat on a commercial jet, with flight attendants who treated us like heroes.

"I can't believe it," Mike said, shaking his head in mock disgust.

We sat and talked for about fifteen minutes. When it was time to go, he walked me out to the Humvee. Sgt. First Class Wilson was dozing in the driver's seat, and when we showed up, he jolted out of his nap. He and Mike greeted each other warmly. Mike knew if he broke protocol, Sgt. First Class Wilson would look the other way, so he followed me as I walked around the back of the Humvee to get in my seat. "Try and stop in again if you get back over here," Mike said. He stole a glance to his left and right, grabbed me, and planted a quick kiss on my lips. I laughed and pushed him away, climbing inside the Humvee.

"See you later," I said, and Sgt. First Class Wilson drove me away.

Over the next ten days I would be lucky enough to visit with Mike twice more on trips to Udairi. They were flying a lot, familiarizing themselves with takeoffs and landings in the dust, which could quickly obliterate the line between earth and sky, a situation called "spatial disorientation." But I was always lucky and caught him in his tent. Mike really liked Sgt. First Class Wilson, and I knew it must have been hard for him not to say to him "keep her safe" or "look after her" or "I'm counting on you"—those things that all husbands and wives feel compelled to say but that Mike kept to himself. His silence gave me the confidence of giants. If Mike respected and trusted my leadership ability, then I knew I could do anything.

————

The 1st Brigade was in Kuwait until the third week of March, and the more days that went by, the edgier we became. It was the inevitable by-product of living in close quarters in a dust bowl—the novelty of our situation had worn off and the daily routine had set in. The fact that the days were getting warmer sharpened the edge of everyone's temper, that and our isolation. We had limited Internet access and only one phone for our entire battalion, which was unreliable at long distances. Cell phones were not allowed, as they could give away our position or allow soldiers to leak information that could come back and bite us. It seemed somehow unfair that vital decisions were being made about our lives while we struggled to track the march toward war.

On March 17, at 0400 our time, our battalion staff gathered around a computer in the TOC to hear our commander in chief set the war in motion. We knew what President Bush was going to say, but we wanted to hear the words for ourselves. A-Day, when the military would begin its air attack, was approaching, and we would be fully committed within forty-eight hours afterward. We got busy cross-loading our trucks, ensuring everything had an assigned place and location down to the smallest phone. On our assigned day, the 426th's ground assault convoy would set out on a marathon thirty-hour drive, punching deep into Iraq on the heels of the Bastogne.

"We hope that fighting will be light to none all the way to Baghdad," I wrote Dad. "It looks like it won't be as easy as we hoped, and the worst part is innocent soldiers will die. So far there is really no doubt in anybody's mind that we will win, but it concerns me that it might not be as easy as we thought. Mike told me he has volunteered to fly missions into the heart of Baghdad if it comes to that. I'm not surprised he volunteered."

A few nights later the air war began. Navy warships began shooting Tomahawk missiles from the Persian Gulf into Iraq, and we figured the missiles would pass overhead on their flight to Baghdad. A couple of us decided to meet as the sun went down and smoke cigars and hopefully get a glimpse of the fireworks. We sat out on cement barriers at sunset, and before long the only visible illumination was the stars and the glowing tips of our cigars. There was little to see overhead, only a few streaks of light that could have been missiles. Finally, the cool air sent me inside to my rubber mat and to sleep.

Once the air war started, it started in both directions. It was like a skeet match going on above our heads: Saddam's Scud missiles flying toward Kuwait and our Patriot missiles knocking them out in midflight. Our calm, quiet nights were finished; the siren went off several times a day. We'd drop whatever we were doing, throw on our gas masks, and run for the nearest bomb shelter, where we'd sweat it out waiting for the all clear to sound. There were always more people than seats in the shelter, so a few of us would sit outside leaning against the sandbags. One time the siren went off during chow, and I found myself leaning against a bunker next to some latrines, holding a plate of food.

In such tight quarters it didn't take long for a nasty respiratory bug, nicknamed the Kuwaiti crud, to make the rounds and find me. What started out as a sniffle evolved into fever and chills. My voice grew raspy and finally disappeared altogether. Nothing could have been worse: having to cross the border unable to speak.

March 21 was G-Day, when the military would begin its ground attack. Infantry units from the various American camps began to head out for the border. We worked until the last minute completing our maps and rehearsing the route and battle drills: what to do in an ambush, what to do under small arms fire, and what to do with obstacles in the road. And the number one threat: what to do if your vehicle broke down.

The twenty-four hours before G-Day was a day and night like any other. The battalion had retired for the night. At 0200, as it had done so many nights before, the siren woke us up. We blearily threw on our gas masks and trotted outside. I had developed a routine of throwing my mask on and standing at the tent door to count the soldiers as they came out. After the tent was empty, I began to run toward a shelter, when the voice of Sgt. First Class Carroll stopped me in my tracks. He didn't have his mask on, which I thought peculiar, and the look on his face telegraphed that something was off.

Sgt. First Class Carroll motioned me into the shadows. We heard an explosion, and I pulled my mask off. "It's not a Scud attack," he said. "It's an attack inside the camp." We drew our weapons and scurried to a different shadow. "I'll do a sweep of the area," he said. "I suggest you report to the TOC to get more information and help run things."

Staying to the shadows, I hustled to the TOC to find our battalion commander, Lt. Col. Gamble, talking on the radio to the brigade TOC along with the commanders of Alpha, Bravo, and Charlie companies. He ordered them to form a perimeter around the camp. "Lieutenant Blaise, you and Captain Boniface grab radios, split the perimeter in half, and keep the commanders and first sergeants informed of what's happening." Within minutes the TOC began to receive calls from our brigade headquarters for ambulance and doctor support.

Tony and I began our perimeter patrol. We walked our sections and then met up on each side to compare notes. Reports were coming in to be on the lookout for enemy soldiers. Their description was constantly changing: how they were dressed, how many there were. The only thing we knew for sure was that someone was injured. Our ambulance crew prepared to leave with a guard of soldiers covering them. Every soldier in our camp was lying in the prone positions with their weapons loaded and drawn. The only sound was the rustle of equipment as they tried to dig themselves into more comfortable positions.

Suddenly to my left I heard a female voice yelling and shrieking. A lone soldier stood up, and I ran to see what was happening. I saw the soldier, a big, burly NCO from another unit, grab the hysterical soldier, drag her to a bunker, and throw her in. I scurried up to the bunker, and he explained what had happened: The anxiety had gotten to her and she'd wigged out. She had ignored a direct order from a senior NCO to sit down and shut up for her own safety. "So I had to take matters into my own hands, ma'am." I quickly radioed the TOC and, in my squeaky-wheel voice, told them that we could leave that section of the perimeter in the very capable hands of that NCO.

Lt. Col. Gamble passed along a scrap of information: Among the wounded was our much-loved and respected brigade commander, Col. Hodges. The news made our blood run cold. Our leader was injured, and we hadn't even crossed enemy lines yet. How was this possible? Our initial reaction was that it was the enemy. We never imagined that the enemy was one of our own.

Tony and I continued to patrol. A few steps from our adjoining corner I saw him stop and stare skyward. A fast-moving object was streaking overhead. As we watched it sweep across the night sky, a second, brighter, and even faster object entered our peripheral vision. The two were on a collision course. When they intersected a few seconds later, the sky exploded with a blinding flash followed by pinpricks of light hurtling toward earth. "Did you see that?" Tony asked, as if he needed confirmation that the explosion had really happened.

"Yeah, what do you think it was?" I whispered. We felt even more under attack. (The explosion was later revealed to be a friendly fire incident, an American Patriot missile intercepting a British fighter jet.)

The radio crackled to life. We were instructed to look for "a Sergeant Akbar, who was unaccounted for, carrying a weapon and possibly carrying live grenades." He would be discovered a short time later sitting in a bomb shelter, acting as if nothing had happened.

Toward dawn we got word that the suspect was in custody. We sent our soldiers back to bed, leaving a small contingent set up on the perimeter. I was tasked to remain on duty as the battle captain, monitoring the flow of information from the brigade and keeping the battalion commander informed. We saw helicopters ferrying the wounded to hospitals. Their names had not been released, but we all had friends in the brigade headquarters and we worried and stewed waiting for news.

Over the next few hours, a fuller picture of the incident developed. Akbar was a veteran soldier in an engineering battalion, who had converted to Islam years earlier. He was acting as Sergeant of the Guard that night, which gave him access to several types of weapons including grenades. Akbar had gone to a tent area where the officers and senior NCOs slept. There, he flipped off a generator to darken the area. Then he went down a line of tents lobbing grenades into several of them and yelling, "We're under attack!" As more soldiers ran outside, Akbar began to fire on them with his M-4 automatic rifle.

After being captured, he reportedly explained that he wanted to take out as many Americans as he could before they entered Iraq "to rape our women and kill our children."

Two officers were killed. Capt. Chris Seifert, twenty-seven, was an all-American kid, an up-and-coming officer whom I saw at the TOC once in a while. He was young and cheerful, always ready with a hello. He had a wife, Terri, and an infant son at home in Clarksville. Akbar shot him twice in the back when he ran out to see what all the commotion was about. I didn't know Air Force Maj. Gregory Stone, forty, but he was a Bastogne soldier and we mourned his loss. Fourteen other soldiers were wounded, many of them my friends. They included our brigade executive officer, Maj. Romaine, whose injuries required him to be sent home, and Col. Hodges, who had light shrapnel wounds in his arm. He refused to be evacuated and received treatment at Camp Pennsylvania.

"We know what we do is dangerous," I wrote Dad, "but you never expect an attack from the inside like this."

The mood in camp the next day was one of subdued disbelief. A quiet settled over Camp Pennsylvania and, it seemed, over the entire desert. Yet we were still preparing for war, and as much as it seemed impossible, there was work to be done. Sgt. First Class Wilson and I had to turn in more paperwork and pick up more soldiers from Camp Udairi. Our convoy was leaving in about ten hours, and we were unable to attend a memorial for Capt. Seifert.

After fielding endless questions about the attack from soldiers at Udairi, Sgt. First Class Wilson and I drove to Mike's area so I could let him know I was okay. We arrived to find a ghost town where the Cav had been. The red-and-white flags were gone; the tents were empty except for rows of abandoned cots. The only sound was of the sand blowing against the tents.

At that moment, the reality and absurdity of war hit home. Last night Terri Seifert had gotten the visit every military wife fears. An Army chaplain and another officer had appeared at her door to deliver news they dreaded to give and she dreaded to hear. She had lost her husband, and their son had lost a father, and we had been here only a few days. And at the hands of a U.S. soldier whose traitorous act was beyond my comprehension. What other impossibilities lay ahead? Long days of danger and unknown challenges stretched in front of us, and I said the first of many quick prayers for Mike's safety.

I walked into his tent and saw one of the crew chiefs from Mike's unit sitting on a cot. Specialist Covian recognized me and filled me in. "The pilots left yesterday and crossed the border," he said. "The ground elements are following tomorrow."

"Will you give Mike a note for me when you see him?" I rasped.

I grabbed a small notebook from my back pocket and dashed off a quick note explaining the events of the night before and reassuring Mike that I was fine. Specialist Covian took the note. "I'll see he gets this, no matter what, ma'am," he said, and he made good on his promise two days later.

By the time we got back to Camp Pennsylvania, it was late afternoon. Sgt. First Class Wilson and I packed the last bags into our Humvee and sat down for a last quiet meal of Meals Ready to Eat (MREs). My stomach was doing backflips and my mind was racing with adrenaline, excitement, and dread. *I was going to war. I wasn't in the middle of it, but I was close.*

Our convoy stretched as far as the eye could see. My Humvee hauled a trailer that was loaded down with everything we would need, from computers to file folders to MREs, to set up an office in the TOC and live off of for the next few weeks. A brand-new second lieutenant, Jason Knapp, would be riding with us, so I set up shifts. Sgt. First Class Wilson and the newbie would ride together up front on the first shift. Sgt. First Class McDaris and I would take a turn riding in the open back. I called a group huddle and whispered our plan to my team, adding that Sgt. First Class McDaris would be the boss of the vehicle. I knew that without a voice, I couldn't be an effective leader if we came under fire. It was hard to assign myself to sitting second fiddle, but it was the best decision for all of us.

The mission was to drive for two days until we got to our first stop, depending on where the fight was. We would head north, Baghdad in our sights. The lead vehicles were equipped with GPS and satellite technology. We'd leave at dusk, following them across the border in the dead of night, entering Iraq through a notch in the berm that separates the country from Kuwait. The moment our tires touched Iraqi soil, we were to lock and load our weapons, the bolt sliding forward to seat the bullet in the chamber. "I want to hear four clicks when we go through the berm," I whispered.

Our vehicles were lined up into at least ten lines, twenty trucks per line. We had a motley assortment of soldiers with us: infantry soldiers, engineers, artillery—you name it. Everyone began loading up into trucks and saying their good-byes to friends who would be in different vehicles. Our faces said the same thing: How would this end? Would we see one another in Iraq or not? We'd been waiting for this moment for weeks, if not longer. I was anxious to get under way and put the waiting behind us. I wanted to see for myself the price Iraq had paid by having Saddam as its leader.

One by one the long snake of vehicles began to move, first one line and then the next and the next, one after the other, out Pennsylvania's narrow front gate. The caravan inched along in the chilly night air, never going more than twenty-five miles an hour in the thick sand. After a few hours of this we drove through a cut in the berm, and I heard the loud click of rounds being chambered and the second click of weapons being put on safety.

We drove until the sun came up. When the convoy finally stopped for a bathroom break, I noticed our company commander, Capt. Swift, walking in a leisurely fashion in our direction. I wondered at his boldness in enemy territory. He stopped at each vehicle and chatted with the soldiers. Then he got to us.

"What the heck's going on, sir?" I croaked.

"We're still in Kuwait. We took a few wrong turns last night. We've been driving somewhat in circles."

We all laughed and joked to mask our frustration. We had gone into this knowing we'd get very little sleep, and now we'd added a day on to the journey. As we unloaded our weapons, I heard the soft *chink* of 5.56 rounds hitting the floorboards of the truck.

CHAPTER 14

FAITH

WE PASSED THROUGH southern Iraq by daylight on a three-day ground assault convoy from hell, heading north. The 1st Bastogne Brigade had been sent there to root out the resistance, and we followed the infantry to provide support. Our three hundred–truck convoy crawled north through the desert, toward a horizon that glowed red where sabotaged oil fields burned. Every now and then, a massive plume of the blackest smoke shot into the sky—another oil well up in flames.

"I know many believe the Garden of Eden lies somewhere in Iraq," I wrote in my journal on March 27. "But it's hard to imagine."

The deeper into Iraq we went, the farther back in time we seemed to travel. The desert was dotted with small settlements whose inhabitants lived in conditions so primitive as to be biblical. Windowless mud huts were clustered around murky watering holes where women and children washed their clothes and collected drinking water. Slender boys with sticks herded sheep, like characters out of the Old Testament. From my passing Humvee, I could see families in robes and no shoes, working their fields by hand—not a farm implement in sight. It was hard to tell what the crop was, perhaps onions or some kind of tall rice. Oil pipes ran over, under, and around every property, though clearly the inhabitants saw nothing of the proceeds from what flowed inside them. Hopefully, I thought, that will change.

I'd never seen such poverty, but I couldn't let it dull my focus. We knew that the enemy could just as easily have been a woman holding a laundry basket as a man dressed in black holding an AK-47. Still, the children got to me. Here and there, families of four or five stood by the side of the road, silently watching our convoy inch by. Sometimes a small child would raise his or her hand to wave, but for the most part they looked completely and utterly forlorn. Or worse, they showed no emotion at all. The sudden presence of hundreds of U.S. Army vehicles snaking past their homes seemed to make no impression. They stood and watched us roll by with the blank expression of the eternally hopeless.

We had crossed the border early on the first morning. Sgt. First Class McDaris and I were in the front seats, and we could feel the eyes of the Kuwaiti guards on us as we passed through a succession of five gated checkpoints. It was hard to fathom what they were thinking—they showed little emotion either for us or against us. We passed through the last gate and locked and loaded our weapons again, this time for real.

Immediately we found ourselves in a small border village. Eerily silent and littered with rusted wreckage and ruined buildings, the village still bore the scars of bombing runs from the Gulf War. "It looks exactly the same," Sgt. First Class McDaris said with a sense of déjà vu. He had been a sergeant back then, and he sometimes commented that he couldn't believe he was back.

Women and children of all ages thronged the streets, silently watching as we drove by. It was a surreal parade from a parallel universe: no cheering or waving, just a sea of blank, hungry faces. The villagers' eyes were locked to the top of our trailer. We had covered its contents with nylon webbing, so it was clearly visible that we carried food and water. Like all the soldiers in the convoy, I had my weapon trained out the vehicle's window and pointed directly at their faces. As sympathetic as we felt toward them, we couldn't assume anything.

The enemy had gotten smart since Desert Storm. They'd come to realize that wars are won and lost on whether the infantry can get food, water, fuel, medical care. The enemy knew that logistics convoys carried less firepower and plenty of valuable supplies, so instead of slipping quietly past, we were now being targeted.

Ambushes were a constant threat. In Kuwait we'd been told that the bad guys were using innocent women and children as decoys, dragging them out into the road and threatening to shoot them in an effort to stop the trucks. We were under strict orders to not slow down for any reason, including this type of brutal blackmail. It could come down to us or them.

About halfway through the village we rounded a sharp curve. Crowds lined both sides of the road five people deep. Suddenly, three teenage boys ran into the street, lugging large chunks of metal wreckage, which they tossed in front of our Humvee in an effort to slow us down. "Hang on!" Sgt. First Class McDaris yelled, and he plowed straight over it, as did the vehicle behind us. Sgt. First Class Wilson and Second Lt. Knapp, who were in the back, were tossed around a bit but came through unscathed. But now the convoy was traveling at only ten miles per hour—dangerously slow. The villagers began to press close to the vehicles as if preparing to rush us.

A small boy of about eight sprang from the crowd and jumped onto our trailer. He clung to the nylon netting like Spider-Man, trying to reach through to the food. We kept on driving. The kid hung on for several moments, all the while tugging fruitlessly at a bottle of water.

A shot echoed throughout the truck. Sgt. First Class McDaris and I looked at each other. The kid fell off, hitting the ground hard. His friends dragged him away.

I lifted the thick nylon flap that separated us from the back of the Humvee and rasped, "Is everyone all right? What the hell's going on back there?"

"I think I shot that kid!" Sgt. First Class Wilson shouted, clearly upset. He'd been sleeping after driving for twelve hours in Kuwait; the impact had jarred him awake and, startled to see the crowd, he'd fired by accident.

"Sergeant Wilson, you did not shoot that kid," I said. "All he had was bloody knees." The boy was the size of a twig; a round from an M-4 would have taken his leg off.

About fifteen minutes later, after we'd exited the village, we pulled over for a pit stop. Some young soldiers in the truck behind us approached Sgt. First Class Wilson and excitedly began asking him about shooting the kid. Sgt. First Class Wilson, who had a son about the child's age, kept asking me what I'd seen, if I was sure the kid was all right. A nylon tarp covered the back of the Humvee, and we climbed on top to inspect the tarp for evidence that the bullet had missed. To make matters worse, Capt. Swift, our company commander, stalked up demanding answers. "I heard someone shot a kid," he said.

I quickly explained the situation to him. "Sir," I said, "I fully believe that Sergeant Wilson did not shoot him." And I pointed out the proof: To Sgt. First Class Wilson's immense relief, we'd found the bullet hole in the tarp.

Crisis averted, the convoy continued north on the first decent road we'd seen in weeks. It was a paved four-lane highway with road signs in Arabic and English. "Check it out!" Sgt. First Class McDaris said, pointing to a sign that read BAGHDAD.

There were four of us in that Humvee, though in a way the vehicle became our fifth soldier. Highly temperamental—she didn't like to start on the first try—and loaded with rucksacks and duffels and boxes of food, she always got us where we needed to go. I considered giving her a nickname, but "piece of shit" more than sufficed.

The four of us said little. All we had to do was follow the vehicle in front of us, scan the horizon through a curtain of dust, and try to stay awake. Every twelve hours, Sgt. First Class McDaris and I switched off with Sgt. First Class Wilson and Second Lt. Knapp. Sgt. First Class McDaris drove; I sat in the passenger seat. Between us we'd cached Twizzlers, bottled water, MREs, and sunflower seeds, which we munched and spat until the Humvee's floorboards looked like the bottom of a bird cage. The team in the back would try to sleep, huddled under sleeping bags against the frigid night. We wore heavy, charcoal-lined chemical suits called JLISTs over our desert camouflage uniforms; I'd written *Blaise* and my blood type on a piece of tape and stuck it on my sleeve in case I was injured and needed blood. We also wore flak vests, Kevlar helmets, goggles to block the sun and sand, and gas masks strapped to our thighs. The whole getup was bulky and uncomfortable but helped to keep us warm. (The in-fantry soldiers came up with novel hand warmers for the cold nights by urinating into empty water bottles. This wasn't so easy for the women to accomplish.) Still sick with the Kuwaiti crud, I shivered with fever, but slowly my voice was returning.

As we drove farther north, herds of wild camels appeared; they would turn slowly to gaze at us, lazily working their jaws. Bedouin tribes led their camels past our convoy, utterly uninterested. Our chaplain gave us daily briefings on the history of Christianity in this region. That, and my reading of *Ben-Hur*, the tale of a Jewish noble-man who crossed paths with Jesus, only reinforced the mystique of the Middle East for me, and sometimes I'd get so enthralled by my surroundings that I felt like a character in the book. The Garden of Eden theory began to seem plausible.

I tried not to let my thoughts stray to Mike. He was up ahead somewhere, flying into the teeth of the war: the tip of the spear. We both had a job to do, and I knew he was performing his with energetic zeal. Worrying wouldn't change anything. I had faith in his ability to do his job, especially since staying alive was part of the job description.

The farther north we got, the friendlier the locals seemed. Adult men in jeans and T-shirts appeared on the roadside, smiling and waving, though this always made us suspicious: They might have been counting our vehicles, discerning what type of convoy we were.

But our biggest enemy turned out to be our own vehicles. They weren't designed for this kind of grinding marathon road trip, and they began to break down in droves. We had old deuce-and-a-halfs—big trucks from the Vietnam era; LMTVs, the newest military cargo/transport truck; fuel trucks, wreckers, long beds; and various types of Humvees, some mounted with artillery guns. They broke down regardless of type.

For almost two days all we did was drive and pull off the road to fix equipment. My truck had no radio, so we knew to pull over only if we saw the trucks in front of us pull off first, one by one by one—a vehicular domino effect. But we couldn't sit on the roadside for long. The mechanics had fifteen minutes to assess the problem and decide if they could quickly fix it. If they couldn't, a wrecker would hook on to the truck and tow it, or we'd have to abandon it—though as far as I know only one trailer met that fate.

These repair sessions doubled as bathroom breaks. The first breakdown happened a couple of hours into our trip, and the logistics of relieving oneself in a line of over two hundred vehicles in a barren desert presented itself. At first I tried using the Humvee doors as a screen, but holding the canvas doors open while doing my business was awkward, to say the least. By the third stop I simply stepped between the Humvee and the trailer and squatted. Modesty was not an option.

Neither was security—in my opinion, at least. Every time we stopped, I assumed the prone position and scanned the horizon for the enemy, helping to guard my small truck and supplies. However, I noticed that many soldiers riding without NCOs or officers seemed to be a little too relaxed, doing more "smoking and joking" than watching and guarding. For some, Operation Iraqi Freedom was still in its field trip phase.

On March 28, two days after leaving Camp Pennsylvania, we limped, exhausted and filthy, into a refueling station. This was no Amoco station with cold drinks and candy bars—just a patch of desert lined with fuel trucks, a secure way station where we could recharge our bodies and our vehicles.

While Lt. Col. Gamble went to a briefing on the security situation, everyone else grabbed a roll of toilet paper and a small field shovel and headed to some small sand dunes beyond the trucks. It must have been a comical sight: two hundred soldiers hovering over "cat holes" in the sand, talking about eating and getting a few hours of precious sleep.

Back at my truck, I saw Lt. Col. Gamble striding back from the briefing tent. He didn't look happy. He called his senior NCOs and officers to the front of the convoy, and as we made our way up, our soldiers followed, until a large crowd had assembled around the boss. He looked tired and grim, as if the weight of the entire convoy was pressing down on him.

"Okay, people, listen up," he said matter-of-factly. "We're not spending the night here. This area was overrun by enemy fire last night, and Intel says they're coming back tonight. We can't afford to get hung up here when Bastogne is further north and needs our support."

He paused for effect, and we knew more was coming. "I need you guys to fully grasp the fact that if things continue to go the way they are, then one of us is not going to make it home. I know I made promises to the families before I left, but I don't honestly think we are going to get out of here without losing somebody unless everyone starts to realize that this is not a game."

Much foot-shuffling ensued as his words settled in. While the attack at Camp Pennsylvania had impressed upon me the danger and unpredictability of war, for the first time I felt personally at risk. This was my "lightbulb moment," when I fully acknowledged that I, a speck in this vast war machine, might not make it home.

I had time for a quick meal and a catnap. But first, I had two letters to write.

For years soldiers have been writing these letters, to be opened only in the event of their death. They write to their wives, parents, or friends, telling them how much they have meant to them and how they should go on and live their lives without them.

After choking down some MRE crackers and peanut butter, I sat in the passenger seat of the Humvee, a notebook propped up on one knee, and contemplated my words carefully. As soldiers slept around me under a soft blue sky, I composed a letter to my dad and a letter to

Mike, sealed them in envelopes and addressed each one, then exchanged them with my fellow officer and friend, Capt. Ed Sleeper,
who'd done the same thing. We made a pact that at the end of the
war, when we were finally back on Tennessee soil, we'd give each other
our letters back. But if one of us didn't make it back, the other would
make sure the letters got mailed.

I ultimately did get my letters back, but I haven't opened them,
and I doubt I ever will.

———

A few hours later, rested and a little less dirty, the convoy continued
on. As we approached An Nasiriyah, our senses went on high alert.
We knew this was a hot zone where U.S. Marines were battling Saddam loyalists in fierce urban combat. We'd also heard that an Army
convoy had been attacked here a few nights earlier, though we knew
little beyond that. To increase our chances of passing the city unnoticed, the convoy turned off the highway and rumbled along a narrow, winding goat track, barely wide enough to navigate, with steep
dropoffs on either side.

Around midnight, the lights of An Nasiriyah appeared in the distance. Tension emanated from the city like heat off a stove, and a
hush fell over the convoy. By the glow of a spotlight moon we crept
along at twenty miles per hour. Every sound from the creaking, rumbling vehicles was exaggerated in the darkness.

Then, truck by truck, the convoy began to come to a halt. The
whispered news raced up and down the line: "Possible enemy vehicles
approaching." We emptied the trucks and set up defensive positions,
gripping our weapons a little tighter and peering into the distant dark
through night vision goggles. Were we finally going to see the enemy?

Two small trucks approached with their headlights off, just out of
range of our weapons. They could have been fedayeen or two farmers
out for a moonlight drive. The trucks stopped and sat there for a few
minutes. We waited to see if they would make a move or if anyone else
joined them. Instead, the trucks turned and drove away—whoever
they were, they'd apparently decided the odds were not in their favor.
Relieved—no one wants a gunfight—the soldiers loaded up and continued on, suddenly fearful of what might lie around the next bend. I
had faith in my abilities and in those of my soldiers, but faith isn't
always enough.

Before we'd left Fort Campbell, I'd arranged with my pastor at the Church of the Beautiful Savior, Matt Brown, to do a sort of independent Bible study while I was deployed. He would e-mail me sermons to read and study, and I would forward them to Mike. As I bumped along in the passenger seat, denied access to Pastor Brown's comforting words, my mind fished for a calming thought or memory. I remembered a hymn my family used to sing in church on Easter Sunday, "Crown Him with Many Crowns." It was Mom's favorite hymn; she would belt it out with particular enthusiasm, and even Dad, the quiet type, sang a bit louder. The rest of us kids tried to keep up, but we hadn't memorized it yet, and I was not tall enough to see the hymnal when Mom was standing. Now, years later, the hymn floated back to me, and I found myself humming it aloud under the roar of the Humvee's engine:

> *Crown Him with many crowns, the Lamb upon His throne.*
> *Hark! How the heavenly anthem drowns all music but its own.*
> *Awake, my soul, and sing of Him who died for thee,*
> *And hail Him as thy matchless King through all eternity.*

The song reminded me of Mom and home, but more than that, it reminded me that we were in God's care. Soldiers at war often discover God for the first time or intensify their personal relationship with Him, and my time here had already brought me closer to Him. I saw Him as my holy bodyguard, someone whom I could count on to protect me and listen to me at all times of the day and night. I fervently believed that, and I knew that Mike, wherever he was, believed it, too.

––––––

On the evening of March 29, three days after leaving Pennsylvania, we reached what we thought was our final destination: a bustling refueling station in central Iraq. After days of wandering in the desert, cut off from civilization, we were suddenly in the thick of things. Soldiers strode busily around the fortified compound, and vehicles and helicopters of every size and type came and went. Hearing the familiar *thwop* of rotary blades high above me, I looked up and saw Kiowas flying. Mike was in the area.

As soldiers collapsed in exhausted heaps around me, I reported to the Humvee for duty as night battle captain. We set up a mini TOC out of the battalion commander's Humvee, where Sgt. First Class McDaris and I, along with a radio operator, monitored the brigade and division frequencies. The sky was black as cast iron and filled with stars, and the smell of tobacco from countless cigarettes drifted along the cool night air. Radio traffic was light. At midnight the other battle captain team relieved us, and we sunk gratefully into our Humvee and went to sleep.

The next morning the battalion commander decided to move the convoy about a mile north. The fighting in An Najaf was unexpectedly intense, and he felt we were too far away to be effective. He had scouted the area and found a suitable spot a few miles outside the city. Not only was it closer to the battle, the area had a water source into which Alpha company could hook its massive water-purification machine. We quickly packed up and made the move.

Once we arrived at our new final destination, there was much to be done before anyone could sleep: lay concertina wire and begin digging a berm around the camp; draw up shifts for guard duty and review our contingencies in case of attack; assemble the TOC and other various tents; hook up computers and phones and Internet connections to our all-important generators. The TOC had to be operational by the evening, when our first night shift would begin. Like sleepwalkers on overdrive, the crews set to work. Soon the TOC rose like a circus tent in the middle of the Battalion Support Area. It was the informational heart of the camp from which we tracked the location of our soldiers, dispatched missions and medevac choppers, and briefed units coming to our area on the enemy situation and the location of friendly forces.

Sgt. First Class McDaris and I wanted to assemble our living quarters so we could go straight to bed after work. After the TOC was done, Maj. Suqi released us to set up our sleeping area and grab a few winks before our shift. We found an isolated spot away from foot traffic where we could rest.

Unfortunately, my ROTC curriculum hadn't included how to build a shelter in the desert without a tent. "Sergeant Mac," I said, "I don't have the faintest idea how to do this."

"Don't worry, L.T." he replied. "I'll show you how it's done."

Sgt. First Class McDaris turned out to be a master at field craft. As I followed his lead, we took two ponchos, some old tent poles, and a little 550 cord and constructed a simple A-frame tent. We assembled cots and stored our gear underneath and placed an MRE box in between for a table. We dug a large hole outside the tent in which our water bottles would stay moderately cool and hung a clothesline from our "house" to our Humvee so we could dry socks and T-shirts after washing them in buckets. We did all this while wearing our chemical suits over our desert camouflage uniforms. We had been wearing the suits for close to a week now; like everyone's, mine was stained with food and sand, and my tan suede boots were covered with urine stains. I affectionately called them my "pee-boots," a nickname I knew Mike would appreciate.

By now, personal hygiene was a fond memory. We didn't have showers yet, so we all stank together, and we relieved ourselves by digging a cat hole, squatting, and then filling it in. After the first few days of tiptoeing around said cat holes, an engineering unit attached to our battalion built us latrines. They were nothing more than large holes dug in the hard earth, but they had wooden seats and tents around them for privacy—the height of luxury. We soon learned to announce our presence because it was easy to walk in on someone, though why this mattered after a week of relieving ourselves in public remains a mystery. Our water intake was restricted, so we wiped down our skin with baby wipes, dreaming of nothing more complicated than soft towels, clean clothes, a bar of soap, and a bathtub full of clean hot water.

Camp life quickly fell into a rhythm of sleep and work. As night battle captain, my shift lasted from 7:00 P.M. to 7:00 A.M. The night staff included myself, Sgt. Mac, and a radio operator, as well as personnel and supply staff from the brigade. Tony, the day battle captain, monitored the battle in An Najaf with a larger crew. The battle captain crews held a battle updating briefing twice a day, once when we came on shift and once when we were leaving. Commanders, first sergeants, brigade representatives, and other soldiers in authority would pack the tent to hear the latest intelligence, any new orders, and ongoing missions. A big part of my job was tracking the infantry's movements so I could brief Lt. Col. Gamble the next morning.

An Najaf still swarmed with fedayeen fighters, and the 101st was going door to door, tracking them down while trying to keep innocent citizens out of the line of fire. Our guys were fighting hard, mainly in the large cemetery on the edge of town called Wadi al-Salem. An Najaf is the holiest city in Shiite Islam, home to many of its most important shrines. The fedayeen were exploiting this fact, storing weapons or hiding in shrines, such as the gold-domed Iman Ali Mosque. They knew the 101st didn't dare destroy them for fear of sparking a public relations disaster.

Trapped between faith and combat, our infantry learned to calibrate its actions. At one point, fearing the fedayeen would damage the mosque and blame it on U.S. soldiers, a battalion from the 101st arrived to place a protective perimeter around the mosque. As the battalion marched toward the mosque, the enemy spread the word through the city that they were going to attack it. When the soldiers arrived, they found a large crowd buzzing with energy and anger. The infantry battalion commander, Lt. Col. Hughes, ordered his men to point their weapons at the ground, take a knee, and smile. This small gesture defused the tension and told the Iraqis that we were there to protect them. The crowd dissipated and the crisis fizzled. After I heard the story, I was amazed and proud at the steely nerve Lt. Col. Hughes and his soldiers exhibited, taking such a vulnerable position in such a volatile situation.

Other soldiers weren't so lucky. As soon as our Internet was up, I learned more about the ambush in An Nasiriyah. A handful of maintenance trucks had become separated from its convoy and taken a wrong turn directly into the city's downtown. Eleven soldiers were killed and six captured, including a nineteen-year-old private named Jessica Lynch. Reports said she had fought off her attackers before being shot and stabbed. Rumors spread like an out-of-control kitchen fire about what was being done to her: beaten, tortured, raped. All female soldiers knew this was a danger if we were ever captured, and I prayed she would be found alive.

Talk of Pvt. Jessica Lynch consumed the camp for days. Her capture and mistreatment made it easier for us to hate our so far unseen enemy, and we wished for our own chance at them.

I kept the camp updated on the Lynch situation, and on April 1, I delivered the news of her rescue to a standing-room-only crowd. Special Forces had stormed the hospital where she was being held and whisked her away without casualties. After a beat of silence, the room went up in cheers. The real story of Jessica Lynch, of course, proved to be less dramatic. It happened that Iraqi doctors had treated her terrible injuries, which are believed to have been sustained when the Humvee she was riding in crashed, and that the fedayeen had abandoned the hospital before the Special Forces arrived. But it didn't matter. I admired her tenacity and courage in surviving her ordeal. After all, on any other day, it could have been my sister or me.

———

I hadn't talked to Mike since entering Iraq, but I had assumed the Cav were nearby. I'd seen a lot of Kiowas flying overheard and heard their pilots communicating with our brigade TOC over the radio. I didn't recognize their voices, but it was great to know they were up there, like old friends who had moved into the neighborhood—an extremely dangerous neighborhood.

The Air Cavalry is one of the few units in the entire 101st that the division commander can use and move at will, wherever he feels it is most needed. A day or two into our support of the 1st Bastogne Brigade near An Najaf, I briefed Lt. Col. Gamble on our new "task organization" for the brigade. This is a list of all the units attached to the brigade at a single point in time. In this case, the mission was An Najaf, and one of the new units was Banshee Troop, 2/17 Cav—Mike's unit. They were based only three miles away and would work for the 1st Brigade for the remainder of the combat in An Najaf. I would be providing logistical support to my own husband.

By coincidence, Mike called me that morning, shortly before I went off my shift.

"Hey, Chubby," he said. "We're finally set up not far from you."

"What have you been doing?"

"Fighting over An Najaf." And then he told me about his own "lightbulb moment."

"For the last few days I've been loving the flying and living on the adrenaline," he said. "Then yesterday, me and Tim were on a mission over the city. We were flying low near the streets and in between buildings. I looked up to my right and saw a fedayeen soldier with an RPG [rocket-propelled grenade] on his shoulder pointed at us. We maneuvered out of the way, but for the first time, that guy made me really think about what the outcome of this place could be. I hadn't really thought too much about it yet. Right then this ceased to be fun."

"Holy shit, Mike!" I understood his excitement flying up there dodging bullets, but no wife can hear about her husband's near-death experiences and chuckle.

His words only confirmed what I knew was happening in the city. I listened nightly to the battle and knew that Mike was in the thick of it. But my faith and confidence in his abilities kept my worry level to a low simmer. At least I got to talk to my spouse, which was more than the other married soldiers got to do.

When my twenty-seventh birthday arrived, I was at my desk minding the war. At the battle update briefing that morning, Lt. Col. Gamble had the soldiers sing "Happy Birthday" and then gave me a big bag of Skittles as a gift. In a short period of time this collection of people from all walks of life had become my family: Lt. Col. Gamble, Maj. Suqi, Tony, Sgt. Mac, Sgt. First Class Wilson, Ed Sleeper. Mike called to wish me happy birthday. It was a short call—he wanted to grab some sleep before his next mission—but I was flabbergasted that he had remembered my birthday in the middle of a war when, back at home, it would often slip his mind.

I headed back to my tent, washed my hair, and collapsed. A few hours later, Tony was shaking me awake, yelling at me to get to the helipad because Mike was on his way to see me.

It still seems like a dream, that day. The Kiowas churning up a dust storm as they landed, and Mike striding toward me and grabbing me up in a giant hug. He had appeared so suddenly out nowhere, like a mirage, only he was flesh and blood and bone. Beyond him I could see Tim Merrell, his pilot in command, waiting patiently for Mike to return to the war. But for two minutes he was mine, and then he was gone. After the helicopter disappeared from sight, I slogged back to my cot and went to sleep, with clean hair and a smile.

———

For a week the fighting raged in An Najaf. The radio chattered all night, sometimes more, sometimes less. The radio telephone operator kept track of the action, but we could hear everything over the speakers. Dispatching the medevac helicopter became an all-too-familiar duty. When the wounded arrived, they were rushed to a mobile hospital in Charlie Company, where surgeons worked heroically to save their lives. I only visited the tent when there no patients, and it was like a M*A*S*H set, only more state of the art. Those doctors were amazing, performing major operations in such challenging conditions.

As word spread of the medical care, Iraqis began bringing us their wounded. They would stand outside the gates, holding bloody children in their arms, and beg for help. They had nowhere else to go. The guards at the front gate would call up and ask us what to do. Tony and I knew we couldn't let a seven-year-old bleed to death outside our gate, and we'd dispatch medics to treat the wounded, but not before the guards had patted down the parents and children to ensure it wasn't a ruse. Eventually locals began showing up with non-combat illnesses and disease, from toothaches to end-stage cancer. Just as the Iraqi doctors had helped Jessica Lynch, our doctors helped the Iraqis and saved many lives in the process.

The twelve-hour shifts were grueling. The days were heating up but the nights were still cold, and even though I'd never liked coffee, I began to drink it to stay warm and alert. We had a few cans of instant, scrounged from the PX before leaving Camp Pennsylvania, but after that was gone we were left with packets of instant coffee from our MREs. They quickly became a hot commodity. Running out was a cause for panic among many of our soldiers, who lived on caffeine and cigarettes.

Some mornings, after I got off shift, I'd take a stroll around the perimeter. It was my job to coordinate our defenses in case of attack, and I wanted to get the lay of the land. My walk would usually take me past the "pen," a circle of concertina wire about 200 yards from the TOC, which held enemy prisoners of war (EPWs). The prisoners, dark-skinned men in loose robes, sat with zip ties around their wrists under the watchful eyes of our Bravo maintenance company, who had been trained in Kuwait to process and guard EPWs. There was no interrogation required; we were simply to keep them in line until they were transferred to the division EPW camp. The number of EPWs averaged from five to twenty-five on any give day. They were given water, MREs, and medical treatment, with some shade in the afternoon. It was hard for me not to stare when I walked past, or for them not to look back. None of them ever tried to escape, though one did fall ill and had to be rushed to the medical tent, where the surgeons removed his appendix.

MIKE AND I IN HIGH SCHOOL

PROM GRAND MARCH, 1994

MY SENIOR PICTURE, 1994

MIKE AND GRAMPY

GRAMPY

ME AND GRAMPY

FORT RUCKER, 1999

*MIKE TAKING THE
OFFICER OATH*

*ME, MIKE, AND LINZ AT MY
COMMISSIONING CEREMONY, 2000*

*NEW YEAR'S EVE, 2001,
AT THE BABUSHKA,
CAMP STANTON,
KOREA*

MIKE HOME ON EMERGENCY LEAVE FROM IRAQ, WITH SCOUT

*MY FIRST IRAQI
HOUSE
AT AN NAJAF*

OUR TRAVELING HOUSE OUTSIDE KARBALA, SOCKS DRYING OUTSIDE

MY ROOM IN THE HEAP

MIKE AND HIS KIOWA, OUTSIDE MOSUL

MIKE AND TIM, TAKING A BREAK OUTSIDE AN NAJAF

*ME AND LINZ
IN BAGHDAD*

THE BANSHEE TROOP OUTSIDE AN NAJAF, MIKE IS CENTER

*MIKE, COLONEL GASS,
AND "COOP" GETTING
THEIR AIR MEDALS
WITH VALOR*

MIKE AND I WITH AN IRAQI FAMILY IN MOSUL

MIKE AND I IN QATAR

PRESIDENT BUSH, CHERYL, TERRY, ME, AND FIRST LADY LAURA BUSH, 2004

By April 6, An Najaf was relatively secure, and Mike began flying missions over Karbala. I spoke with him once on the field telephone; his helicopter had been badly shot up the night before, but he'd kept flying for four more hours. My war experience was comparatively mundane, but Mike was experiencing enough excitement for both of us.

Over time, my quality of life improved at the Battalion Support Area. My shift was changed to midnight to noon so Sgt. First Class McDaris and I could sleep during the cooler night hours. We didn't have to wear our chemical suits all the time. On the advice of a friend who'd served in Afghanistan, I'd brought a small camp shower. It was basically a rubber bladder that held water, which warmed in the sun until you were ready to use it. Using pulleys and a poncho for a shower curtain, the staff section rigged the camp shower up for communal use. I stood under the water at sunset and felt weeks of grime wash away like the sins of the newly baptized.

As fighting in An Najaf tapered off, my shifts grew less intense and the days began to melt into each other. During slow times I'd scribble a few notes on the world news to brief Lt. Col. Gamble in the morning. This evolved into the *Sandy Club Gazette*, a daily newsletter I put together that soon became required reading around camp. It was a collection of the latest news on the war (both good and bad) and around the world, sports, a "Daily French Bashing" (this was very popular), and a Bible passage from the chaplain. I dashed off journal entries as often as I could muster the energy and time. I described the ground assault convoy from hell, my living conditions at the Battalion Support Area, Mike's brief visits and phone calls. I wrote in a small spiral notebook, and when I was done I'd rip out the pages, put them in an envelope and stick it in our mailbag. Thousands of miles later, Dad would open the letters, read the entries, and then put them in a binder for safekeeping, for a day when they would matter.

E-mail was a godsend; I felt blessed to have it, unlike troops in the past who had to depend solely on the mail. On April 8, during some downtime at the TOC, I sent a mass e-mail back home briefly filling in the family on recent events. At the end I wrote my sister a personal note. Lindsey had been training with her National Guard platoon at Fort Leonard Wood in south central Missouri in preparation for their deployment to the Middle East. "Linz—have a safe trip over—hope to get a chance to see you." The next day, in the middle of a field training exercise (FTX), she managed to send me a reply.

> *Kate: It's so great to hear from you. . . . I have been thinking about you constantly . . . people are probably sick of hearing about you. Ha Ha. You're a real hero in the eyes of my entire platoon. . . . I have such an awesome group of soldiers and this FTX has really, really brought us together. Anyway, we "End-Ex" tomorrow and then it will be all downhill from there . . . pretty much just have to pack up and get on the plane. Still looks like about three weeks until we leave country. I still have no idea where we are going . . . there's rumors of some huge EPW compound going up in Kuwait and that we'll be there, who knows. The 1138th flew out today and we're next on the list.*
>
> *Take care and keep your head down. I miss you terribly. You are such an amazing person . . . your strength and dedication motivate me. Love you, Linz.*

But the biggest morale booster was the care packages that began to arrive toward the end of our stay. One day I arrived at the TOC to find a huge box addressed in Dad's handwriting. It was packed with cookies, candy, and two of my favorite foods: black olives and canned oysters. For the next weeks and months, the care packages poured in for me and Mike. They came from people we knew and loved—Dad, Wendy, Mike's aunt Linda—not to mention half the population of Macon. I loved coming to work to find my desk overflowing with boxes containing beef jerky, Pringles, crackers, fruit cups, pudding cups, decks of cards, Charmin, corn chips, Hot Tamales for Mike. Dad sent a baseball and a Missouri flag, two things he thought represented the United States the best. I proudly hung the flag in my tent and kept the baseball sitting on my desk. It had an almost magnetic quality: No one could resist the urge to pick it up and feel the smooth white leather and laces in their hands. Eventually Dad mastered the art of sending a loaf of bread so that it arrived still soft. More than once I opened a box from Grandma Decker to find a batch of her molasses cookies, smelling so deeply and richly of home.

The best part was there was plenty to share with others. "It's the one thing I can do to make myself feel useful," Dad said. So the boxes kept on coming, much to the delight of my coworkers. And it was always nice to see Dad's handwriting and the old Callao stamp.

After receiving the first box, I e-mailed Dad my thanks right away:

> *It was like heaven and just in the nick of time. I was on day fourteen of straight MREs and needed a break. The box was so big and jam-packed with goodies, there were murderous looks sent my way—but once the mongrel horde realized I was planning to share the contents with the troops, all was well. Many days were brightened and all agreed you were a great American.*

This was truer than my humorous tone let on. Dad, Terry, Cheryl, Peg, and countless parents like them have been the unsung heroes of the conflict, providing support, sustenance, and prayers for their children stationed in harm's way. Dad read books on Islam; followed the war news with more attention than his beloved Cardinals; shared scraps of information with Terry; opened bank accounts; and gave the bank in Macon a photo of us to post in their lobby. He forwarded my e-mails to friends and family, often attaching his own addenda.

"I can't imagine what it would be like to be in battle with my wife, or in Kate's case, husband, nearby," he once wrote. "I simply don't know how they do it. Only with a strong faith that God is watching over the other would it be possible."

———

We stayed in An Najaf for two weeks, though it seemed like forever. We were supposed to jump ahead to our next Battalion Support Area on April 9, but at the last minute were "op-conned"—attached to work for a short time with another division, the 82nd Airborne. Two of our infantry battalions moved forward, one to work with the 3rd Brigade Rakkasans and 2/17 Cav in Al Hillah and the other up north, near Baghdad. We would meet the 82nd Airborne at Karbala, but I was itching to get to Baghdad—I'd hate to have come all this way and not move all the way forward. The statue of Saddam famously came down on April 9, but we knew that it was mostly symbolic. Taking Baghdad wasn't going to be that easy.

On April 12 we pulled up camp for a move to the outskirts of Karbala. We sent an advance party to find a suitable area and began the tedious task of packing our belongings. Like conscientious campers in a national park, we tried to eradicate all signs that we had been there. We filled in the holes we had dug for defensive positions and latrines, and everything that couldn't be loaded or tied onto our vehicles was burned, particularly the latrines, which had been dismantled and set on fire. (Maj. Suqi later told me that a large herd of wild camels soon made itself at home on the site.)

The local populace had been keeping a sharp eye on us during our stay. Now, as they saw us preparing to leave, they became emboldened. As soon as our concertina wire came down, small groups of men and women began to move furtively into camp. I watched them from my Humvee, where I was running an interim TOC. Wordlessly, they began a well-executed plan of trash excavation, foraging for the smallest scraps of lumber. Finding the small bonfire where the latrine lumber was burning, two men reached into the flames, pulled what had been our toilet out of the fire, and dragged it away as if it were made of gold.

———

Our next destination was seventy miles north, an area between Al Hillah and Karbala. Later I described the journey in a mass e-mail home:

> *Our route took us directly through the center of An Najaf. It was our first opportunity to see the city up close. It was like something out of a movie. Thirty years ago this city was probably very beautiful; you can tell from the architecture of the few remaining buildings. The city is home to about 423,000 people, but doesn't look it. For the most part it all looked bombed out and uninhabitable. Fighting positions dotted the landscape—most of them not ours. Citizens lined the streets as we drove through—small children ran from their houses just to give us the thumbs-up sign. There was a lot of traffic, mostly old beat-up cars. The people were very intrigued any time that they noticed women—the men kept riding up near my vehicle to smile and wave at me or they'd point and talk excitedly as I passed. (Of course this has ALWAYS happened to me so I handled it with my usual calm—ha, ha.)*
>
> *Once through the city the landscape began to change dramatically. We went from a desolate, barren desert to a lush area with lots of water and forests of palm trees. It's a refreshing change. . . .*

We are fairly near the Euphrates, so there is farming in this area. We paid a farmer some money to take over his field and bulldoze it up.

We soon discovered that the locals near Karbala were not as shy as their southern brethren. Lt. Col. Gamble paid a local farmer to set up shop in one of his wheat fields next to a main highway. As our convoy reached the site, Iraqis on two-wheeled donkey carts, on foot, and in small pickups approached us brazenly, offering to sell everything from soda to old money bearing Saddam's photo. We were under strict instructions to have no interaction with the locals. Things were still dicey, and the enemy didn't wear uniforms.

Sgt. First Class McDaris and I set up our cots in a nice spot only to discover the field was carpeted with sheep droppings, but my farm girl sensibilities were not offended. (I also noticed that the field could have used some earth rotation.) The next morning I awoke to a cool breeze, the smell of fresh sheep poop, and a twittering sound so sweet it seemed heaven-sent:

"Listen, Sergeant Mac. It's birds."

CHAPTER 15

PILGRIMAGE

WHEN WE REACHED our second Battalion Support Area near Karbala on April 12, our immediate concern was the announcement that, for the first time in decades, devout Shi'a Muslims would hold their pilgrimage to Karbala, where Hussein bin Ali, the grandson of the prophet Mohammed, was martyred and buried in A.D. 680. Saddam Hussein had long denied the Shi'a this opportunity, but his fall from power had, as expected, opened the floodgates of religious expression. This meant that Shi'a Muslims numbering in the hundreds of thousands would arrive in Karbala on foot from all parts of the country. Not only would we have a firsthand view of the people passing by, but they would have a firsthand view of us. Naturally, the thought of countless Iraqis, not all necessarily favorable toward the United States, walking within spitting distance of our camp was a cause for concern. But the U.S. Army wanted to demonstrate its support of the Iraqi people in all their endeavors, and the command scrambled to work with Shi'a and Sunni Muslims to ensure the pilgrimage, or *Ashura*, was conducted peacefully. I was happy that they could express their religious beliefs again—after all, how would I feel if our president prohibited me from attending church simply because he didn't like Lutherans?

Every soldier in the Battalion Support Area, especially the perimeter guards, needed to be briefed on how to handle the pilgrims. These rules of engagement were formed at the Army's highest levels, and they dribbled down to us in the form of operation orders, which were disseminated to our company commanders. The rules of engagement were simple: Don't engage them. The Army was more concerned that the rival Sunnis would cause trouble.

A few days later, around April 15, the first pilgrims began to appear on the highway outside our Battalion Support Area. What began as a trickle of two or three quickly swelled into a river that silently flowed past our front gate. Many of the pilgrims carried the Iraqi national flag or black banners with messages in Arabic that, we assumed, declared their religious and political sentiments. Our initial concerns about raised tensions evaporated as we realized they simply wanted to pass peacefully into the city, where they would congregate at the shrine of Imam Hussein.

I made the pilgrimage the lead story in the April 22–23 edition of the *Sandy Club Gazette*. I included a black-and-white photo of bloodied Iraqi men, along with an explanatory caption, which read in part: "Some men use swords to cut their heads as part of the ritual. Some women weep, hammer their chests, and whip their backs until they bleed. This pilgrimage and these rituals have been illegal since Saddam Hussein was in power."

For a week the pilgrims were a constant presence, a human backdrop to the military life within the confines of our Battalion Support Area. The pace in the TOC remained fairly brisk, characterized by spurts of activity and sporadic radio calls. We were still working with the 82nd Airborne, which was continuing to flush out pockets of resistance in Karbala and Al Hillah. We worked to a sound track of howling dogs that shimmied under our concertina wire and rooted through our trash. Once the sun went down, the wild, mangy mutts sent up a coyotelike baying that echoed through the Battalion Support Area and kept the soldiers awake.

Mike and I rarely spoke. We were on different schedules—he was flying when I was sleeping. Or should I say, trying to: The days were heating up, and sleep came, like the radio calls, in sporadic bursts. Every hour or so Sgt. Mac and I would wake up, flies swarming our faces, our clothes soaked with sweat. Between the heat, the flies, and a cricket that never stopped chirping, like an alarm clock that couldn't be shut off, I managed to piece together, at most, three hours of rest a day. We were flying on autopilot, but so was everyone else. Exhaustion was part of the drill.

Since sleep was nothing to look forward to, I made a habit of walking the perimeter in the morning after my shift, just as I had at An Najaf. The boundaries of our Battalion Support Area were constantly being improved, with more wire, more fighting positions, and a newly finished berm and I wanted to have a mental map. Besides, the greenery made this Battalion Support Area so much more bearable; it was amazing what a small grove of palms and a few straggly stems of grass could do for my morale.

Once I reached the front gate, I'd stop for a few minutes to chat with the guards and watch the pilgrims pass by. The men and women tended to segregate themselves into groups. Most of the men wore long, loose, light-colored garments, perfect for the heat, as well as red-and-white-checked head wraps. The women, on the other hand, wore long black abayas from head to toe, only their eyes visible. They intrigued me, not only for their stoicism in such hot garments but for the manner of their passage. They walked silently and steadily forward, seemingly lost in thought. The dust was hardly disturbed by their passing. Nothing jostled their meditative silence—not the pitiless heat, not the few passing cars, not the sight of a female soldier from America standing seventy-five yards away, watching them go by.

At the same time, I didn't expect a reaction. I had not spoken directly to a single Iraqi woman since entering their country four weeks earlier. They seemed like living shadows, huddled in back rooms and under flowing robes or walking in dark groups by the side of the roads. This lack of interaction was partly a function of the fact that for the first two months of the war, I left the confines of our Battalion Support Area only to relocate to another. But in May, when I began to venture out into the countryside, it was the men who stared at me or waved, as they did when our ground assault convoy passed through An Najaf. Of the few women I did see in those early weeks, they seemed to be confined to the background, as if they weren't allowed to be curious about me or anything else. Or perhaps they disapproved of me, a woman doing a man's work.

If these women had any opinions about me, they betrayed nothing. Not one gave me more than a cursory glance, if that. We were separated by much more than armed guards, an eight-foot berm, and reams of concertina wire. I couldn't fathom what they were thinking. I couldn't imagine living in their world, and I suspected that they couldn't imagine living in mine. I had grown up believing that I could do or be anything that I wanted to be. What had these women grown up believing? What were their dreams? Was my presence in their country changing their lives at all, or was that beyond my control? I had come here to help improve the lives of the Iraqi people, but did they see me as an invader or a liberator—or both?

Did they care? I couldn't tell.

I was no expert on the state of women's rights in Islam. We'd received a small booklet on Islamic culture and common Arabic phrases, but it contained nothing explicit about the role of women except the warning to "never discuss issues of women's rights, equality, or liberation." Most of what I knew came from following the news in Afghanistan and the efforts of women there to assert themselves in society after years of life under burqas. But I knew that Saddam's Ba'athist regime wasn't as repressive as the Taliban. As I began to read about Iraqi society, I learned that for women, these religious ceremonies served several important purposes. Not only were they an opportunity to express their Islamic beliefs, they were a type of entertainment, a social happening. The pilgrimage, for example, gave them a chance to watch the reenactment of ancient battles and reconnect with friends and relatives they hadn't seen in years. I went to church back home for the same reasons. While our faiths were fundamentally different, our devotion wasn't.

I stood a stone's throw and several worlds away from these women, but I was in no position to judge or assume anything about their lives. All I knew for sure was how lucky I was to grow up in a country and an era that placed few limitations on women. Ironically, I'd chosen one of the few lines of work that explicitly restricted the role women could play, but I'd accepted that role. If I could have been on the ground knocking down doors in An Najaf, I would have. Not because I was trying to strike a blow for women's rights, but because it was where my natural inclinations took me. It was what I wanted to do, but my gender made me ineligible.

We all follow a path to somewhere, and mine had led me here.

Today, thinking of those pilgrims and their trek to Karbala gets me to thinking about my own journey as a woman in a man's world. Ironically, I had almost as little interaction with American women as I did Iraqi women, but this was purely a function of being outnumbered. There were plenty of women in the battalion doing every job imaginable, from mechanics to medics to supply sergeants, and we had several female lieutenants down in our companies. But as the only woman on the Forward Support Battalion staff, I interacted mainly with men day in and day out.

For two months I had been immersed in the male culture, and during that time I'd struggled to be recognized as a soldier first, not as a woman in a uniform. I soon realized this was about as likely as Saddam turning himself in to CENTCOM. I noticed subtle differences in the way my male peers reacted to me, whether they knew it or not. "You sure do look nice this morning," they'd say if I'd combed my hair for a change, or "Hey, you smell good," if I'd run a few baby wipes over my dusty skin. A man would never make such comments to another man, and while I came to realize they were harmless in most instances, they also telegraphed that men saw me as a woman first, and nothing could change that. My dual identities as officer and woman were fused together like conjoined twins who shared the same brain; separating them was next to impossible.

But it was a tender balance. Act too masculine and you're considered butch. Act too girly-girl, and you're considered a lightweight. For a female officer, trying to be too "womanly" can sabotage a career. Years earlier I had worked with another female officer who wore a lot of perfume and makeup, even in the field. I used to overhear what her male peers said about her—how her perfume was "in their face" and reminded them that their wives weren't there. While the female officer was competent enough, her overzealous application of Obsession by Calvin Klein so distracted and annoyed the men she worked with that they didn't always recognize the job she was doing. In the war to earn the men's respect, she and Calvin were fighting a losing battle.

And so I learned that earning my soldiers' and fellow officers' respect meant suppressing my femininity to a degree. While I enjoyed wearing perfume and a little blush and lip gloss for social occasions, I avoided doing so in uniform, especially when we were in the field. My soldiers needed to think of me as a respected officer they had to listen to, not a woman they might want to date. However, I did have to deflect one senior officer's advances—a desert camouflage uniform can go a long way to camouflaging curves, but there's nothing like being five thousand miles away from your wife or girlfriend to make a woman look good in anything.

Yet I refused to abandon all girly indulgences just because I was going to war. Instead, I adopted a policy of stealth femininity. Take my feet, for instance. I left for Kuwait with my toenails painted fire engine red (Mike called the color "whore red" because it was a color you'd see on prostitutes in bad cop shows). I brought the bottle of polish, too, tucked in my rucksack next to ten pairs of cotton panties from Victoria's Secret—bright colors and stripes, no lace. During my tenure in the Middle East, I didn't wear makeup, style my hair, or wear any color other than brown, so just knowing I had bright red toenails under thick green Army socks inside my suede "pee boots" made me feel a bit more like a woman. I later found out that, purely by coincidence, Lindsey had brought a bottle of red nail polish, too.

One of the worst things about being a woman at war was wearing a bra in 120-degree heat. Nothing made me more miserable than having a contraption with wires and tight straps sticking to my sweaty body. I always looked forward to the end of the workday when I could take it off and feel twenty degrees cooler.

On the other hand, I insisted on wearing clean socks every day— putting on a pair before work improved my attitude immensely. On laundry days, I'd pour powdered detergent into buckets of water and scrub and slosh my socks and T-shirts like a pioneer woman beating her clothes against rocks in a stream. The water turned so filthy that I could hardly distinguish between clean and dirty clothes. I'd drape the wet garments on the line tied from our tent pole to the Humvee's fender, though I always hung my Victoria's Secrets inside the Humvee. Having bright red underwear flying from the line for all to see could only undermine my best efforts.

Personal hygiene was nonnegotiable, especially since dysentery had started going around. While I did my best to stay clean, a few of our soldiers happily reverted to caveman status. Between a lack of bathing and wearing the same desert camouflage uniform for a month, they could get pretty gamey. There were times when a guy would walk in the TOC and nearly clear the place out. Toward the end of our stay near Karbala we were saved from ourselves when a National Guard Shower, Laundry, and Clothing Repair crew pulled into camp with showers and washing machines on tractor trailers. Still, some of the cavemen refused to come clean, and their commanders literally had to order them to take showers. I don't recall any women having to be so convinced.

———

It was a friend and fellow officer who taught me how to balance being a woman with being an officer. Jenn Hull held the same job as I did in the Forward Support Battalion that supported the 101st's 2nd Brigade; when the division left for Kuwait, her battalion commander kept her at Fort Campbell to run things in the rear.

Jenn was an Army brat from Maryland who, like me, had grown up wanting to serve her country. We'd met in the summer of 2000, during my first job in the Army, working at the ROTC Basic Camp at Fort Knox. As I was unloading my car outside the barracks, she approached me and said, "Hi, my name's Jenn."

"I'm Kate."

Then she said, "I had to come talk to you because you're the first female officer who's pulled up who is nicely dressed and who's wearing a bit of makeup. I knew we'd get along." As a soldier, I had never been singled out for those reasons before.

Jenn was living proof that when holding your own with men, a sense of humor and a healthy serving of self-esteem go a long way. Tall and slender, with long, curly auburn hair and green eyes, she always looked like a million bucks, whether in uniform or civilian clothes. She was equal parts girly-girl and hard-core soldier; she could shovel dirt with the best of them and not ruin her manicure. While she'd wear mascara and eye shadow on the job, she didn't need heavy perfume or lipstick to get attention. That's because Jenn's best feature was her confident attitude. A good leader and well respected, she was funny and hardworking and unwilling to take any shit off anyone. She was herself, like her or not. If you didn't respect her, that was your problem; she wouldn't give you another thought. Her utter refusal to try to impress men was what impressed them the most; that and her work ethic earned their respect.

Jenn's "be yourself" philosophy worked well for me in Iraq. Being one of the boys has always come naturally to me, and this extended to a tolerance for the male sense of humor. If, while talking in the TOC, the conversation turned to *Maxim*'s latest cover model, it didn't ruffle my feathers. Or if one of my soldiers cussed up a storm and then said, "Sorry, ma'am, I didn't mean to cuss in front of you," I'd reply, "Shit, I don't care!"

Ultimately, I was more of a confidante than an object of desire. In their free time, the guys sought me out to talk about their personal issues: frightened wives, unfaithful girlfriends, sick parents, unhappy kids, or the big soccer game they just missed back home. Maybe they'd had a bad day at work or the brigade had lost soldiers. Or maybe it was just simply one of those days when you were sick of being in Iraq. (Believe me, we all had them.) They found it easier to talk to a woman about issues they held dear, and I didn't mind playing the role. Everyone needs someone to talk to, bitch to, and laugh with.

If I needed a laugh, I knew where to go. During my stroll of the perimeter, I'd often drop in to see First Lt. Jesse White in Bravo Company. Jesse was in charge of our Shop Office, which meant that every piece of brigade equipment or weaponry that needed repairs came through him. He worked out of a small office in a trailer, while his maintenance crew toiled a short distance away. I always enjoyed visiting the mechanics. Grease-covered and rough around the edges, they were some of our most efficient and good-natured soldiers. They smiled and joked even on the hottest days, lying on their backs on the hot sand under a broken truck.

Jesse was typical of my male friendships, full of good-humored banter and an easy camaraderie completely lacking in sexual tension. We each knew the other had a spouse we deeply loved, and there was no question of that changing.

A Tennessee native with the twang to prove it, Jesse was in his late thirties, married to Sheila, a former Air Force soldier with whom he had two young boys. Jesse had started out in the Air Force in the 1980s before switching over to the Army and becoming a warrant officer; then he got his college degree and became a commissioned officer. We called him "Mr. Midlife Crisis," because he was always changing careers. And he was fanatical about golf; in his downtime I'd find him cranking golf balls into the desert with his sand wedge.

More than anything, Jesse was one of the funniest people I'd ever met. He was always telling stories about growing up in Tennessee, his brother "Bones," or funny things his soldiers did. He had arrived in our unit the previous summer, a newbie like me. The officers were required to attend Army functions such as Hail and Farewells, and on one such occasion we'd been seated next to each other. We began to talk and soon discovered a mutual love of cards and beer; by the end of the night we had cemented plans to start a lieutenant's poker night.

The first one was at my house. This was during the run-up to the war; Mike was in the bedroom, studying for a flight test the next day. But he soon ended up on the living room couch, drawn by Jesse's sense of humor. Poker night became a ritual, and Mike and Jesse learned that if they put their heads together, they could have everybody gasping with laughter. Jesse also felt that his closest friends needed ridiculous nicknames; mine was "Bleezy," and he never called me anything else.

A world and a war away, I stopped by the shop to bring Jesse the latest copy of the *Sandy Club Gazette*, hot off the presses. He and his crew were some of my most loyal readers. "Hey, Bleezy," Jesse said when I entered the trailer. "What's the latest French-bashing in the *Sandy* today?"

"How many Frenchmen does it take to change a lightbulb? One. He holds the bulb, and the rest of Europe revolves around him."

"How about the weather?"

"I'm going out on a limb here: hot and dusty." And we both had a good chuckle.

"What have you heard from Mike?" he asked.

"Not much. All I know is they're flying missions over Baghdad."

"Next time you talk to him, tell him to keep an eye on the sky and kick some ass for us."

———

The next day, I left the TOC for my daily perimeter stroll, but when I got to the front gate, the pilgrims were gone. The highway was empty. "Guess that's that," said one of the guards, sounding relieved.

Soon thereafter, we received orders for the next stop on our driving tour of Iraq. At Fort Campbell, the plans had always been for the 101st to end up in Baghdad, but like all battles, this one had shifted and changed. Securing An Najaf had held us up longer than anticipated, and the 3rd Infantry Division had done its job so well its soldiers were now firmly entrenched in Baghdad. The Army and Maj. Gen. Petraeus wanted us up north in Kurdish-dominated territory. Marines in Mosul were battling anti-American violence and needed reinforcements. I was disappointed that I wouldn't get a chance to see the famed capital city, and I hoped a chance to do so would present itself later. But going north would give me a chance to see the entire length of the country, which could prove interesting, even if no one was quite sure where Mosul was.

Our convoy left Karbala on April 27, hundreds of military trucks rumbling along the same highway that the pilgrims had walked. The ground assault convoy to Mosul took two days, and was far less stressful than our first trip. The roads were paved and the Iraqi people were less fearful. They knew Saddam was in hiding, and anti-Saddam demonstrations were breaking out all over. The weather was sunny and so was the mood of the people, from what I could see. Outside Al Hillah, we passed the ruins of Babylon, the wealthiest, most powerful city in the ancient world. We skirted the edges of western Baghdad, where I saw nothing but terrible slums, endless acres of trash, and columns of smoke rising into the hot blue sky.

The closer we got to Tikrit, Saddam's hometown, the more we saw how the regime had favored the Sunni minority. The homes were more impressive, the roads better maintained. Every few miles we'd see a huge mural of Saddam in action: in a military uniform, holding a small child on his lap, and so on. Usually his head and face were gouged out with automatic weapons fire, a sign of the locals' new defiance.

The roads had gone from zero traffic to a steady flow, mostly small white pickups packed to capacity with livestock or people. They'd drive up next to us and point and yell. Their proximity was a little unnerving, especially since Tikrit had been the site of much unrest. But as with the pilgrims we soon realized they meant us no harm. We even began to smile and wave back.

At the halfway point we stopped at an abandoned Iraqi Air Force base for the night. We pulled out our cots and set them up next to our vehicles, a row of cots as far as the eye could see. The desert wind blew mightily that night, and all the flapping and snapping of canvas on the trucks made it difficult to sleep. We were up at sunrise, and after a breakfast of cold MREs, our convoy was on the move again.

We were headed to a dot on the map called Qayyarah West, an abandoned Iraqi air base that had been bombed by coalition forces. In the late afternoon, a few hangars appeared on the horizon, and we rolled down the airfield's main road like the conquering Army that we were. Its name was immediately shortened to Q-West. I didn't know it at the time, but Q-West would be home for the duration of my stay in Iraq.

The base was in a pretty spot. There were mountains in the distance, a few olive trees, and some grass and flowering shrubs. Q-West was quite large; it took almost fifteen minutes to drive around the entire post. It was also evident security was going to be a problem for a while: Local shepherds had turned the grassy expanses into prime grazing ground, and there was nothing but sheep as far as the eye could see. It took two weeks of coaxing and a lot of perimeter wire to convince the shepherds to take their flocks elsewhere.

The buildings here seemed relatively new. There were large jet hangars, bunkers of all sizes, and a long airstrip pocked with huge bomb craters. Several metal buildings had literally been torn to shreds by bombs and looters, who'd hauled away most of the usable steel, along with just about everything else on the post not nailed down, though half the stuff nailed down was gone, too. Every building on post had been picked clean as a Thanksgiving turkey—wires were yanked out of walls, plumbing was plundered, garage doors were yanked from their hinges.

A good portion of the 101st was scheduled to roll in here over the next months. Since my battalion was among the first to arrive, we had first dibs on where to settle. We picked a small street with bunkers, one for each company to work out of. The bunkers, which were made of solid concrete and had heavy iron doors that required a forklift to open, would protect us from the dust and, if necessary, incoming rounds.

Sgt. First Class McDaris and I set out to find a place to pitch our tent. Next to our bunkers we found a cement slab covering an old septic tank—perfect for the floor. Since it looked like we'd be here for some time, we gave this "house" a few upgrades. We made it taller so we could stand upright inside, and furnished it with a table and two chairs made from old barrels and plywood. We hung mosquito netting on one side for a "screened porch" and invented a pulley system so that from our cots we could pull a rope and roll up the side of the tent to get some air. That next day, the weather decided to throw us a curveball by turning rainy and cold, and we lay shivering and wet in our makeshift tent.

We soon settled into a routine. The TOC went up and we set to work. A few days after we arrived, I got a phone call, and I was ecstatic to hear Mike's voice on the other end of the line.

"Guess what," he said, sounding excited. "The Cav is coming north to work in Mosul, too. We'll be staying just outside of the city limits—where is that in relation to you?"

"We're about forty-five minutes south. But that's awesome! We'll get to see each other, maybe, once a month!" Our paths had crossed again.

CHAPTER 16

KIOWA DIARIES

AS A WIFE, I worried about Mike, but as a soldier on the ground, I quickly came to appreciate the heroic work he and the other Kiowa pilots were performing. I heard daily testimonies from the infantry soldiers who came through our TOC and shared the pride and trust they felt for their brothers in the air.

Kiowa pilots performed invaluable support to the ground troops. The Kiowa's tight turning radius makes it maneuverable at low altitudes; the aerial equivalent of a roadster, it can turn, swoop, and stop on a dime. Its small cockpit allows the pilots to look out the window directly at the action. They would often remove their doors so they could look straight down to do the mission, becoming, as they called it, "all eyeballs."

Chief Warrant Officer 3 Tim Merrell, who was forty-one to Mike's twenty-nine, flew with Mike in the early days of the war, when infantry troops were waging bloody battles in the southern cities against Saddam loyalists and the fedayeen. In the air, Mike's job was to operate the radios, talking with headquarters and ground elements. He would relay what was happening in the battle as well as inform headquarters of their actions. Tim was in the right seat of the aircraft; Mike was in the left. Tim did the flying; Mike did the talking. His nickname was Mikey B.

As a former infantryman, Mike had a particular affinity for the soldiers on the ground. He poured his heart and soul into his job, whether scouting, taking out enemy positions, or providing extra firepower during gun battles. As a result, the infantry guys treated him and the other Kiowa pilots like celebrities. Whenever they spent time with infantry guys, "Someone would always shake our hand and tell us the story about how we really saved their asses," Mike told me once.

The Apache is the Army's star helicopter, but it's more suited to high-altitude flying. It is what's called a "deep attack" aircraft, capable of going far behind enemy lines, destroying armor and returning unscathed. It doesn't like to fly low, which makes it ineffective for supporting the guy on the ground. The Kiowa, on the other hand, can fly so low it practically skims the ground. Scott White recalled one mission over Karbala where they were ordered to check out a funeral procession. Suspecting there were weapons in the coffin, he and his copilot hovered over the funeral party and demanded they open the lid. All they found was someone's late relative.

Mike had a similar story, also over Karbala. He and Tim were performing aerial security for a ground checkpoint when a horse-drawn wagon full of straw and men began to approach the checkpoint. They knew that innocent-looking locals could be couriers carrying large amounts of money, weapons, or messages to the enemy, so ground forces asked Mike and Tim to stop the wagon. The Kiowa hovered in front of the locals trying to get them to halt. But the wagon continued to move toward the checkpoint, ignoring warnings to stop. Finally, Mike took his M-4 off the dashboard, leaned out of the cockpit, and pointed it at them. That worked. The men turned out to be harmless.

Though they didn't fly together over southern Iraq, Scott and Mike became brothers there. They'd been close at Fort Campbell, but in Iraq they formed an ironclad bond forged in the crucible of combat. After their missions they'd smoke cigarettes and talk about "their day of adventure," as Scott puts it. Their often ate dinner together—ramen with tuna, cheese and crackers. They'd take turns cooking and cleaning up, and Mike "Big Country" Young would often join them. "On the days we didn't fly," Scott said, "we would catch up on laundry and sleep and try to call home."

Both Scott and Mike told me that sometimes they felt helpless. There was nothing more frustrating than seeing soldiers injured by roadside bombs and not being able to land and help. The pilots were committed to the ground forces, and sometimes they flew in weather they had no business flying in. "We did whatever it took to get up there and fly," Scott told me. "Because when we didn't fly, that's when bad things would happen. We did it for the guys on the ground, who were dying on a daily basis. Our only help was to make them feel secure as they convoyed through the cities or did IED [improved explosive devices] sweeps or just walked security patrols."

I had gotten a firsthand taste of the Kiowa's capabilities in Korea. I was visiting Mike at Camp Stanton, and he asked me if I wanted to go for a ride. "Are you kidding?" I said. "Of course I do." Chief Warrant Officer 3 Tom Castagna, who lived across the hall from Mike, would be my pilot. As I was boarding the aircraft, another pilot asked me what I had eaten that day. "Just a few Twizzlers," I said. He laughed and said, "Good luck."

It turned out that Tom was notorious for making people vomit on their first flight. I had never had motion sickness before, so I wasn't worried. I pulled on a helmet and let Tom buckle me into the narrow seat. I was amazed Mike could wedge his big body into that tiny cockpit.

Mike and his copilot had a mission, and they took off right behind us. For a few seconds the two Kiowas hovered next to each other before Mike waved and flew off in the other direction.

Flying in a helicopter was an amazing feeling. We soared up high, near the clouds, and skimmed down low, above the trees. As we flew, Tom talked into his headset about the aircraft and what it could do, and I felt proud and excited knowing that Mike possessed the skills to put a bird like this through its paces. About twenty minutes into our flight, Tom said, "Since your stomach doesn't seem to be too bothered, I'm going to show you the limits of the aircraft."

He proceeded to yank the Kiowa all over the sky. We swooped up, down, right and left. On the last maneuver, my stomach stayed somewhere to the left. Grinning, Tom glanced over at me, saw my chalky face, and yelled, "Hold on, I'm landing, I'm landing. . . . You'd better open the door!" I promptly did so, but not before upchucking Twizzlers in the aircraft. As we proceeded back to the hangar, Tom radioed Mike and said, "Well, buddy, I made her sick."

After we landed, I was walking from the hangar when one of Mike's other neighbors walked by and said, "Hey, Twizz." Word had spread.

Such lightheartedness was a far cry from what Mike and his fellow Cav pilots experienced in Iraq. Their days were grueling and dangerous. They were crammed into that tiny cockpit for eight hours, stopping only to land for fuel and more ammunition. They had little time to do anything except stretch, relieve themselves, grab a bottle of water, maybe wolf down some MREs. Mike would get out and stretch one time, Tim get out and stretch the next, so someone was always at the flight controls of the running aircraft.

Not long ago, I spoke with Tim and Scott about the missions they went on in the early, dangerous days of the air war over southern Iraq. They shared memories of the battles and of Mike's role in them with me, some of which I knew, some I didn't.

————

According to Tim, when the air war kicked off, Saddam was expecting the ground troops to wait two weeks before crossing the border into Iraq. In fact it was a simultaneous, two-pronged attack. The 3rd Infantry Division moved ahead, and the 101st went a day or two behind them. The 101st would swing around using its air assault mobility to travel large distances quickly. The five troops of the 2/17 Air Cav, totaling forty-eight pilots in twenty-four aircraft as well as twelve staff pilots, left Kuwait before daylight on March 21. They flew 150 miles to a refueling stop, Forward Ammunition/Refuel Point Shell, and then another 150 miles to its first Forward Operating Base about thirty minutes by air to An Najaf.

The pilots set up a defensive perimeter around the aircraft and dug into their fighting positions: holes six feet long, three feet wide, and four to five feet deep. Both Mike and Tim were old country farm boys—Tim was raised on dairy farms in New England—so neither of them minded the hard work of digging in. The weather was perfect for hard labor: mid seventies in the daytime, forties at night. They dug in quickly and waited for their vehicles, which took two to three days to drive the distance the Kiowas had flown in six hours.

Tim said they were excited to finally get into the action. "We'd been training for this our entire military careers," he told me. "I'd been in the first Gulf War so I knew some of the desert flying we were about to do, but Mike was completely new to combat. There we were with our hopes up, and the first mission we got was to go look for some cargo boxes containing parts and supplies for the brigade. They were being airlifted to us by Black Hawk, but the pilots had run into bad weather and had had to cut the loads. It wasn't the mission we were hoping for, but it did give us some time to get used to flying together."

After the cargo box mission, sandstorms grounded them for several days. There were total brownout conditions; they couldn't see ten feet in front of them. There was one twenty-seven-hour period where the two men didn't see each other at all. "We were holed up in our tents, and we'd occasionally holler out to each other to see how the other was doing, but that was about it," Tim recalled. "The tents were all-weather, but nothing keeps that fine sand from finding its way in. We could read by flashlight or write a letter, but not without the hue of brown and orange around you. For the most part, surviving the sandstorm kept our minds occupied. We wore goggles, and a T-shirt or kerchief over our mouths and nose to try to sleep; in the morning we'd dump an inch of dust out of our goggles. We'd choke through the dust to draw a breath. You would hear the wind start dying down and you would get pretty excited. You got through it to the clear days."

Tim recalls that Mike was always the one to lighten the mood. The pilots would be sitting around, silently studying the information, and Mike would break the quiet with a typically sarcastic comment, always followed by laughter. "I remember waiting in the sandstorms to go into An Najaf, and our commander was briefing us on the day's losses," Tim said. "It had been a bad day for the allies: several dead, setbacks at a few objectives. It all seemed so gloomy. All was quiet until Mike said, with that slow, deliberate farm-boy drawl: 'Well, hell, I guess we might as well go home.' We all laughed, picked ourselves up, and prepared for the three-day assault on An Najaf."

Their first mission was a reconnaissance flight over the city in support of the 1st Brigade, which was planning to drive its tanks through town in a show of force called a thunder run. They had to identify enemy forces ahead of them. Their wingman was Lt. Monica Strye, one of the Banshee Troop platoon leaders, and J. C. Carter. Here's how Tim remembers it:

We flew into An Najaf expecting to see desert, but the landscape quickly turned into date groves and palm trees. It was pretty heavily forested, more so than we expected. It was the first time our team had conducted a tactical flight over an urban environment. We had prepared for a more open terrain type flight, where Saddam's forces would be arrayed outside the cities. Our first mission gave us a taste for flying over the cities: the wires, the different types of buildings, some of the forested areas.

As we found different parts of the route that were of interest, Mike wrote them down and radioed the information back, either to the other aircraft or to headquarters so they'd know what to expect the next day.

On the following day, the ground forces moved into An Najaf. It took an hour and a half for our forces to penetrate the city. The ground forces met some resistance but quickly and methodically overcame it and cleared the enemy fighters out of a few buildings. We flew into the southeast corner of the city, supporting the ground units, but did not receive any fire for the first hour or so. Then, about an hour and fifteen minutes into the mission, RPGs began to explode in the air around the aircraft. That was the first time we received fire.

Our flight helmets and the noise from the turbine engine muffled the sound of the explosions, so that the RPGs sounded like pops from a BB gun. We first saw the blasts around the tail of our wingman's aircraft, then saw a few near us. As a team we immediately went into evasive maneuvers, turning quickly and erratically, first left, then right, mixing it up and all the while continuing to conduct reconnaissance for the ground elements. Mike began to report information down to the ground forces, letting them know the enemy's fire was intensifying. We continued on with our mission without taking any hits to the aircraft.

It was Mike's first time under fire. He was rock solid. It's kind of funny—when you're in that situation you just fall back to your training. He dealt with it well. He was aware of it—he got bright-eyed—but he never shut down on me. He kept on going.

The guys on the ground were clearing a housing compound of some kind. We provided cover for them as they went building by building, door by door. If we saw any movement, we would radio it down to them. We had our flight of two working this area; Scott White was working another area, then he came over also. He'd received enemy fire and damage to his aircraft that day, in the tail area. The metal used on the Kiowa is so thin that when we got back he repaired the hole with a flattened Coke can.

Eventually our four aircraft were relieved. We were expecting to go home after we landed back at infantry headquarters, and that's when we received the most challenging mission so far. They wanted us to go behind enemy lines and identify the location of some truck-mounted, large-caliber machine guns and verify the location of large groups of enemy fighters. The suspected location was a good five or six miles into the city. As a team, we huddled for a few moments around a map and came up with a workable course of action. We decided that we could approach the location from different angles, flying around the backside of the city and entering it from the northwest. We took off from headquarters. We were aware that there was a threat of SAMs [surface-to-air missiles] from inside the city, so we used some of the mission optics on the aircraft to see if we had any indicators that the surface threat was there. We determined that it wasn't and positioned ourselves for a run through the city. North of An Najaf, we moved in as fast as we could. Once we got into the city, it erupted. There were a hundred or more fighters on rooftops and in windows. They were firing RPGs at us, and we could hear the rat-tat-tat of machine guns. It was coming from all sides. We were flying at our maximum airspeed about fifty feet above the rooftops. It's all geometry at that point: You want to be as close as you can to limit the angle of the enemy's fire. If you're moving that fast it's hard for them to get a sustained look at you. We also had to look out for the wires. Iraqis had run hundreds of wires off of one large generator and the streets and alleys are crisscrossed with them. Everyone has wires and antennas. Thin wires, thick wires, power lines, all at varying altitudes.

Flying into wires can be catastrophic. The Kiowa has a wire strike protection system that will "pinch and cut" through wires, but failure of that system results in a loss of the aircraft and/or the crew. If Mike saw a hazard coming up he would say, "Large wire, ten o'clock at flight level, two hundred meters."

We made three passes that day and got the information that the intelligence officer wanted. The large-caliber machine guns were mounted on the back of small pickup trucks and were, in fact, moving through the city. With the intensity of enemy fire it was impossible, in my estimation, for us to successfully engage the vehicles and live to tell about it. We radioed the information, then flew back to headquarters for a detailed debriefing with the 1st Brigade Intelligence Officer.

The third day over An Najaf, we received a report of a large grouping of artillery pieces and ammo trucks behind enemy lines. Once again, we were asked to confirm or deny the report. This time we were given the order that we were to take them out if we saw them.

The artillery pieces and ammo trucks were hidden in a long, rectangular, forested park. We flew in and found the targets; we lit up

*the ammo trucks and called in the Air Force. The Air Force was re-
luctant to drop because it was too close to the civilian population so
we resorted to ground artillery.*

*That was when Mike's strength as a former infantryman became
evident. He knew infantry tactics and procedures, and calling for artillery was one of those tactics. It's very difficult for the left-seater to
keep his head down, looking at a map, while the pilot flies erratically
to avoid ground fire. It's kind of like trying to read a book on a
roller coaster, the difference being there's little room for error. An
incorrect location results in the deaths of friendly forces or innocent
civilians. Even though it was pretty hectic, Mike was able to pin-
point the location on the map and pass on those grid coordinates
for the artillery to fire on. He was busy doing that and running the
radios but was still able to get off the artillery call for fire. We were
able to destroy most of that equipment. We didn't receive much fire
that day and we expended about two thousand rounds of .50 cal
and forty-nine rockets or so into that area. We carried five hundred
rounds of .50 cal and seven rockets at a time; once that was gone,
we'd switch out with another team and go back to get gas and more
ammunition. It was a pretty busy day.*

*At the end of the day, Mike happened to mention that it was
Kate's birthday and asked if it was okay if we dropped in on her camp.
Since we were done with the mission, I saw no problem with it. Mike
asked Lt. Strye, our team's air mission commander, for approval. She
quickly agreed, then called in our intentions to our headquarters.
The rotor wash from the aircraft created a large dust cloud as we
landed. We set down outside their perimeter and Mike climbed over
the berm to talk to Kate. It was good to see them give each other a
hug, good to see someone get to be with his wife on her birthday.*

From An Najaf, the 2/17 moved to Karbala, another city where the
resistance remained strong. They spent the first two weeks of April
2003 dodging bullets and RPGs. Tim and Mike's first mission over
Karbala was the worst of the war, and they came very close to being
shot down. The 1st Brigade was airlifting troops into the city as well
as assaulting it with ground troops. The plan was a coordinated attack on different sections of the city. The city was big enough that the
squadron used all three air troops to support the ground forces. Here's
how Tim remembers it:

The mission started with Mike and me conducting reconnaissance for a landing location for a sortie of Black Hawks. The city was divided into sectors for support. Our troop was given the eastern side of the city, conducting the reconnaissance for the Black Hawks and also supporting the southern ground assault.

U.S. forces arrived simultaneously, enclosing the city and pressing forward into the urban areas.

As Mike and I began the mission, all was quiet; the enemy forces were waiting for our ground forces to get into the city before engaging us. Their plan was to get us bogged down in an unwinnable urban fight.

Our first combat engagement came as we overheard a radio call from two Humvees, one of which had hit a land mine. I believe there was one dead, one seriously injured, and several okay but shaken. As we arrived, Mike was instrumental in assisting the vehicles in finding their way out of the minefield. Our specific mission was to provide over-watch for our guys on the ground and identify any enemy forces that might attempt to ambush them. The ground forces moved all personnel from the destroyed vehicle to the intact vehicle and proceeded to get out of the area. They reported taking small arms fire; however, we later determined that it was the ammunition from the burning vehicle exploding—secondary explosions. No ambush had occurred. We escorted them back to friendly locations and continued our mission.

After assisting the vehicle out of the mined area we continued to fly through our sector conducting reconnaissance ahead of our forces. I remember it was getting quite hot that day, probably in the mid to upper nineties. The ground troops were pushing hard and were having difficulty getting water resupply. Mike commented on the difficulty of having to run through the city with all their gear on. He had been there himself once.

J. C. Carter's aircraft was having maintenance problems due to the heat, as were several aircraft that day. We returned to the Forward Ammunition/Refuel Point to attempt repairs. Carter's Kiowa was deemed irreparable, so Mike and I picked up another. We went back into the city and continued the mission.

Meanwhile, in the sector to our north, Scott White and his team had come under fire from an enemy stronghold. They proceeded to pound away at the enemy stronghold. Black smoke arose from the target area as we watched their aircraft make several passes at the enemy's location. Mike and I could hear their conversations on the radio and could see their aircraft just north of our sector.

At that time we received a frantic call from a ground unit within our sector that had come under sniper and sporadic ground fire. The soldier on the ground sounded excited, stressed, and young. As a former infantryman, Mike understood the uncertainty of not knowing what you were up against, and he helped translate what the guy on the other end of the radio was going through.

Prior to the mission, the crews involved had set up boundaries using map coordinates and prominent geographical features or landmarks (mosques, traffic circles, cemeteries, major roads, etc.). Each team had a sector of responsibility and was under orders not to cross into another team's sector. The call from the ground unit under fire was on one of those boundaries, a road running east to west.

We could hear and see the teams to the north engaging the enemy stronghold and decided to work our way toward the ground unit. As Mike and I talked through the plan, we decided to use sweeping flight paths each time, edging closer to the area and attempting to identify the enemy positions shooting at our forces. What we didn't know was that the enemy stronghold to the north continued all the way into our sector, and it was the southern tip of that enemy stronghold that was firing on our ground forces.

Mike and I continued our flight paths unscathed, not seeing any enemy activity except that to the north. As we moved closer, Mike talked with the ground elements and asked them to identify the specific area from which they were receiving fire. Mike then showed me where the ground elements were and where the suspected enemy units were. As he talked to the ground elements, I let our wingman know what the situation was and what our plan was for dealing with it.

We made several passes drawing no fire, seeing no enemy. It was common for us to attempt to draw fire from the enemy, which helped the ground units to identify them as well. We made one lower, fast pass in an attempt to identify the enemy position, and suddenly the buildings came alive with fire. They had waited until we were right on top of them.

The buildings were small, two-story adobe type dwellings, no different from what we had been flying over all morning. The build-

ings were set close to each other, with small alleys between them. There were narrow roads in the front and small courtyards in the back. Unknown to us, the fighters were moving through the courtyards and alleys and then onto the roof stairwells and into second-story windows.

We heard the burst of fire, followed by the thud and ting of bullets hitting the aircraft. Mike and I immediately looked at each other, half to see if the other was all right, half out of the surprise of being hit. We conducted a quick analysis of the aircraft systems and found that all instrument indications were normal, meaning no vital components were hit. Mike got on the radio and told the guys on the ground about the hostiles and then radioed headquarters to fill them in. The friendly ground forces were moving into that location and we continued to support their movement.

One of the governing rules of armed reconnaissance is to not get so wrapped up in one area that you leave the remaining areas unattended. Lt. Col. Schiller ordered artillery and air strikes on the area and additionally ordered us back to center sector, avoiding any seam infractions by the two adjoining friendly ground units. The concern was having too many air assets on one targeted area, leaving the southern part of the city without Kiowa support.

As we proceeded back to the center of our sector we came across a soccer field, similar to a small city stadium, surrounded by twelve-foot concrete walls. At first look it was empty. Then Mike noticed, tucked away under trees and against concrete walls, two work trucks loaded with ammunition. We again proceeded to contact ground forces who were in the area. We attempted to engage the truck, and though we hit the trucks with our machine gun, we couldn't hit the ammunition tucked up under the trees. Mike then called in the ground guys to the area. He provided a "set of vertical eyes" for the ground troops: He looked around the corner they were approaching, telling them what to expect. He told them what was on the roof of a building that they were scurrying to next. His assistance gave them a sense of security.

Mike directed the ground troops through the streets and into the stadium. The ground troops then engaged and blew up the trucks. Enemy fighters had rat-holed ammunition all through the city; Mike's find that day took away a good piece of it.

After flying over the city of Karbala for nearly eight and a half hours, we were told to return to base; another air troop would relieve us. We were exuberant and tired. Mike was all smiles and much more talkative and animated than usual after a mission. We gathered around the aircraft with the rest of the pilots and realized that we had literally dodged a bullet. A postflight inspection of the aircraft revealed over ten bullet holes, several of which took the aircraft out of action for the next several months.

In the second half of April, Mike and Tim flew some of their last combat missions together. They flew over Al Hillah for a couple of days, but Mike saw little action. He was bumped from the cockpit by a senior officer and didn't like it.

It was an off day for Banshee Troop. The 3rd Infantry Brigade was not going into the city until the next day, and Alpha Troop was assigned to do the pre-mission reconnaissance. Despite having the day off, Banshee Troop prepared for every day the same way. While the crew chiefs worked on the birds, Tim and the other pilots in command assigned crews and aircraft and reviewed intelligence briefs and operational plans. They were always ready to go, if needed.

As the communications officer, Mike had to make sure all the radios were up and running. Keeping the sand out of the radios was a constant battle. In any downtime between flights, Mike and Tim would clean the sand out of the aircraft with their crew chief, Specialist Johnny Salvador, whom everyone called Sal. He was a native of Guam, and his work ethic made him one of Mike's favorite soldiers. "You can count on him to get it fixed fast and right," Mike always said.

They'd remove the doors and, using paintbrushes, clean as much sand and dust as possible out of the components. Tim recalls how Mike would put on his headphones and sing country songs while he was working.

Mike spent the first day of Al Hillah doing maintenance on B Troop's ground radios. A captain who had been working with the 2nd Infantry Brigade rejoined the squadron, and since Mike was working on the radios, Tim switched him and the senior officer. Mike didn't seem to mind—at first. Then, as Tim told me, things got exciting.

Shortly after A Troop took off, the radios came alive. A Troop was taking heavy fire from wooded areas outside Al Hillah. We were told to "spin up" and stand by: engines running, blades turning. When Mike saw Capt. Wiernusz join me in the cockpit, his demeanor changed quickly. He wanted in on the mission. I could see the disappointment and frustration in his eyes. He hadn't said anything to me up to that point, but then he calmly came over and asked, "Am I sitting this one out?" I explained to him that it had nothing to do with his performance; in fact, he had been stellar up to that point. It was a decision made to circumstances.

Alpha Troop's aircraft came limping back in. One had been hit by small arms fire and smoke was pouring from its engine. Another had been shot through the crew station in an intense, short-range firefight. Yet another had taken direct hits to the main rotor system. Remarkably, all crews returned safely.

Capt. Wiernusz and I took off with J.C. and Lt. Strye as our wingman. Due to the early enemy contact, 3rd Brigade was moving up, considering an option of starting the offensive a day earlier than planned. Once again, our team found itself in the heat of it, ahead of the friendly forces. We approached Al Hillah from the south and were assigned the eastern outskirts of the city. The area we flew over was forested and sparsely populated. Large power lines ran into the city from the southeast. In some places we flew over them; others were high enough that we could fly under them.

The enemy had switched tactics and moved out of the city, setting up strong points in remote areas. Proceeding to the east, approximately five miles from the city, we began to receive fire. This time I was not so fortunate. My fuel tank was hit and onboard systems told me that my fuel pump was failing. We continued another thirty minutes, destroying several enemy-held buildings with our rockets and calling in artillery on other enemy locations.

When we returned, I could see the anger and anguish in Mike's face. He wanted to be there, to be part of it. But he quickly got over it, and we moved on to Baghdad.

The stress of nonstop flying over lethal urban areas was making itself known. Baghdad had fallen a week earlier, but sporadic resistance remained, and the Cav flew most of its missions in support of ground units securing remote areas of the city. Flying combat missions for three weeks straight in triple-digit heat took its toll. Tim began to get short with both J.C. and Lt. Strye, and Mike was on the receiving end of that as well. They disagreed over tactical flight profiles and troubles with aircraft equipment. "But the disagreements didn't last long," Tim said. "We'd talk it through and get past it. We all knew what we'd been up against."

Baghdad was relatively tame compared to the first three cities. Mike and Tim hadn't flown over Baghdad for too many days when they received orders to fly farther north. They flew a few more missions together, primarily searching for caches of weapons and munitions. Mike had been a pilot-in-command in Korea, and after passing an academic and flight evaluation, he began to fly with other crew members—only now he was the one in charge.

On April 30, Mike dashed off a quick note to my father. In it he asked after our dog, Scout, and revealed his pride at the Kiowa's abilities as well as his optimism that he'd be home that summer. He also referred to the news that my sister Anna had filed for divorce after ten years of marriage. I left in the run-on sentences—Mike wrote like he flew, fast and furious.

Dear Steve,

How are you and my number one son? I'm doing fine by the time you get this the war will be over and I will be a pilot-in-command again. Thanks a lot for the letters and packages and all the other things you are doing and have done. It has made it possible for us to concentrate on our tasks over here.

There are all kinds of rumors about when we will be home. I'm sure Kate has given you some dates via email but if she hasn't here are a few shithouse lawyer guesses. Some have said as early as 1 June and others before Labor Day. The Colonel said we should be standing on the parade field by 4 July. I put more hope in the last date and it seems to be the most realistic. Don't tell anybody for fear it may cause trouble if we don't get home by the 4th. Oh yeah I nearly forgot I am betting the 15th of June (I don't know why just optimistic).

This isn't far from the truth but the OH-58D really won the war because of its low flying abilities over the cities. I was over almost every city in the Army's sector (before ground forces) from the border to Baghdad. I have lots of stories and pictures and beer to drink with you, all while the steaks are cooking and I'm petting ol' Scout on the back deck. Tell Anna that I am sorry and I feel the worst for those girls and they are all in my prayers.

          P.S. I received the Scout pics. Thanks again!
          Love, Mike

CHAPTER 17

HARVEST

IN THE EARLY MORNING HOURS of April 28, I was at my usual post in the TOC, which we'd set up in a huge concrete hangar. It had been a slow night. The 101st, which was now at full strength up north, had managed to head off a good deal of looting in the city. The 2nd Brigade Combat Team, after skirmishing with opposition forces, had secured Mosul enough that our convoys were moving unmolested through the streets. The 1st Brigade, which my battalion was attached to, was responsible for the rural areas, encompassing dozens of villages and towns.

The 101st's major missions had turned to peacekeeping and nation building. Northern Iraq is a crazy quilt of different ethnic groups, and the 101st's division commander, Maj. Gen. David H. Petraeus, was working with the Arabs, Assyrians, and Kurds to create an interim provincial government. Our engineers were putting in water pipes to bring fresh water to villages, many for the first time; working to restore electricity; distributing propane; and building and stocking hospitals and schools.

Most of my time was taken up with personnel issues and monitoring the brigade's movements. But the exciting stuff seemed to be behind us.

That night, I was trolling the Internet for news for the latest edition of the *Sandy Club Gazette* when I switched over to check my e-mail. I saw a message marked *urgent* from Cheryl Blaise, Mike's stepmother. I opened it up, and my heart flip-flopped. Grampy had had a heart attack and was in intensive care in Columbia. He was scheduled to undergo a triple bypass and an aortic valve replacement—major surgery made even more major by the fact that he was eighty-six.

It was hard to fathom Grampy lying in a hospital bed, helpless and perhaps dying—he seemed as permanent as the earth itself. Like Mike, Grampy wasn't a big writer; I'd received several greeting cards from him on which he'd written a few sentences along the lines of "The great-grandkids were out to see me today." Still, Mike and I had heard how deeply worried he was about us. Now Grampy was the one in danger, and we were thousands of miles away.

The Cav was ensconced at Stetson Assembly Area, a makeshift base in a wheat field overlooking Mosul that didn't have Internet access. Mike and I talked regularly now that things had quieted down some, and I picked up the phone to call him, dreading his reaction. His happy hello fell off into silence as he absorbed the news. When he finally spoke, his voice was suffused with emotion. He asked me for details, but I knew little. I could tell he was scared, so I just kept repeating, "Everything's fine. Cheryl said he was doing okay."

The next day, Mike called me at the TOC. "My troop commander is letting me come down for a day on a convoy," he said. "He knows how close Grampy and I are, and he thought I could use some downtime."

I hadn't seen Mike since his surprise appearance on my birthday two months earlier. I was excited to lay eyes on him, yet sad that it had to be under these circumstances.

I met Mike's convoy in the late morning, after my shift. He jumped out of a cargo truck, a far skinnier version of the man I'd last seen. But then I'd lost weight as well. "Hey, Chubs," he joked as he scrambled into the Humvee. He was wearing his flight suit and a floppy desert hat just like mine. As we drove back to camp he barraged me with questions: Had I heard anything more from home? What were Cheryl's exact words? How did his surgery go? The weight of concern sat around our necks like lead collars.

We drove straight to the TOC, where we called home on the unit satellite phone to get the latest news. We talked to Terry, pressing our ears together so we could both hear.

"Grampy came through the surgery like a trouper," Terry said. "He's recovering and doing well. He's going to be released in about a week, but everything looks good. He'll stay with Dale and Linda until he's up and around."

Mike and I grinned at each other with relief. Grampy was going to be okay.

We returned to my house on the cement slab and settled into folding chairs on our porch to talk. Sgt. Mac wasn't there. Now that the temperatures were routinely in the triple digits, he'd taken to sleeping in an underground bunker where it was about twenty degrees cooler. I preferred to sleep in the tent—after spending twelve hours a day in a giant cement hangar, I needed to be outside, no matter how hot it was. After my shift I'd collapse on my cot, trying not to think about all those years of easy-access air conditioning, and try in vain to sleep. Finally, after an hour of sweating and sipping warm water to lubricate my dusty throat, I would pass out.

Within minutes Sgt. Mac showed up, and I introduced them—he and Mike had met only briefly before we deployed. I'd spoken to each of them about the other, so they felt as if they knew each other.

Mike and I needed some time alone to talk about Grampy, so I said we were going to go inside and play cards. "Can I join in?" Sgt. Mac asked eagerly. I couldn't say no—it was his house, too—so the three of us played a few rounds of spades while Mike cast me amused looks. I'd gotten used to losing my privacy, but it was harder to give it up on those rare occasions when Mike was around.

After cards Mike and I found Jesse White at his shop, and we headed to the chow hall for dinner, where Army cooks heated up mass quantities of MREs, such as beef and noodles and burritos. We pulled up chairs at the outdoor "café" the battalion had set up using plastic chairs and tables bought in Mosul. After dinner, Jesse grabbed his digital camera and took a picture of Mike and me standing in the middle of Q-West with our floppy hats on. Back at the TOC, I forwarded the picture to Mike's cousin Stephanie to take to the hospital.

She wrote back, "This looks like that painting *American Gothic*, only you have M-4s instead of pitchforks." She nicknamed the photo *Iraqi Gothic* and taped it to a wall in Grampy's room where he could see it.

(*Iraqi Gothic* became rather famous back home. Since Mike had gone to school in Atlanta, a family friend decided to blow up the photo and put it on a float for Atlanta's annual summer parade. The giant photo was surrounded by stripes of red, white, and blue tissue paper. The handwritten words *Our Heroes* were glued above it and *Mike & Kate Blaise* were affixed underneath. The billboard-size display was mounted on a small trailer adorned with patriotic streamers and banners and pulled behind a pickup. Kids sat on the trailer waving American flags, and the float won first place.)

Mike sat in the TOC with me that night. While I was working, he used my e-mail account to talk to folks back home and search the Internet for truck parts. We had dropped his precious '70 Chevy at a body shop before leaving for Iraq, and he was excited to see what it would look like when completed.

When Mike left that night he looked refreshed and upbeat. We were confident that Grampy was going to pull through.

———

On May 1, I went to yahoo.com and saw a photo of President Bush on the USS *Abraham Lincoln*. He'd landed on the aircraft carrier in a fighter jet and declared an end to major combat operations. A banner behind him famously read, MISSION ACCOMPLISHED. This wouldn't quite be the case, of course, but at the time, the war seemed to be winding down.

Local politics were keeping the 101st busy, and the foremost issue was the impending harvest. Our allies, the peshmerga Kurds, were intent on reclaiming land that the Ba'ath party had confiscated and given to Iraqi Arabs. Wheat and barley grown on that land was ready to be harvested, and since the Iraqi Arabs had paid for and tended the crop, they were loath to give it up. My boss, Lt. Col. Gamble, was one of the senior officers helping to broker an agreement. He spent many evenings at the homes of various Iraqi officials, sipping tepid brown water straight from the Tigris and eating what he called sheep "ass-flap": the fatty part of the sheep's rear end, stewed and served as a local delicacy.

On May 7, I got an e-mail from Dad. "I talked to Terry a while ago and Grampy seems to be doing well. He is already out of ICU, about two days early. He is pretty tired according to Terry, but who wouldn't be? Terry says he is going to Linda's when he comes home." Then he added: "Stay safe, don't let your guard down, this thing is not over yet, and may be getting ready to enter a new phase."

It was as if he could see what was coming, as if he knew that someday U.S. forces would look back ruefully on these early days, when a wheat harvest was one of our biggest concerns.

On May 10, in the farming village of Makhmur, the Kurds and Arabs signed an agreement that called for splitting the profits from the sale of the crops. Anyone who owned a combine could bid to harvest the crop at a particular field. "At one point there was talk that I would have to climb up in the combine and harvest all the wheat," I wrote in a mass e-mail. "Apparently, everyone assumes that I know how to run a combine—I don't think I would have had much luck, but at least I have been in one, which is more than most can say."

Five days later, as our sixth wedding anniversary approached, Mike called with a great idea. "I have two days of downtime coming up," he said. "Is there any way you can hitch a ride to Mosul to spend the night with me in our sector of the city?"

It just so happened that Sgt. First Class Wilson and I had a meeting the next day at brigade headquarters at Mosul's airport, which the 101st had commandeered for its air assets. The meeting was a bureaucratic hoedown for all personnel officers and NCOs in the 101st, and would cover such topics as how the division planned to handle the new R and R trip program, emergency leave, and awards submissions.

"I'll pick you up there," Mike said. "I can guarantee you a Kiowa ride home to Q-West early the next morning, but you'd have to miss a night of work."

"I'll make it happen," I replied.

"And don't worry about sleeping arrangements—I'll set us up a tent at the edge of camp."

I asked Tony Boniface, the day battle captain, if he could take my shift, and he readily agreed, even though it meant he'd be on for twenty-four hours. Things had been fairly slow, so he said he could bring his cot into the TOC and sleep during the night while Sgt. Mac kept things rolling, waking him if he needed to.

Next I had to secure the approval of my immediate supervisor. Maj. Suqi was a bit reluctant—such a request was completely unorthodox, not to mention risky—but in the end he agreed. With a caveat: "Lieutenant Colonel Gamble has to give you the green light."

I headed to Lt. Col. Gamble's desk in the TOC to ask permission. He was the big cheese, and he could be tough. One of the NCOs had traded some MREs to an Iraqi for a donkey ride, and when Lt. Col. Gamble found out he blew a gasket and chewed the soldier out royally. The boss and I had a pretty good relationship, but I knew that this was not a normal request. It was like taking a day off from the war to goof off. No one else got this opportunity, but I figured I had to at least ask.

I found Lt. Col. Gamble working in the TOC as usual. "Sir, I was wondering if I could interrupt for a minute."

He seemed a bit distracted as I made my request, fingers crossed.

He gave me a brief grilling: "Where exactly will you be going? How will you get picked up in Mosul?" I felt like a teenager asking her dad for permission to go on her first date. In the end he acquiesced. "I don't see why it would be a problem, since you have to be in Mosul anyway."

"Thank you, sir!"

The next morning after my shift I caught a ride with a convoy into the city. It was one of my first ventures off post, and I was almost as excited at the prospect of seeing the real Iraq as I was at seeing Mike.

As the convoy entered Mosul, we passed under a magnificent archway supported by massive stone columns; it looked like the entrance to an ancient temple. That was the architectural high point, from what I saw. Mud homes stacked into hillsides loomed up from the roadsides, and trash was heaped everywhere. The streets zigzagged randomly, reminding me of older sections of Seoul. We soon rolled into the airport, where a tent city was springing up. The Army camp was dusty, and a nasty stench drifted up from the Tigris. When the rainy season hits, I thought, this place will become an even bigger dump. I took a moment to thank God for placing me at Q-West.

I'd heard rumors that the Cav was going to relocate either to this airport or to Q-West, where our battalion was based. The Kiowa pilots hoped to move to Q-West, and none more than Mike. What an amazing piece of luck: to find ourselves neighbors.

Mike was waiting for me in a Humvee at the main doors to the airport terminal, along with another pilot named Coop. Before long he was negotiating the twisting, turning city streets with the assurance of someone who'd driven them before. At one point, he said, "We have to make a stop and pick up some soda for the crew chiefs."

He pulled over at a small store on the side of the road. It looked like any convenience store you'd find in the States—outside were racks of candy bars and a cooler of ice cream bars—except for the racks of Iraqi head scarves and sandals. I had heard nothing but the dangers of making oneself an easy target, how the enemy looked like innocent Iraqi citizens. Mike must have seen the look on my face because he quickly added, "Don't worry; we stop here all the time. You want some ice cream?"

Of course I wanted ice cream.

Mike and Coop hopped out and entered the store while I stayed with the Humvee. Car theft was a big problem, so I stood guard with my weapon in case someone wanted to take it for a spin.

Soon they returned with their arms full of soda, ice cream, and chocolate bars. Mike had bought me a black head scarf printed with red hearts, and he laughed as he tossed it to me—he knew how much I hated hearts.

The store's owner followed them out, children trailing behind him. I spotted movement in a second-story window and looked up to see two women peering down from behind a curtain.

The owner was a portly man with glasses and a mustache, dressed in a striped shirt and loose cotton pants. He had seven boys ages four to seventeen and a little girl who looked to be about two. One of the older sons spoke decent English, and he served as translator. Mike and Coop conversed with the father and the older kids while I entertained the small ones. The little girl peeked from behind her father's leg, her eyes as big as quarters. With my pale skin and light eyes, I struck the children as rather unusual looking. The Iraqis boys gestured for me to take off my helmet—they wanted to see my hair color. When I did as they asked, they looked a bit disappointed; I think they'd hoped I'd be a blond.

Grampy was never far from my mind, and their curiosity reminded me of an episode at his farm the previous summer. Mike and I had gone over for dinner and cards, and when we arrived, some Amish workers were there, putting a new roof on the house. Grampy was sitting outside smoking his pipe and chatting to the workers, a family he'd known for years. One of the men had brought his six-year-old son. I was wearing shorts, sandals, and a short-sleeved shirt—hardly typical attire for Amish women—and that little boy was so intrigued by me he could hardly walk up the ladder, which made Grampy chuckle. I didn't have to come to Iraq to be considered an oddity.

While I was being ogled like a rare butterfly on the end of a pin, the older boys were giving Mike the third degree about his personal life. The sons asked him if he was married. He nodded his head and introduced me. Their jaws almost hit the dirt.

"How long have you been married?" the boy asked.

"Almost six years," Mike said.

"Do you have children?"

"No, not yet."

"You have been married for almost six years without children?" The father and his sons looked at one another and shook their heads. In fact, our childlessness caused quite a bit of consternation among the menfolk. They continued to shake their heads and press the subject. "What a shame," the storekeeper repeated time and again. "I have many children. I am so proud."

It turned out he had three more daughters for a total of eleven children, as well as two wives, whom I'd glimpsed in the window. The father recruited a kid from another family to take their photo with us. Before we took off, one of the boys presented me with a small denomination Iraqi bill, which had the former dictator's picture on it. This was something of a hot commodity among the soldiers in my unit. We drove off, Saddam's face clenched tightly in my fist.

We bumped along a dirt road that ascended into hills. About ten minutes later Mike pulled to a stop at the edge of a field. Acres of tall wheat, golden in the afternoon sun, swayed in the warm breeze. "Wow, it's so different here," I said, hopping out. "It reminds me of home." The wheat was ripe enough to harvest, and I could have been on Dad's farm running my hands lightly along the brittle kernels. Kiowas dotted the hillside, attended to by enlisted crews in desert camouflage uniforms. Pilots in flight suits sat on MRE boxes and smoked or played cards. Another troop was encamped on the next bluff over, and then another and another.

Mike gave me a tour of the camp. Banshee Troop slept in two large tents, one for the pilots and one for the crew chiefs. A smaller tent in the middle served as a dining hall, briefing room, and makeshift theater with an overhead projector. "We show movies on the side of the tent," Mike said. Then I spotted Scott and Big Country. They gave me large, manly hugs and sat me down to share news from home. Scott said Sonja was lonely and worried but holding up. Then they asked about what I was doing, where I was, how the war was going from my perspective. "We're making progress," I said, "but the citizens seem as if they won't be able to relax until Saddam and his sons are dead or captured. We have a long way to go."

Accustomed to sleeping during the day, I'd been up for almost twenty-four hours. "I could use a nap," I said. So Mike led me to the pilots' tent. He didn't have to tell me which cot was his. Like me, he had been overwhelmed with care packages from home, and his cot was stacked with open boxes overflowing with beef jerky and Hot Tamales. "Don't worry, I'll put up a tent for us tonight," he said again.

"What would General Petraeus say?" I said and laughed. I was referring to the major general's edict that banned fraternization between soldiers. Sexual relations can lead to all sorts of drama—love triangles, fistfights, pregnancy, which is an automatic ticket home (for the woman, anyway). Maj. Gen. Petraeus felt such distractions could be detrimental to the war effort. Such a rule is next to impossible to enforce, and I wondered how they'd handle the gray area of punishing two soldiers who happened to be married to each other.

Mike cleared a space on his cot and gave me his headphones for the minidisc recorder I had gotten him before we left. He had made a disc of some of his favorite songs by Alan Jackson, Chely Wright, and Travis Tritt. Mike could make do without a lot of things, but country music wasn't one of them.

"I'll wake you up when the insect wars start," he said. "You won't want to miss 'em."

Iraq is home to some of the nastiest critters on earth. One of the most notorious is the camel spider. If looks could kill, this creature could have won the war single-handedly. Camel spiders are ugly in a science-fiction, aliens-attacking-Earth sort of way. They have hairy bodies, long spindly legs, and nasty pincers, though fortunately their bite, while painful, isn't poisonous. They're not spiders at all but an exotic type of arachnid. They grow to the size of a man's hand, and they're fast—they can sprint at a speed of ten miles per hour, though they seem completely incapable of climbing. I'd gotten my first glimpse of these nasty guys while driving through the southern deserts. Camel spiders like dark places, and Sgt. Mac and I soon learned to shake out our clothes and combat boots before putting them on.

After an hour or so Mike gently shook me awake, and we walked to the center tent. Like men at a cockfight, the enlisted soldiers had crowded around a spot on the ground. Scott had donated a huge camel spider that he'd discovered in his sleeping bag to his crew chief. One of the other crew chiefs had a small black scorpion in a jar. Apparently the scorpion was the champion, the camel spider the challenger. Whichever one was left standing at the end of the round got to come back the following day.

The camel spider proved to be easily intimidated. It kept trying to run away, but the scorpion stung it again and again until the larger critter expired. I laughed and cheered like everybody else—any kind of entertainment was appreciated. Besides, one less camel spider was always something to applaud.

After the epic battle, we sat outside on the ground for a dinner of cold MREs with Scott and Big Country. We talked shop, and the guys were interested to hear my side of the war—they didn't get many new people or stories. They said they'd been flying the same type of missions over Mosul as they had over the southern cities but receiving far less return fire. Their biggest hazard was the millions of electrical wires strung all over the city like a lethal web.

Afterward we stayed up to watch a movie under a full moon. I can't remember the movie—I was too busy trying to stay awake. Finally Mike said, "You've got to see the city at night." We walked to the edge of the hill and gazed down at the intricate lacework of lights. I thought back to our first date, when he had suggested we drive around town and look at the Christmas lights. It seemed like another lifetime, when we could never have guessed we'd be married, let alone married in a war zone.

Between the lights and the conversations and the stargazing, Mike and I stayed up so late that we didn't have time to put up a tent. But I could tell by the look in my husband's eyes that he would not be deterred. He walked over to one of the big cargo trucks, peered inside to find it empty, and said, "This'll do." As I watched in amusement, he grabbed air mattresses and blankets to cushion us from the ridged floorboards. I hopped up and over the tailgate while Mike climbed in behind me. The sides and roof were covered with canvas but the back end was open to the moon and stars.

Mike's dog tags jangled as he arranged our makeshift bed. I saw he was also wearing a small silver medallion around his neck. It had a shield with a cross on one side and an inscription on the other.

"Where'd you get that?" I asked.

"A disabled veterans group back in the States sent them to the entire squadron," he said. He held it up as if to read the inscription, but I could tell he knew it by heart: " 'Be strong and courageous. Do not be terrified; do not be discouraged, for the Lord your God will be with you wherever you go. Joshua 1:9.' "

"I like that. Do you wear it a lot?"

"I never take it off except when I shower."

"I never take mine off, either," I said, fingering his wedding ring on my dog tags.

Afterward we curled up together and fell immediately to sleep, blessed to have this privacy, these stolen hours in the midst of chaos and confusion.

The next morning we woke up early so I could catch the Kiowa back to Q-West. I climbed out of the truck and walked through camp, trying to ignore the knowing grins everyone tossed my way. My pilot, Jeff, had to bring the aircraft there to pick up the chaplain and bring him back for services, so it all worked out perfectly. Mike adjusted his flight gear to fit me as best he could. His large helmet made me look as if I had a melon on my shoulders, and he got endless amusement out of watching the helmet bob back and forth as I walked. We took some pictures for the family back home, and he threw my gear inside. He grabbed me up in a hug, kissed me, and buckled me into the aircraft. We took off and I watched him wave good-bye.

My second ride in a Kiowa was short but fascinating. Jeff pointed out villages and ridgelines that I had seen only on our maps. There is something about seeing the land from on high; the distance puts every aspect of the landscape into perspective and you can finally see where you are. Jeff dropped me off fairly close to our area, and I walked to the TOC to report in.

Somewhere between the airfield and the TOC, I ran into Maj. Suqi. He laughed when he saw me. "Hey, Kate, you did ask the BC if you could go up there and spend the night, didn't you?" I looked at him blankly. "Yes, sir, of course I did."

"Well, somehow his wires got crossed, because last night when you weren't here for your shift he got ticked off. You'd better go talk to him right away."

I had that queasy feeling in my stomach like when you're sent to the principal's office for a sin you didn't commit. I threw my gear in my tent and went to find Lt. Col. Gamble. I hated the thought that he might be upset with me, but at the same time I knew I had asked his permission. I found him doing paperwork in the TOC.

"Sir, I hope you know that I am not the type of soldier to go off half-cocked and not tell you the whole story. I absolutely would not have gone if I didn't think I had your permission."

Lt. Col. Gamble tossed his pen on the table and settled back in his chair. "Well, that's basically the conclusion I came to. I must not have been paying close enough attention because I thought you were flying back last night, not this morning. But now you're back. So how's Mike doing?"

"He's great, sir." I filled him in on what the Cav had been up to in Mosul and headed back to my house to get some sleep before my shift.

While I was visiting Mike, Grampy was being discharged from the hospital. On May 18, I called Dale and Linda's house, but no one was home, so I left a message on their answering machine. I couldn't have known this, but they were on their way back to the hospital—Grampy was having stomach trouble. I got an e-mail later that night from Linda telling me how upset Grampy had been to miss my call.

The diagnosis this time was a herniated bowel. Grampy had more surgery, and he seemed to be recovering. Suddenly his health began to deteriorate. He needed another operation, but the doctors told the family it probably wouldn't help. They should prepare themselves to lose him.

Terry called the Red Cross to contact Mike so he could come home on emergency leave. The worker he talked to was less than helpful. She had unilaterally elevated her job from passing on the message to deciding for the Army who would get to come home or not. She told Terry that "soldiers couldn't come home for just anything, and after all, it was only his grandfather." Several phone calls and almost two days later he finally got the message passed by telling her that Grampy had practically raised Mike. I knew my chances of getting sent home were slim to none. The Army allows soldiers to return home from a combat zone only for immediate family. But I had to try. I approached Lt. Col. Gamble in the TOC, and with a big lump in my throat I asked him if it was possible. I was known as the completely unemotional type, and when Lt. Col. Gamble saw how upset up I was, he stared at me with shocked surprise. Then he turned me down.

"Kate, I would love to be able to send you home," he said. "I've heard a lot of Grampy stories from you, and I can tell he means a lot to you. But the division won't allow it. I'm sorry."

Not long after Mike left for Missouri, the Cav moved to Q-West. When my husband returned to Iraq, he'd be living only one mile away.

———

Mike had to hitch a ride with a cargo plane to Kuwait and catch a flight from there. He called me before he left, and I could hear the concern in his voice about leaving me behind. "If you need anything while I'm gone, Scottie's just a phone call away," he said. "I'll tell Grampy you love him and he'll see you soon."

A day and a half later, Terry picked Mike up at the airport and brought him straight to the hospital. "Prepare yourself," he told Mike. "This isn't the Grampy you remember."

He was bruised, emaciated, and limp in his bed. Mike took one look and his knees buckled. Terry walked over and woke his father up. "Grampy," he said, "there's somebody here I figure you'll want to see."

Mike walked over to his bedside. When Grampy saw him, his eyes widened and a huge smile creased his gaunt face. Mike sat and held his hand and talked to him for a while, though Grampy couldn't speak because of the respirator. But he didn't have to. The look in his bright blue eyes spoke volumes.

Back in Iraq I called home every night and checked my e-mail obsessively, though I dreaded opening any from home. And I worried about Mike. Not only was he losing the most important person in his life, he was dropping into this tragic situation fresh from full-blown combat with no buffer, no decompression time, like a scuba diver who rises to the surface too quickly and pays a price.

On May 24, Dad sent me this e-mail:

> *Mike came over to the house this morning to check on Scout, who was very glad to see him. He remembered him. Now that Mike has gone, Scout is in a funk! Goodness knows what he will do when you get home.*
>
> *He looks good, Mike, just a lot skinnier. Maybe I should go back as a replacement. I hear you are also thinner. Do remember to eat, even when it is hot.*
>
> *It is raining today so no bean planting. I am going to Hannibal to see your mom. We are trying to arrange a barbecue for tomorrow evening. Mike requests a steak, so he will get it. Wish we could send one your way with all the trimmings. Will keep one on ice till your return and then we will have a heck of a party.*
>
> *Thanks for serving your country. Americans are reminded this*

Memorial Day of all those who have served, especially those who paid the ultimate price. We celebrate rather than mourn, which is probably the way we should look at it.

On May 25, I called the hospital, and Cheryl held the phone to Grampy's ear so I could talk to him. "I love you, Grampy. I miss you," I said, all the while thinking, *I've got to be strong. It's not over yet. I don't want him to think I've given up on him.* Cheryl told me later that Grampy's eyes lit up as soon as I started talking but that he was frustrated that he couldn't talk back.

The inevitable came two days later. I had been calling Cheryl every few hours on her cell phone. This time I got Terry. I could tell by his voice that Grampy was gone.

I called Scott to give him the news. "I'll be there in five minutes," he said.

Scott and I sat outside in the cool night air and hardly said a word. We were both thinking about Mike and wishing we could be there to help him through the loss. For me, Grampy's death was simply un-fathomable. I couldn't imagine home without him. What would happen to the farm, to all the traditions he had anchored all those years? It didn't seem real.

"Kate, I want you to know that Mike gave me strict instructions to look after you," Scott said. "Anything you need, you know I'm here for you." For all my bravado and independence, I did need looking after, and I was glad that Mike understood that.

"Tell me some Grampy stories," Scott said. I described Grampy's house and the kitchen table where he presided over family gatherings. How he always wanted to play cards. How, throughout his marriage to Fern, he would go to auctions for farm machinery but come home with some beautiful old serving bowls, a romantic gesture over a forty-year marriage. Finally, exhausted from remembering, I stood up, rubbed my eyes, and did what I did every night: I went to work.

―――

Grampy's memorial service was held at the Elliott Funeral Home in Atlanta, Missouri, on May 29. Dad wrote me that it took an hour and a half to get through the receiving line, and that it was just as long when he left as when he'd arrived. Grampy was buried in the Blaise family plot at the Shelby Memorial Cemetery, about twenty-five miles from Macon.

On June 4, Mike called to tell me he was back. I hitched a ride over to the Cav's home, which I'd never visited before. Mike was standing outside of the Banshee Troop's area, waiting for me. His troop occupied a small barracks, built around a courtyard. Each room had a tile floor, doors that opened to the outside, and a bathroom with a nonfunctioning shower. Mike and Scott were roommates, and Big Country lived next door.

We went to his room and sat on his bunk to talk. Mike was tired from the marathon trip home. He'd had a few hours to kill in Kuwait, so he'd tracked down his good buddy from Fort Rucker, C. D. Foster, who was heading home from a few months of flying medevac missions in Iraq. "We spent a few hours catching up and had a chew of tobacco together," Mike said. Maybe seeing C.D. was one reason he didn't seem as sad as I thought he would. More than anything, he seemed relieved to be back.

Mike filled me in on his time in Macon. He'd caught up with family and had a long visit with Lindsey. She was about to leave for Kuwait, and he gave her some tips on packing for the sand. Yet as I suspected, his visit had been extremely difficult. He was easily frustrated and quick to anger. "Riding in a car with Dad driving made me a nervous wreck," he told me. "If he had to jerk the wheel to go around another car, it reminded me of being in the air and jerking the aircraft to avoid incoming rounds."

Terry stored Mike's Harley in his garage while he was gone, and Mike rode it every chance he got, enjoying the speed and the freedom. But one day he backed his dad's pickup into the bike, leaving a small dent in the rear fender. He was so mad he almost cried. Later, after he cooled down, Terry broached a subject that had been on his mind. Mike recalled the conversation this way:

"So Dad said, 'You know, Mike, I've been pretty worried about you. I pray that both you and Kate will get home in one piece.' And I said, 'Dad, I don't want you to worry. But I also want you to know that if something does happen to me, that I'm proud to be serving my country, and I'm doing what I love to do.' "

Mike was quiet for a few moments, and then he went on. "Kate, it was great to have a cold beer and a steak, but I kept thinking about you and Scott and how I wished you could've been there to enjoy it with me. I felt split in two. I was grateful to be there, but I couldn't stop thinking about all of my buddies risking their lives while I was at home.

"In a way, I'm glad you didn't come," he continued. "I know it was hard for you to be stuck here, and it would have been nice to have you with me. But I'm thankful you didn't see Grampy looking so sick. You'll always remember him at the farm healthy and happy."

And so I have.

CHAPTER 18

HONEYMOON IN IRAQ

AND SO WE HAVE COME to the central irony of our time in Iraq: It took a war to bring Mike and me together. Of the seven years we were married, we saw more of each other at Q-West than at any time except when we were in Clarksville. Our military union, once defined by stolen moments, coincidental sightings, and long-distance longing, now resembled a normal marriage. We saw each other every day, even if for only fifteen minutes, and we usually ate at least one meal together. We had mutual friends and common interests. We eked out a shared life in the midst of a shared war and created our own version of a family in the process. Granted, we lived on opposite sides of an airfield, but this one-mile buffer was crucial—it never let us forget that, as important as our marriage was to us both, our jobs had to come first.

The possible length of our deployment was a constant source of speculation. Our initial hopes for a June homecoming, based on early, optimistic estimates of the war, were dashed in late May, when the bosses said that September or October was more realistic. Scuttlebutt had us staying as long as February 2004. When the news broke in May that the 3rd Infantry Division, which had been in Iraq eleven months, would be kept in the country longer than anticipated, a collective groan went up across theater. We knew this would likely delay everyone else's homecoming as well. Clearly we were in Iraq for at least the summer.

In mid-June, several commands changed hands as high-level officers were shuffled to new assignments. Our battalion commander, Lt. Col. Gamble, was assigned to division headquarters in Mosul. His replacement, Lt. Col. Jeffrey Kelley, was a fun-loving officer who was crazy about golf. Maj. Whitson, the support operations officer, replaced Maj. Suqi as battalion executive officer. While I hated to see

Maj. Suqi leave, I was excited to be working with one of my best friends in the Army. Since I'd first worked under him at Fort Camp-bell in 2002, Maj. Whitson had become a combination older brother and favorite uncle. He always took time to listen to me, and we could discuss almost anything.

We also had a new S-3 operations officer. Capt. Chip O'Neal, the former company commander for our Charlie Medical Company, was a tough commander with a baby face, a shaved head, and a sarcastic remark for every situation. Chip oversaw the soldiers' training, mak-ing sure they stayed combat ready. During the early days of the war, we'd often met for an MRE supper before the evening brief, and as we talked, we discovered a mutual love for the Army life and culture. Soon he was one of my best buddies. Chip had an offbeat, unpre-dictable sense of humor. At Q-West, he would spend hours at his lap-top, creating briefing slides in which he'd superimpose photos of the staff onto movie posters. I'd be listening to him drone on about range safety when a slide of Han Solo and Princess Leia would pop up, only my head was on Leia's body, and I was kissing the new battalion com-mander, Lt. Col. Kelley.

It was Chip's idea to move out of our tents. By June the tempera-ture was in the nineties at 10:00 A.M. and climbing, and we weren't even into the hottest months yet. Other units had commandeered abandoned buildings on post, and Chip suggested we do the same. "It would be a helluva lot cooler," he said. So while Mike was still on emergency leave in Macon, Chip and I had gone house hunting. After passing on an underground space that was cool but claustrophobic, we found a condemned building near the airfield and the TOC. We picked through the decrepit structure like potential buyers examining the ultimate fixer-upper. This had been one of the newer, nicer build-ings on post until two large bombs fell through the roof. Only half of the building was in ruins, and for some reason it hadn't caught fire, so was quite habitable. Every window was blown out, which provided a refreshing cross breeze. One area had three small garages, giving us each a room to share with a roommate. The garages opened onto a large common area, and a small staircase led to what was left of the roof—perfect for sunbathing. But what sold me on the place—other than the price—was the wide sidewalk that encircled the building (this became our porch) and the olive trees and flowering shrubs that grew out front. "We'll have trees!" I exclaimed.

Our new home was hardly in move-in condition, so we set to work. We cleared rubble for two days and knocked a hole in a wall for a front door. Sgt. Mac had brought a hammock, which we hung between two pillars where the cross breeze was best. We covered the porch with tarps for shade and rummaged through looted bunkers for anything we could use ourselves. We built several benches and a table out of floor tiles and a piece of plywood. We set metal shelves on cinder blocks to store food and water. Sgt. Mac built a latrine over an old septic tank, constructing walls from scavenged boards. (The guys installed a piss tube by the front entrance, but after several unintended exposures, I asked them to put up a privacy screen so I wouldn't have to watch.) Hooks pried off an electrical box came in handy for keeping our equipment off the floor and away from scorpions and camel spiders. (A well-aimed combat boot quickly took care of them.)

Afterward we stood outside and eyed our new home, a Flintstones special.

"It needs a name," said Chip.

"It looks like a big heap of crap to me," I said. "How about calling it 'The Heap'?"

We all agreed. I painted the name on a large rock beside the front door, and wrote "The house that bombs built" underneath.

Six people moved in, two per garage. Sgt. Mac and I continued to share a living space since we worked the same shift. Chip and one of his NCOs, Staff Sgt. Jerry Salyers, took another garage, and Capt. Clay Curtis and his Iraqi interpreter, Abdul, took the other one. Staff Sgt. Salyers was one of the best NCOs in the battalion. He was short, with reddish-blond hair and a no-bullshit attitude. Capt. Curtis, the brigade's medical officer, worked with local communities to set up clinics and hospitals. Abdul, who was from Kirkuk, was quiet and didn't seem to mind living with a woman who was not a relative—surely a novel situation for him. He was about twenty-three years old, college-educated, and was being paid about ten dollars a day. He gave the money to his family; the only thing he ever bought for himself was a small CD player on which he listened to the Backstreet Boys and Islamic prayers.

Living with five men in a bombed-out building was like being the token girl in a ratty frat house. Staff Sgt. Salyers and I kept an ongoing chess game, and Chip and I caught rays on the roof together. I did my best to make The Heap homey. I dug up some flowers from around the building and replanted them in an old ammo box, and filled in the landscape with plants that Ed Sleeper had bought off the locals. I taped up the calendar I'd made in Kuwait, one month per sheet, even the months that were behind us. It was a morale boost to look back at the days we had lived through. Usually I checked off each day at a time, but when I got busy and forgot a few days, I suddenly had an entire block of time to put behind me. I loved that.

All around me I put reminders from home. Dad e-mailed photos of the farm, and I taped them together into a 360-degree panoramic view. I taped photos of Mike, Scout, Grampy, and the rest of my family on one wall and artwork from my five nieces and nephews on another. I ordered shower shoes, towels, an electric razor for Mike, and two small refrigerators off the Internet, one for his room and one for The Heap.

The Cav area where Mike lived was off by itself, near the front gate about a mile from the battalion TOC and The Heap. He shared a small room with Scott. I helped them find some metal shelves for their room, and they set up a camp shower in their "bathroom" so they didn't have to drive to the shower tents. They insulated their room as best they could using plywood, and set up a swamp cooler they'd bought off the local economy. Mike had what Scott called a "floor fetish." The sand was always getting trapped in the cracks between the floor tiles, so eventually they pulled them out, leaving an easy-to-sweep concrete floor.

But the first thing they did was tape up a small poster of the Miller Lite girl. She was a seductive brunette in a white bikini, the name Sofia written in cursive letters below her. They'd pulled the poster out of *Maxim* magazine in Kuwait. Just as I did with my calendar, they took Sofia everywhere, rolling her up and taking her from location to location. Taping her up at each new camp was a ritual. No doubt she reminded Mike of beer, a beverage he was sorely missing. "At least she's a brunette, not a blond," I said when I first saw her. "I know you're not wishing for something you can't have."

In retaliation, I cut out a tiny picture of a male model with killer abs from *People* magazine and taped him near my bed. Every one of my male roommates commented on it. "I can't believe you put that up there!" they'd say, offended, forgetting some of their rooms were wallpapered with semiclad women. Except for Abdul—he didn't decorate much.

Like The Swamp in *M*A*S*H*, The Heap became *the* place to hang out. Lt. Col. Kelley loved it so much that he began hosting biweekly "smokers" for the battalion's officers and senior NCOs there. About thirty of us would sit on benches in the large common area, puff on fat cigars, and drink near beer. By Q-West standards, we were living like royalty.

Today I look at photos of The Heap and can't believe I ever considered that dump a home. I was living without running water, indoor plumbing, air-conditioning, or any other amenity Americans take for granted. Yet at the time, it could have been featured in the home section of the *Army Times*, had the paper had a home section. The Heap was a monument to resourcefulness. Consider the process by which I obtained cold water: I'd get a sock good and wet, pull it over a full water bottle, and leave the bottle sitting out on the porch in a small breeze. Twenty minutes later, as if by magic, the water was icy cold. I learned this trick from some infantry guys on the ground assault convoy to Mosul; they'd tie the socks from their side mirrors so the water bottle inside the sock would cool as they drove.

Early in our residency, we had to evacuate The Heap for two days. The airfield was cratered with unexploded ordnance, which the engineers had to wire and detonate. The Heap was next door to the airfield, close enough that the explosions could jar the walls, which were barely standing as it was. One two thousand–pound bomb was too large to detonate in place, so the engineers gingerly moved it out to the desert and blew it up out there. We could feel the explosions in the TOC. For a millisecond the world would be shaken like a snow globe, but the blast passed so quickly that I might as well have imagined it.

I recounted this and other experiences and hardships in long e-mails to dozens of friends and family back home. The weather was an endless source of material. Dad never let an e-mail go by without a mention of rainfall, temperature, or tornadoes, which were particularly bad that year. I am, after all, my father's daughter. Besides, Iraq's violent and unpredictable climate was hard to ignore, and it wasn't just the heat.

"We have had a lot of 'squalls' here lately," I wrote in June. "Back in the States we call them dust devils, which is basically what they are but bigger and more powerful. For instance, as we waited in the chow line about a week ago, a squall came out of nowhere and completely tore apart the chow tent. Then it was gone. Very strange. No one was hurt, and all you could do was stand and watch it happen."

But that didn't compare to a storm I called "The Big One":

"The day had dawned less sunny than normal and quite cool for a change," I wrote. "I should have guessed that something was up. I worked until noon and then returned to The Heap and headed to the roof for some rays. Chip was already there. We noticed the sky had turned an odd yellowish-green. Now, any good Missouri girl should know that a sky this color means trouble. I mentioned to Chip that in Missouri we'd be battening down the hatches right about now. No sooner had the words left my mouth than the wind began to BLOW, and I mean sticks, large chunks of sand, and debris flying through the air. Chip grabbed his cot and ran for the door—it was very evident by his speed that his thoughts were solely for his own safety. Meanwhile, I struggled to get to the door; it was like walking through water, the wind was blowing so hard. Beyond the roof I could see nothing but a swirling vortex of wind and sand. Finally, I made it inside. . . . Our best guess was that it was a tornado. We had no warning and no idea that Iraq even had tornadoes. You would think the sandstorms would be plague enough for one country. You would also think that a born and bred Missouri girl would recognize the signs, but sometimes you just have to show me.

"Afterward we assessed the damage: ten large Army tents ripped in half or blown away; countless sleeping mats, personal tents, clothes, and three camouflage nets lost; two computers broken; shower tents blown away, leaving men with soapy hair to wonder where their roof had gone; and one junior officer's pride completely shattered, thanks to her failure to predict a dangerous storm."

If the weather was a distraction, food was an obsession. We got one meal a day at the chow tent and ate MREs the rest of the time. "You know you're in the Army and deployed when you walk in and sit down to breakfast and there is a mustard jar on the table," I wrote. "You lift the lid off your food to discover hamburgers, baked beans, and corn. You look around to see if anyone else thinks this is odd and then you grab your drink to find grape juice. Does this make sense to anyone—grape juice and hamburgers for breakfast? I think I may be going crazy."

I sent Dad long lists of food we wanted, from Velveeta to tortellini to dill pickles. Dad passed along our request to friends who wanted to contribute, but our lack of creature comforts left him exasperated, as he wrote to friends: "We are the richest country in the world and we can't provide our troops with decent food? Ridiculous!"

Mike flew mostly at night and I worked at night, so our schedules tended to coincide. I'd get off shift around noon and head to his area, lugging a bag of DVDs and groceries from the care packages that arrived regularly from people I knew and people I didn't. The Cav area was off by itself, so if the Humvee was broken down or in use, someone would take pity on me and either give me a ride or lend me their vehicle.

I'd usually find Mike in his room, listening to music or watching a DVD on Scott's laptop. Mike "Big Country" Young would come over, and we'd hang out and talk about what we'd do after the war. Big Country and his wife were planning to go on a cruise, and I was assigned the task of finding a suitable vacation spot for Scott, Sonja, Mike, and me. "What are you guys looking to do?" I asked Mike and Scott one day.

Mike immediately sounded off. "I don't care where we go, as long as it has the three B's: beer, beach, and bed, all within easy stumbling distance of each other." He and Scott hooted and high-fived, and I had to agree that after a year of brown, gritty sand, the soft, white, powdery kind would feel pretty good.

When dinnertime rolled around, we'd take stock of our grocery situation. All four of us stockpiled certain care-package foods, which we could combine into an improvised meal. I'd contribute canned meat such as tuna fish, Big Country would add a canned vegetable, and Scott would offer up a can of tomato sauce that Sonja had sent him. We'd whip up some concoction on a camp stove I bought on the Internet, and then sit on the bunks and eat together. After dinner Big Country would head next door to his room and crank up the tunes, and Scott would sit and talk with us for a bit. Eventually he'd say something like, "Well, I guess I'd better go check on the radios," and leave the room so Mike and I could have twenty minutes to ourselves. After dinner, Mike would walk me to my Humvee and we would both go back to work.

Sometimes I'd get to the room and Mike would be off flying. In that case I'd take over his cot so I could sleep in the coolness. If I didn't come over, Scott and Big Country would get offended. We'd become a family, and they wanted to see me. Scott liked the fact that if I were in a charitable mood, I'd take their sheets and wash them at The Heap, where we'd installed an Iraqi washing machine. "We have our maid," Scott joked to Sonja in a letter.

I was living on a meager ration of sleep, and some days I'd be so tired that I'd simply run over there, hang out with Mike for ten minutes, and then go home to try and grab a few winks. Or I'd go to The Heap for a nap before heading over. I never blew him off. It was vital that we see each other every day; it was almost our responsibility. We knew how blessed we were to be this close together, and begging off because we were too tired or busy felt like a disservice to those who weren't so lucky as to have their spouses a mile away. Besides, it was the biggest morale boost of the day for both of us.

Living together at Q-West wasn't an option, but even if it had been, Mike and I would have lived apart. Accountability of personnel in units is of the utmost importance, and our bosses needed to know where we were at all times. In The Heap, I was constantly being awakened with a request for my signature or to answer a question. Mike needed to be near his aircraft and his unit in case of an alert or attack. If rounds came in, I didn't want him worrying if I'd taken cover or trying to protect me. If something came up at work that required my full attention, I didn't need the competing lure of Mike at home, waiting for me. He needed to focus on his job, and I needed to focus on mine.

In a conventional marriage, where time together is laid out like a vast banquet there for the taking, it's easy for couples to take each other for granted. Our time together was too precious to squander on squabbling or hard feelings. We could both be cranky or inconsiderate, but we'd talk it through and let it go. Pilots are required to get a certain amount of sleep, but I could go days with only an hour or two. Once in a while, Mike would drop by The Heap and wake me up because he was so excited to see me. In a conventional marriage, I would probably have lost my mind. In a combat marriage, I'd gave him a sleepy smile and say, "Hey, what's going on?"

By July, five thousand members of the 1st Brigade were living at Q-West, including several infantry battalions as well as squadrons of Apaches, Black Hawks, and Kiowas. My battalion was centrally located, since we had the fuel, showers, and medical and maintenance facilities. Every battalion and squadron had its own neighborhood, each with a sign to distinguish one area from the next. The Brigade TOC was near the front gate, in office buildings close to the Cav. But wherever we lived and worked, we felt as if we were being cooked alive.

The heat had taken on a life of its own. In July the average temperature was 120 degrees—one day it spiked at 137—and went no lower than 100 at night. I was stunned by the blank consistency of the weather. For two months it had been sunny—no rain, not even a cloud. At The Heap, we stopped running our fans because it felt as if someone was blowing a hair dryer on us. Imagine the wave of heat you feel when you open the lid on a barbecue grill to flip a burger. Now imagine climbing inside that barbecue and living there. Throw in a hot, relentless wind and you have an idea of life at Q-West.

Keeping up troop morale under such conditions wasn't easy, and the senior leaders were constantly inventing ways to keep the soldiers occupied in their off-hours. We bought new TVs and satellite dishes on the local economy so they could watch sports and a few primetime shows. We built a gym and had flag football games on the holidays, NCOs against officers. We held softball games, organized runs and holiday parties. We built Internet cafés all over post so that people could e-mail loved ones and buy things online. We got new uniforms and new boots. But the biggest morale boost in months came in the form of Porta-Johns set up throughout Q-West and cleaned by local laborers. This meant we no longer had to burn our latrine buckets, a despicable process that involved gasoline, a match, and a very long stick.

We also hoped the Porta-Johns would help to cut down on the dysentery that had become epidemic. Chip came down with a terrible case in the summer. By the middle of July, only three people in the battalion hadn't gotten it, and I was one of them. Ed Sleeper was the other, and we jokingly created an "Iron Person" contest to see who lasted the longest.

Q-West began to take on the trappings of any entrenched workplace, complete with inappropriate office romances, lax work ethics, and piss-poor attitudes. Drinking alcohol was banned on post, but soldiers managed to find it. Hard liquor, beer, wine—you name it—were for sale all over Mosul in the new liquor stores that had materialized. As soon as you exited the post you saw countless little kids selling whiskey on the roadside. Families back home sent booze in care packages. Take a bottle of mouthwash, dump it out, fill it with vodka—who's to know? Everybody knew somebody who had alcohol, but as great as a cold beer sounded, I never had a drink at Q-West. Part of my job was writing up and processing the paperwork for soldiers who got in trouble, usually for drinking or bad behavior, and in some cases I recommended appropriate punishments to my bosses— extra duty, a loss of rank. I would have felt like a complete hypocrite doing that while breaking the rules myself.

Infidelity and fraternization among the troops had become rampant, too, but Maj. Gen. Petraeus's no-sex mandate was difficult to enforce. One female soldier who was transferred to our unit turned out to be pregnant. She was on the next Black Hawk home.

And as with any workplace, there was the inevitable grumbling about the bosses. When word trickled down to our soldiers that Maj. Gen. Petraeus had taken over one of Saddam's palaces in Mosul for division headquarters, the rumor mill began working overtime: They had a pool, air-conditioning, and bathrooms with toilets that actually flushed. Its nickname was the TOC Mahal.

I went to the palace a few times for meetings and found that the rumors were not only true, they were inadequate, except for the air-conditioning—they didn't have any, either (though the marble structure did stay at least ten degrees cooler). But I saw large ornate rooms, grand staircases, marble and gold in every nook and cranny. I used one of the toilets, which did indeed flush, a reassuring sound if ever I heard one. Hundreds of soldiers were encamped there, and in their downtime they'd lounge around the pool in P.T. shorts and T-shirts. The palace was straight out of a fairy tale, only in this case there were no rolling green hills filled with smiling peasants, just rolling trash heaps with starving children. It blew my mind that the Husseins had been living high above the city with a 360-degree view of all that misery without ever feeling a speck of guilt about causing the suffering below them.

In the end, I was perfectly happy at Q-West. The palace had way too much brass walking around—we would have had to stay on our toes a lot more. Q-West was more like living in the countryside. It was just my speed.

Keeping Q-West tidy, however, was a constant battle. More people meant more trash, and that meant varmints. Packs of wild dogs roamed the area foraging for food, and they were unafraid of anything or anyone, including the U.S. Army. They lay in packs on the roadsides, sleeping in the midday heat, and came to life at night. They'd root through our garbage cans and run alongside our Humvees, snapping at our legs and arms. We nicknamed them the Fido-yeen. I learned to carry one or two smooth river stones wherever I went and kept a stack outside The Heap so I could pick up a few on my way out.

One morning before dawn, I was walking back to The Heap from the TOC. The sun wasn't up yet, but it was light enough to pick my path without a flashlight. Suddenly the shadows began to move and a low growling emanated from several directions at once. I began to finger the stones in my pocket. As if on cue, four dogs, more wolf than canine, jumped out of the scrub and started to bear down on me. I could see their teeth, their mangy hides. I fired off the rocks and scrambled for more, but by the time I reloaded they had scattered, yelping into the night. I never saw them in my neighborhood again.

Finally the dog problem got so bad that we implemented a policy of removal. We were allowed to shoot them if they attacked, or we could call the MPs and have *them* shoot them.

Naturally we weren't allowed to befriend the mutts, but Mike was a softie for animals of every stripe. One night, not long after I'd moved into The Heap, I woke up to find him and Capt. Curtis sitting on our porch, looking dejected. They had heard something moving near the trash in the dark and, thinking it was a field rat, Mike had picked up a rock (with Clay's encouragement) and smashed the critter with it. A few minutes later, four baby hedgehogs emerged from their nest, looking for their mother. It had been an honest mistake—who knew Iraq had hedgehogs?—but they felt terrible.

So when Mike saw the puppy by the side of the road, he couldn't resist. He and Coop were on their way back from the infirmary where they'd been visiting Scott, who had a bad case of the Big D. Suddenly, Mike told Coop to pull over. "It was obvious the puppy was old enough to be weaned, but the mother hadn't done it," he told me later. If the puppy didn't learn to eat normal food, it was going to die of malnourishment. It needed to leave its mother, so Mike took matters into his own hands. He rushed over, snatched the puppy, ran back to the vehicle, and yelled "Go!" By the time I showed up, the dog had already been fed, washed, and named Sofia, after the Miller Lite girl.

A retriever/spaniel mix, Sofia had a sweet personality and a cute face, two things an all-male unit didn't see much of. When I wrote Dad about Sofia, he told Chuckie Hall, and Chuckie said, "I'll bet they bring her home, just like Scout."

"Kate," Dad wrote, "I have a bet going that you will not bring back another dog. So keep that in mind. I don't want to lose five dollars."

One day I said to Mike, "Just curious, but what do you plan on doing with Sofia when it's time for us to go?"

"I'll cross that bridge when I come to it," he replied, and went back to scratching her tummy.

Operation Iraqi Freedom had been in its honeymoon phase for a few weeks, but that came to an end that summer. Like the squalls that kicked up out of nowhere, Saddam loyalists began launching a series of small guerrilla-type actions against U.S. troops. The division switched from straight stability and support operations (SASO) to combat and SASO operations, and began conducting regular searches for weapons and bad guys. Anti-American violence was escalating rapidly in Baghdad, and cities like Fallujah and An Najaf were becoming more dangerous by the hour.

"The situation in Mosul has been heating up," I wrote in my journal. "The threat level has skyrocketed. Mike said last night in Mosul they were fired on by small arms fire and had to blow some trucks up—nice day at the office. I'm a realist though—and would be stupid if I didn't thoroughly grasp what he's doing."

Back in Macon, Dad watched the news and read the papers with a near-obsessive interest, and was beginning to formulate some definite opinions about what America had gotten itself into.

"War news continues to be bad," he wrote me. "I think we are not prepared for an aftermath that would take so long to stabilize. We were prepared for a long combat phase. Probably the Administration should not have declared the war is over quite so quickly. Still, most people feel the whole thing was worth doing, and we should stay the course to see it done right. However, it is going to take more personnel, and that debate can't seem to get started. The politicians don't want to touch it. They should."

On June 9, while in Europe, Secretary of Defense Donald Rumsfeld was quoted as saying that the resistance "looks as though it has an element of organization as opposed to being random," and that more ground forces were coming, especially infantry and military police.

As the need for troops grew, the Reserves and the National Guard began to play a vital role. Lindsey and her Guard unit, the 2175th Military Police Company, arrived in Baghdad in the middle of June. She was living on palace grounds in a tent city in what was fast becoming a full-on war zone. They had one phone for 750 soldiers and no Internet, so Linz asked me to e-mail the unit's Family Readiness representative, Carl, to reassure the frightened families that everyone was okay, which I gladly did.

For the first few months in Iraq, the 2175th was in charge of collecting prisoners from the Iraqi police stations around Baghdad and delivering them to detainee camps. I spoke to Lindsey several times that summer, and she had nothing but praise for her soldiers: how tough they were, how uncomplaining. Like so many newcomers to this region, Linz was suffering from a chronic, dust-induced cough, weight loss, and dehydration, but she still sounded upbeat.

"I've gotten two marriage proposals from civilians," she told me once. "They call me Snow White because of my pale skin. They want to know if the sun hurts it. I brought plenty of sunscreen, but Kate, tell Dad to send baby wipes, bug spray, and shower gel."

Meanwhile, I'd become increasingly frustrated with my part—or lack thereof—in the war. The 1st Brigade was responsible for activity outside of the city of Mosul, and the area was relatively quiet compared to Mosul. The twice-daily battle update briefings, where the commanders updated the staff and officer corps on their units' activities, had become so short that Lt. Col. Kelley eventually scrapped them altogether. There wasn't much for me to do besides shuffle papers and surf the Internet for material for the *Sandy Club Gazette*. My buddies were helping to build hospitals and water systems; I could go a whole night without the radio going off.

Every job seemed more important than mine, even the daily mail run. I'd see Sgt. Wilson, my other NCO, at the morning battle update briefing, and afterward he'd drive in a convoy to the Mosul airfield, load up several trucks with the battalion's letters and boxes, and drive back. It took a good part of the day, and Sgt. Wilson felt responsible for carrying it out safely. Driving anywhere in Iraq had become dangerous, and I admired his willingness to make the trip every day, in heat and later in cold and rain. These letters and care packages from home were a vital link in the morale chain, and I think delivering them to the troops made him feel like Santa Claus. By comparison, my job seemed unimportant and ineffectual. I wasn't making a difference.

A huge fire kept the TOC occupied for much of July. One of Saddam-era Iraq's most successful business ventures was the Al-Misraq sulfur plant outside Mosul, which exported sulfur to several Middle Eastern countries for use in everything from gunpowder to hair dye. In late June the plant caught fire, either by accident or sabotage. Because the factory's fire-fighting equipment had been looted, the fire quickly raged out of control. In a matter of days, a massive cloud of toxic fumes covered northern Iraq, forcing residents of villages indoors and wiping out crops. When the acrid smoke hit Q-West, panicked soldiers began calling the TOC, asking if we were being gassed. The fumes made breathing difficult and burned our throats and eyes; everyone on post developed a chronic cough. We wore our gas masks when the smoke was heaviest, and sometimes it got so thick I'd get lost walking from one building to another.

The 101st had worked hard to develop trust with the local population, and in a way, that fire symbolized their coalition. For three weeks, several hundred of our engineers and National Guard firefighters battled the blaze around the clock, side by side with Arabs, Kurds, and Turkmen. Bulldozer drivers in gas masks spent hours in the noxious smoke pushing dirt onto the flames; several had to be treated for smoke inhalation. My unit worked overtime coordinating the firefighting and relief efforts. We oversaw the movements of the firefighting teams and the evacuation of several villages, and got food, drinking water, and medical care to the displaced locals and their firefighters. By July 17 the fire was extinguished, but not before one Iraqi firefighter was killed and two others had been severely burned.

After the fire, an exhausted lull settled over the TOC. But when the shit hit the fan, it hit big-time.

I would often stop by the TOC in the late afternoon to catch up on paperwork and check up on any news from our sector. On July 22, I showed up to a flood of excited chatter. This was unusual. I found Chip to get the scoop.

"We're waiting on news," he said, "but it looks like the Cav and 2nd Brigade have Uday and Qusay Hussein holed up in a building in Mosul. The word is we're sending a lot of firepower into the building, but they're also returning fire." We had been searching for the brothers for so long that it came as a shock to hear we'd gotten them. I'd heard no warning or even a whisper of the operation.

The brothers weren't interested in going quietly, and a full-blown firefight erupted. They were killed, along with six bodyguards, and four soldiers from the 101st were wounded. This was the biggest news of the war, and I rushed to get it onto the front page of the *Sandy*.

Bringing Saddam's sons to justice did wonders for everyone's morale, Americans and Iraqis alike. After putting the *Sandy* to bed, I headed over to Mike's. The Kiowa pilots were often the last to hear anything, and I didn't want them to miss out on this. "The Iraqis will sleep well tonight," Mike said. We were excited and thankful that the manhunt was over.

But our satisfaction was short-lived. Over the next few days, the body count rose for the 101st. Two 3rd Brigade soldiers were killed in an ambush, possibly by Saddam loyalists, and an infantryman died when his Humvee hit an improvised explosive device (IED) outside Mosul.

The night of July 24 was quiet. It was about 2:30 A.M., and I was on shift. Sgt. Mac was outside, leaving only the radioman with me in that big empty hangar. I was checking a stack of awards one of the companies had submitted. Normally, requests for help or backup went to the brigade TOC, which radioed me, but that night we happened to hear the call come in from the infantry unit out in the sector.

A soldier's desperate voice crackled out of the speakers, speaking to the brigade TOC. A small convoy on patrol had been ambushed, and the shaken infantryman was calling for medical assistance and some additional firepower from a unit in the area. One scrap of information caught my attention:

"Three KIA. Repeat, three KIA."

I immediately got on the radio to Charlie Company and got its commander, Capt. Hooten, on the line. I gave him the grid coordinates for the patrol's location as well as the possible injuries and number of casualties. By the time Brigade called me to dispatch the medevac chopper, it was already in the air. A few minutes later, I heard it land with its load of wounded. With serious injuries, seconds count. If I'd waited for Brigade to radio me to send the medevac chopper, it might have arrived too late.

That was a moment of clarity for me. War is as much about monotony as action, and we all play our roles, some more violent than others. While I'd been hoping to see more action, that single minute of time made my entire stretch in Iraq worthwhile. For twenty minutes, what I did mattered. But losing three soldiers in one night is a huge blow to a platoon and a battalion, and I knew that for the soldiers who survived, the wounds from bullets and shrapnel would heal far sooner than the wound from the human loss.

That morning I got off shift feeling not quite right. Mike was flying, so I headed back to The Heap for some sleep. A few hours later, I woke up with severe stomach cramps, and soon I was making trips to the latrine every ten minutes. The Big D had finally gotten me. I walked as quickly as I could to the TOC to let them know I was headed to Charlie Company. The medics put me up on a cot and stuck an IV in my arm. I felt the medicine travel to my head, and then I remember nothing else. Six hours and five IV bags later I felt a lot better. Maj. Whitson had sent word to send me back to The Heap for the night, and that someone else would cover my shift. When I left the infirmary I weighed 114 pounds, down from 130 pounds when I first deployed.

I enjoyed sleeping during the night hours for a change, and I woke up feeling refreshed and thankful I hadn't suffered more. Some soldiers got dysentery so bad they had to be evacuated to the Army hospital in Mosul.

Like everyone else, Mike had a lot of bad bowel days, but nothing to keep him out of the cockpit. From IEDs to well-armed insurgents, the ground troops had their hands full, and the Kiowa pilots did all they could to help. The recent casualties had angered and reinvigorated everyone, including my husband. On July 30, I wrote Dad this e-mail:

> *You can see a big shift in the attitude of the entire division since we had two soldiers killed in the Rakkasans and the three killed in my brigade. The soldiers are mad and they seem to be moving much more aggressively. We had fallen into a bit of a lethargic mood and sadly those deaths woke us up. Those guys are really out there hunting now. It does appear that we are getting close to Saddam—what a boost that would be if SOMEBODY would get him!*
>
> *Mike is doing well. Between you and me and NOT his family and friends, he had a bad night a few days ago. He was spotting and another pilot was flying as they were chasing a suspicious vehicle. It was unusually windy, and when they turned to follow the vehicle the wind caught them just right and they dropped about seventy feet*

*in a millisecond. The pilot had to over-torque the aircraft to keep it
in the air (this is about a one-million-dollar repair job). Probably
wouldn't have killed them but a half body cast would have been in
order. Anyway, a reminder to him that what he does is dangerous.
He said he smoked about half a pack of cigarettes with shaky hands
once he got on the ground. That is a day in the life of Mike.*

———

In early August, the official word came down from on high: The 101st
was not going home until February or March of 2004. I made some
new months to add to my calendar.

Everyone around me faced up to this depressing thought surpris-
ingly well, though I felt especially bad for the guys whose wives had
given birth while they were over here. I couldn't imagine not getting
to see my child until he or she was almost a year old. It was always
exciting when guys had babies; it made that day a little more special.
Chip's wife, Linda, who was also a captain (she had not deployed),
gave birth to a daughter that August. He was happy that his wife and
daughter were okay, but he hated missing the birth. I'll never forget
how he passed out cigars and smiled the broad, bittersweet grin of the
deployed new father.

I wrote Dad an e-mail to this effect, and he responded, "I, too, feel
sorry for all those fathers that can't see those new babies. But I was
seventeen months old before I first saw my father, and he me, so it is
not unheard of for sure. Remind the troops that their grandpas did it
during World War II and they can, too."

Now that we were at Q-West for the long haul, the government
floodgates opened and money began to pour in. Workers for Kellogg
Brown & Root, the engineering and construction arm of Halliburton,
showed up with a multitude of projects, including a dining facility,
showers, and better sleeping quarters. The thought of hot, freshly prepared food made us giddy. To encourage grass-roots entrepreneur-
ship, the 101st invited Iraqis to open small businesses on post, and
before long kebab shacks, a pizza restaurant, and small stores selling
anything from DVDs to ice cream had popped up.

Saying he needed a place to "relieve some stress," Jesse White decided to build a golf course, so he scraped together a few holes using
carpet scraps for putting surfaces. Lt. Col. Kelley, himself a fan of the
game, encouraged Jesse to expand the course. Jesse laid out several

holes, from 50 to 250 yards. The fairways were dusty, bumpy, and littered with aircraft debris. Jesse secured the cups with a special mix-
ture of sand and mud, and rimmed the tee boxes with stones from the
Tigris River. The first tee sat atop a bunker with a beautiful view of
the northern mountains. They dubbed it South Course at Mosul, and
the first tee time was 6:30 A.M. Jesse even began giving me lessons.

We continued to refine The Heap. Chip and I commandeered
some plywood from a recent shipment, and Mike called upon his ancient woodshop skills to build me a nightstand and a bed frame using
power tools from the supply shop. It was a very husbandly thing to
do. We had never lived anywhere long enough to own power tools, so
I got a kick out of watching him use an electric saw. "I can't believe
we had to come all the way to Iraq to start doing home repairs," I
said. He would have laughed if he hadn't been cussing so hard at the
saw, which was refusing to cut straight for some reason.

Unfortunately, we lost our garden. One afternoon, Sgt. Mac was
burning trash in an old, dried-up well. We'd had no rain in ages, so
when the wind lifted a burning ember out of the well, everything was
ablaze within seconds. Awakened by Sgt. Mac's cries of "Wake up,
get out of the building, there's a fire!" I ran outside to find tall flames
racing toward one of our Humvees, which sat disabled in the driveway. We put out the fire with the help of two other captains and every
spare soldier who saw the smoke, but not before it ravaged our yard
and sent our latrine up in a pillar of flames. Every tree, bush, and blade
of grass was turned to ashes. Burnt, blackened olives, still smoking,
dropped to the ground, and the smell of charred vegetation lingered
for months.

———

In the second week of August, a troop's worth of Kiowas, including a
lot of the squadron staff's, were assigned to take out some terrorist
camps. It was a joint unit mission encompassing aircraft from several
other units besides the 101st. Banshee Troop was stuck on rotation as
the Quick Reaction Force (QRF) that week. If Q-West was ever attacked, the QRF had to be ready at a moment's notice to get in the
air and take out the enemy. (We had QRF ground forces for this purpose as well.) Tim Merrell, now the squadron's senior instructor pilot,
was flying the mission, and he could choose any pilot he liked to fly
with him. Mike was elated when Tim chose him. They hadn't flown

together in a few months, and Mike missed his commonsense country attitude.

Unfortunately, the mission itself proved less than exciting. Word had leaked of the raid, and U.S. forces arrived to find the camps had been abandoned shortly before they arrived. They did discover weapons caches, cell phones, and money, so it wasn't a total loss. The weapons had to be destroyed, so Mike did get to "blow a lot of stuff up," as he liked to say.

Deployment had its advantages: We were putting away every dime we made plus combat pay. Dad handled our finances, paying off the Tahoe and the Harley. By August we had a nice sum stashed away in Army savings accounts, and we put some aside for a new boat. When we got home we'd get special combat stipends of a thousand dollars each, and we agreed that each of us could spend it on whatever we wanted and the other person couldn't say a word.

"By the time we leave, we'll have sucked it up it over here a year," Mike said. "Let's invest some, but let's do something fun with part of it." He wanted to upgrade his Harley, and I wanted a mountain bike.

On the recommendation of a friend, I ordered a book from Amazon.com called *Smart Couples Finish Rich*. It was a guide for people who don't know much about investing yet who want to make smart choices about their future. Mike and I read it together. The book included all sorts of exercises, and one night we sat on my bunk and did a few. One of them required us to make a list of the things that mattered most. We were supposed to draw a series of arrows in a circular pattern, and on each arrow write something that was important to us. The closer we got to the center of the circle, the more each thing was supposed to mean. Finally, when we reached the very middle of the circle, we would write the thing that mattered the most in our lives.

With Sofia sleeping at our feet, we talked through what we wanted on our "wheels" and discovered that our hopes and desires for the future were still the same. Having a family. Buying a house. Building financial security for our old age, when we could do those things together that we'd always wanted to.

We drew our wheels on sheets of green notebook paper and exchanged them. When I looked at Mike's, I saw that he had written my name in the middle of his circle, just as I had written his.

CHAPTER 19

MR. MOHAMED AND ME

BY AUGUST hundreds of Iraqis, all men, were working on post. They drove water trucks, cleaned Porta-Johns, flipped pizza dough, and hammered nails. They called the members of the 101st the "Eagle People," after the Screaming Eagle patch we wore on our uniforms. In the TOC we called them local nationals, but in the field, when we wanted to get their attention, we'd call out, *"Haji!"* This term has taken on a derogatory connotation, but we picked it up from the Iraqis themselves; it was a word they used for one another. Paying the locals not only infused money into the region, but also provided a much-needed workforce that could improve our own living conditions—we needed to get our soldiers out of their sweltering tents and into buildings with roofs and air-conditioning.

Most of the Iraqis we hired capitalized on the opportunity to make money, but a few exploited it. Before any Iraqi worked on post, he had to be screened by the brigade's S-2 intelligence section to weed out Ba'athists, fedayeen sympathizers, car thieves, petty crooks, and so on. But the screening process wasn't always foolproof. In An Najaf the brigade hired a local as an interpreter. We called him Joe, and he worked directly with the infantry. One of his jobs was handing out humanitarian supplies to the citizenry—until some locals pointed him out as a bad man. We discovered that prior to the war, he had worked in the city as one of Saddam's henchmen. And now, instead of distributing food, water, and medical supplies, he was giving them to his cronies to sell on the black market. When Joe realized that we were on to him, he skipped out with an American uniform. The last I heard, he had declared himself the prime minister of Iraq and was running around Baghdad.

The Iraqis' help sometimes came at a high personal price to themselves. Workers all over Iraq were being killed for working for the coalition. Saddam loyalists kidnapped the son of an interpreter who worked for an Army officer I knew in Mosul; fortunately, U.S. forces found and rescued the child. The foreman at an oil refinery we were helping to repair was shot dead on his way to work. Yet despite the risks, Iraqis continued to step forward and place their lives on the line. I believe they did so not so much out of a desire to help America, but out of a desire to help themselves.

By late August 2003, under Maj. Gen. Petraeus's stewardship, the 101st had spent almost two million dollars to rebuild northern Iraq. The division had repaired and built water pump stations, power plants, roads, hospitals, and schools and had even brokered a deal to privatize a five-star hotel in Mosul. We were importing certain American ideals—democracy, free enterprise, pepperoni pizza—but sometimes our influence had an unintended effect.

Christianity was more prevalent in northern Iraq, and one day Tony Boniface visited a Catholic monastery and orphanage outside Mosul as part of a charitable mission. (I took his shift; I owed him for covering me the night I spent with Mike in the wheat field.) After services, our unit held a picnic for the orphans, where Tony helped to hand out toys and other goodies. Before church he had met an Iraqi college student who spoke excellent English. The young man had grown up in the orphanage, and he pointed out his sister, who still lived there. Tony could see that the girl wore a T-shirt and jeans, but when she walked past him after services, he had the opportunity to read the shirt. It read, "This isn't a beer belly, it's a fuel tank for a sex machine." Tony could barely refrain from laughing. He asked the young man if he and his sister knew what the words meant, and he said no, that she had received the shirt in a donation of clothing from the States. Tony tried to explain, but the nuances of redneck humor defied articulation. When he described the episode to me later, we agreed that in this case, ignorance was bliss.

To me, that T-shirt represented the challenges we faced translating American ideals to the Middle East. "We need to find the key to showing Iraqis how to develop their country without letting 'America' insinuate itself too much into their culture," I wrote in a mass e-mail on August 21. "I am very proud of everything American, but I don't think all countries need to be exactly like us. As long as they emulate the part of America where we fight for the underdog and refuse to let evil, corrupt murderers run the country, where kids can be whatever they want and actually have something to look forward to, then I think we all will be okay. Iraq has some interesting traditions and history; I hope the citizens understand that we are not here to change that."

———

After we arrived at Q-West, Ed Sleeper, the support operations transportation officer, took on the additional duties of overseeing the improvement and business projects on post. He and an interpreter went looking for a local who could help us get supplies and do contracting to improve our living conditions. In the village of Qayyarah, Ed found Mohamed Kharmeese, an out-of-work engineer with perfect English, a hungry family, and a vision for a better future for his four-year-old daughter.

Mr. Mohamed, as we called him, was in his late thirties or early forties, of medium height and build. Polite and reserved, he was a secular Muslim, like Abdul and most of the educated men I'd met. He had a mustache and glasses that gave him the look of a college professor. He wore Western-style clothes: loose pants and button-down shirts or golf polos. Mr. Mohamed was a nice man, very forward-thinking. Because he had refused to openly support Saddam, he'd been unable to get a job or travel. His brother, Akhmed, had a degree in French and dreamed of moving to France to continue his studies, but like his brother was unable to leave the general area, let alone the country. The 101st gave both of them a chance to start over.

Every morning the two brothers drove to the front gate, where they lined up with the other workers to be searched and let pass. Mr. Mohamed was hardworking and ambitious; no job was too big or too small. Whatever supplies we needed, he got; whatever structure needed building, he hired a crew and got it built. So when Ed asked him if he'd be interested in running a restaurant, Mr. Mohamed said, "Of course, and it will be the best restaurant in northern Iraq."

They struck a bargain. The U.S. Army would provide funds to renovate an old building near the TOC, but it was up to Mr. Mohamed to supply the restaurant with food, set the prices, and manage the day-to-day operations.

I'd seen Mr. Mohamed before from a distance, but I met him for the first time in June. I was about to get off shift when Ed showed up with him in tow. When he introduced me, Mr. Mohamed looked me in the eye and shook my hand, something few Iraqi men were willing to do. Yet there was a shyness about him.

"Mr. Mo was just telling me how his mother's having trouble with her skin being too dry," Ed said. "Since you're the care package queen, I was thinking you might have some sunscreen or lotion you could spare."

As Ed spoke, Mr. Mohamed stood off to the side, looking a little embarrassed—clearly this visit had not been his idea.

"Sure," I said. "I've got tons. I was just heading home, why don't you two come with me and I'll see what I've got."

We hopped in Ed's Humvee and drove the quarter-mile to The Heap. While the men waited in the vehicle I ran inside, emerging a few minutes later with a boxful of sunscreen and lotion. "This is for your mother," I said, and handed Mr. Mohamed the box. He seemed genuinely moved by my gesture. He bowed his head and said thank-you over and over, all for some simple items that most Americans find in our medicine cabinets.

The next day, at the TOC, Chip said, "There's someone here to see you." Mr. Mohamed was waiting for me outside. "My mother says thank you," he said.

———

The restaurant was coming along. It had an air-conditioned dining room with plastic tables and chairs and a grassy courtyard for out-door dining. Ed hired a local artist to paint scenes of mountain ranges and prairies on the walls. Using spices sent by his sister and recipes off the Internet, he showed the cooks how to make spaghetti and ham-burgers à la McDonald's. The soldiers were craving pizza, so Ed said to Mr. Mohamed, "We need a clay oven." Before long those Iraqis were back there tossing dough like natives of Naples. They called their establishment the Eagle's Lounge.

Going out to eat was a welcome respite from the chow tent and MREs, and by opening day the place was packed with hungry soldiers who were tired, hot, and impatient to get their food. The waiters, a couple of teenage boys whose English didn't extend beyond "ham-burgers, no onions," struggled to understand orders rattled off like machine-gun fire, and when the food was slow to arrive, some of the soldiers got cranky. In the kitchen, the cooks felt overwhelmed by the flood of orders. Ed came to find me.

"Kate," he asked, "how are your waitressing skills?"

After my shift I tied on an apron and went to work. When the Iraqi waiters got confused, I took the order. When the soldiers, most of whom I knew, demanded to know why their food was taking so long, I said, "Look, this is the opening day. You can leave or you can wait." Ed helped out in the kitchen, and Mr. Mohamed was running the cash register, smiling with every bill he rang up. No one had expected this much business.

By late afternoon, the place had finally emptied out. Ed and I sat exhausted but hungry, eating our first slice of pizza in months. Mr. Mohamed came over and thanked us profusely for helping, and I could tell by the gleam in his eyes that he was already thinking about the next day and the business he would do.

With Ed as his battalion liaison, Mr. Mohamed soon became the Donald Trump of Q-West. In no time he'd built a thriving construction business from the ground up and was overseeing dozens of projects around post, including new office buildings and a gas station so we could easily refuel the post's vehicles. He built an office at the restaurant from which he ran his businesses, and eventually added a small convenience store on the front that sold everything from movies to foam mattresses to chocolate bars. Soon other "haji shops" opened up all over post, kebab stands being particularly popular.

Mr. Mohamed wasn't the only construction guru at Q-West; at one point, Jesse White hired a local to build new quarters for Lt. Col. Kelley and Maj. Whitson. A structure that strongly resembled a double-wide trailer soon materialized, and my bosses christened it Morning Wood, for no other reason than the obvious.

Spurred, perhaps, by a sense of competition, Mr. Mohamed felt that as officers, those residing in The Heap deserved better quarters as well. We had focused on the enlisted quarters before our own, but when they were completed he said to me, "I could make your place nice."

In mid-August his construction crew set to work. Years of making do with very little had made them resourceful, and in one week they turned a bombed-out building into a small house using nothing but rubble, cinder blocks, and cement. They walled in the garages and put on doors and walled off part of the big common area into three smaller rooms and installed an air conditioner, which turned out to be too small to make much of a dent in the heat. Earlier that month, Sgt. Mac had left the 426th for a new job in Mosul, so my bedroom was now mine alone, a place where I could walk around naked, paint my toenails, or drool in my sleep without anyone knowing or caring. Nancy sent me a blue sheet printed with colorful fish, and I strung it up to divide the room into sleeping and living areas. Mike began to stop by, something he'd never done when I had a roommate.

But Mr. Mohamed was more than a capitalist in training. He always had his ear to the ground, and he was our conduit to what was going on among the local population.

One day, when I showed up for work, Tony told me that there had been an incident with one of the water truck drivers. These workers were crucial. They brought us water from the Tigris for showers. They would drive around to different stops on post and fill up the showers and washbasins. Since we couldn't have the drivers roaming around post in a big truck by themselves, soldier escorts accompanied them, sitting in the passenger seats.

There was one driver who took the same route every day. The security escorts changed daily, and on this particular day, the escort was a female soldier from my unit. The 426th was in charge of the water, but I knew her only by face and name.

As Tony told it, they were driving along when the Iraqi casually reached over and touched the soldier on her breast. She slapped his hand away, and he slapped her face. She locked and loaded on him— stuck the rifle barrel in his face—and immediately turned him in. He was arrested and his water truck was confiscated.

As with any small town in the United States—Macon comes to mind—the news spread like a head cold to the local villages. The next day, at the Eagle's Lounge, Mr. Mohamed filled us in. "The man is from a village not far from mine," he said of the culprit. "His actions have brought shame on his entire village." He shook his head. "No one likes him. He was a rascal, always making trouble."

"We want good relationships with the locals, but I hope they understand that this type of behavior is unacceptable," I said.

"He was just one bad man. Don't worry about him causing trouble. His family will take care of him."

When Ed moved to a new job in Division Headquarters at the palace in Mosul, he asked me if I'd be interested in taking his place. He and Mr. Mohamed had gotten to be good friends, and Ed wanted to be sure that he was well taken care of.

I worked with Mr. Mohamed until I left Iraq, and in all that time, he never had a problem working with me, a woman. While other Iraqi men averted their gaze, he looked me in the eye. While other Iraqis gawked at a woman in uniform giving men orders, he treated me with nothing but respect. When I stopped by the restaurant, he always greeted me warmly and refused to let me pay for my pizza. If he needed help getting paid or hiring more workers, he'd stop by The Heap in the afternoons to ask my advice, and he usually left with a sack of beauty products for his wife and mother. I may have been supplying his entire village by that point, but he never asked for anything. I was happy to share.

I never did meet Mr. Mohamed's wife and mother, but one day he brought his daughter to meet me. She was a beautiful child in a frilly dress with huge brown eyes and glossy curls. She hung out at the restaurant for the day, as giggly and rambunctious as any little girl in Macon. Her eyes lit up when her father walked in the room, and he in turn was extremely proud of her. Holding her in his arms, he toured her around the kitchen, speaking softly in Arabic and pointing out the stove, the sink, a lump of floured pizza dough on the counter. Mr. Mohamed and I never did talk about Saddam or the Iraq before America came, but we didn't have to. The little girl he carried told me everything I needed to know.

CHAPTER 20

SISTERS IN ARMS

ON THE MORNING OF September 2, I hopped a convoy to Mosul for a meeting and then begged a ride on a Black Hawk to Baghdad. There were two other soldiers on the flight, but the engines were too loud for conversation so I sat by the open door, trying to enjoy the hot wind on my face as we skimmed over the desert. The pilots stopped in Tikrit for fuel and new passengers, and about four hours later, Iraq's capital came into view. After seeing its ragged outskirts in August, I had assumed that the city, on full examination, would look more prosperous. Instead, it simply looked ancient, decrepit, and cramped. The Black Hawk set down at Baghdad International Airport, where Lindsey and I had planned to meet. I called her unit from the airport phone to let her know I'd arrived.

"I'm working in the area," she said. "I'll be there soon."

U.S. forces were running the airport, and it felt odd not to be surrounded by soldiers from the 101st. I waited in the terminal, watching fellow soldiers come and go. The airport had become a hub for military personnel heading to or returning from R and R in Qatar or the States. It was easy to tell who was who: The outbound soldiers buzzed with excitement and anticipation; the returning soldiers were slumped over with dejection.

While I was excited to be in Baghdad, it was yet another double-sided privilege. I got to visit my sister, but it meant that she was in Iraq, too. It was the same dilemma I faced with Mike.

About twenty minutes later, I saw two Humvees pull up outside the terminal. There were four soldiers in each vehicle, which bristled with armor and ammunition. Linz was sitting in the backseat of the first Humvee, holding her weapon. She hopped out of the vehicle and ran inside, and when she saw me, we shared a big, long hug. We hadn't seen each other since Christmas, nine months and a lifetime ago, and even through her flak vest she looked and felt thin. But then so did I.

"You're so skinny!" she cried.

"It's the Operation Iraqi Freedom Diet," I said. "Guaranteed to take off fifteen pounds in a matter of weeks."

"Come on," she said. "I want you to meet some of my soldiers."

Outside, Linz introduced me around. We had heard a lot about each other, so the soldiers seemed as excited to see me as I was to see them. Like a distant relative visiting from out of town, I gave this surreal situation a veneer of normalcy.

"We're still working," Lindsey said. "We're headed to a detainee camp near here called Camp Cropper. I thought you might like to come along."

"You thought right," I said and jumped in next to her.

"It's a short drive," she said, "but you need to stay alert."

Within minutes we were at the camp. Strung with miles of concertina wire, Cropper was a high value detention site whose detainees included everyone from low-level petty criminals to big-name prisoners such as Tariq Aziz. There were rows and rows of tents for the prisoners and a main building that served as a processing center. As we walked to the center, I took in the scene. Using translators, soldiers interviewed the detainees, who waited in line, hands bound behind them with plastic zip ties.

While Linz did paperwork I met many of her soldiers, putting faces to names. Most of her platoon and company were men who in the civilian world were college students, cops, and prison guards. Lindsey worked for the Missouri Supreme Court, assessing the way cases were processed and documented in the staff computer system. I'm sure that when they signed up for several weekends a year, few of them thought they'd end up dodging bullets in Baghdad.

When it came time to leave the camp, we locked and loaded and climbed into the Humvees. "We have to drive through the nice part of town to get to our quarters," Lindsey said. "It's closed off to the general public and is supposed to be relatively quiet. But we don't take chances anywhere." A few minutes later we entered another world of quiet streets lined with beautiful mansions on impeccably landscaped grounds. "Most of Saddam's rich supporters lived here," Lindsey said with the authority of a tour guide. "We're going to drive right past the presidential palace and parade grounds. I thought we'd stop and take a few pictures."

I had seen pictures of the famous gateway to the parade grounds: two giant hands holding sabers, which crossed to make an archway. I was excited to see the gate firsthand, and it didn't disappoint. Then Lindsey pointed out a detail the news videos and pictures tended to omit: Nets filled with Iranian helmets anchored the base of each hand. We inched toward the parade grounds, our speed impeded by countless Iranian helmets that were buried in the ground, only their tops showing, like hell's speed bumps. With an inner shiver I wondered if there'd been heads in those helmets when the concrete was poured.

We stopped and snapped a few pictures under the arches. But as always in Iraq, you should never stop in one place too long.

The sun was setting by the time we arrived in the southeastern section of the city, where Lindsey's company shared a camp with soldiers from the 82nd Airborne. She gave me a quick tour of her barracks, which resembled a seedy motel. Small rooms, some air-conditioned, opened off a narrow hallway. There was one bathroom for the entire floor and showers and rows of Porta-Johns outside. In one common room Linz pointed out a tiny brown leather sofa. "We got this from one of Saddam's palaces," she said. She plopped down on it, I followed suit, and we asked a soldier to take our picture.

"It's nice to see where you work," I told her. "When we're eighty and sitting on the porch with our grandkids swapping war stories, I'll be able to picture where you were."

Linz shared a tiny, crowded space with another lieutenant and their two platoon sergeants, all men. She'd crammed every spare inch with packaged food, toilet paper, and other necessities from Dad's care packages. After washing the hot day off our bodies, we changed into our off-duty uniform of P.T. shorts and T-shirts and hung out for a while, enjoying being together.

Once it was dark and the air had cooled, we headed outside to smoke cigars, away from the constant drone of the generators. Some of Lindsey's NCOs joined us, and they peppered me with questions about the early days of the war and our living conditions at Q-West. In the matter-of-fact tones of soldiers who had settled into their dangerous new jobs, they talked some about getting shot at and being on constant alert for mortar attacks, rocket-propelled grenades, and IEDs.

The soldiers were older than those I worked with; some were Vietnam vets in their fifties. Mostly we all talked about home and all the things we wished we could do—take a real shower, go fishing and hunting— and the food we wanted to eat: fresh fruit, vegetables, and a thick Missouri steak.

Lindsey let her soldiers do most of the talking. She didn't like to discuss her mission and its dangers, and to this day she doesn't open up about it. I knew this much: My sister had seen more action in two months than I had in six, and while I admired her courage and achievements, there remained that part of me that envied the job she had—getting bad guys off the streets.

Linz and her company were preparing to add a new mission to their résumés. Because the company commander and many of its soldiers were from law enforcement, the 2175th was selected to start a Major Crime Unit that would train and work with Iraqis to develop an undercover police force. Lindsey would eventually be the officer in charge, which entailed coordinating raids and searches between Iraqis and Army units. In addition, her MPs would accompany Iraqi forces on missions to offer guidance, gun power, and help. "It's a big responsibility," she said, "but these guys are up to it."

As for myself, I'd been told I was being promoted to captain. For the most part it's an automatic promotion—you practically have to be serving time in Leavenworth not to make captain. Regardless, I was proud to make the list.

"Dad says I'll be the first captain in the family since the Civil War," I said. "The ceremony is in October. It would be great if you could come up for it."

"You tell me when," she said. "I'll do my best to be there."

In the days before my arrival, Lindsey's soldiers had tortured her with threats of the information about her that they were going to extract from me. I laughed when I heard they'd actually prepared a list of thirty questions to ask me: "What was her most embarrassing moment?" "What did she get in trouble for?" But I proved to be a master at evasion and in the end gave up nothing—the sisterly bond is a powerful thing.

Sitting there watching Linz and her soldiers trade gentle barbs, it occurred to me how similar we were, and yet so different. When I'd call for her from Q-West, the soldiers who answered the phone would say, "Your voice sounds identical to Lieutenant Decker's!" Once the soldiers saw us sitting side by side, the similarities became even more pronounced: We may look different, but our inflections and our mannerisms are eerily similar, like identical twins without the identical part. Our leadership styles were similar, too. Like me, she didn't want her soldiers to think of her as a woman first. We both believed in praise, not criticism, as a motivational tool, but at the same time we were straight shooters.

But we diverged when it came to rules. I was a much more "by the book" officer, who tended to see things in black and white. Lindsey, on the other hand, was more easygoing. Maybe it stemmed from the wild ways of her youth, when she learned to appreciate and exploit the gray areas between good and bad because that was where the fun stuff happened. Whatever she was doing, it was working: Lindsey's soldiers clearly liked and respected her.

After a raucous dinner in the chow hall, our next order of business was calling Dad. We knew he'd find comfort in hearing our voices and knowing that we had gotten to see each other for a few hours. The soldiers were allocated a certain number of minutes on the company satellite phone, and Linz had been saving hers up so we could call him together. "Hi, Dad, it's us!" we said at his hello. He sounded overjoyed to hear our voices; I swear his even cracked, though I couldn't be sure. Lindsey talked to him first. "Kate's too skinny," she said, throwing me a look, "but I've managed to put some weight back on." She talked to him about her new job and the pictures we had taken that day, then put me on.

"How's Mike?" Dad asked, his voice crackling over the long distance.

"Mike is flying a lot; he's logged more hours in the air in the past few months than he did during his entire tour in Korea. And they flew a lot in Korea. He was in a major operation a few days ago and got to shoot up some weapons and ammunition."

"I think I saw something about that on the news," Dad said.

"Tell everyone back home hello," I said. "Lindsey's going to try and come up for my promotion to captain in October. We wish you could be there."

"I wish I could, too," he said. It took him a few beats to say his next two sentences. "I'd tell you girls to take care of yourselves, but I know you're good at it."

"We love you, Dad. Talk to you later."

After I hung up, we e-mailed him some photos of the two of us standing on the parade grounds and at the airport. He made sure the newspaper got copies.

I often wondered what Mom would have thought of all this. Dad later told me that he would arrive at the nursing home to find her watching the news about the war. Because current events would stick in her memory for a few moments, he liked to discuss them with her.

"There's a war on," Mom would say.

"Yes, and Lindsey, Kate, and Mike are over there, in Iraq."

"What are they doing there?"

"They're in the Army, all three of them."

"They're in the Army? What are they doing in the Army?"

"They're fighting for our country."

"Oh, that's good." And then Mom's mind would wander elsewhere.

"Mom couldn't have fathomed that she'd have two daughters fighting in a war," Dad told me. "But she believed you girls could do anything you wanted. I have no doubt that, had she been able to, she would have been your biggest cheerleader."

———

One of the platoon sergeants had offered to sleep elsewhere, and I sacked out on the cot next to Linz. It had been a long time since we'd shared a room, and we talked about Dad and Mom and Mike and life for a few minutes. But sleep consumed us quickly. I had a dawn Chinook ride to catch back to Mosul, and Lindsey and her platoon had to get back to nabbing hoodlums and terrorists.

As our Humvee pulled out of the compound the next morning, all jokes and laughter ebbed. We understood the gravity of leaving these walls. Once those helmets went on, we were back in soldier mode, serious and focused.

Lindsey and I rode in the back of the truck through the city, facing each other, weapons locked and loaded. The tarp was off, so I could clearly see the streets and people as we zipped along. Most of the citizens were so used to soldiers passing by that they didn't even give us a glance. The streets were a noisy, dingy collision of Iraqi hustle and bustle meets twenty-first-century urban warfare. Humvees full of Americans sped past, and soldiers with weapons watched from rooftops. Linz and I scanned faces, buildings, vehicles, and overpasses, saying nothing, knowing we didn't have to.

Suddenly Lindsey spoke up. "We're going to cross a really danger-ous intersection. Military vehicles get hit here all the time by bombs and RPGs." We adjusted our weapons and tightened our helmets. *How do soldiers deal with this stress every day?* I wondered. I was relatively sheltered at Q-West; my biggest fear when walking to and from The Heap was wild dogs, easily scared off by a few smooth stones. Her enemy was not so skittish.

As we approached the crossroads, I glanced up and caught Lind-sey's eye. I knew what she was thinking, because I was thinking it, too: Here we were, two sisters holding loaded weapons, watching each other's back. Two sisters playing guns again, but this time it was real.

CHAPTER 21

ROCKET DAYS

ONE EVENING in early September, days after I returned from Baghdad, Chip and I headed out for a four-mile walk. We'd started doing extra P.T. both to stay in shape and to catch up on the day's events at the TOC. After Sgt. Mac left Q-West, I returned to the 2200 to 1000 shift. I'd wake up at 1800, grab something to eat, and head out with Chip at sundown, striding down the road that ran through camp. That day, we planned to follow our usual routine: make the two-mile straight shot down and then turn around and head back. We'd finish our workout by relaxing and stretching out on top of a bunker.

We set off into the darkness. The lights from local villages provided little illumination, making us feel as if we were on an island in a black sea. Our only weapons were flashlights. P.T. was our one break from carrying a weapon, and we welcomed dropping the burden for an hour.

We headed up the road, chatting. We could see all the way to the other end of the post, where the 5th Black Hawk Battalion was based.

We had been walking for five minutes when we saw a series of explosions strike near the Black Hawks, followed by a muffled boom. We stopped in our tracks, looked at each other, and, without saying a word, turned around and sprinted toward The Heap and our weapons. Seconds later a blinding light exploded on the airfield a mere forty feet away and sent us jumping into a ditch. My ears ringing and heart thumping, I felt as if I were inside a large church bell at noon. Chip and I exchanged a quick "Are you all right?" and were off again, this time for the TOC, where we knew we'd be needed. Stumbling over rocks and shrubs, we headed toward the hangar, a dark shadow in the near distance, as explosions went off all around us. We still don't know how we escaped getting hit by shrapnel.

As we approached the Alpha Company area, a voice in the darkness called out, "Halt!" We skidded to a stop, breathing hard. Several soldiers were backlit against a bunker, weapons pointed straight at us. We quickly identified ourselves. "Okay, you can continue," the voice said, and the weapons were lowered.

The TOC was in chaos. Calls were coming in from all over the post, and soldiers were streaming into the hangar, talking excitedly. We couldn't hear the radios above the din. Chip and I caught our breaths and went to work. "Okay," I yelled, "anybody who doesn't need to be here, clear out!" As explosions continued to go off, we assigned two soldiers to record any news from the units and brigade about the locations of hits, and we fed the information to the brigade TOC as we got it. Then we began to account for all weapons and personnel so we could determine who, if anyone, was injured.

Thirty minutes after the attack began, it stopped.

The only reported injury was a soldier who had tangled with some concertina wire trying to enter a bunker. And there was only minor damage—a small miracle considering how close the explosions had come to our aircraft and work areas. At first light the engineers determined that the attackers had fired some type of small Soviet-made rockets—quite a few of them—from multiple locations. Stories of lucky breaks and near misses emerged. One of our NCOs, Master Sgt. William Presley, was in his bunk when a rocket exploded outside his building; we examined his room to find shrapnel lodged in everything except him. A rocket had also landed at the front door of Morning Wood with both Maj. Whitson and Maj. Spencer Smith, the support operations officer, inside, but no damage had been done.

Finally, there was Chip and me, walking along when a rocket exploded a stone's throw away from us. Such a close call made one reevaluate life, especially Chip. As the father of two kids, one only a few days old, he got to thinking about the cost of going to war and leaving his family behind. "It makes me realize how important they are, and the many sacrifices they make so I can do a job I love," he said in a moment of uncharacteristic seriousness.

For a few days the post was a bit shell-shocked. We had lived here for six months and done so much good for the surrounding communities, from fighting fires to building hospitals and schools. But evidently there were certain parties who didn't appreciate our presence. In a way, the rocket attacks were a wake-up call: No one could escape the ever-widening violence.

A few days later the attackers struck again, and then again and again. Over the next few months the rocket attacks became part of life at Q-West, and the 426th area was almost always in the target zone. This made us think that the attackers may have had inside information, perhaps from one of the local workers. It didn't take a genius to understand the importance of this unit. We were the only logistics unit on post, so everyone needed us for one thing or another—not to mention the fact that we had huge barrels of gasoline at which to aim, had the attackers actually been able to hit anything. But their aim was so bad as to be laughable. Every few days, usually at night, a couple of rockets would smash into the desert and light up the sky, and we'd shrug and go about our business.

In return, our guys would lob artillery fire out into the no-man's-land beyond the perimeter, but it was more of a scare tactic than anything. Over time we found several abandoned firing sites that were so crude that it was a wonder they weren't blowing themselves up.

I had been watching the fourth season of *M*A*S*H* on my new Army laptop (the dust having dealt a fatal blow to my portable DVD player). In a way, the rocket attacks reminded me of one of my favorite episodes. A North Korean fighter pilot would fly over, always at the same time, and drop a bomb, missing the camp by a mile. Eventually the camp's residents began placing bets on what "One O'Clock Charlie" would actually hit. They'd sit outside and picnic, drinking martinis, and wait for the hapless bomber to strike.

Sometimes I seemed to be playing a supporting role in the show's Middle Eastern spin-off. Take our golf course, for instance. Hawkeye and McIntyre liked to tee off into a minefield and trigger an explosion. When I'd get off shift and leave the TOC, I'd often see Jesse White, Lt. Col. Kelley, Maj. Whitson, and Maj. Smith teeing off a bunker. Their balls landed in a "fairway" littered with charred debris. They played a game called Army skins—whoever recorded the lowest score on a hole earned a quarter from the other players. Because of the rocky greens, scores weren't a true indicator of victory. Bragging rights were the real reward.

TPC at Mosul was making quite a splash back home. A reporter from Jesse's hometown paper in Tennessee wrote a short article about it. Several regional papers picked up the story, and *The Times* (London) had sent a reporter to write a piece. Before long, donations of clubs, balls, flags, and hats were pouring into Q-West. Then the Professional Golf Association got wind of it. The PGA listed the course as an honorary site on its official course list and sent boxes of golf gear, movies, and supplies to all the soldiers, as well as several dozen caps they'd had specially stitched with a TPC AT MOSUL logo. Jesse was pleased and a little stunned to think that all these golf-obsessed folks back in the United States were interested in him and the makeshift course he'd scratched out of the desert. He'd intended it as a place to relieve stress and exercise his passion for golf, but the course had grown into something larger: It had become a way to keep America close.

I'd get out with Jesse every chance I got, and once in a while Mike even picked up a club and whacked a few balls. But Mike's free time was becoming scarce. He'd been given the job of unit movement officer for his squadron, which meant he was responsible for moving every bit of equipment back home when the time came. It was a tough job, heavy on paperwork, and entailed endless documentation, inspections, and so on. "All that extra work means I'll be flying less," he said, and sighed. "But I like the fact that the squadron commander thinks enough of me to give me the job."

He became harder to track down. When I'd stop by his barracks, more often than not he was out running around, checking containers and hazmat paperwork, though he always left a note or word with Scott on where he was going to be. And instead of flying less, he began flying more. As two of the more experienced pilots, Mike and Scott flew security for Secretary of Defense Rumsfeld when he visited the 101st on September 5. They followed his convoy from the Mosul airfield to city hall, flew circles above the meeting area, and then followed the convoy back to the airfield. Immediately afterward Mike and his troop left for a mission, hunting terrorists in southern Iraq.

Both Mike and Scott had the most combat hours in their troop, and they adopted a bit of swagger as a result. One day I showed up for lunch to find both of them gone. I started to leave them a note when I heard the familiar *thwop* of rotor blades overhead, very low and very close. I stepped outside to see a Kiowa swooping down over Banshee headquarters, rattling the windows. I couldn't make out the pilots, but I had a sneaking suspicion. Later, Mike and Scott walked, laughing, into the room.

"How long have you been in here?" they asked.

"Long enough to see you two yahoos flying over the roof," I said, amused.

They attempted an innocent look neither could pull off. "It was his idea," Mike said, wagging his thumb in Scott's direction, and they dissolved into fits of laughter like two little boys who'd been busted for TP'ing their neighbor's yard.

Mike could be cocky, but he was not a braggart. He won two Air Medals for valor in Iraq, but you wouldn't know it from talking to him. "Now don't be goin' and writin' your dad and tellin' him all about how I won a medal," he said to me once in his room. "Next thing we know there'll be a big old article in the paper and another float."

————

For all the dangers he'd faced, Mike thrived on being a combat pilot, though I think he would have given it up in a heartbeat to go home and have kids. We discussed his putting in his twenty years and retiring on a full military pension in his late thirties. He and Scott talked about transitioning to the elite 160th Night Stalkers, which flew missions for the Army's Special Operations. It would have meant shorter, more targeted missions instead of long, grinding deployments. But we also talked about returning to Missouri, maybe buying some farmland near Macon so we could be near our family. Dad and Mike were very close, and while we never discussed inheriting the farm directly, we all knew, without saying, that Dad felt he'd found someone who would appreciate and work the farm as it deserved to be. That person was his son-in-law.

My four-year stint would be up in May 2004, forcing my decision to reenlist or not. Mike had introduced me to a major in his squadron who, with his wife, had adopted a child from Russia. "He's willing to walk us through the paperwork once we get home," Mike said. This process would take up most of my time, and once we had a child to raise, I'd need more flexible work hours. Ironically, having to reach this decision while at war only made it harder. I had grown so close to the guys in my unit that it was difficult to imagine moving on. I believed in our mission in Iraq and what we were accomplishing here, and I felt guilty leaving the job to others to finish. On the other hand, if Mike and I did have children, I never wanted to be in the position where both of us had to leave them to come to a place like this.

I agonized over my decision, but in the end the draw of a family was overpowering. After all, I would still be married to the military.

I'd start transitioning out of the Army shortly after we arrived home, but I needed to submit the paperwork before I left theatre. This meant I had to tell my chain of command of my decision, and that started with Maj. Whitson. As close as we were, he deserved to hear it first. In the third week of September, he stopped by The Heap to go over my latest performance evaluation, giving me a chance to talk to him one-on-one.

I asked him to pull up a plastic chair. After he'd given me my review, I told him that Mike and I wanted to start a family.

"Congratulations," he said. "Are you going to try soon after you get home?"

"No. . . ." I hesitated and took a deep breath. Then I told him that we were adopting because I wasn't able to have children. "So you see, it's a little different than the norm."

Maj. Whitson looked quite surprised at my bombshell. He shifted in his chair a bit and said, "I'm sorry. I didn't know."

"It never really came up," I said lightly. "But Mike and I have put our lives on hold long enough. We feel we're ready to move forward. This is our top priority."

"I understand," he replied. "I know how important being a father is to me, how much I love my kids."

"Do you think Col. Kelley will be okay with it?"

"I think the boss is going to understand," Maj. Whitson said. "He'll want to talk to you about it, a lot of people probably will. I hate to lose good officers, but I understand the reasoning behind it, so I won't try and convince you to stay."

My decision wouldn't be official until I told Dad. I dreaded doing so: For some reason I thought he would be disappointed in me. I knew this was irrational, but I thought it just the same.

"I have decided to continue on my present course and leave the Army," I wrote to him on September 21. "I could leave theatre in

January but I have decided to stay until the 'bitter end' here. I can't imagine having started this whole thing with this group of people and not ending it with them as well. The downside is this will cramp my timeline for finding a new job and all that goes with leaving the Army. . . . I imagine initially I will try and find something that pays right off the bat and then settle into figuring out what it is I want to be now that I AM grown up. I am considering getting my teaching certificate in H.S. history. I would enjoy job satisfaction, good hours but poor pay and little variety—so pros and cons."

Evidently the stress of having two daughters and a son-in-law in combat was weighing heavily on Dad because he took my news quite well. "I know it is a tough decision," he replied. "I will get you some information on teaching certificates in Missouri. You will find civilian life to be, shall we say, tame."

And so my promotion was bittersweet. I was becoming a captain, but my career would stop there. Yet I couldn't help but wonder if my love affair with the army was really going to end like this. Maybe it wasn't as final as I was thinking it to be.

My promotion ceremony was scheduled for October 1. Two weeks beforehand, I had the tailors in the laundry service sew the new rank on my Kevlar and two of my three uniforms, leaving one uniform with lieutenant rank for the ceremony. But two days before the big day, Mike found out that as the unit movement officer, he was required to attend a ten-day class in Mosul on transporting hazardous materials.

"It doesn't seem right to get promoted without you there," I told him. "I'll just postpone it until you get back."

It also meant that he'd be gone for his twenty-ninth birthday on October 10. Joining the Army ensured that he was rarely home for his birthday, so I planned to give him his present when he got back: a Harley-Davidson T-shirt I'd ordered from a shop in Tennessee. Back home Mike's wardrobe staple was blue jeans and Harley T-shirts, so I figured he'd appreciate having one here.

While he was in Mosul, Mike gave someone a note for me. He'd folded it several times, and in typical Mike fashion, he had written "CPT Blaise" on the front, then put a line through "CPT" and written "1LT" instead.

Delaying my promotion meant I had to wear the same uniform for ten days, but at least I had a washing machine. I'd stopped using the locals' laundry service since the clothes had started coming back smelling like gasoline, and certain cherished items, such as my favorite towel, began to disappear. Ordered online, the towel was big and plush and a light-green color—a huge improvement over the thin Army issue towels that barely covered half your body.

October arrived on the heels of a dust storm so severe we needed our gas masks to breathe. The storm brought thunder, lightning, and rain, along with a small tornado for good measure. But Q-West survived unscathed, and the next day dawned cool and fresh. The lower temperatures continued—autumn in Iraq had officially begun—yet no positive development went unpunished in this country, as I wrote in a mass e-mail entitled "Of Mice and Men":

> *In The Heap we are currently surviving a mice infestation. I guess the cooler temperatures have them venturing out. They are very small mice that have proved difficult to catch. We have witnessed them sitting on the traps, eating the food and moving off without ever having tripped it. We are told they can fit into a hole the size of a dime. Due to the fact that we live in a bombed-out building, I'm afraid we are fighting an uphill battle. I have moved all my food into containers impervious to mice and taped or filled every hole in my room. I did notice a cat and two kittens have moved into our building, so I am hoping they will start to feast and help the situation out.*

In the same e-mail, I also vented a bit:

> *I have to say that although I think men are excellent beings, I really feel I could do with a large dose of female companionship. I was reflecting on the lack of females in my world just the other day as I had to teach a class on how to do laundry. I work with ALL men, no women. I live with seven men, no women. For the most part this doesn't bother me too much, but there are days when I do long for a little female conversation. You know, emotions, irrational thoughts, and can we get a little fashion talk please?*

I soon got my wish. Delaying my promotion ceremony meant Lindsey could attend. She was waiting for her platoon replacement to arrive before taking over command of her company, and the lull gave her a few days to come north. She caught a Black Hawk to Q-West, and I picked her up in my Humvee and drove her to The Heap. "I like what you've done with the place," she said, only half joking. "Wow, you have so much space." Fortunately the mice had made themselves scarce, and it was too cold for camel spiders—Lindsey hates spiders of all kinds.

She slept on an extra cot in my room and came to work with me at the TOC, where she caught up on e-mails and we called Dad again. I gave her the tour of post; at the pizza place I introduced her to Mr. Mohamed, and we visited Scott and Mike. The four of us talked, not about Baghdad but about normal stuff like home and how the family was doing; the war had been our world for months, so it was the last thing we wanted to discuss. Mr. Mohamed's crew had built offices in the TOC hangar, so Linz and I watched the National League playoffs in the briefing room; the Cubs were closing in on their first World Series appearance since 1945, and I was devastated when they lost to the Florida Marlins.

Linz stayed for two days and caught up on her sleep, but she seemed preoccupied. I know her so well that I can read her mood, and I sensed that the burden of command was beginning to settle on her shoulders. She was responsible for the lives of more than a hundred soldiers, but I knew it was a job that she would manage brilliantly. Those soldiers couldn't be in better hands, and I told her so.

We held my promotion ceremony right outside the TOC. I asked Maj. Whitson, Mike, and Lindsey to do the honors. Maj. Whitson stood up and talked about me and how great it was to have Mike and Lindsey there. Then the three of them pinned on my new rank: Maj. Whitson did my collar, and Mike and Lindsey did my hat. Then I gave a short speech thanking everyone who helped me along the way, and so on. One of those people was Col. Hodges, the brigade commander, and I was thrilled that he had made time in his busy schedule to be here. I had worked with him at Fort Campbell and had gotten to know him better over the long months in Iraq. He was a great soldier and leader, and I appreciated his support. Col. Hodges had met Mike at a couple of the "smokers" at The Heap, and Mike had a lot of respect for him as well.

In the States, the soldier getting promoted throws a big party. You are supposed to spend whatever your additional pay raise is on the celebration. It was hard to spend five hundred dollars at Q-West, but I loaded up on near beer and put them out in coolers.

Linz couldn't get a ride out that day, so she stayed an extra night. I had to work, but I made dinner first at The Heap. Mike came by, and the three of us ate together. But her job was calling, and when she gave Mike a hug good-bye on October 15, her mind was already in Baghdad.

That month we got some big news: Our "head south" date was to be January 15. "Of course this is give or take a few weeks, but the general opinion is that it will be fairly accurate," I wrote Dad on October 22. "This means we will start packing stuff up in November and sending it south so that we are ready to move out on the fifteenth. Looks like we will be GACing again—hoped that we would find a better route than that. It's a little depressing to think that we have been here a year and the convoy south won't be that much safer than the convoy north. It's good to hear all the redeployment talk and to be starting to look in that direction. I just hope it doesn't slow the days down, they have been zipping by pretty quickly. Mike will be leaving about one to two weeks after I do. Generally we should arrive home about that same time apart, which isn't too bad. I will just wait for him before I go on leave.

"I can't wait to get home—really looking forward to some good old-fashioned country QUIET! No generator noise, no helicopters, just birds and bees and quiet. I won't feel like I am actually home until I get to the farm. We were watching a movie the other day and it took place in the country. Looked a lot like Missouri, but in the background you could hear the insects and some red-winged blackbirds and I felt VERY homesick. Weird what will do that to you. In all my daydreams about things I miss and where I can't wait to be—Grampy's house and yours were always at the top of my list."

———

When the war started, the Army had instigated a "stop-loss" policy, meaning that soldiers in theatre had to serve beyond their enlistment phase or stay with the unit even if they had orders taking them to a new posting. That policy had been over for several months, and soldiers had been leaving for home or for their next assignments. This meant we were losing people who knew how to "sling-load" equipment and conduct air assault operations. In an effort to curb this loss, the division commander and division sergeant major decided to bring the Air Assault School to Iraq for two months, to train existing personnel on the techniques.

As the only air assault division in the world, the 101st moves troops and supplies via helicopter, and we're known for our "quick insertion" into battle zones, where infantrymen rappel down ropes dangling from Black Hawks and drop into the combat zone, ready to fight. At Fort Campbell, Air Assault School is a tough ten-day grind; once you pass all the phases you're awarded the coveted Air Assault wings: a small badge in the shape of a helicopter with wings, worn proudly over the left breast. Those wings and the respect they garner make walking around Fort Campbell a whole lot easier. Mike had gotten his wings after joining the infantry, and I didn't want to leave the Army without mine.

This was the first time that Air Assault School had been held outside the United States. It was a kinder, gentler version—you couldn't take an infantryman straight from combat and yell at him because he didn't tie a knot correctly. The physical challenges, such as the six- and twelve-mile road marches, were axed, and the course was dropped from ten days to six. I looked forward to a new challenge and new people for a few days. Always an adrenaline junkie, I couldn't wait to rappel down a ninety-foot rope.

The school's cadre was quartered at Q-West, though soldiers from throughout the division attended. It was set up near the Brigade TOC, where we had classes on setting up sling loads for everything from boxes to Humvees and artillery pieces. We also practiced hooking the equipment up to a helicopter that hovered above us. We spent days practicing various types of rappelling with rucksacks and rifles.

I was used to knowing what was happening in every corner of Q-West, but for those six days, I was out of the loop. It was both liberating and disconcerting. But one night, when rounds started going off, I knew exactly what was going on.

"Don't worry, it's just the friendly neighborhood rocketeer," I said wryly. A couple of students and I went outside to watch the rockets hit in the distance, as if we were taking in a fireworks show.

The final test was a rappel from a Black Hawk. As the helicopter hovered ninety feet above the ground, I hooked in and backed out over the edge, my legs and feet straight out in front of me, one hand on the rope behind me. Once I was in position I bounded off the side of the helicopter and zipped to the ground, pulling the rope close with my back hand intermittently to control my speed. It was exhilarating to hear the rotor blades above my head and see the ground loom closer as I zipped down the rope.

Afterward we received our coveted wings. "Never take any flak off people who think you didn't work hard enough to get your wings," one of the instructors told us. "You're in a war zone and you were even rocketed while in school. You've earned them."

Our attitude toward our attacks may have been relatively casual, but make no mistake: We knew what was happening in Mosul and beyond, and it was worrying. The enemy had become a mix of Saddam loyalists, disaffected Iraqis, Al Qaeda followers from Saudi Arabia and Pakistan, and assorted troublemakers who were crossing the porous borders from Syria and Iran. The welcoming Mosul of the previous spring was a mere memory; stopping at a roadside stand there was now out of the question. The brigade sergeant major from 2nd Brigade and his driver were killed and dragged through the streets after taking a wrong turn. Politicians were beginning to make the inevitable comparisons to Vietnam, as Dad described in an e-mail on November 12:

> *I think it has turned into "the quagmire" the Administration feared. We are very naive I think about the capacity of other cultures to accept democracy or a republican form of government in a few days or months. Look how long it took ours to evolve, and we didn't even get the Constitution right on the first go. . . . Winning the initial war was a whole lot easier in terms of loss of life than getting the peace we desire or want.*

A week after Air Assault School, I was working at the TOC when word came down that two Black Hawks had collided in midair over Mosul, killing seventeen soldiers from the 101st. It was the highest death toll from one incident since the war started. I didn't know any of the soldiers who had died, but the 101st is like an extended family; any loss affects the entire division. I went to see Mike, only to find that he was out on a mission. But Scott was there, so as always I tossed myself on Mike's cot to talk. Soon enough the conversation turned to the accident and how tragic it was to lose so many soldiers in an instant. The conversation turned to the notification of next of kin.

I propped myself up on an elbow and said, "Scott, I can't imagine being here and having some chaplain or soldier I don't know coming up to tell me Mike's been hurt or worse. I want you to promise me that if anything ever happens to Mike, that you will be the one to tell me."

"I know what you mean," Scott said. "I can't imagine being in the same situation with someone telling me about Sonja. I will promise to make sure and be there, but only if you'll promise that if something happens to her that you'll be there for me through the whole ordeal."

We smiled and shook hands on the deal. Then Scott punched me in the shoulder and we started talking about something happier.

————

That fall, the division started handing out R and R slots to either go home or go to Qatar. They were handed out according to a complex priority list. Home R and R was the toughest to get; soldiers with new babies and ill relatives got them first. Part of my job was prioritizing who got to go. Soldiers went before officers, and since I was the one sending the soldiers, I put myself at the bottom of the list. I figured since I had the advantage of having a husband in theatre, I didn't need to go. Mike had used his slot when he'd taken emergency leave to see Grampy.

"I don't think my number will ever come up, and Mike's won't at all," I wrote Dad. "I really don't think I want to come home—well, I WANT to come home but not for just a break. I would be so tired through most of it and it would make coming back that much harder. Right now we are all kind of numb to home and starting to forget a lot of things we miss—don't want to start all over again."

I knew that the only way I'd get R and R was if we went through all the soldiers and officers and still had slots left and time to take them. By the beginning of November, there were only a handful of people who hadn't been on R and R, and Maj. Whitson and I were among them. There were slots available, and they'd go begging if we didn't take them. Finally, Lt. Col. Kelley ordered us to go, and we accepted the invitation. We started planning a date to head to Qatar, a popular getaway for war-fatigued soldiers.

When I told Sgt. Wilson that Mike couldn't go with us, he was appalled. "That ain't right!" he said. "If you're going, he should go."

"He went home on leave," I explained. "And he's not going to take a slot from a soldier."

"It still ain't right," Sgt. Wilson said, and huffed away.

Two days later, Sgt. Wilson came back from a visit to our higher headquarters in Mosul. He walked into the TOC with bags of mail and we started sorting through them, small-talking as we sifted through letters. Then, a smile twitching on his lips, my NCO looked up at me and said, "Ma'am, I got Mr. Blaise a slot for R and R the same time you're going."

I looked at him hard. "What do you mean? All our slots are taken."

"I know, but Division had extra slots, so they gave me one. You shouldn't go on R and R without each other."

It turned out that Sgt. Wilson, who had worked in Army personnel his entire career, had put his connections to good use. I'm convinced he did it because he liked Mike so much. I was so excited that I almost picked him up in a bear hug, but decided against it since he probably would have fainted. Instead, I thanked him about a million times. When I told Mike the news, he was as excited as I was. We'd leave right after Thanksgiving for Camp As Sayliyah outside Doha, Qatar's capital. We had heard other soldiers talking about Qatar, so we had some idea of what to expect. We started mapping out where we wanted to go and what we wanted to eat. We were headed to the land of civilian clothes, real showers, frosty glasses of beer—and, rumor had it, an Applebee's.

Holidays are a crucial milestone for soldiers in theatre counting the days until they go home. When Thanksgiving rolled around, we knew we'd be out of there in no time, though in fact we had about fifty days until we left for Kuwait. Our little family was split up for the holiday: Scott had gotten two weeks of R and R back home with Sonja, and Big Country was celebrating with a good friend of his from a different unit.

The Army pulled out all the stops for Turkey Day. The cooks, who were from India, decorated the chow hall with carved pumpkins and gourds, and the tables groaned with turkey, rolls, mashed potatoes, homemade pies of every type, and a rarity in these parts: ham. There was sparkling grape juice in Styrofoam cups. True to military tradition, the officers served the enlisted soldiers their Thanksgiving feast, and every unit's officers took a turn serving. Mike showed up shortly before I was done, and we sat down to turkey and potatoes with some guys from my unit.

All we could talk about was Qatar. Mike's crew chief, Specialist

Johnny "Sal" Salvadore, had gotten a slot, too, so he and Maj. Whitson rounded out our R and R foursome. We'd have almost four days away from the Army, and we looked forward to them with an almost manic anticipation.

In the meantime, The Heap needed some festive cheer, so after Thanksgiving dinner I ordered The Heap's inhabitants to show up that evening, ready to work, and to my surprise, they did. The chaplain had given us a small artificial tree, some lights and bows, as well as a CD of Christmas music that I played while we decorated, just as my family had done when I was little. We also drank near beer and smoked cigars, which my family didn't do when I was little. I asked everyone to bring a food item they'd stockpiled from their care packages, and we laid out a huge spread. Mike and Maj. Whitson came over for the food. Staff Sgt. Salyers put up the tree by our front door in the common area while I wrote everyone's name on gold and silver balls with the date and location, for example, Capt. Chip O'Neal, Christmas at The Heap, Q-West, Iraq, 2003. We strung lights in our rooms and taped big red bows on the doors and nailed stockings on the wall. Most of us didn't have official Christmas stockings, so our old black Army socks, gnarled and nasty from months inside combat boots, had to suffice.

Qatar, a peninsula off the coast of Saudi Arabia, sticks out like a hitchhiker's thumb into the Persian Gulf. On November 28, Mike, Maj. Whitson, Specialist Salvador, and I left our weapons behind and caught a ride on a C-130 cargo plane to Camp As Sayliyah outside Doha. R and R in Qatar was like a reward challenge on *Survivor*: We had won the challenge—live for nine months in hostile territory with lousy food and little sleep—and were about to be rewarded with some of the creature comforts we sorely missed.

Mike and I had heard that the barracks at As Sayliyah had private rooms for married couples, and we couldn't wait to sleep in the same bed together. "Sorry," a soldier told us at the in-processing center. "The private rooms are being occupied by colonels and generals who are transitioning out of the country." Mike had a few choice words in response. (Fear not, we managed to be resourceful.) The barracks had four long hallways of rooms, and each room housed eight to ten soldiers. We made plans to meet out front in a few minutes, and I headed to the female officers' quarters. There I took a long hot shower, letting the water flow over me, but nine months of war are tough to wash away.

When we'd left Fort Campbell all that time ago, our packing list had included one set of civilian clothes in case we needed to venture out among the locals without drawing attention to the fact that we were soldiers (as if that were possible). My light cotton pants and T-shirt had remained buried in the bottom of my duffel bag since early March, and clothes that fit me then hung on my body now. And I wasn't alone. When the four of us met outside the barracks, we laughed and pointed at one another: We all looked like children dressed in their fathers' clothes. Our first stop was the PX. Junk food, jeans, magazines, new socks: We reveled in getting to actually choose what we wanted to eat, read, and wear. It felt odd to spend money, but I managed. Mike bought new clothes and tennis shoes.

Lugging shopping bags, we stepped outside the PX and saw a Subway, a Burger King, and a coffee shop. After debating where to head first—we briefly considered a roving junk food smorgasbord—we finally settled on Subway. I ordered an Italian sub piled high with fresh vegetables, but between the big meal and the months of little sleep, I could hardly keep my eyes open in the restaurant.

Suddenly I jerked awake and felt for my weapon. *It's missing!* I thought with a rush of panic. Then I remembered it was back in Mosul, yet I could almost feel it slung across my chest, like a phantom limb. Mike did the same thing a few times, and sometimes we'd share a look that said, "Oh, yeah, we're on vacation."

That night, clutching two beer coupons each (that was the Army limit; it's hard to get drunk on two beers), we hit the bar on post. It was a dark, smoky hole in the wall with food, dancing, and, much to Mike's delight, karaoke. He immediately put his name on the list to sing. The place was packed with R and R soldiers from Iraq, but we found a table, and a few minutes later we were sipping our first real beers in nine months. "Shit, that tastes good," Mike said, a blissed-out look on his face. While Sal flitted from table to table, talking people out of their unused beer coupons, Mike eagerly awaited his turn to sing.

"Mike puts Travis Tritt to shame," I said to Maj. Whitson. "He's really good."

"Really, you sing?" the major said. Mike just nodded and replied, "I'm all right." Most of the singers were lousy, and the crowd kept yapping over their valiant yodeling.

When Mike's turn to sing came around, he walked up to the stage as the first notes of his song came over the speakers. A hush fell over the crowd as he belted out that loud, rowdy country song, "Here's a Quarter (Call Someone Who Cares)." (He always started off a karaoke session with it, and this time was no exception.) Maj. Whitson was speechless. Afterward, as Mike made his way back to the table to loud applause, people stopped him to compliment him on his singing and to ask him if he'd sing some more, so he did. Mike was on cloud nine, and so was I—listening to him sing was like watching my favorite band perform.

Before we'd left Q-West, Wendy's husband, Chris, had put me in touch with an old Air Force buddy of his who was working at As Sayliyah, and Dan had agreed to sign us off post and show us Doha, Qatar's capital. The four of us were eager to see more of the Middle East world than brown sand and sad cities, and as one of the wealthiest countries in the world, oil-rich Qatar fits the bill. We drove along manicured boulevards lined with soaring palm trees and modern buildings. Mercedeses and Bentleys zipped by. Our first stop: the Doha City Center Mall, a lavish, Western-style shopping center. Palatial and palm-studded, the mall had everything, including an extravagant food court (we ate yet again out of respect for American fast food), hundreds of upscale shops, an epic games arcade, and a Starbucks. The mall teemed with women in robes wearing designer shoes and carrying Gucci purses. Mike tried on some clothes in a men's apparel store and came out shaking his head. "The men wear strange underwear in this country," he said. "They look like diapers." We capped off our day with a dinner of USDA prime steak and potatoes and slept the sleep of the extremely well fed.

The Army offers all kinds of activities at As Sayliyah that soldiers can sign up for, so the next day Maj. Whitson, Mike, and I took a desert safari in Land Rovers. The dunes were what I'd always imagined dunes should look like: mountains of white, powdery sand rolling as far as the eye could see. Our local guides drove those Land Rovers like dune buggies; a few times we actually went vertical and bottomed out so hard our heads hit the roof of the car. It felt great to laugh and have fun without worrying about a rocket spoiling our good time. At the end of the day they drove us to the Persian Gulf, where we took a quick swim in the chilly water just to say we'd done it. The guides set up tables by the water and lit a bonfire, and the three of us ate by the light of flickering tiki torches, laughing and talking until midnight.

My last act in Qatar was to drag Mike to the post salon for his first massage, manicure, and pedicure. "I'm looking forward to a massage," he said.

"I'm looking forward to watching a lady file your nails," I replied. Mike was no pretty boy, but after we got married he'd become more interested in his appearance. He kept his nails cut short, but his feet were easy to make fun of. I called them "Fred Flintstone feet." They were square and flat on the bottom, and Ranger School had left them permanently gnarled. I got a huge kick out of watching Korean women file down his calluses and clutch his huge paws in their tiny hands, ordering him to keep still.

The R and R served its purpose: We headed back ready to face our last two months in Iraq. "It was nice to get away," I told Mike as the C-130 rumbled toward Mosul, "but it was hard to have a good time knowing our guys were still back there sucking it up in harm's way."

This feeling intensified when we found out there'd been a rocket attack while we were gone, though once again, the attackers had missed.

––––––––

By mid-December the Iraqi rainy season was in its full soggy glory. There was nothing but eternal rain, day after day of it, and the Army doesn't issue umbrellas. Q-West became a boot-sucking, tire-trapping, soul-sapping swamp. "Just when you think this place can't get worse, it starts to rain and doesn't stop for weeks," I wrote in a mass e-mail on December 8. "Sand is bad enough when it's dry, but now we have nothing but muck everywhere we turn. The last week it has turned really foggy, and I mean can't-see-five-feet-in-front-of-you foggy. Mike has been grounded a lot, which is both nice and frustrating at the same time. When you have time off there isn't always a lot to occupy your time. In addition, it is now getting COLD. On the bright side, The Heap has proven to be very waterproof. Not the warmest building around, but hopefully we will have heat soon and, to be honest, I'd rather be cold than wet. Some people, including my boss, have been flooded out of their buildings and/or tents, and THAT would be miserable."

The constant downpour dampened everyone's mood. Despite being fifty-five days away from leaving Iraq and only eighty days from getting home, we felt as if we were running short on things to be happy about.

That changed two weeks before Christmas. I had just reported for duty at the TOC when Chip ran up and said, "Did you hear? We got him! The ace of spades!" Soldiers from the 4th Infantry Division had pulled Saddam Hussein out of a hole near Tikrit, looking mangy, dirty, and disoriented. I found it fitting that he was checked for lice. It was sweet justice that he'd experienced a bit of the misery his people had lived with for years.

The headline on the December 15 edition of the *Sandy Club Gazette* quoted Paul Bremer, the U.S. administrator in Iraq: "Ladies and gentlemen, we got him." More than one soldier I knew grumbled that his captors should have "killed him and been done with it," but I was proud of the fact that they had restrained themselves. The Iraqi people deserved to put this guy on trial. Maybe now, we said, they and their country could move forward.

The news kept getting better as we got new "going-home" dates. Instead of leaving Kuwait in early March, we'd be heading home between February 9 and 13. We had always assumed we wouldn't get out of the country until we had at least hit the 365-day mark, so this meant we would be home about three weeks earlier than we thought. We stood there momentarily stunned, and then everyone cheered. I immediately sent out a mass e-mail. "I am SO excited, I can hardly type," I wrote. "This means we will be HOME much sooner than expected and should be on leave around the first of March. Of course in the Army things can change, but they won't change by much because once the boats are on their way your timelines are pretty much set. Hopefully Lindsey will be hot on our heels!!! Hip hip hooray!"

"Hallelujah and praise the Lord," Dad wrote back. "Now how will I break this to Scout. Maybe better do it outside so he won't have an accident. He will undoubtedly run about the house in circles, jumping and prancing. I may even give him a fresh chew bone tonight."

A week before Christmas, I was hanging out with Scott and Mike when suddenly, out of the blue, Mike reached into his pocket and shoved a small box, beautifully gift-wrapped, into my hand. "Open it," he said.

He had been saying for some time that he had a Christmas present for me. This being Iraq, I assumed it was probably some sort of gag gift. He kept insisting he didn't want to wait until Christmas to give it to me, and finally he could take it no longer.

As I sat there looking at the present, Scott stood up and said, "I guess I'll be going."

Inside the wrapping I found a blue Tiffany & Co. box wrapped with a red ribbon. I stared at him in wonder. "How in the world did you get Tiffany to ship here?" I asked.

"Scott got it for me when he was on leave," said Mike, barely able to contain his glee.

As I slipped the small card from its envelope, I looked at him and said, "I can't believe you did this. I didn't think you were seriously getting me a present. I feel terrible—I didn't get you anything."

"Don't worry," he replied. "You always take care of me. Whenever I've needed anything, you've always found a way to get it for me."

I read the card out loud: "Merry Christmas. Why should this one be any different from all the rest? Love, Mike." Inside the box was a simple silver necklace with a tiny tear-shaped pendant. "I love it!" I said. I tried it on in front of a little mirror while Mike beamed, thrilled with his success. By this time, his accomplice was back in the room. The necklace was too short to wear with my uniform but I couldn't wait to wear it when I got home.

That night at the TOC I showed it off to all the guys. They were pretty impressed—and a little ashamed. Like me, they hadn't put a whole lot of thought into getting their wives something special. This was Iraq, after all.

As Christmas approached, the TOC overflowed with white priority mail boxes from across the United States. The place looked like a postal service shipping center. Our chaplain had signed up for several online programs that let people "adopt" units in Iraq by sending them needed supplies, and the American people had come through, no more so than at Christmas. There was far too much for just our unit, so the chaplain systematically sorted through all the boxes and divided them into categories—hygiene, games, books—and distributed them across Q-West.

Thousands of miles away, Dad was trying on the unit sweatshirt that read TASKMASTERS, and Mom, Grandma Decker, Peg, and Cheryl were admiring the flowers I'd ordered for them on FTD.com.

On Christmas Day, the officers and the NCOs played one last game of flag football in country. I couldn't play because I had to watch the TOC, but the game was still going on when I got off shift, so I ran over to get Mike and Scott. The weather was cool and sunny—what I'd come to call "a pretty day in Iraq"—and I wanted to drag them outside to enjoy the weather and the game. When I got there, Mike was up and around but Scott was still sleeping.

"Do you think we should wake him up and bring him with us?" I whispered.

"We are not leaving him here by himself," Mike said, shaking him awake.

We all had times where the war got to us, where a sort of combat fatigue set in and turned our minds and bodies to mush. Today was one of those for Scott. We could tell by the look on his face that he wanted to be in his own bed at home, not here with us.

"I'm not going," he snarled and rolled over, showing us his back.

Mike just shook him harder. "You may want to lie here all day, but it's Christmas and we are family. So you're getting up and coming with us, and we are all going to do something together."

"All right," he growled and threw on some clothes. We went to the football game, watched Maj. Whitson score the winning touchdown, and then enjoyed a big spread at the chow hall. We'd received two copies of Mike's favorite movie in a care package from home, and the three of us watched *National Lampoon's Christmas Vacation* on Scott's laptop, just as we used to do at home. To this day, Scott likes to tell the story of how Mike and Kate wouldn't "leave him the hell alone" on Christmas Day in Iraq.

By the end of the year the rocket attacks had ebbed, thanks to our artillery barrages and a few tanks the brigade had parked around the perimeter. "Tanks just sitting there can be quite a deterrent," I wrote Dad.

But the rocketeers weren't done yet. They managed one last salvo, and this time they hit a little too close to home.

I was in the TOC when news came over the radio that the Cav had been hit. The 2/17 squadron commander, Lt. Col. Schiller, was out at the airfield preparing to go on a mission when a rocket struck near his aircraft, sending shrapnel into his thigh. "I'm headed to Charlie Company to check on Colonel Schiller," said Maj. Whitson, who was a good friend of his. Though I knew Mike was okay, I wanted to see for myself. I grabbed a Humvee and headed over to find him in his cot, getting some sleep before that night's mission, oblivious to the world.

CHAPTER 22

SHORT-TIMERS

IN EARLY JANUARY 2004, I moved out of The Heap and into a "living container," a trailer divided in two by a wall, creating two compartments. Kellogg, Brown and Root had deposited an entire neighborhood of them at Q-West to replace the tents. Chip had moved into one in December and couldn't stop raving about how comfortable it was—and warm. As hot as The Heap had been in the summer, it was freezing in the winter, and the ceilings were so high that space heaters made little difference. So I packed up and left The Heap for good. On the one hand, I was sad to go—I'd worked hard to make it a home. At the same time, most of my friends had already moved out, and I'd have to go anyway since I was leaving the country in a few weeks. I was one of the last to leave.

I took my photos and artwork off the walls and carefully packed them in a box to send to Dad, along with a few boxes of clothing and pots and pans. The only thing I brought from The Heap to the living container was my calendar, now a thicket of Xs. My days in Iraq were dwindling.

Our replacements at Q-West were several Stryker Brigade combat teams. They were named after the new Stryker vehicle that was being tested in these new brigades. It is the cutting edge in light armored vehicles, designed to withstand RPGs, roadside bombs, and various armor-piercing rounds. But we had mixed feelings about the new guys. Like people selling a home they'd remodeled with love and care to new owners, we almost hated to hand Q-West over. We had invested our blood, sweat, and tears into improving the base and developing relationships with the locals, and we hoped our improvements would stick.

The living container was an improvement over The Heap in most respects. It had bunk beds, a wardrobe, a table and chairs, and a space heater. But it lacked windows and the walls were paper-thin, so I was glad I wouldn't be in it for long. Mike liked the fact that the container was warm. The Kiowa pilots flew with their doors off for better visibility, but this made it miserable to fly when it was cold, windy, or rainy. His unit had no heat in their buildings, and even though I gave him and Scott a space heater to use, they felt guilty using it when no one else had one.

As our departure date approached, my days got busier. I had awards to process, countless manifests to check and change, office equipment to pack, and records to catalog. Mike was working overtime overseeing the shipping of the squadron's equipment. He was also desperately searching for an Iraqi veterinarian who could give Sofia the shots she'd need to enter the United States.

On December 31, Mike dropped Dad a line.

> *Well we are busy as ever here but the added work is in preparation for the trip home so it's definitely bearable. I enjoyed my visit, although short, with you on the phone. I will try and do it again soon. I am very thankful that I was truly blessed with an extraordinary family. Your multiple care packages and heartfelt letters that seem to say just what I needed to hear. I would like to tell you that I have been taking care of your little girl but I have to say the opposite has happened. What a lucky man I am!! She does so much I am not sure where she finds the time. We are counting the days until we arrive in what Grandma Decker called in her last letter to me "God's Country." I can't think of a more fitting title. Well I will talk to you again soon. Again I know you don't truly know what you mean to me. Take care of yourself and I will be squeezing the crap out of you soon, about fifty some days.*

Things were shaping up on the home front. Mike and I had gotten a house on post at Fort Campbell, around the corner from Scott and Sonja. It had a fenced yard and was across the street from a large field, perfect for Scout. "I'm hoping to be moved in and unpacked before Mike gets home," I e-mailed Dad. "He is generally in my way during moving time, trying to convince me not to throw away his T-shirt from Atlanta Homecoming 1980! Ha."

Dad and I arranged to meet in Clarksville. He would bring a

trailer of household belongings he'd stored for us in Macon, such as our hunting rifles and antique dishes. I also asked him to bring Scout. Since I didn't know exactly when my battalion would land at Fort Campbell—our window was February 9 to 13—Sonja agreed to be the liaison. She and Dad had traded numerous e-mails while I was gone and had become friendly. She'd let him know when our flight left Kuwait City; and they'd agreed to meet on post and take a bus to the parade field to wait for me.

The first units from the 101st had begun to arrive at Fort Campbell on January 7. We had seen their homecomings on television, but I tried not to dwell on what was sure to be an emotional moment. I still had the long ground assault convoy to Kuwait ahead of me, and Mike had a few more missions to fly.

On January 14, Mike made his last call home, which Terry described in an e-mail to Dad (note how father and son shared an aversion to punctuation):

> *I had a call about 1 am this morning from Mike. We were able to visit for about 15 min or so. He thought that this would be the last time we would be able to talk until Kuwait or possibly the states. He was excited as he was telling me of a medical helicopter that went down. He heard the mayday call and as he was in the air flew right to the downed aircraft and was able to direct rescue people to them. Everyone was okay and the area was secured until they were able to fix the helicopter and fly it away. It was later he learned as I understand it that he was the only one who heard the mayday call. Other than that, everything sounded pretty normal, just all this talk about packing up to come home. Doesn't that just sound great.*

On January 21, I put the hundredth edition of the *Sandy Club Gazette* to bed and completed the 101st, which I planned to hand out to the battalion as we boarded the plane in Kuwait to go home. A special six-page edition, it included a passage from *All Quiet on the Western Front*, a compendium of my "French Bashing Favorites from Throughout the Year," "Five Reasons We Can't Wait to Get Home" (No. 1: "Having to look at other people's POO every time you go the latrine") and "The Latest World News and Sports News" ("Who cares, you'll be home in a few hours and you can watch SportsCenter and CNN").

On a more serious note, I wrote an open letter to the entire 426th, which read as follows:

Dear Sandy Club *Subscribers,*

Soon we will return to Fort Campbell and before long everyone will start to go our own way. Some will go to new duty stations, some will leave the Army and some will stay at Fort Campbell. Chances are you may never experience anything like this again and throughout your life you will meet even fewer people who can relate to the same experience. Regardless of what you choose to do, you have now become part of a "club" of sorts. Whether you realize it or not, this is the end of one of the most influential and important years of your life. Friendships you have made here will last your lifetime. The freedom and help we have brought to this country will have changed a whole generation of young Iraqi children's lives for the better. The American people will hold you in awe until the flag is folded for you one last time.

In 345 days you have endured a grenade attack, Scud missiles, the GAC from hell; fought the battles of An Najaf, Karbala, Al Hillah, and Mosul. You have dealt with fear, death, unbearable heat, euphoria, and an endless work schedule. This "club" you are now part of will continue to affect your life no matter what you choose to do in the future. You will always have a unique perspective of Iraq and will remember this year every time Iraq is mentioned in a book or on television.

Few people are given the opportunity to make history, not just live it. Your "club" is made up of the American people, the soldiers in the 101st, the Bastogne Brigade, the 426th FSB, your company, your platoon, your squad, your circle of friends, the guy who sleeps next to your cot.

So that's the true meaning behind the name of the "Sandy Club." It's not just about the "Bastogne" symbol of the club, it's about belonging for the rest of your life to a group of people who spent a year in the desert and made a difference. So stand tall when you get home, drink a beer down at the VFW and tell war stories, live long and happy, take every opportunity to continue to make history and never forget your brothers and sisters in arms and the "club" you forged in the desert. God speed and good luck!

—The Editor.

I had one last conversation with Dad, a mop-up call about home-coming logistics.

"The next time you hear from me, I'll be in Kuwait," I told him.

———

My last night at Q-West was January 23, a Friday. Our advance party, which included Chip and Jesse, had already left. They would arrive in Kuwait almost a day and a half ahead of us to prepare for our arrival. Our trucks were lined up and ready to leave first thing in the morning. After that night, we would have one more night to spend on Iraqi soil, somewhere between Mosul and the border—wherever we took a break on the drive south. I'd packed all the gear I had to pack, taken all the pictures I was going to take. I was ready to leave, minus a quick good-bye and good luck for Mr. Mohamed in the morning.

Mike had two more nights at Q-West. They would fly south on Sunday, providing air security for a different convoy from the 101st that was also bound for Kuwait.

That night was my last on duty in the TOC, or what was left of it. Almost everything was packed up, and our radios were already in the Humvee, ready for the drive south. It would be a slow night, with nothing but administrative radio traffic.

On Friday morning, Maj. Whitson turned to me at breakfast and said, "The boss, Commander Sergeant Major Stokes and I are playing cards and drinking near beers at his place tonight. Why don't you and Mike join us for one last hurrah?" He must have seen the look of concern cross my face because he added, "If you're needed for something, you'll only be a few seconds away. The radio operator can come and get you."

"Okay, sounds fun," I agreed. With his blessing, Mike and I would have a few laughs before we said our good-byes.

Mike wasn't flying that night, so we planned to spend the afternoon at his place with Scott and Big Country before heading to the TOC for a game of spades. It was unusual for us to get a block of six hours together, and we both looked forward to the visit. I got off work on Friday morning, grabbed a Humvee, and headed over to his place. When I opened the door, I was surprised to find him sleeping. At this hour, that only meant one thing.

The sound of the door opening woke Mike up. He rolled over, saw it was me, and said, "Bad news, Chubs. I've got to fly after all. Captain Fredericks has a meeting, and he asked me to take over his flight tonight."

"Really? Who are you flying with?"

"Another pilot from the new Cav unit that's taking over. We're going to provide security to the guys in Mosul like normal, but it's also a chance to show him some of the obstacles we've found these past few months."

"That sucks." But that was life in the Army: The mission comes first. I sat on the end of his cot. "So what's the plan?"

"Let me sleep a few more hours and come back around four. We can eat dinner together before the mission brief. The weather isn't supposed to be the greatest, so we may not even fly."

"All right. I'll go get some sleep myself and catch up with you around four." And I headed back to my trailer to grab some shut-eye so I'd be ready to win at cards later.

At around three thirty in the afternoon, I hitched a ride back to Mike's and found him lying in bed, awake. Scott wouldn't be back until later. I lay down next to Mike in his cot. His gear was packed and stacked by the door—he was as ready to leave Iraq as I was.

A few days earlier, Maj. Gen. Petraeus had issued an order saying that all soldiers had to make sure their equipment was clean so that when they disembarked at Fort Campbell they'd look presentable. I may have been the more straitlaced of the two of us, but to me "clean" meant beating your vest a few times to get the dust off. I wasn't going to go out of my way, and I wouldn't have expected my soldiers to, either.

To my surprise, Mike had hand-scrubbed every piece of equipment with a toothbrush and rubbed it until it shone. When I commented on this, he began to pick pieces up off the floor and show me his handiwork. I found it hilarious that he had gone to such lengths. I began to tease him so mercilessly that soon he was doubled over with laughter, his eyes tearing. It always felt like a gift when I made him laugh that hard since it happened so rarely, and I began to laugh, too.

Finally we paused to catch our breath. "We have to make dinner," I said, and I started to stand up, but Mike grabbed my hand and pulled me back down onto the cot. He looked at me very seriously, though his eyes were still laughing.

"You know," he said, "I'm really glad this year's over, and I wouldn't want to do it again. But I just wanted you to know that I've had a really good time with you this past year."

"Really?"

"Yeah. I know we're at war and it sucks and it's dirty and we're tired, but looking back, I actually had fun with you."

I smiled and said, "I had fun with you, too."

We whipped up a care-package dinner on the camp stove and headed to the TOC. Two Kiowas would be flying that night. Chief Warrant Officer 3 Dan Hoff would be in the lead bird with his new aviator, and Mike would be in the second bird with his new pilot, Chief Warrant Officer 2 Brian Hazelgrove. They were supposed to meet Mike in the Banshee TOC so he could give them their mission and route brief. "When Scott gets back, he'll take you home," Mike said as he gathered his gear.

I zipped a black fleece jacket over my uniform and we walked outside to take a look at the weather. It was a tar-black night, and the wind was blowing hard.

"The weather's not looking too good," Mike commented. "I wouldn't be surprised if we decided not to fly after all." He grabbed me, gave me a kiss and then a hug. We stood there for a moment, looking at each other, our foreheads touching. We were excited to be going home, moving on to the next phase of our life together.

When we walked inside the Banshee TOC, Mike tossed me a black fleece stocking cap. The aviators had been issued these, and I had envied Mike this cap for the last few months. It was warm but thin enough that I could wear it underneath my Kevlar on the long, cold drive south. "You're going to need that," he said.

Big Country showed up, and the three of us sat and talked while we waited for the new pilots to arrive. Mike stood up and started to walk toward the briefing room, but before he entered, he stopped and looked over his shoulder.

"I'm still not sure if we are flying tonight or not, but regardless I'll come by in the morning to tell you bye." And with that he went inside and shut the door behind him.

A few minutes later, Scott walked in. "Are you ready? Do you want to go back there and say good-bye?"

"I don't want to interrupt him."

"Hell, yeah, we're interrupting him!"

He grabbed my arm, dragged me to the briefing, and opened the door. "Mike, we're leaving. I'm taking Kate back."

"Okay."

I said, "I'll see you later, right?"

"Yeah, no matter what, I'll find you in your vehicle before you leave in the morning. Don't worry, I'll find you."

———

"We'll bid seven." I looked over my cards as Maj. Whitson recorded our bid on the score sheet. The four of us sat around the table laughing and trash-talking as we threw our cards down and outbid one another. Outside the wind howled.

Just as I was about to throw down a card, I heard a familiar *thwop-thwop* and I paused. Concern skittered across our faces.

Lt. Col. Kelley noticed it as well. "That sounds like our medevac chopper. They must be doing some last-minute training."

"Do you want me to go check on it?" I asked.

"Nope. If we're needed, someone will come and get us."

I nodded and played my card as the sound of the rotor blades faded into the night.

CHAPTER 23

GOING HOME

ABOUT FIVE MINUTES after we heard the medevac chopper fly off, an officer entered the TOC. I looked at his name—Royer—and knew who he was: the former squadron executive officer for Mike's unit. Mike had often talked about him—he and his wife were adopting a Russian child—but we'd never officially met. He looked in my direction, and I could tell he recognized me as well.

"Hey," Lt. Col. Kelley said casually. "What's goin' on?"

I saw Maj. Royer glance quickly at me with a poorly disguised look of alarm, as if thinking, *Holy shit, what do I do, what do I do?*

Then he said, "Lieutenant Colonel Schiller sent me over here. He wanted to see if you could come to Cav headquarters for a visit." Maj. Royer seemed to be attempting a relaxed tone, as if his request was no big deal.

"Sure, does he need something?" Lt. Col. Kelley said. "Is it important?

"Yeah, well, we thought maybe we could use some of your equipment. We had a bird go down, we just need something to help recover it."

When I heard the words *a bird go down*, my heart dropped and I looked at Maj. Whitson. His face had gone white. He said, "Mike's flying tonight, right?"

"Yeah." I looked back at Maj. Royer and Lt. Col. Kelley, who had adopted the major's attitude of forced nonchalance. But the request was unusual since we'd had helicopters go down before and never had to use any of our assets to help recover the wreckage.

"Okay," Lt. Col. Kelley replied, "I'll come with you and see what we can do."

Then Maj. Whitson said, "Kate, I think you need to go with the boss."

"No, I'll stay here. I'm sure it's nothing, but I should get to the TOC to wait for word on getting a recovery team ready." Something felt wrong, but I didn't want to go over there and confirm that my gut feeling was right.

He leaned toward me across the table. "Kate, I think you need to go. I'll go to the TOC and I'll cover your shift, but I think you need to go."

"Okay, maybe you're right."

I left the TOC and climbed into the colonel's vehicle. Maj. Royer climbed into his and took off down the road as fast as he could go, as if trying to beat us to squadron headquarters.

A creeping anxiety was setting into my bones, an alarm bell clanging, *Something's not right, something's not right.* I wedged my hands between my legs to stop them from shaking.

"I'm sure it's nothing," Lt. Col. Kelley was saying as he drove. "I've been by a couple of times this week and missed seeing Schiller. He probably just wants to shoot the shit." The wind carried his words away as soon as they left his mouth.

I said, "You're probably right. But if we pull up and see Scott there, then something's wrong."

We pulled up to Cav headquarters and parked. Through the large glass doors I saw Lt. Col. Schiller, Maj. Royer, and Mike's troop commander, Capt. Adam Fredericks, huddled in conversation. Scott was there, standing off to the side.

Lt. Col. Kelley got out of the vehicle and jogged inside ahead of me.

My next moves happened in slow motion, methodically, as if I were giving myself orders. *Take your seat belt off. Shut the vehicle door. Walk inside. Look at Scott and smile because maybe it's not what you think it is, maybe it's completely innocent; maybe it has nothing to do with Mike at all.*

"Hey, sir, what's going on?"

Everyone was way too quiet. Lt. Col. Schiller walked up to me and looked me right in the eyes. There was no foot shuffling or looking at the ceiling, and I have always appreciated that.

"Kate, we had a Kiowa go down tonight, and Mike was flying. I'm really sorry, but right now it looks like he didn't make it."

My first reaction was to walk away. *I'm dreaming. I have to be having a nightmare. This couldn't happen, we've worked so hard and we are going to have kids and Mike is going to be a great dad. I just saw him, smiling, joking, and picking on me. This is Mike, he's larger than life, everybody likes him, he's a good person, he's religious, he's lived a clean life. If I were God I would want him to entertain me, but there are a lot of worse people out there.*

I stood and stared for a few minutes into the building's courtyard. They silently waited to see what I would do because if I believed it, then they could, too. Scott came up behind me and wrapped me in hug and said he was sorry. Then he started to cry. And that's when I knew it was real—because Scott doesn't cry. Behind him I heard Adam Fredericks crying, too.

Lt. Col. Kelley walked over and said, "Kate, I am so sorry. What can I do?"

"Can you send Major Whitson over here?" Every part of me shook, and I felt as if I would fall apart were it not for a thin band of steely resolve holding me together. I prayed it wouldn't snap.

"I'll go get him."

They put Scott and me in Lt. Col. Schiller's room while he went to brief Maj. Gen. Petraeus. We sat down on the cot and Scott put his arm around my shoulder and we sat there in silence. It was cold, so cold; the hard wind blew through the cracks in the building, and we were both shivering. I couldn't stop my teeth from chattering, couldn't stop saying to Scott, "This isn't really happening. It seems all made up. But I know Lieutenant Colonel Schilling wouldn't tell me he was gone if he weren't really sure. He wouldn't do that."

"No," said Scott softly. "He wouldn't do that."

"He wasn't even supposed to be flying. He was supposed to go home. We were both going home." And then there was nothing left to say.

A few minutes later Lt. Col. Schiller returned, clutching a black satellite phone. We stood up automatically because that's what soldiers do when a higher-ranking officer walks in. He looked me in the eyes and spoke gently yet firmly.

"Kate, there are two things I want you to decide. One is, do you want to notify the family or do you want the military to notify the family?"

This was easy. "Sir, I want to do it. Let me have the chance to tell Mike's parents myself. It'll be easier coming from me." I didn't want two strange men in uniform showing up at Terry's door and Peg's door. I didn't want them to open the door and see them, feel the fear and pain pierce their hearts when they realized why they were there.

Lt. Col. Schiller continued. "Now the other question is, what do you want to do? I know you're close to the guys in your unit. Do you want to go back now, or do you want to go back with your unit to Kuwait?'

"I need to take Mike home. My family is going to need me at home."

"Okay, now is there anything I can do for you right now?"

"I would like your permission to allow Scott to escort me home."

The Army wouldn't allow us both to escort Mike home, so they gave me the choice of sending Scott with Mike or with me. I handed the decision to Scott.

"Mike would want me to take you home," he said. I was grateful for his decision because the thought of that long plane ride by myself was unfathomable.

"Scott's coming with me," I said to Lt. Col. Schiller.

"Done." And he handed me the phone so I could call our families.

Scott and I headed out to stand on the top of a bunker so I could get a better signal. The wind gusted and the sky spat rain intermittently. The night was black, too black to see.

I stood on top of a bunker in the middle of the night, shaking uncontrollably, looking at the phone as if it had suddenly appeared out of nowhere in my cold hand. I called Terry at home, but got the answering machine. He and Cheryl were probably at work, and I'd never bothered to write down their cell phone numbers because Mike had been my human Rolodex, remembering every phone number he'd ever heard. Standing on that bunker, freezing and shaking in the wind, I dialed Dad's cell number.

He was at the grain bin on the Halls' farm, helping them grind feed. When he heard my voice, he said excitedly, "Hey, Kate! Are you in Kuwait?"

"No." The word snagged in my throat.

"Is there something wrong?"

"Dad, Mike was flying last night and his helicopter crashed."

"Is he okay?"

"Dad, he's gone."

"Oh no, oh no." The last time I heard my father sound like that was in the hospital after Mom's accident. It was the saddest voice I had ever heard.

Saying *he's gone* out loud made it true. The thin band of steel inside me broke, and the tears and sobs crashed over me so hard I could barely speak. I was crying and shaking, my teeth were chattering and I thought, *Every time I say it out loud it means it's really true and I don't want it to be true.*

"Dad, I need you to help me track down Terry and Peg. I don't know their cell phone numbers and I don't know their work numbers."

"I'll take care of it."

"Okay, I'll call you back in a few hours."

Dad turned to Chuckie Hall and said, "Something terrible has happened. I've got to go."

He ran home to his landline. He called Terry at his job at the Macon Electric Cooperative and was told that he was in Kansas City. He called the Blaise family pastor, Sheila, and asked her to meet him at his house. He'd no sooner hung up than his cell rang—it was Terry. "Work called, they said you were looking for me." He said he and Cheryl were at the hospital in Kansas City, where Mike's brother, Josh, had been admitted with pneumonia. He was sitting at Josh's bedside.

A minute later, Terry dropped the phone.

"Terry, what's wrong?" Cheryl picked up the phone, put it to her ear, and walked out into the hallway, listening. Then she reached out to steady herself against the wall.

Pastor Sheila arrived at Dad's, and from there they drove to Peg's, where Pastor Sheila broke the news. Dad stayed at Peg's for about an hour until friends arrived to comfort her. Then he drove to Grandma Decker's to tell her and then drove to the bank where his sister Teresa worked as a receptionist, but somehow word had already traveled, in the way it does in small towns, and by the time he got there she already knew.

About two hours later I called Dad back and he told me that he had notified Mike's parents. I hadn't expected him to do that, and I was surprised but also grateful.

"I've also told our family. I'm trying to get ahold of all your sisters now. Is there anyone else you need me to call?"

"Please call Mollie. She can let Nancy and Natalie know. Her number is in the phone book."

Dad was my oak. He seemed so unemotional, and I was grateful for how well he was handling the situation. I found out later that he was a wreck, pulling himself together long enough to talk to me, falling apart when he got off the phone.

My next mission was to get ahold of Lindsey. Her unit had just moved and the number I had didn't work. "I can't find her!" I said to Scott, welling with frustration. Scott found a computer so I could send her an e-mail. When I opened up my account, there was a message from one of Mike's buddies, Bubba, whom we knew from flight school and Korea. Bubba wrote that he heard a Kiowa had gone down from the 101st and wanted to check in with Mike and Scott. He was worried, was sure everything was fine but wanted to be sure. I e-mailed him and Mike's best friend, C. D. Foster. I wanted them to hear it from me, not from the grapevine.

Sleep was an impossible notion. We sat in a room near the TOC waiting for news on our departure. By now Maj. Whitson had showed up. He was calm and solid, just like Dad. I asked Scott to find Big Country; it didn't seem right that he wasn't with us.

When Big Country walked in the door, he bent his tall frame over and sobbed on my shoulder. He wiped his eyes and apologized. "I'm sorry for crying on you."

"It's okay, I know how much you love Mike."

"I'm supposed to be comforting you and you're the one comforting me. It's not supposed to work that way, Kate."

Col. Hodges stopped by to give his condolences, and I was grateful for his compassion. Lt. Col. Kelley said he was going to keep the news quiet in our battalion so I wouldn't have to deal with countless questions and concerns. He would tell the battalion shortly before they left Q-West.

By now it was three in the morning. The sitting around had become too much, so Scott and I decided to try for sleep. We stopped by the Banshee area to see the soldiers in Mike's troop, who looked as if they'd been hit by a fleet of buses. But I wanted them to see me so that they'd know everything was going to be all right, even if I wasn't so sure of that myself. Then Maj. Whitson gave us a ride back to my living container. I'd already packed my bags and stored my belongings on the truck for next day's ground assault convoy departure. I made a mental note to track my stuff down in the morning. Right now, I just needed to sleep.

Maybe I can forget about this day. Maybe I'll wake up to a differ-
ent one.

Scott, ever the watchdog, didn't sleep a wink, afraid to nod off in case I needed him. He spent what remained of the night propped up in the corner of the bunk bed.

The downside of going to sleep was waking up the next morning and realizing all over again what I didn't what to know.

We went to track down my bags. The work area was humming with activity and high-spirited soldiers preparing to head out. No one knew about Mike, and it was awful to walk around and talk to my friends while harboring this terrible secret. People would stop me and ask, "Are you okay? You look a little out of it."

A sergeant with whom I worked came up to me. He'd never met Mike, so when he saw Scott, he said, "This must be Mike, coming to see you off, huh?" We mumbled a reply and shuffled off to collect my personnel file from the back of a Humvee.

My job was to account for every person and every detail in the battalion, no matter how minor. I noticed that a few people were loading up onto our ground assault convoy who weren't supposed to be going with us. It was hard to stop worrying about my job. When I told Maj. Whitson, he said, "Don't worry, Kate, We'll take care of it."

We gathered my things and got back to Scott and Mike's room to find that Big Country had already packed their bags for the plane ride home. Though Mike would follow Scott and me home on a later flight, his belongings would come with us. Combined with my bags, we had ten large pieces of military baggage, a mountain of belongings that would later overwhelm me to the point where I wanted to dump them into the ocean.

The room was stripped clean. Someone had written on the wall above Mike's cot, "Rest Easy Banshee 22."

For the first time in nine hours, Scott left me alone to check on our ride to Mosul. I lay down on Mike's bunk in that empty room, where just hours before we had been laughing. I had never felt lonelier or more lost. Big Country was guarding the door, and I could hear people cajoling him to let them in so they could talk to me.

A Black Hawk flew Scott and me to Mosul later that morning. Maj. Royer and the aviation brigade command, Sgt. Maj. Glidewell, accompanied us. Col. Samuel Holloway, the division support commander who ran the airfield in Mosul, had secured us seats on an Air

Force C-130 that was running its regular route from Mosul to Camp Doha in Kuwait.

When we touched down at Mosul airfield, Maj. Suqi and the division chaplain were waiting for us in a Humvee. "We've got the plane lined up for you," Maj. Suqi said as he helped us load our bags in the back. "I'll take you over there. Is there anything you want to do before you get on the plane?"

"I want to see Mike."

"Are you sure you really want to do that?" Scott asked.

"I'm sure."

I knew that he had been brought to the division mortuary. I knew that I needed to see him before he changed beyond recognition. I needed to see him in order to believe that my Mike was the one who was gone.

The chaplain said, "Now I have to warn you, I haven't seen him, but he was in a bad accident, so be prepared that he might not look as you remember him."

"I know. I want to see him."

A few minutes later, we pulled up next to a refrigerated container sitting on the ground next to the mortuary office. We had to slosh through a vast puddle to reach it. Maj. Suqi went into the office while we stood waiting for him. A young specialist who looked straight out of high school came out with him and asked us to give him a minute while he unlocked and entered the container. He reemerged a moment later. He seemed sad and scared, and I thought it was probably the first time he had ever had to see a family member in this job. "I'm so sorry," he said, trying not to cry as he beckoned me inside the container. Scott followed me inside, his arm tight around my shoulders.

The kid had uncovered Mike's head and chest. How strange it was to see my husband lying there, and a liquid sadness filled my soul and poured itself into the empty hole that had opened inside me.

He was absolutely untouched. There wasn't a scratch on him. He had suffered severe head trauma, but swelling had not set in yet.

I knelt on the floor and Scott knelt behind me and put his arms around my waist and held tight, like a shipwreck survivor clinging to a mast, crying softly. Blood was dripping from Mike's ear, and I could hear the soft splash as it hit the stretcher. Had it not been for the blood and the fact that his eyes were open, it could have been

Mike sleeping next to me, his chest rising and falling. But his chest was still.

I looked hard at his face and his body, at everything about him, no matter how small or imperfect, imprinting him on my memory one last time. I didn't want to forget any detail: the scar above his right eyebrow, the freckle on his left ear, his big hands that required a custom-made wedding ring, his chest hair, which had only begun to grow in the last three years. "I'm almost thirty years old, why am I getting chest hair?" he would say, exasperated, plucking the offending hairs with tweezers. "That's just making it grow more, stop that!" I'd say, laughing.

The doors to the container were open, and I could sense Maj. Suqi, the chaplain, and the young soldier hovering in the doorway. I wished they would all walk away, even Scott, and leave me alone for a few minutes to say good-bye. But it didn't occur to me to ask them to leave, and in the end we were in a hurry to catch a plane.

I looked into Mike's eyes. They were brown and clear. I ran my hand through his hair, which had grown longer in the field. This was Mike as I wanted to remember him, as I'd always remember him.

I kissed his forehead and took one last long look, committing him to memory, and rose to my feet. It was time to go home.

———

It took Scott and me two days to get home. We flew from Mosul to Kuwait City, from Kuwait City to Cairo, from Cairo to Frankfurt, from Frankfurt to Chicago, and from Chicago to Kansas City. True to his word, Scott was there for me every step of the way, pulling me along in his sturdy wake. But I can't forget the guardian angels, from baggage clerks in Frankfurt to security guards in Chicago, who smoothed the way for us, whether they knew about our loss or not.

From the mortuary at Mosul, Maj. Suqi had driven us to Col. Holloway's office, which was in a hangar on the airfield. We hadn't eaten in about thirty-six hours, so when Col. Holloway offered to get us something to eat, we gratefully agreed. He dispatched Maj. Suqi to one of the Iraqi restaurants on post, and when he returned with hamburgers and fries, I said we could eat them on the plane.

"Sit down and eat your food," Col. Holloway said. "That plane's not leaving until I tell it to leave."

It felt good to sit and eat, to take our time. Even though hamburgers aren't my favorite dish, I ate it eagerly.

The C-130 was the same type of plane we'd flown in to Qatar, and this flight was just as noisy and uncomfortable. We flew to Camp Doha, where the crew dropped us off at the Army airfield. We knew we had to get to Camp Wolf, where our tickets were waiting for us, and then to Kuwait International, but we didn't have the slightest clue how to make that happen. Finally Scott parked me on the mountain of luggage and went to find a phone, where he called a shuttle service. We waited and waited and waited. Scott's blood pressure rose and rose and rose. Just as he was about to completely lose it, an elderly African-American gentleman, probably a civilian worker on post, walked by. We must have looked utterly forlorn, because he stopped.

"You guys waiting for somebody?" he asked.

"We're trying to get to Camp Wolf," Scott replied.

"I know where that is. I'll give you a ride." Then he stopped and stared at the mountain. "How much baggage do you have?"

"All of this," Scott said, gesturing to the pile. "Look, don't worry about it, I'm sure you don't have room."

"Just give me a minute," the man said and left.

"We'll never see him again," Scott muttered.

A few minutes later the man pulled up in a big white van, jumped out, and began tossing our bags in the back. He drove us to Camp Wolf and waited to make sure we were in the right place, then helped us unload our baggage onto another waiting bus. We gratefully thanked him, but what we really wanted to do was nominate him for sainthood. Then we were off, racing for the airport.

Still in our desert camouflage uniforms, we arrived at our gate with only about forty-five minutes to spare. "You'll be first-class all the way home," said the Army sergeant behind a desk reserved for military passengers. Then the other shoe dropped.

"I'm sorry, but you can't fly in your uniform on a civilian aircraft," the sergeant added.

"Excuse me?" I was incredulous.

"People aren't supposed to know you're in the military."

"Look," I said, "we've got ten pieces of military baggage. I think people are going to figure it out."

"I'm sorry, you've got to change."

Our one set of civilian clothes was at the bottom of one of those duffel bags. I looked around and spotted a fancy clothing boutique. Somehow, shopping was the last thing I wanted to do at that moment, but we didn't have a choice. We left our bags with the sergeant and ran over.

The boutique sold expensive resort wear for men and women. We didn't even look at prices—for the first time in my life I was going to hand my credit card over to a salesclerk and say, "Whatever it costs, charge it." I picked out a pair of loose cotton pants and a purple boat-neck top with three-quarter sleeves. I didn't want to wear my uncomfortable desert boots, and I'd been wearing my socks for three days. The only footwear in the store was a pair of black sequined flip-flops that, under any other circumstances, I would have scoffed at.

The bill came to two hundred dollars. Scott bought some jeans and a button-down shirt but kept his desert boots on. His bill came to about the same.

Scott stayed with the luggage while I went to change. I walked into the men's room by mistake; a flustered attendant quickly pointed me in the right direction. In the women's room I changed, splashed cold water on my face, and brushed my teeth. The desert combat uniform went into my bag, but I couldn't imagine hauling my boots all the way home. I stuffed them into a trash can. After Scott changed, we looked at each other and agreed it felt odd to be without our uniforms and weapons.

Dirty, exhausted, numb with grief but nicely dressed, Scott and I collapsed in our first-class seats to Cairo. I was out before we left the ground, but Scott was too worried about me to sleep. What if something happened and I needed him? He decided he needed a drink. One rum and Coke became four rum and Cokes.

I woke up to Scott whispering my name and shaking my arm. "Kate! Kate!"

"What?"

"How're ya doin'?"

"I'm fine, how are you?" He was clearly buzzed.

"I'm doin' pretty good. You think you're gonna be all right? I think I'm gonna have to go to sleep."

"I'm fine, just go to sleep."

In Frankfurt we had ten minutes to make our connection to Chicago. We had to get our baggage, load it onto carts, pass through security, and get to the gate. We missed that flight. We got a new flight with yet another small window to make it. Our prospects were looking bleak when the German security and baggage clerks came to the rescue. An older woman who spoke excellent English ushered us over to her line and moved us through as quickly as she could. She sent us off with a smile and a "good luck."

We boarded the plane and found our seats. They were in the last row. We'd be wedged between two other people, within smelling distance of the lavatories. A rum and Coke was in order for both of us. As soon as we could, we ordered the drinks, gulped them down, and asked the flight attendant for another.

"You can't order another drink for thirty minutes," she said snippily. "Airline policy."

I thought Scott was about to go ballistic. He got up from his seat, grabbed the nearest flight steward, and explained our situation. The steward smiled sadly in my direction and proceeded to take care of us for the rest of the flight.

At Chicago, the cycle repeated itself: disembark, collect the baggage, take it through security, board another plane. Scott and I must have looked a fright with our summer clothes, our mountain of bags, and our thousand-yard stares of exhaustion and grief. "Welcome back to the United States," the security guard said. "Good to have you back. Thanks for what you've done for the country." I wanted to hit him with my carry-on.

The final leg of our journey was blessedly short, just over an hour. Dad, Terry, Larry, and Richard Young, Terry's best friend, would meet us at the airport, with two vehicles to hold all our bags. Scott and I longed to get there and not to get there. For a year I'd dreamed of stepping on Missouri soil, but how could I have ever guessed I'd return under these circumstances?

As I stepped off the plane onto the Jetway, a baggage handler opened a side door and a blast of cold Midwestern air hit my bare toes in the black sequined flip-flops. I was home.

CHAPTER 24

THE LAST MISSION

WE BURIED MIKE next to Grampy during the snowiest winter in years. Grampy was buried next to his favorite grandfather, Peter, in Shelby Memorial Cemetery, so it seemed only right that Mike should be laid to rest next to his favorite grandfather, too.

Macon County dedicated two snowplows to clearing the twenty-mile stretch of Route 63 from the National Guard armory in Macon, where the funeral was held, to the cemetery in Shelbyville. I assumed few of them would make the slippery drive through the snow and ice to the cemetery. I was wrong—two hundred people attended Mike's funeral.

Soldiers don't usually return from a war zone all at once. There are weeks of debriefings and counseling sessions, all designed to ease them back into a world not of life and death but of families and mundane concerns. I didn't have that. I rappelled directly into the sorrow zone, and it was sensory overload. Every nerve in my body felt frayed. Sometimes you have to tap into the deepest well of will you possess, and that's what I had to do to be able to make the decisions I had to face, one after another.

As Mike's wife and friend, I'd always taken care of him as best I could. When it came to his funeral, I knew what he would want and how he would want it done. Above all, I knew that if he could, he'd say to me, "Kate, I know I always gave you a hard time about being so strong and independent. But I need you to do this one last thing for me. I need you to be strong for my parents. They are going to need you to get through this." Somehow I buried my immense sadness and found a way to help Terry, Cheryl, and Peg get through this difficult time. I kept telling myself I'd have a chance to fall apart later. I couldn't do it right now, not yet. I had one last mission to complete for Mike.

The two weeks between my arrival home and Mike's funeral live in my mind as a series of images and experiences. Like slides at a briefing session, they flash, one after another, across my memory.

The arrivals corridor at Kansas City International seemed to go on forever. Finally I saw the four men standing behind a wall of glass, looking sad, tired, and bewildered by the circumstances that had brought them there. Dad and Terry wrapped me in a long hug and said, "We're glad you're home."

Scott's wife, Sonja, arrived on a flight from Nashville minutes later, bringing a care package of comfortable clothes from Old Navy and Victoria's Secret.

We still had a three-hour drive ahead of us, and I sat in the backseat of one of the vehicles with Terry. He asked me to tell him everything that had happened in the last forty-eight hours, from beginning to end, and I did. As for the accident, I told him as much as I knew: that Mike had been flying to a routine combat mission over Mosul, that the weather had been bad, and that this somehow had caused the crash.

It was past midnight when we got to Macon. Scott and Sonja checked into the Phillips Place Bed and Breakfast, where the owners, Scott and Carol Phillips, had offered rooms for close family and friends. I bunked down at Dad's. I couldn't wait to see Scout, but when we got there, he rushed to meet all of us equally. He didn't single me out, didn't seem to know me anymore. My dog had become a stranger, and his inattention hit me like the final blow in a long, punishing boxing match.

I dropped my bags in the basement and rode into town to see the rest of the family: Cheryl, Peg, Josh, Kris, and Stephanie. I was accustomed to seeing nothing but brown sand, and the snow-covered fields looked startlingly white in comparison, even at night.

Terry's house was crowded with casseroles, marshmallow salads, fresh-baked bread, pans of lasagna. Living in a small town is like having a huge extended family, and the food represented an amazing outpouring of support and love. My visit was brief yet intense. Peg was distraught, overcome with grief. Kris tried to comfort her, and Josh, who was still sick with pneumonia, looked thin and drawn. He would go back into the hospital after the funeral.

I wasn't ready to be alone, so I brought Stephanie back to Dad's to spend the night. I took a shower, standing for an hour under water as hot as I could get it. Dad's guest bathroom was stocked with fancy soaps and lotions left over from four daughters coming and going over the years, and I emerged trailing a scented cloud behind me.

In bed I felt a familiar lump settle over my feet: Scout had remembered me after all.

The Army's casualty assistance officer showed up the next day. Maj. Mark McLemore was an active duty Missouri National Guard aviator and a godsend. Every day he showed up with a list of questions and a stack of papers for me to go over and sign. It was the kind of paperwork you're never prepared to fill out: the final resting place for the remains; where I wanted the life insurance money sent; did I want the Army to set a marker, and if so, what kind? Maj. McLemore quickly explained each sheet and moved on to the next. I didn't mind the task. The family needed me to take charge, but I wished I had my uniform, as if wearing it could help me channel the firm captain who could make decisions without thinking twice.

The snow was falling. I had no winter shoes, so after Maj. McLemore left, Dad took me to the local shoe store, J. P.'s, to replace the sparkly flip-flops. I hated the sight of them.

The next day, January 27, I checked my e-mail to find a message from Maj. Whitson, letting me know the unit had made it safely to Kuwait. I had been praying for their safety during their two-day GAC south, and knowing they were safe and sound was a huge relief.

Wendy and her family flew in from Florida. Anna drove in from St. Louis, Tiffani from Columbia, and Joe from Springfield, Missouri. Lindsey came home on a ten-day emergency leave, and Anna picked her up from the airport. I don't remember Lindsey arriving; suddenly she was simply there, and her presence instantly lifted my spirits. She became my constant companion, entertaining guests, making phone calls, helping Cheryl to prepare meals, listening when I needed to talk.

I stayed at Terry's during the day and Dad's at night, where the peace and quiet of the farm and his calm, reassuring presence were my retreat from all the comings and goings, all the decisions and planning.

At Terry and Cheryl's house, the phone and doorbell rang and rang. Terry, who had lost his father and his oldest son in the space of nine months, put on a brave face; he loved talking about Mike, but his blue eyes, always so expressive, glistened with pain. When reporters and local news stations called the house for interviews, I couldn't turn them down. Sharing who Mike was with Missouri was another aspect of my mission, and so when the media slid out to the house with cameras and microphones and notebooks, I gamely answered their questions.

Every morning one of Terry's coworkers showed up to shovel his driveway before heading to work.

The only thing Mike had ever said about his funeral was that he wanted our pastor from Clarksville, Matt Brown, to preach the sermon. I made the call, and without hesitation Pastor Brown agreed to be there. Pastor Sheila from Mount Zion would give his eulogy.

We chose a young funeral director, Brian Hayes, a former Marine with a quiet presence who had also handled Grampy's funeral. We decided to hold the visitation and the funeral at the National Guard armory. Macon has only a few buildings large enough to hold the crowd that Brian expected, and it seemed fitting to have it there instead of some random school gymnasium.

C.D. and Stacie Foster drove in from Texas. C.D. and Scott became my rocks. While C.D. had met the whole family before at Fort Rucker, Scott knew no one. The two of them greeted people, told funny stories about Mike, answered questions, and did their best to explain the risks of flying in a combat zone.

Mike arrived home a week after I did. Dover Air Force Base in Delaware, the military's East Coast mortuary, had been snowed in, delaying his arrival. I tramped over to the funeral home with the immediate family as well as C.D. and Scott. This would be Terry and Peg's final confirmation of their oldest son's death. I glanced at Mike in his coffin and turned away. I wanted to remember him as I'd seen him in Mosul, not made up by a well-meaning mortician. I waited outside in the snow, which was still falling.

Thousands of miles away, in a country where snow never fell, the squadron held a memorial service for Mike. Several of his fellow pilots spoke, including Big Country, who was with us in spirit if not in person.

Friends and family wouldn't let me out of their sight. When I said I needed a winter coat and clothes for the funeral, Natalie, Stephanie, Sonja, and my sisters all took me to the mall in Columbia. "I refuse to wear black," I said. Anna's three young daughters had also come, and our flock of females wandered from one store to the next debating over my wardrobe. Finally I turned to Natalie and said, "Help me." She discreetly steered me away from the flock. Green was Mike's favorite color, so we picked out a bright-green turtleneck and gray wool slacks.

There was something else I needed to do. I wanted to send flowers to Brian Hazelgrove's funeral. Because I didn't know his wife, I was unsure how she would react to such a gesture. People can be irrational in grief—what if she blamed Mike, who was flying that night, and by extension, me?

I called Maj. McLemore to find out where he was being buried. The major gave me the name of Hazelgrove's hometown in Indiana, and I called information and asked the operator to find me a florist there. All I knew about Brian Hazelgrove was that he was in his late twenties, married, and had several children. It turned out that the florist was a friend of the family, and when I asked her how his wife was doing, the florist replied, "Kimberley is a strong woman. She's handling everything really well, even with four kids." I wanted to send yellow roses, but the florist said they'd run out, so I picked something else.

The visitation was on February 1 in the armory's drill floor, a cavernous space that resembled an airplane hangar. Scott braved the bad roads to drive Mike's Harley-Davidson from Terry's house to the armory and parked it in a corner of the room. Brian put pictures of Mike up on boards throughout the room, and a blown-up copy of *Iraqi Gothic*, the photo Jesse White had taken of us at Q-West, the same one that had appeared on the float, was hung on one wall. Flower stands occupied every inch of wall space. I noticed a huge bouquet of yellow roses with my name on them near our photo. They were from Kimberley Hazelgrove.

Mike lay in an open casket at the front. He wore his green dress wool uniform with all his medals and ribbons. About fifteen hundred people stood in line for four hours to see him and the family, including a contingent of Amish who came as a tribute to Grampy. The line snaked through the room and out the armory entrance. For eight hours Terry and I greeted the mourners. We refused to sit down—they had stood for hours to see us, so we could at least do the same. Lee Greenwood's "God Bless the U.S.A." played to a slide show of photos of Mike. It ran on an endless loop, and afterward I swore to myself I never wanted to hear that song again.

On the day of the funeral, I arrived early with Terry, Cheryl, and Dad to have a few minutes alone with Mike. Gazing at his face for the final time, I took off my dog tags with the wedding ring from around my neck and placed them in his left breast pocket. Then I walked straight into the side room reserved for our coats. Dad followed me and hugged me, and I cried as hard as I had ever cried, until my soul, like a well, had run dry. Terry and Cheryl joined us and we all huddled together. No one had seen me cry since I'd gotten home. "You needed to do this," Cheryl said.

The mourners represented a cross section of our lives: Josh and Kris and her three small children; Natalie and Mollie and their husbands (Nancy was almost nine months' pregnant and unable to come for more than a day); friends from high school, from college, from Fort Campbell; wives and parents of other Cav pilots who wanted to pay their respects for their husbands and sons, who were still in Kuwait; my friend Jess Umentum and her husband, who had come over from Germany; two of Mom's sisters, Zoe and Joanna, along with their kids; friends of Mike's and Terry's whom I didn't know.

Mom wasn't there, but Dad had driven out to tell her before I'd arrived back in the States. He described the visit to me this way: "I told your mother that Mike had passed away when his helicopter crashed in Iraq. She shed a little tear, but a few minutes later, she'd already forgotten what I'd told her."

I sat in the front row between Terry and Dad, looking straight at Mike's flag-draped casket. My sisters, Scott and Sonja, and C.D. and Stacie sat behind me. The Army sent a general to express his condolences. He awarded Mike a posthumous Bronze Star Medal. C.D. and Scott presented the medal, and the general pinned it on my turtleneck.

In his opening remarks, Pastor Matt confessed that this was the first funeral he had ever officiated. The reason, he said, was that he didn't feel comfortable delivering a sermon for someone whom he hadn't known, whom he wasn't sure, in his heart, was in heaven. With Mike, he said, it was different. With Mike there was no doubt about where he was. He described numerous talks he and Mike had had about faith, and he shared stories of Mike's participation in church that even Terry and Peg hadn't known. For example, only members of our Lutheran congregation are able to take communion. When an elderly visitor with poor hearing mistakenly tried to join in, Mike knelt down on one knee in the aisle beside her. He gently explained the situation to her and promised to answer any questions after church.

At the end of his sermon, we all felt lifted a bit. Pastor Brown's words had comforted us and renewed our hope that we would all meet again someday. The stories of his deep faith gave us the strength we needed to finish this day.

Pastor Sheila told funny and poignant stories about Mike that she had gleaned from his family and friends. It helped remind everyone of one of their own memories of Mike. A choir sang classic country hymns like "The Old Rugged Cross," "Amazing Grace," and "In the Garden." I had chosen these hymns, and I knew Mike would approve.

Finally the pallbearers carried Mike's casket out to the waiting hearse, and we got our coats and walked to the cars for the drive to the cemetery. I wore my new black coat and the black cap Mike had given me before his last flight. I rode in a black Suburban with Terry, Cheryl, Dad, and Lindsey. Led by a police escort, we followed the hearse out of the parking lot. I looked through the rear window to see one car after another follow us onto the snowy roads until a line of vehicles two miles long was inching along behind us.

The drive, which normally took twenty minutes, was at least twice that. People clustered along the roadside, braving the blizzard to show their support. Children in winter coats solemnly waved tiny American flags. Drivers going the other direction honked their horns in salute. A tent had been set up at the grave site, but the crowd of mourners spilled out across the hillside.

I wanted a short, simple interment ceremony. I knew the military honors would be extremely moving and hard to get through. Pastor Matt said a few words and a prayer, and then a twenty-one-gun salute jarred the still and silent scene. The rest of the soldier detail removed the flag from the casket and folded it into a triangle with crisp, precisely choreographed movements. A soldier placed three of the spent shell casings inside the folded flag and passed it to the general, who walked over and handed it to me with the words "On behalf of a grateful nation."

Peg and Terry received flags as well, but I clutched mine tightly, the special one. Finally a bugler played taps, the song I had been dreading. The notes echoed through the trees and along the country road, and I knew I would never feel sadder than at that moment. I watched the bugler finish and walk silently out of sight. When it was time to return to our cars, I strode ahead of the others, eager to leave this place of finality as quickly as possible. On my way I passed Scott and C.D. walking through the snow, heads down, searching for the rest of the spent shells. I saw these two men who had never met before this tragedy stop, embrace each other, and cry silently on each other's shoulder. I looked away, depleted. My mission was complete.

CHAPTER 25

EIGHT CANS OF PEAS

FOR THE FIRST THREE MONTHS, I slept.

I slept to make up for the sleep I had missed during the war. I slept hoping to dream about Mike, to wake up, and for a few fleeting moments to have forgotten the heartache. I slept because I had nothing else to do. I slept in a room I'd rented from a Special Operations pilot in Clarksville named Will who was rarely home and needed a roommate to keep an eye on his house. Post housing was available only to married couples, and in the eyes of the world I was no longer married. Yet in my heart I still was. How did I make that feeling stop? When would I feel no longer married? I took those vows with forever in mind; marriage had always been more than a ring on my left finger and a new last name. I had embraced the idea of being half of a complete whole. What did I do now that my other half was gone?

When I wasn't sleeping I was lying around, too exhausted to think. When I wasn't lying around I was a sleepwalker, going through the motions of living. There were tributes and homecomings to attend, homecomings in which Mike and I were supposed to have been participants. Instead, I was a bystander. Just as Mom's accident had transformed our family dynamic, Mike's death upended all my expectations. I was improvising, and I've never been very good at that. I prayed for peace and acceptance, prayed as hard as I could.

After Mike's funeral, I spent a week at the farm. Lindsey left soon after the service, eager to get back to her company for the remaining few months of her deployment. "I'll see you in June," she said as she hugged me good-bye. After she left, there was no one but Dad and Scout there, and I relished the peace and quiet, the time to do nothing but sleep.

A few days later, I went to Terry and Cheryl's to help them write thank-you notes. The uneaten pans of lasagna were in the freezer, the funeral flowers donated to nursing homes. People were still dropping by to give their condolences, and as we sat at the dining room table addressing envelopes, the doorbell rang. It was a family friend who hadn't been able to attend the funeral. She had recently buried her teenage son, her only child, killed in a car accident, and she couldn't face another funeral so soon. I didn't know her very well, but clearly she was still reeling from her loss.

We chatted for a few minutes, and she asked about Mike's accident. I told her what I knew. "Mike wasn't even supposed to be flying that night," Terry said with a hitch in his voice.

"I don't understand why these things have to happen," the friend said. "I don't understand why these boys had to be taken from us."

"When God calls you home, he calls you home," I said. "There's nothing you can do about it."

"Do you honestly believe that?" she responded, her voice rising sharply. "I don't believe that for a minute. Do you really think it was Mike's time?"

Her anger caught me off guard. I put down my pen and looked at her. "Well, Mike believed it," I replied. "We had a conversation about it a week before his accident. He said, 'I used to think you could side-step an accident. But after your mom's accident and being here and seeing friends injured and killed, I believe now that when God calls you home you have to go. It's just your time.'"

"I don't buy into that," she said.

I struggled to respond. I wasn't trying to tell her what to believe, simply what I believed. "Well, that thought gave us a little bit of comfort," I said quietly. "And it gives me comfort now."

The friend shrugged stiffly and glared at no one in particular. We sat there for a few moments, stewing in tension, and finally Cheryl, bless her heart, changed the subject. We all have our personal mechanisms for processing grief, and I prayed that she would find a way to deal with hers.

In a way, my mechanism was to be the strong one. My habit of being too independent to ask for help was never more pronounced; being everyone else's rock helped me take my mind off my own sorrow. Like an officer directing troops in a losing battle, I didn't want to show weakness lest my soldiers falter.

The next day, Maj. Whitson called me from Kuwait to tell me the

426th Forward Support Battalion was arriving back in Fort Campbell on February 13. "Wear your uniform and be at the tarmac," he said.

Scott, Sonja, and Dad offered to come with me to the homecoming. "No," I said, "I want to do this by myself." I figured I'd have to handle a lot of hard stuff alone, so I should start now.

On February 11, I packed Scout and my luggage into the Tahoe and drove the six hours to Fort Campbell, a route I'd taken so often I could drive it in my sleep. I'd decided to stay in Clarksville permanently. Scott and Sonja would put me up in their guest room until I found a place of my own.

On Friday 13, 2004, I put on my desert camouflage uniform and drove from Scott and Sonja's house to the airfield. The tarmac teemed with big signs, new babies, and sobbing fiancés. Standing with Holly Petraeus, the major general's wife, I watched the commercial jet land and taxi into position. Our battalion guidon bearer, Staff Sgt. Jackman, leaned out the cockpit window, waving our battalion flag as the families cheered wildly, and it made me smile.

The plane stopped and the door opened. A worker wheeled the stairs to the door, and an officer escorted me to the top. I could feel the confused stares of the expectant families, as if wondering, why does she get to go first? At the top of the stairs "my guys" met me: Jesse, Chip, Maj. Whitson, Maj. Smith, Col. Kelley, and Sgt. First Class Wilson. The colonel gave me a giant hug and said, "I told them we weren't getting off without you."

There is a protocol to coming home. The families stand behind a roped area on the airfield. Returning soldiers are supposed to march past them without stopping, but of course they do. Once inside a hangar, the families sit in bleachers and the soldiers stand in formation. A general welcomes them back, a band plays the Screaming Eagles anthem and "The Star-Spangled Banner," and then the families rush onto the floor like concertgoers charging a stage. The soldiers get about thirty minutes to mingle with their families before going back to the unit, where they turn in their weapons and perform other formalities before being released for the night.

Ironically, the homecoming ceremonies for all the units of the 101st were held in the hangar for Mike's cavalry unit, the 2/17. That day I stood in formation with the 426th while Maj. Gen. Petraeus spoke and the band played. Then the soldiers scattered to greet their families, leaving me standing alone in the ecstatic crowd.

The next day, after I came back from an errand on post, Scott handed me a piece of notepaper with a name on it: Kimberley Hazelgrove, the copilot's widow. Her phone number was written underneath. "Her casualty assistance officer called," Scott explained. "He said she wanted to get in touch but felt like she should leave it up to you to call. That way, if you don't feel like getting to know her, you won't feel pressured." I left her number on the dresser in the guest room, knowing I'd call her eventually, yet having no idea what I'd say.

———

I stayed with Scott and Sonja for two weeks. During the days I slept on their sofa in the living room; Scott slept in his favorite recliner. This was how we spent our days. Sonja, on the other hand, was full of energy as always, a butterfly fluttering over two fallen trees. She came and went to her job and the gym, cooked us meals, asked us if we wanted to do something. "No," we'd mumble. We felt bad, but we also felt extraordinarily tired.

I couldn't stay there forever, so Scott and Sonja helped find me the room in Will's house. His upstairs bonus room became my studio apartment, and I had my own bathroom downstairs. Because he had little furniture, I took some of my furnishings out of storage. His bonus for having me as a roommate was that he also got a couch to sit on, dishes, and a TV with surround sound.

The Army is big on checklists. We have a saying known as "check the block"—do that item (whether you need to or not), check it off, and move on. I still had to in-process and go through the training they give soldiers their first two weeks back in the States. My unit had gone through the training in Kuwait, so I sat in a big briefing room by myself as a civilian counselor clicked through slides and spoke in a monotone about coping with postwar stress and the demands of family life. After what I'd been through, I felt as if I could teach the class myself. But like a lot of things in the Army, you have to "check the block" and move on.

Even though I was an officer until May 12, Col. Kelley told me he didn't want me to come back to work. "Take your time to do what you need to do," he said. I had to take classes designed to prepare me for the civilian world. The Army will help you write your résumé, find a job or a school, line up health insurance. I had to go and check the block, but I didn't need help finding a job. Mike and I had saved up enough money, and I had no bills except my minimal rent. I planned to spend my free time with my family and worry about a job when the time came. The Army offered me grief counseling, but I turned that down, too. Maybe down the road, I thought, maybe with someone who had the same religious background.

At the end of February, the Air Cavalry had its own homecoming. I wanted to see those guys walk in, especially Big Country, since he hadn't been here to say good-bye to Mike. I didn't want to give this happy occasion any sad edges, but Scott and Sonja talked me into going. "The troop will be glad to see you," they said, and they were right. We sat with Big Country's wife, Jennifer, and their young daughter, Morgan. When the pilots were released to greet their families, I was gratified that they all seemed glad to see me; many brought their wives and parents over and introduced us. Some of the guys got choked up when talking about Mike—it was still so hard to believe he wasn't there with us.

A few days later, Capt. Fredericks, Banshee Troop's commander, gave me a call. Mike had been the last soldier from the 101st to die in that rotation to Iraq (Brian Hazelgrove was part of the next rotation), and his troop wanted to have a ceremony for the soldiers and the family. They held it at the American Legion hall in Clarksville. Dad, Terry, and Cheryl drove down, and Maj. Gen. and Holly Petraeus came as well. They took the time to talk at length with everyone from my family. When the major general got to me, he said, "This is going to be a really tough year for you. Everything is going to be a first. I'll have you in my thoughts." His words were direct, but I preferred that to the false optimism some people had dealt me: "Oh, you'll feel better in a few months!"

The Cav showed the video of Mike's life that we'd played at the visitation, and afterward Capt. Fredericks and Lt. Col. Schiller presented me with the first bottle of Cav wine from a local vineyard and the "widow's quilt." It's a small quilt with red, white, and blue stars; in the corner is a label dedicating the blanket to me in memory of Mike. I had never heard of this military tradition until then, but I accepted the quilt gratefully. I had written a short speech, and afterward I stood at the front of the room and read it:

"Thank you all for coming tonight to celebrate Mike's life. I tossed around a lot of different ideas about how to do this, what to say and how to say it. If Mike was here he would tell me to make it short and sweet so we could get to the karaoke and beer portion of the evening."

At that everyone in the room chuckled and nodded their heads.

And then I told some stories. I talked about his '70 Chevy and his Harley-Davidson, the time he landed to wish me happy birthday in An Najaf and buzzed the Banshee command post with Scott at Q-West. (More chuckles and nods.) I talked about how his friends could count on him, how important his family was to him, especially Grampy, and how he'd always been a positive influence in everything I'd done. I talked about his faith in God and the necklace he wore in Iraq with the cross on one side and the Bible verse on the other.

I ended the speech by saying, "I and everyone who knew Mike well are always going to be a little lonely for him. We are always going to tell our Mike stories, and the new guys in the unit will regret never having the chance to meet him. Thanks for coming tonight to remember and celebrate Mike's life. He would have really loved to drink a beer with all of you."

Afterward, I mingled with the guests. Chief Warrant Officer 3 Dan Hoff, the pilot who was flying the second Kiowa that night Mike died, called me over to sit with him and his wife. Dan got to talking about the accident, and he filled me in on a few details only he could have known.

"That night was the darkest I'd ever seen in Iraq," he said. "About fifteen minutes into the flight I radioed Mike and told him to call when they had reached their comfort zone as far as the weather was concerned. Shortly after, Mike called me and said, 'I think we're there.' He said it in that real sarcastic tone that Mike had perfected." Dan paused and then went on. "You know how changeable the weather was between Q-West and Mosul, especially at that ridge that was the halfway point? That's where the weather always went bad. The visibility was pretty much zero. I suggested they turn toward a local village to get some illumination so that they could continue the mission. Mike said okay. I turned, and he followed. But shortly after the turn, I tried to contact Mike on the radio and got no reply. After several more calls, we began searching the ground for signs of the Kiowa. We saw a small fire smoldering on the ground. We immediately called for assistance and landed to try and help, but there was nothing we could do."

I thanked Dan for giving me his account. It didn't explain what exactly happened in the cockpit that night, yet I didn't want or need to know. God had taken Mike, for reasons only He knew, and nothing was going to change that.

The tribute took its toll. Afterward I collapsed in bed for several days, exhausted by the energy it took to keep my emotions in check. I still had to go through all the boxes I'd kept in storage for a year, and I didn't know how I was going to manage it.

Dad drove down to help, and Scott and Sonja pitched in, as did Big Country. I felt I could manage the task alone, but I also felt I had to invite people into my life. If I didn't, they'd get worried about me, and I hate it when people worry about me. That's why I kept coming up with ways to ask them for assistance: to make them feel needed, to see that I was okay. I was helping them by letting them help me.

Dozens of boxes were delivered to the house. Mike and I had moved so many times that many of them had been filled and then never opened again. I decided now was the time to open them all, yet I did so with mixed feelings: They were packed with memories that I wanted both to remember and to forget.

Mike and I had lived apart so much that we had assembled two of everything: two sets of dishes and Tupperware, two televisions, two desks, and so on. It was a Noah's ark of domesticity. I could sell some of it at a garage sale, but many items were too sentimental to discard. Mike had never explicitly told me his wishes for his possessions, but I could sense them. The John Deere flag went to his cousin Larry; his guitar to his uncle Dale; his pocketknives to his brother, Josh, step-brother, Aaron, and best friend, Mark; his leather flight coat to Scott. A Ranger tab that he had worn on his hat throughout Ranger School— a sergeant had given it to him for motivation—went to Big Country, and his Harley T-shirt collection went to C.D. The Harley itself went to Terry. One of the reasons Mike had always wanted to get a Harley-Davidson was to be able to ride with his dad. I transferred the title to Terry and gave it to him on Father's Day.

Slowly, over a few weeks' time, I whittled the pile down to the things I couldn't let go of, objects that would have seemed silly to any-one else but were important to me because they were Mike's. Things like the ticket stubs from the putt-putt golf place we'd go to when we were poor and couldn't afford movies or bars, and the blue hand-kerchief he'd used to wipe paint off my face that summer we painted Terry's barn. It was his fault I was wearing paint in the first place, and I could see him laughing as he cleaned it up.

In one box I came across a videotape. The label read, "Mike and Johnny in Panama." Then I remembered: It was the tape his old friend Johnny had given me of him and Mike singing in their barracks room all those years ago, before we were even married. I had never watched it, and I put it aside, thinking that someday I'd get up the nerve.

A week later I came across Mike's electronic label maker he used when making aviation maps. I turned on the gadget, and an LED readout in a little window said, "Label ready to print." Curious, I pushed PRINT. Mike had last used it a few months before we deployed, so I assumed it was the name of a route or a city in Iraq. The gadget spat out the label, and I stared in disbelief at the words printed on it: *Kate is Chubby.* I literally looked around to see if someone was standing there, laughing at the practical joke. Sixteen months ago he'd hatched a scheme to use this label maker to get a chuckle out of me, and it actually worked, even after everything.

That laugh led me astray. It made me think I could pop that video-tape into my VCR and watch it without repercussions.

I pushed PLAY. Within minutes there was Mike, walking, talking, and singing his favorite warm-up song, "Here's a Quarter (Call Some-one Who Cares)." It was the same song he'd sung in Qatar on R and R, and I recalled how the audience had loved his singing, how he'd beamed for hours afterward. Now, to see him alive, to hear his voice, shook me to my core. I pushed the OFF button and just sat there, feeling a numbness like frostbite creep over me.

The video brought me so low I could barely muster the energy to move about the house. I stayed home for three days eating pizza, un-able to sleep. Scott had gotten into the habit of calling me regularly with his "daily motivational speech," so when the phone rang and I saw it was Scott, I picked up.

"Hey, Sonja and I are going to dinner, you wanna join us?"

"No, I don't feel like going out."

"What's the matter?"

I told him about the label maker and the video.

"Look, just because Mike is sending you messages from the beyond is no reason why you shouldn't eat," he said. "I'm coming to get you."

I managed to laugh and got up to get dressed.

———————

On March 16, I got a phone call from the personnel officer for Fort Campbell. He said that President Bush and the first lady were coming to Fort Campbell to thank the troops and welcome them home. They wanted Mike's family to be there. "That's in two days," I said.

"Sorry about the short notice."

Terry, Cheryl, Peg, Josh, and Kris immediately drove down to be there. A large area on the parade field was set aside for the president to make his speech. We sat in the special section of bleachers reserved for the families of soldiers killed in Afghanistan and Iraq. All the soldiers on post were clustered on the field in front of the stage. The president flew in on a helicopter and the Secret Service forged a path through the crowd as he made his way to the stage, shaking hands and patting backs along the way.

After the president spoke, the families of the fallen were bussed to the division's museum to wait for him and Mrs. Bush to arrive. We knew he was on his way when a flock of Secret Service agents appeared, wires in their ears, and canvassed the room.

At that point, sixty soldiers from the 101st had died in Iraq, and there must have been about 150 people in that room. We were instructed to form a line, and the president began to make his way from one family to another. I was wearing my uniform, the first in line in my group. President Bush shook my hand and gave his condolences. He looked tired and pale; clearly the war and the presidency had aged him. He then moved on to talk at length to Terry and Cheryl.

The first lady, pretty in a dark suit, approached me. "Are you the sister of the fallen soldier?" she asked.

Surprised, I smiled politely and said, "No. Actually, he's my husband."

Mrs. Bush recognized their blunder; my uniform must have thrown them off. She quickly expressed her sympathies, slid over to the president and, plucking his sleeve in a wifely manner, steered him back to me. "George, this is the soldier's wife," she said. I had never seen the president look as disconcerted on television as he did the moment he recognized his mistake. He again expressed his condolences and said,

"I know it's probably not proper for your commander in chief to kiss you on the cheek, but I'm going to anyway."

After accepting his peck on the cheek, I steered him to Peg. "This is Mike's mom," I said. The president looked confused again—he hadn't realized Cheryl was Mike's stepmother.

The president was supposed to take only thirty minutes with the families, but he and the first lady spent hours in that room. I respected the fact that he didn't turn the visit into a public relations spectacle. I always thought that was classy. It was if he understood what his decisions had cost us.

That evening, after Mike's family had left, I dialed Kimberley Hazelgrove's number. I'd mentally rehearsed the greeting I'd use when she answered the phone, an elaborate statement explaining who I was. But I figured that since she had called me, just saying my name should be enough. In the end, I went with the simple approach:

"Hi, this is Kate Blaise. I got your number, and I've been wanting to call you for a while and was waiting for the right moment."

Kimberley recognized who I was immediately. "I'm really glad you called," she said warmly. "I was hoping you'd want to talk to me."

Instantly, we felt like friends who didn't need small talk or conversational warm-ups. "How is your family doing?" I asked. "How are the kids?"

"As well as can be expected," she said. "The older kids miss their dad, but the little ones don't really understand that he's gone. Especially the baby—I had a daughter right before Brian deployed." She told me the kids' names and a little about each one and how each was coping with losing their father.

She had a lot of questions about the accident: What had the weather been like? Where exactly had it happened? What went wrong? How much did I know?

I told her everything I knew, which was quite a bit. In a way, I felt fortunate to have been there, to know things firsthand rather than to rely completely on the accounts of others.

"You see, I was in Q-West at the time."

"You were?"

"Mike and I were stationed there together. I was there the night he and Brian died."

This information surprised her. "I'm in the Army, too," she said. "I'm a Sergeant First Class in military intelligence. But I'll be transitioning out in six months. I can't take the risk of being deployed and leaving my children behind, especially now that I'm a single mom." Her next words told me she was a dedicated soldier who, like me, had mixed feelings about leaving the Army. "I wish I could have gone to Iraq," she said. "It was hard to watch other soldiers do the job without me."

"You shouldn't feel like you needed to go there," I said, trying to sound reassuring. "You've done your duty. You shouldn't feel any sort of guilt."

As for the accident, the notion of guilt or blame never came up. Maybe, as a soldier, Kimberley understood that in the military, fatal accidents are an inescapable part of a dangerous job description.

I told her that I had gone to the mortuary to see Mike.

"Did you see Brian while you were there?" I discerned a hint of hope in her voice.

"No," I said. "He was covered up, so I couldn't have seen him unless I asked. And that seemed disrespectful."

Our conversation lasted about thirty minutes. The more we talked, the more we discovered our husbands had in common. They were both from small towns and very close to their families. The florist had told me that Brian's father had taken his death particularly hard, just as Mike's had, and I asked after him. I also found out that Brian's pride and joy, besides his four children, was his Harley-Davidson. I imagined our husbands getting to know each other during the flight, talking about riding motorcycles, the thrill and the speed. Through their deaths, Kimberley and I were forever linked, a reality she came back to several times. "For whatever reason," she told me, "you've been brought into my life, and I'm going to embrace that fact."

"Me, too," I replied.

We said good-bye with a promise to talk again.

March 19, 2004, was the first anniversary of the invasion. It was hard to believe that twelve months earlier, I'd been sitting in Kuwait with the rest of my unit, poised to cross the border. Three days later the fragging incident had occurred, an unthinkable act of treachery and cowardice committed by an American against other Americans. Two days after that, we'd been driving around lost in the desert, looking for the way into Iraq. Now here we were, looking for a way out.

These were the thoughts crossing my mind when I turned on the TV that evening. I wanted to keep up on the situation in Iraq, especially with Lindsey still there. I had the TV tuned to one of the networks and was half listening while I made something to eat.

Then a story grabbed my attention. It was a piece about the antiwar protests that had been held around the United States and the world that day, so I turned to watch. I saw a film clip of marchers, each holding a sign with the photograph of a fallen soldier and reading off their names. With a start, I recognized one of the faces on one of the signs. It was Mike.

I was horrified. Who were these people to use my husband to further their agenda? I served my country to defend people's right to express their beliefs, but in this case, freedom of speech had crossed the line. No one forced Mike to serve his country; he did it willingly, and with honor. He believed in our mission there, just as I did. He would never have condoned using his image to send the opposite message.

I threw a few choice words at the television and called Terry, who said a few choice words as well. It took me hours to calm down.

A week later, a sportswriter from the *New York Daily News* called my cell phone. He was doing a story on the golf course at Q-West and wanted to interview me. We spoke for about fifteen minutes, and toward the end of our conversation the writer asked about my feelings toward all the antiwar sentiment. Recalling the protest, I said, "I was watching the news, watching this antiwar demonstration, and they were reading off names of soldiers who had fallen in Iraq and they read off my husband's name. That made me very angry because he very strongly believed in what he was doing and they were using his name for a purpose that he would not have approved of."

The writer thanked me for my time and hung up. The article, which ran on March 28, turned out to be my favorite of the many stories run on TPC at Mosul. Jesse White was the focus, as he should have been.

On April 2, I turned twenty-eight. I have no recollection of any celebration.

Later that month, the Banshee Troop's Kiowas finally arrived at the port in Jacksonville. Scott, Big Country, and the rest of the Cav pilots were flown to Florida so they could then fly the Kiowas to Fort Campbell. Sonja called to invite me to go to the airport and watch them fly in. I readily agreed—seeing a whole troop fly in at the same time would be a proud moment. It was an informal occasion, with just a few family members on hand.

The helicopters appeared on the horizon, a cluster of black dots against a blue spring sky. They grew larger and larger as they approached the airfield, six Kiowas flying in formation. As Sonja and I watched, they landed as lightly as dragonflies about two hundred yards away. The pilots disembarked and mingled for a few moments around the aircraft. In their helmets and brown flight suits, we couldn't tell who was who. Finally, three pilots broke off from the group and headed in our direction, helmets in hand. From a distance we couldn't tell who they were, but one of them could easily have been Mike walking toward me, laughing and swinging his helmet and talking about a cold beer and a hot steak. I blinked. The pilot waved, turned toward the hangar, and walked toward his waiting family. A cloud passed over the sun.

I know a woman in her mid-forties whose father had died during the Vietnam conflict. He was a Navy pilot, shot down over Laos in 1969. "The local paper ran his name, but otherwise, it went unnoticed by the world at large," she recalls. "No one mourned him but his family and friends." That was thirty-six years ago, before the Internet and twenty-four-hour news channels, before losing a husband meant losing your privacy.

Toward the end of April, news surfaced that on the April 30 broadcast of *Nightline*, Ted Koppel planned to read the names of all the soldiers who had been killed in Iraq and show their photos. This created a lot of controversy. Some people saw it as a tribute, others as a statement against the war. Sinclair Broadcast Group, one of the largest owners of TV stations in the country, ordered eight of its ABC affiliates not to air the program.

Naturally, a lot of people were interested in my opinion. When asked, I replied that I felt the program was honoring the memory of the fallen soldiers. "I see no reason why it shouldn't be aired," I said. It struck me as a spoken version of the Vietnam War Memorial, which had given my friend so much comfort: Just seeing her father's name up there, etched among so many others, reminded Americans of his sacrifice.

Personally, I didn't want to watch the program—not out of any ill feelings, but because Mike's death was still too fresh, the wound too new.

A few weeks later I was chatting with Chip on the phone. He told me that he had recently Googled his name. "It was fascinating what people with my name have accomplished," he said. "You should Google your name and see what comes up."

That night, having nothing better to do, I gave it a try.

What I found amazed and dismayed me. I found a letter posted on the Sinclair Broadcast Group Web site to Senator John McCain from its CEO, David D. Smith. I remembered the controversy surrounding the stations that had decided not to air the show, but I was shocked to discover that I was planted squarely in the middle of it.

In the letter, Smith defended Sinclair's right not to air the program. "*Nightline* is not reporting news; it is doing nothing more than making a political statement," Smith wrote. "In simply reading the names of our fallen heroes, this program has adopted a strategy employed by numerous antiwar protesters who wish to focus attention solely on the cost of war." Then he said a lot of other things before winding up.

"In closing," Smith went on, "I would like to quote for you the words of Captain Kate Blaise of the U.S. military. Captain Blaise served in Iraq as a member of the 101st Airborne Division and suffered the loss of her husband, Mike, who was killed while also serving in Iraq. In commenting on exactly the type of practice that *Nightline* intends to employ, Captain Blaise had this to say."

And then the letter ran the aforementioned quote I had given to the writer at the *New York Daily News*, which Sinclair's people had obviously pulled off some clip service: "I was watching the news, watching this antiwar demonstration, and they were reading off names of soldiers who had fallen in Iraq and they read off my husband's name. That made me very angry because he very strongly believed in what he was doing and they were using his name for a purpose that he would not have approved of."

I felt personally betrayed. I saw a difference between Mike's name being read by an antiwar protester with an obvious agenda and by Ted Koppel, a television journalist. By taking my comment out of context, Smith had done virtually the same thing as the protesters—manipulated a personal tragedy to his own purposes. Besides, they missed the whole point: Soldiers need to be remembered. One of the families' biggest fears is that people will forget what they stood for and how they fell. Reading their names out of a sense of loyalty to what they sacrificed was a sign of respect. Reading their names to further a cause that goes directly against what they were defending only cheapened that sacrifice.

To make matters worse, numerous chat sites, assuming I'd made that statement to Sinclair, had sprung up criticizing me and telling me to mind my own business. If my husband's death wasn't my business, then whose was it?

All I wanted was to grieve in peace, to sleep and dream of my husband and remember him as he was, not as others wanted him to be. Yet far from being a private matter, my loss was taking on the quality of a community project. Well-meaning strangers from across America sent me pictures, quilts, pins. On the one hand I appreciated the support of all these people; on the other, I wanted to crawl into a hole and disappear. Every tribute was one more confirmation that this nightmare was indeed a permanent condition.

My career in the Army ended without fanfare or parades. On May 12, 2004, I put on my BDUs for the last time, drove to the post personnel office to sign the final paperwork, and then drove off post. Back at my rented room, I changed out of my uniform into shorts and a T-shirt. I was a civilian.

When I wasn't sleeping or lying around, I was driving home to Macon. I felt I needed to be there for every important occasion: Memorial Day, Father's Day, my nieces' and nephews' birthdays, Tuesdays—whatever excuse I could come up with to find my way home.

I spent a lot of time on that highway between Clarksville and Macon. I was torn between the two worlds, unsure of where I fit in. In Macon, Terry and I would ride Mike's Harley, and it seemed as if he was right there laughing along with us. In Clarksville I felt at loose ends. Most of my friends from the unit were getting new jobs and moving on. I was in a holding pattern, hovering above my own life.

I thought I was going to stay in Clarksville for good, but I'd begun to have second thoughts. Everything in Clarksville reminded me of Mike. I'd hear a song, see Kiowas flying over, drive past an old house we used to fantasize about living in or a favorite restaurant where we'd had so many good times. Well, I thought, I'll give it the summer.

In June, a local bar in Macon sponsored a surprise welcome home party for me and another soldier who had recently returned from Iraq. Cheryl tipped me off beforehand—she knew I hated surprises. So when I walked in and saw the crowd and heard them yell, "Welcome home!" I pretended I hadn't seen it coming. The bar's owner, who has a son in the Marines, is very patriotic, and I appreciated her gesture even though I didn't feel in the slightest like being welcomed back. I had a piece of cake in one hand and a beer in the other when she said to me, "I have another surprise for you!" A camera crew from a local station walked through the door; she'd invited them to cover the event. I prayed quickly for the floor to swallow me up, but when it didn't, I knew I'd have to talk about Mike again and how it felt to be home. By now the question-and-answer sessions were becoming robotic, but when the reporter approached me, I smiled and took a barstool, clutching my beer and hoping that Grandma Decker wouldn't see me on the news sitting in a bar.

The cameraman turned on his big bright light, but before the reporter started he leaned in to me and said, "Um, you're going to have to put the beer down first."

———

Lindsey did not come home in June. Days before they were to leave for Kuwait, she and her company had their tour extended to August. Morale plummeted. Not only were they facing another summer in the Middle East, they were heading to An Najaf, the new hot zone in Iraq. In April, the Al-Mahdi army, a militia loyal to radical Shiite cleric Muqtada al-Sadr, had seized control of the city, and the Iraqi police needed help taking it back. Heading south from Baghdad to An Najaf, Lindsey's convoy was hit with three IEDs and two of her soldiers were slightly wounded. But that was only the beginning.

As her company rolled into An Najaf, Lindsey could see Al-Mahdi soldier walking openly in the city, dressed in black, their faces covered like ninja warriors. They were an eerie sight and a clear indication of the magnitude of this mission. The newly formed Iraqi police stations had fallen into the Al-Mahdi's hands. Lindsey's company was directed to retake the stations and hold them.

It was a tough job for any commander, let alone a woman. Lindsey found herself working with some skeptical Iraqis, but she won them over with her ability and nerve. During one mission to retake a police station, her company and the Iraqis came under continuous mortar fire. Lindsey stood in the midst of it, her map spread out on a Humvee, while debris from incoming rounds rained down around her. Every time her map got covered with debris, she would calmly wipe it clean and continue her briefing. After witnessing that, all those skeptics became believers.

Lindsey needed more firepower, so she was given two tanks to command. And that's how my sister became, to the best of my knowledge, the first woman in Army history to command tanks in a combat situation. Within a matter of weeks, the police stations were in American and Iraqi hands; even so, her company came under daily attack.

Naturally, Lindsey's new mission in An Najaf caused Dad a lot of worry. He'd become the ultimate news hound while three of his kids were at war, and once again he spent his days glued to the television. One day while I was visiting, Fox News announced that U.S. forces had turned An Najaf over to the Iraqi police and had left the city. Dad gave a big sigh of relief. "I wonder where she is now," he wondered aloud.

"Dad, I hate to tell you this, but she's still right in An Najaf up to her armpits in work."

"Kate, they wouldn't announce something like that on the news without having something to go off of. I'm sure she's moved somewhere else."

I shook my head. "We're due for a call from her soon," I said. "And trust me, she'll call from An Najaf."

As it happened, Linz called the next day. "Where are you?" Dad asked. He listened for a moment, then turned and scowled at me. We both hate being wrong, although in this instance, I wished he'd been the one who was right.

"It's not that it's irresponsible reporting," I told him later. "It's just that they often don't have a way to fact-check but still need a story. I've been reading the news for a year wondering why they were reporting the 101st's movements that were completely contrary to what we were actually doing. It's unfortunate for parents like you who are glued to the television, but I guess it's just the nature of reporting a war."

This is especially true in an age of embedded journalists, who are directed away from certain missions because they're too secretive or dangerous. Lindsey would tell me later about their embedded reporter, who would complain that he'd been taken to watch soldiers distribute food to locals when the bullets were flying elsewhere.

Lindsey finally made it home in August. Her state job was waiting for her, but she had a month of leave to take first. She needed to find a place to live and get her belongings out of storage. But first she needed a vacation. It goes without saying that no one, female or otherwise, returns from such intense combat unchanged. Linz seemed quieter and a little angry, like a jar with the lid screwed on too tight.

For three years, Linz and I had promised each other that we would go somewhere special, just the two of us, and have some fun. Unfortunately, every time we started to make plans, one or both of us would get deployed. After a lot of debate we decided on an Alaskan cruise. We wanted a destination that was the polar opposite of Iraq, and Alaska's beautiful scenery and cool weather fit the bill. We quickly booked the trip and a week later headed off to this new frontier.

The cruise didn't turn out to be the big party we had anticipated. We discovered this our first night on board when we found ourselves alone in the biggest bar on the ship. The next morning, at breakfast, we ate our eggs surrounded by senior citizens. Apparently Alaska is popular with an older crowd. "Well, we were mainly interested in spending time with each other," Lindsey said.

The best thing about the cruise was the free champagne and the scenery. The Alaskan coast was calm, quiet, and utterly pristine—just what we needed. Floating past icebergs and mountain ranges, soaking in the outdoor hot tub and sipping our cocktails, we talked about what we wanted to do with our new lives. I was confused as to where my home really was. I felt strongly that I didn't want to be in Macon or Clarksville for the rest of my life, but I had to choose one or the other for now.

"Everything is so jumbled up," I said to Lindsey. "My life plan has been demolished. For the first time in a long time, I don't know what I want." We soaked for a few minutes in silence, sipping our drinks. Then I said, "You know what? Macon has always been home. Even when I lived for so long in Tennessee, Mike and I always referred to Macon as 'our real home.' "

At that instant, I knew where I was going.

That night I said one of my favorite prayers: "Lord, help me to be smart enough to know the path You have chosen for me and to take it."

As with everything, once I made a decision I executed it with military efficiency. After a two-day house hunt, I bought a ranch-style house on a grassy one-acre lot, with big trees for me and a big yard for Scout. The rising and setting sun gives the walls a rosy glow. I knew I could call it home for a while anyway, even if it did need some painting to make it a little more "me." I live down the street from Grandma Decker, two minutes from Terry, fifteen minutes from Dad. When the windows are open, I can hear a woman employee speaking over the loudspeaker across the road in the car dealership—"Service, line 101"—a disembodied voice drifting through the house.

There was one other big-ticket item left to acquire. Mike and I had saved up to buy a boat when we returned, but the thought of going nautical by myself wasn't all that appealing. Yet I also knew that Mike would be mad at me if I didn't take that money and spend it on something fun.

Back in February, C.D. had called me. In a few days he'd be shipping out to Iraq for a year, but there was something he wanted to tell me besides good-bye.

"I don't know if you know this," he began, "but Mike and I made a pact a few years ago that by 2005 we would both have Harleys and we would go to Sturgis." (The Sturgis Motorcycle Rally is one of the biggest Harley gathering in the country, held in South Dakota every August.)

C.D. went on. "I've been thinking about it, and I want to keep up my end of the bargain. So I'm going to start saving, and I'm going to get a Harley. In August I'm driving up to Missouri, I'm going to pick up you, Terry, and Lindsey, and then we're going to ride to the cemetery and pick up Mike before heading north to Sturgis. I'm absolutely going to keep my promise."

Terry had Mike's Harley, but that left Linz and me without a ride. During the cruise, I'd asked her what she thought. "When I was at Q-West visiting you guys, Mike was working on me to get one," she'd recalled. "You know—outlining what a great investment they were and how much fun I would have coming along with you guys on rides. He convinced me, but after the funeral I figured I'd never do it. Lately, though, I've been thinking that Mike would be far more ticked off at me for not getting one just because he's not here to ride it with me. So I say, let's do it."

We ordered our Harleys right after we got home from Alaska: a Sportster for her and a Softail Standard for me.

———

I moved home to Missouri in October and spent the fall settling into my new home. I stripped wallpaper, pulled up carpeting, and painted over paneling. I put up shelves, gave the bathroom a face-lift, and ordered an island for the kitchen. I haunted the local antiques mall for vintage kitchen accents in red and white, my color scheme.

Inevitably, driving around town became a trip down memory lane. Everywhere I went I saw landmarks of my life with Mike: the C & R Market where I cashed his checks; the Pizza Hut where he first made me laugh; Crossroads Christian Church, where we got married one hot spring day a long time ago.

But it was the small, unpredictable moments that got to me the most; the subtle reminders of day-to-day life affected me more than big holidays or anniversaries. One day, not long after I moved in, I came across two unopened boxes of canned goods and spices left over from our last move in Clarksville, between our deployments in Korea and Kuwait. I ripped off the tape, unsealed the flaps, and found myself staring at eight cans of peas. I hate peas. Mike liked them, so I'd bought them for him. Now here I was, stuck with eight cans of peas and no one to eat them.

I put them in the kitchen cabinet and promptly forgot about them. A few days later I was putting my groceries away, and the next thing I knew I was staring at eight cans of peas and remembering Mike. I also came across a box of Lever 2000 liquid soap he had bought in bulk so he wouldn't run out of his favorite scent. And the cards he would buy and address for family and friends' birthdays and anniversaries and then forget to mail. These small moments would catch me off guard and literally stop me in my tracks. Still, the memories were good ones, and I'd laugh, smile, or shake my head in exasperation. I was thankful to have as many memories as I did.

From the moment I grasped that Mike was gone, I knew I was going to be okay. Part of the gift of knowing and loving him was finding the confidence to go on. I knew he would have been disappointed in me had I given up. He would have demanded that I find the strength and purpose to navigate my new life. He would have wanted me to be happy.

Most days, knowing this was enough. But there were other days when it wasn't, days when I felt as if the forces of mourning and the forces of self-reliance were waging war in my head. Giving away Mike's possessions meant I'd accepted he wasn't going to use them again. Mike had always insisted the heat be turned to seventy degrees, so turning it up to seventy-five made me feel like I was somehow reveling in his absence. If I heard myself talking about Mike in the past tense, I'd hate myself for it. My confidence in my own survivorship felt like a form of betrayal against Mike, and it would take more than a long time to forgive myself for it.

In the eyes of others, my finding a new man seemed to be some kind of litmus test that I was going to "be all right." It took about four months for friends, acquaintances, and even total strangers to begin asking me when I was going to date again. Not only did this question trivialize my marriage to Mike—as if he could be so easily replaced—it implied that I couldn't take care of myself. I am fully capable of creating a happy, fulfilled life on my own.

As accustomed as I'd been to being alone, this was a different kind of alone. Before, *alone* meant separation. I would stockpile lists of stories, memories, and jokes to tell Mike when I saw him or talked to him next. Now, alone meant a permanent loneliness, a heartache. I missed the easy way we could be in the same room together, the way we were always touching each other—my hand on his shoulder when I told him a joke, his swatting my butt every time he walked by. I missed that human contact.

By November I was settled into my house, just in time for the opening day of deer season. Terry asked me if I wanted to go hunting, and as always, I said yes. I knew we would enjoy being outdoors in each other's company, but I didn't look forward to a different kind of first: my first hunt without breakfast at Grampy's.

On a chilly morning before Thanksgiving, I zipped up my coveralls and laced my heavy insulated boots. The .270 Winchester, Mike's old rifle and now mine, stood ready at the door. I looked forward to firing it again. Terry picked me up and we headed out into the dark before dawn. I loved being awake that early, before the first rays streaked across the sky and the first cars hit the road, when the world was sleepy and quiet. This time of day felt like a secret that everyone who was sleeping didn't get to share.

Terry and I spent the early hours in a small hunting shack that Larry had built years ago in a clearing by a small pond. Our small heater roused the flies out of their stupor and sent them to buzzing against the windows. Otherwise, the scene was quiet as we took up positions, scanning the forest and field for signs of movement.

Holding that old Winchester, I recalled the day when Mike had taught me to shoot with it—how alien and powerful it had felt. Now it felt so familiar. The Winchester was actually heavier than my M-4, but after a year of carrying an automatic rifle everywhere I went—even to bed—I was happy that I didn't have to baby-sit this one all the time.

The sun rose over the pond and the firing began, so loud and all-encompassing that it sounded like a Wild West shootout, just as it did every opening day. This always amused me—it seemed as if the hunters were firing their rifles into the air for the sheer exuberance of being outdoors on the hunt. Ironically, I had never fired my weapon in Iraq, though I knew, with every fiber of my being, that I would have if necessary. Here, bullets were as common as confetti.

Time and war had taken their toll on the family, but our rituals remained, however modified. Dale and Linda adopted the morning breakfast tradition. A nice young couple was renting Grampy's house, so Mike's aunt and uncle had breakfast at their place up the road. Terry and I headed over there around 0800. It was nice to see the family gathered in a kitchen, everyone pitching in. But without the familiar scent of tobacco mingling with cold air and bacon grease, without the morning light flooding Grampy's kitchen, the meal seemed a little bitter just the same.

Terry and I hunted all day and the next. As the sun was setting on the second day, a doe walked into my sights. It was an average doe, nothing special, and I probably wouldn't have taken the shot. But this was my only chance to bag a deer this season.

I had shot several deer over the years, and doing so had never bothered me much. When I had a deer in my scope, I never got weak in the knees and thought about Bambi. But this time I did not take the hunt as lightly. Seeing a trail of bloody Iraqis lined up outside Charlie Company, children ripped open by roadside bombs, had impressed upon me the damage that weapons can inflict on the human body. Hunting had seemed fun before, almost frivolous. Now it seemed like a privilege. I still dropped that deer cold with one shot through the neck, and I'll continue to hunt and like it. But this time I found myself thinking about my rifle with a new respect and, I must confess, a bit of distaste.

———

As my year of firsts ended, I tried to stay busy. I got a night job at the front desk at the YMCA checking people's ID cards and directing them toward the locker room. And when I couldn't stand being alone with myself anymore, I drove. At the drop of a hat I'd jump in the car with Scout and visit a friend. I visited Mollie, Nancy, and Natalie, all of whom had had babies within the past few months. I took some time to reacquaint myself with my brother, Joe, who was living in Missouri again. I visited Scott and Sonja several times. I watched so much television that I eventually disconnected the cable because it was sucking from me whatever life force I had left.

Scout was my constant companion, but even he was not unchanged. He had always been protective of me when we were by ourselves, but he would always relinquish the job of bodyguard to Mike as soon as he came home. Soon enough, Scout sensed that Mike was never coming home, and his behavior shifted. He never let down his guard. He growled at people he knew well, even Dad.

You know your current situation is dire when you look back fondly on Christmas in a war zone. Christmas had always been such a happy day with Mike, even in Iraq, when even The Heap had glittered with the season. Mike had sat there eating care package food, puffing on cigars and making wisecracks about the decorations.

This was my first Christmas as a widow. I hated that word *widow*—or, as I called it, the *w* word, which sounded less heinous. Wendy and Chris didn't come home for Christmas, and Anna had to sing in church. Getting through this particular holiday was like putting on a play with half the cast out sick.

I would just as soon have ignored the day altogether, but again, I didn't want to give people a reason to worry. Like a soldier who goes to war because she must, I participated in the customary rituals of the season out of a sense of duty. I tramped out into the woods with the Blaise family so we could all pick out our trees; I put up mine in my living room and decorated it by myself. I watched *National Lampoon's Christmas Vacation* and laughed in all the usual places. On Christmas Eve day, Dad, Tiffani, Lindsey, and I visited Mom and gave her presents. I spent Christmas Eve service at Mount Zion with Terry and Cheryl; Christmas morning unwrapping presents with Dad; Christmas dinner at his sister's in the afternoon. Without Mike, I didn't fit into the picture the same way anymore. If I had been a silver skater on a mirrored pond, a giant hand could have reached down and plucked me out of the scene with no one the wiser. I was going through the motions, checking all the blocks. Go to Terry's, check. Go to church at Mount Zion, check. Go see Mom, check. Go to Aunt Teresa's for Christmas dinner, check. If I hadn't gone, I could just see my family sitting around the table at Aunt Teresa's house, thinking, *Well, Kate's finally cracked.*

As for New Year's Eve, 2004 ended in much the same way it had begun. I slept hoping to dream of Mike, Scout a familiar lump across my feet when the rest of the bed felt so empty.

CHAPTER 26

THE HEART OF A SOLDIER

AUGUST 2005, MACON, MISSOURI

IT HAS BEEN more than eighteen months since my life was upended by the sound of rotor blades on a black, windy night. Many
people, in an attempt to reassure and comfort me, have said, "It will
take time, but you'll make it through this and get over it." If there is
one thing I've learned, it's that you never "get over" losing a loved
one. Instead, you find a way to learn to live with it.

I thought writing the book would help me do that—a literary self-
help exercise of sorts. In some ways, it has. Like flying high above a
desert landscape, looking down on the broad outlines that shape it,
telling my story has given me a chance to examine my feelings and experiences, to put them in perspective. The hard part was that I had to
keep Mike close throughout the process. At times I could almost sense
him sitting next me as I sat down at the computer. "Don't tell them
that," I'd hear him say, or, "Wait a minute, what about the time you
and Lindsey stole Tootsie Rolls from the Ben Franklin when you were
kids?"

It's funny, but when Mike was putting his life on the line in Iraq, I
didn't sit around and wring my hands and worry about losing him. I
had faith in his abilities and those of his copilot and wingman, and
fixating on the dangers of his job would have paralyzed me, rendered
me incapable of doing mine. Any fear and worry I had got shoved
into a corner. That's one reason why his accident was so shocking.
That mission seemed so routine, something he'd done a hundred times
before.

Ironically, I never feared for Mike's safety in the war, but in making him come alive while writing, I struggled with the fear of losing
him, for the first time and all over again.

The results of the crash investigation mirrored what we had suspected all along. There was zero visibility that night, and Mike lost orientation with the ground and the sky. The accident was a matter of split-second timing in which they probably had little or no time to react and correct the situation. It's assumed the two men died instantly, and photographs of the crumpled Kiowa left little doubt in my mind that either man had suffered or lingered.

The results of the crash investigation brought me neither comfort nor pain. Ultimately, we will never know what happened in the sky that dark night. All I can say for sure is that Mike died a hero, trying to help the soldiers he cared about.

As I write these final paragraphs, I'm sitting at my desk in Macon; Scout lies on his dog bed nearby. Whenever I start writing he follows me into the office and keeps me company, alerting me to the presence of traffic and visitors. I'm comfortable in this house, even if I don't know how long I'll live here. As this story has evolved, so has my home, in subtle ways. A year ago I couldn't look at photos of Mike, but now memories and images of him surround me. Above my computer is a photo of the two of us on the beach in Qatar. It's a picture of a loving couple on vacation. What it doesn't show is that the moment after it was taken, Mike laughingly pretended he was going to push me down the sand dune we're standing on. That was our marriage in a nutshell: full of adventure, full of fun.

I look at him and smile and feel the twinge of pain that accompanies it. That twinge will always be there, just as there will always be a part of me that is lonely for him. But I've found some peace; I laugh more easily now, and I feel blessed to have been loved and to have loved in return a very good man. Mike is always going to be a voice in my head telling me that I can do anything I want. The voice that tells me the correct way to pass a vehicle, the best way to tuck a rifle in my arm to cushion the weapon's kick, the right way to saddle a horse without spooking him.

In my bedroom sits a recent addition to my home decor: a large, rough-hewn toolbox about the size of a sea chest with sliding shelves and small compartments. It had belonged to Grampy's brother-in-law, Malcolm, who had worked for a while in the shipyards of Virginia. He had made the box himself, and it was still full of his old tools from the 1930s. A few months after I got home, Terry assembled all the kids and let them go through an assortment of belongings he'd found at Grampy's house after his death. No one wanted the box except me. "We could refinish it and store Mike's military stuff in it," I said to Terry. He loved the idea, and we worked on the box for a year until I was ready to bring it home. Like my parents' cedar chest full of personal mementos and Dad's Army medals, it's a box of memories: the gold heart locket that was Mike's first gift to me, his high school letter jacket, the .270 rifle shell from the first shot I ever fired under his tutelage, and the watch I got him when he graduated from flight school that became one of his most prized possessions.

Mike also lives on in the memories of all his family and friends. Last spring Brendan Cullinan, a pilot we had gotten to know at Fort Rucker and later in Korea, had his first child with his wife, Becky. They named their son Aidan Michael, after Mike, and asked me to be his godmother. I love being a part of Aidan's life. I love the fact that whenever someone laughs at his antics or says that little boy's middle name, Mike will be there.

It's not easy for a small-town girl to put down her most personal thoughts, feelings, and memories on paper, knowing everyone in town will read them. How people decide to grieve is very personal. I am a private person, but since privacy seems to be a rare commodity these days, I decided to push my personal limits. Mike would have wanted me to. "Kate," I can hear him say, "this is your chance to share a story that many soldiers in your combat boots will never get a chance to tell." And he's right. This story is for all of the spouses, parents, and children who have a million tales about the loved ones who sacrificed so much for this country, tales that will never be heard.

As for Iraq, some people may quibble with my memory or description of certain events. This book is solely based on my thoughts and observations at the time. I feel privileged to share some of the memories and stories of soldiers and a unit that I loved, respected, and considered my family. I knew firsthand the positive changes that the 101st Airborne Division made in Iraq, and believe those changes are still in place.

More important, I knew firsthand the soldiers who made it all happen. I was lucky, in a way—I got to sit back at a fairly safe distance and watch our soldiers work hard and take care of the Iraqi people. I often wonder about Mr. Mohamed and our translator, Abdul—how they're doing, if they're safe.

If you had told me in the spring of 2003, when the war looked won, that we'd still be fighting so fiercely, I wouldn't have believed it. Like many Americans, I too find the war situation frustrating and, at times, deeply saddening. Yet for every terrible incident we read about, there is a positive development that goes unnoticed. There are thousands of Iraqis who have decided to change the course of their country by becoming policemen, teachers, politicians, and shopkeepers. It's a tough battle. Wars are not fought and won like they once were, when there was decisive victory and everyone went home.

As I write this, the role of women in combat has again become a hot topic. Some politicians think that women would be better suited away from the front lines, and many Americans believe this as well. They even want to ban female soldiers from working in forward support roles—something I know a little bit about. This shows a lack of understanding of the new face of war. The lines separating the good guys from the bad have become smudged. The enemy has decided that anyone hailing from a particular country is the enemy whether they are soldiers or not, or men or not.

In June 2005, a suicide car bomber targeted a truck of mostly female soldiers being driven to checkpoints around Fallujah, where they assist in searching Iraqi women. Three women were killed and eleven wounded. But I read something else that says a lot about the character of women serving in today's military. Because the checkpoint searches frightened some little girls, the female Marines asked that friends send teddy bears to give to the children to calm their fears. The military needs that kind of compassion, and it is a vital attribute that women bring. I am proud of those soldiers and the job they were doing, and the fact that they were doing it from the heart.

The enemy doesn't care about teddy bears or best intentions. But like it or not, women are part of that situation, and we belong there. It is absurd to assume that the military could fight as effectively by removing women from forward positions. Units have been integrated— men and women working side by side—for years. We would be hard-pressed to find male soldiers to fill our slots and, in many cases, do as good a job as we do.

As women, we have just as much right to defend our country as any male soldier. This means, inevitably, we will die for it as well. Are women suited to be in combat? Some are, but many aren't, just as many men aren't fit for combat, either. Lindsey and I are both proud of our service. We are not interested in moving to the back and letting the men get the job done. This genie is out of the bottle, and no amount of politicking will coax her back in.

————

In these pages, I've recounted a good many memories of those days at Q-West, but there's one involving Abdul that I've saved until now. To me, it represents the possibility of peace.

Abdul tended to keep to himself at The Heap, but one night he taught me a lesson that will stay with me the rest of my life. Chip and I were sitting on the porch, enjoying an unusually cool evening and watching the star show. Abdul came outside and asked if he could join us. We said of course. He had his CD player with him. "Is it all right if I play a few songs?" he asked.

"Sure," Chip said. "I could use a little Backstreet Boys right about now."

Abdul played some pop songs, not too loud, and we all sat there nodding our heads to the beat. Then he put in a third CD, and a male voice began to sing in Arabic. I had heard this voice again and again in Iraq, drifting on the wind from the slender minarets. Abdul apologized over getting the CDs mixed up, and he started to remove it when we stopped him.

"What does that song mean, anyway?" Chip asked.

"This is the Muslim call to prayer," Abdul answered, and he translated part of the lyrics for us:

> God is great, God is great
> There is only one God; there is only one God
> Come to pray, come to pray.

The song had always sounded sinister to my Christian ears, but now I was glad that I knew what it meant. As a deeply religious person, I understood the call to prayer was one way that Muslims expressed their own beliefs, and it occurred to me how easy it is to judge those things and people we don't understand. That is one lesson I brought home from Iraq, as surely as that mountain of luggage. I never want to forget the other lessons I learned there, starting with how lucky I am to have been born an American, with access to so much. Everyone should be so lucky.

My love affair with the military is not over yet. Last winter I called up the closest Missouri National Guard recruiter, and a few months later I was buttoning up my uniform and polishing my black boots again. I am now a weekend warrior, and the Army is again part of my life. Many people seem surprised by my decision, and they ask me if I want to go back to Iraq. This question makes me laugh—no one who's been there wants to go back to the heat, the lousy living conditions, the danger. But being a soldier means I embody the will to serve. If called up, I will salute, pack my rucksack and not look back. For better or worse, no matter where I go no matter what I do, I will always have the heart of a soldier.